Farm Life in Northeast Scotland

1840–1914

THE POOR MAN'S COUNTRY

Ian Carter

JOHN DONALD PUBLISHERS LTD
EDINBURGH

Paperback edition 1997
ISBN 0 85976 457 5

I Gwenllian, Angharad a Rhiannon.
I chi y rhoddaf y gwaith gorau byth y byddaf yn ei gyflawni.

Phototypesetting by Burns & Harris Limited, Dundee
Printed in Great Britain by Bell & Bain Ltd., Glasgow

Preface to the Paperback Edition

WHEN asked by his publisher to satisfy 'popular demand' by producing a paperback edition of a book first published eighteen years earlier, an author has two choices. He can change everything, or he can change nothing. Let me explain why I choose the second course.

Farm Life in Northeast Scotland was widely and generously reviewed when it first appeared in 1979. No significant error of fact was identified then, or has been found since. One reason for rewriting the text disappears. In 1982 I decamped to New Zealand, escaping devastation wrought on Aberdeen University by Margaret Thatcher's policies; so I have no new research to report in this edition. A second reason evaporates. There might be some point in recasting the book's theoretical framework. Many reviewers appreciated its detailed evidence but deprecated the Marxist machinery organising that material. Clearly, after eighteen years this machinery looks a little rusty. I decline to change it, for two reasons. First, one must remind today's readers that important social issues about the rural northeast (and about Scottish society more generally) still are excluded from public debate. This book's first edition was published in Jim Callaghan's last months as prime minister, when he presided over an Old Labour cabinet tilling the intellectual ground for Margaret Thatcher's elected tyranny. This paperback edition is published while Tony Blair settles in as prime minister, presiding over a New Labour cabinet content to implement Thatcher's policies with a (somewhat) less brutal face. An exile should bear witness against policies which forced him from a loved land. In declining to change this text I anathemise The Old Iron Woman's fanatical dictum that There Is No Alternative. Alternatives always exist. If academic life has any purpose, then it is to give them life.

My second ground is less polemical. If, as a young academic building a career, I were writing this book today then I would be forced to start from today's fashionable theories. You would hold a book built around notions of discourse; of presence and absence; of deconstruction; of post- this, post- that and post- the other. A book of that kind on this topic would be a feeble thing. Karl Marx may be an unfashionable figure today, and any text looking to the disgraced Louis Althusser's structural precepts (in a less inhumane manner than he managed, one hopes) risks our deepest disfavour: but Stuart Hall's qualified defence for structural Marxism remains true and potent.[1] We could not have got to this place without following this road. The argument in *Farm Life* only makes sense within a structural Marxist framework. Destroy that framework and the argument crumbles to dust. Attempting to disguise this knobby fact would be dishonest, misleading today's readers.

Almost thirty years after beginning the research reported here, I am astounded at my foolhardiness in tackling this topic. As the Introduction makes clear, I had no preparation for the task. I was English, with no direct knowledge of Scotland. I was born and raised in an engineering town, with no direct knowledge of agriculture. This book is my attempt to understand the social world to which an impersonal academic labour market transported me. Jim Hunter's review[2] made *Farm Life* an indictment of Aberdeen University. Such a magnificent research topic, he insisted, should not have been left lying around for a raw southern immigrant to find. His point was well taken. Somebody else, somebody born and raised in the region, should have recognised the remarkable wealth of material about northeast rural life which lay sleeping in Kings Library. That nobody did — with the partial exception of the admirable Malcolm Gray — was my good fortune. Chris Smout's review of the book[3] (a generous review, given that I had used him as a stalking horse — but only *good* Old Turks merit Young Turks' criticism) led Tom Devine to construct a collection of historical essays on Scottish regional differences in farm labour organisation.[4] That apart, *Farm Life* seems to have settled down in Scottish academic circles to tombstone status: a relic to which authors give a respectful nod before plodding off in other directions. When last I looked, this still was the only book-length study of nineteenth century agricultural change in a lowland region. That still puzzles me.

Two men did most to take this book furth of Scotland, turning it (as Ronnnie Frankenberg said of the book which got him his university chair) into the thing which made me what I am. Through his peasants' seminar in London University T. J. Byres, Aberdeen's loyal loon, knocked important bits of my argument into shape at important times; and then grilled the finished book in a comradely searching review.[5] A little later, Raphael Samuel recruited me for the then-exhilarating History Workshop movement, giving me a fleeting hint of what academic celebrity might look like.[6] Only one agricultural historian gave *Farm Life* a lousy review, claiming that he had made all its essential points years ago when discussing Norfolk agriculture. But later, several less blinkered scholars tried to use the book as a template against which to investigate nineteenth century agrarian change in English rural districts.[7] These efforts, and my own attempt to develop comparative work in New Zealand, all foundered on the paucity of necessary local cultural materials when compared with the northeast's riches. As so often, Jim Hunter had got it right.

Finally, let me record one anecdote which still affords me guilty pride. Late in 1979, the library van which trundled south Kincardineshire's roads did not appear in Auchenblae on its appointed day. It was being serviced in Stonehaven. When next it ground to a halt outside Charlie Minty's shop, a shocked driver told me that something had been stolen in Stoney: the van's single copy of *Farm Life,* so heavily requested that it had to be kept in the driver's cab rather than shelved among the main stock. He probably still cannot understand why I did not share his outrage at this larceny, why I took it to be the sincerest flattery which an author can enjoy. Wherever that thief is today, I thank him: and hope that he found the book as enlightening as (with luck) a new generation of readers will find it.

Ian Carter
Mount Eden
June 1997

Notes

1. S. Hall, 'In defence of theory', in R. Samuel (ed), *People's History and Socialist Theory,* London, Routledge, 1981, pp 378–385.
2. *Aberdeen University Review,* 1979, IL, 213–5.
3. *Social History,* 1980, V, 482–5.
4. T. M. Devine (ed), *Farm Servants and Labour in Lowland Scotland, 1770–1914,* Edinburgh, John Donald, 1984.
5. T. J. Byres, 'Of slumbering academics and peasants' sons; perspectives on the peasantry of the northeast of Scotland', *Journal of Peasant Studies,* 1981, IX, 110–17.
6. I. Carter, 'The changing image of the Scottish peasantry, 1745–1980', and 'The Scottish peasantry', in R. Samuel (ed), *People's History and Socialist Theory,* London, Routledge, 1981, pp 9–15, 85–92. Also see Gwyn Alf Williams' review of this book in *The Guardian,* 5 February 1981.
7. See for example N. Gregson, 'Tawney revisited: custom and the emergence of capitalist class relations in northeast Cumbria, 1600–1830', *Economic History Review,* 1989, XLII, 18–42; M. Reed, 'The peasantry of nineteenth century England: a neglected class', *History Workshop Journal,* 1984, XVIII, 53–76; M. Reed, 'Nineteenth century rural England: a case for peasant studies', *Journal of Peasant Studies,* 1986, XIV, 78–99; C. E. Searle, 'Custom, class conflict and agrarian capitalism: the Cumbrian customary economy in the eighteenth century', *Past and Present,* 1986, CX, 106–133. For another island see R. Breen, 'Farm servanthood in Ireland, 1900–1940', *Economic History Review,* 1983, XXXVI, 87–102.

Acknowledgements

I AM grateful for permission to make brief quotations from the following works that are covered by copyright regulations: J. R. Allan, *Farmer's Boy*, London, Methuen, 1935; J. R. Allan, *North-East Lowlands of Scotland*, London, Hale, 1974; J. R. Allan, *The Seasons Return*, London, Hale, 1955; E. H. Carr, *What Is History?* Harmondsworth, Penguin, 1961; R. Douglas, *The History of the Liberal Party 1895-1970*, London, Sidgwick and Jackson, 1971; G. Evans, 'Trade Unionism and the Wage Level in Aberdeen', unpublished PhD thesis, Aberdeen University, c 1950; A. Fenton, 'Farm Servant Life in the 17th-19th Centuries', *Scottish Agriculture*, 1964-5, Vol. XLIV; 'Lewis Grassic Gibbon', *A Scots Quair*, London, Hutchinson, 1946; 'Lewis Grassic Gibbon', *A Scots Hairst*, London, Hutchinson, 1967; H. Hamilton, *Third Statistical Account of Scotland: the County of Banff*, London, Collins, 1961; H. Henderson, 'The Bothy Ballads', *Journal of Peasant Studies*, 1975, Vol. II; R. Molland and G. Evans, 'Scottish Farm Wages from 1870 to 1900', *Journal of the Royal Statistical Society*, 1950, Vol. CXIII; A. C. O'Dell and K. Walton, *The Highlands and Islands of Scotland*, London, Nelson, 1962; J. H. Smith, 'The Cattle Trade of Aberdeenshire in the Nineteenth Century', *Agricultural History Review*, 1955, Vol. III.

I am also grateful for permission to use photographs from the Country Life Archive of the National Museum of Antiquities of Scotland to illustrate this book. For permission to reproduce Plate 5, I am indebted to Mr N. Halket, Elgin.

Ian Carter.

Contents

List of Tables

List of Figures

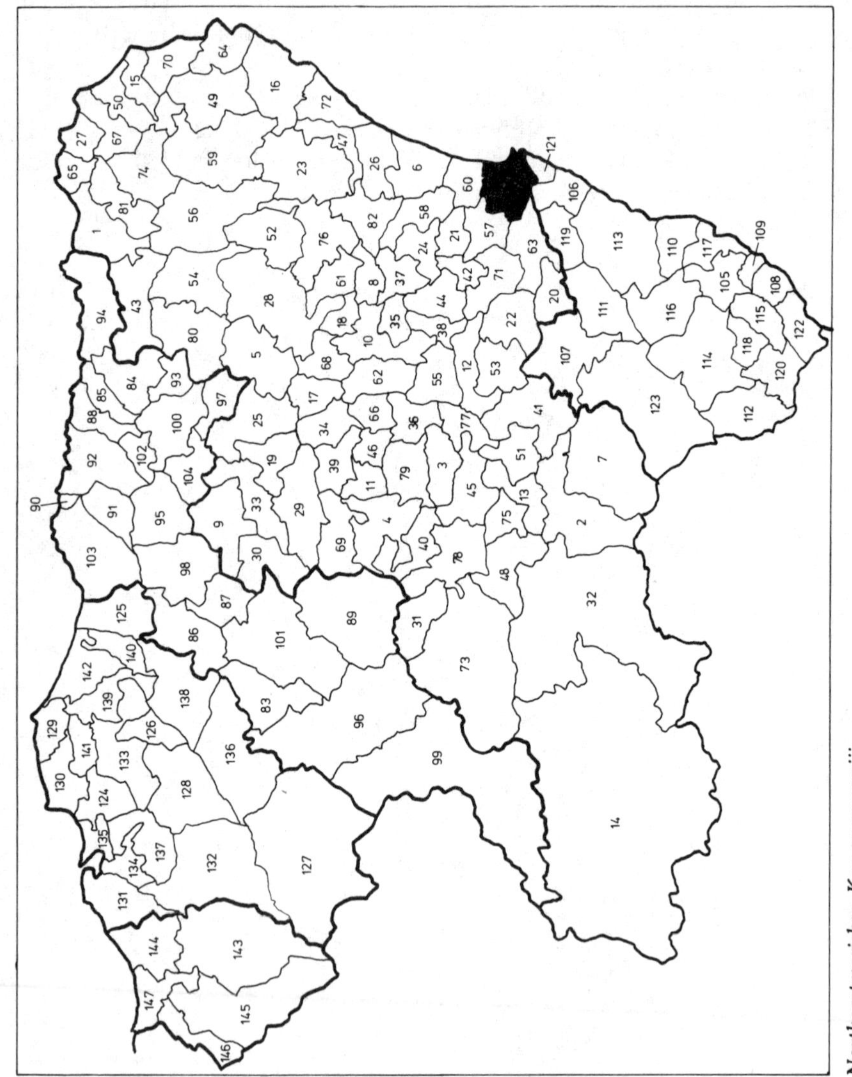

Northeast parishes. Key on page xiii

Key:

Aberdeenshire
1 Aberdour
2 Aboyne
3 Alford
4 Auchindoir and Kearn
5 Auchterless
6 Belhelvie
7 Birse
8 Bourtie
9 Cairnie
10 Chapel of Garioch
11 Clatt
12 Cluny
13 Coull
14 Crathie and Braemar
15 Crimond
16 Cruden
17 Culsalmond
18 Daviot
19 Drumblade
20 Drumoak
21 Dyce
22 Echt
23 Ellon
24 Fintray
25 Forgue
26 Foveran
27 Fraserburgh
28 Fyvie
29 Gartly
30 Glass
31 Glenbuchat
32 Glenmuick, Tullich and Glengairn
33 Huntly
34 Insch
35 Inverurie
36 Keig
37 Keithhall
38 Kemnay
39 Kennethmont
40 Kildrummy
41 Kincardine O'Neil
42 Kinellar
43 King Edward
44 Kintore
45 Leochel Cushnie
46 Leslie
47 Logie Buchan
48 Logie Coldstone
49 Longside
50 Lonmay
51 Lumphanan
52 Methlick
53 Midmar
54 Monquitter
55 Monymusk
56 New Deer
57 Newhills
58 Newmachar
59 Old Deer
60 Old Machar
61 Oldmeldrum
62 Oyne
63 Peterculter
64 Peterhead
65 Pitsligo
66 Premnay
66 Rathen
68 Rayne
69 Rhynie
70 St. Fergus
71 Skene
72 Slains
73 Strathdon
74 Strichen
75 Tarland
76 Tarves
77 Tough
78 Towie
79 Tullynessle and Forbes
80 Turriff
81 Tyrie
82 Udny

Banffshire
83 Aberlour
84 Alvah
85 Banff
86 Boharm
87 Botriphnie
88 Boyndie
89 Cabrach
90 Cullen
91 Deskford
92 Fordyce
93 Forglen
94 Gamrie
95 Grange
96 Inveraven
97 Inverkeithny
98 Keith
99 Kirkmichael
100 Marnoch
101 Mortlach
102 Ordiquhill
103 Rathven
104 Rothiemay

Kincardine
105 Arbuthnott
106 Banchory Devenick
107 Banchory Ternan
108 Benholm
109 Bervie
110 Dunnottar
111 Durris
112 Fettercairn
113 Fetteresso
114 Fordoun
115 Garvock
116 Glenbervie
117 Kinneff
118 Laurencekirk
119 Maryculter
120 Marykirk
121 Nigg
122 St. Cyrus
123 Strachan

Moray
124 Alves
125 Bellie
126 Birnie
127 Cromdale
128 Dallas
129 Drainie
130 Duffus
131 Dyke
132 Edinkillie
133 Elgin
134 Forres
135 Kinloss
136 Knockando
137 Rafford
138 Rothes
139 St. Andrews and Llanbryde
140 Speymouth
141 Spynie
142 Urquhart

Nairn
143 Ardclach
144 Auldearn
145 Cawdor
146 Croy
147 Nairn

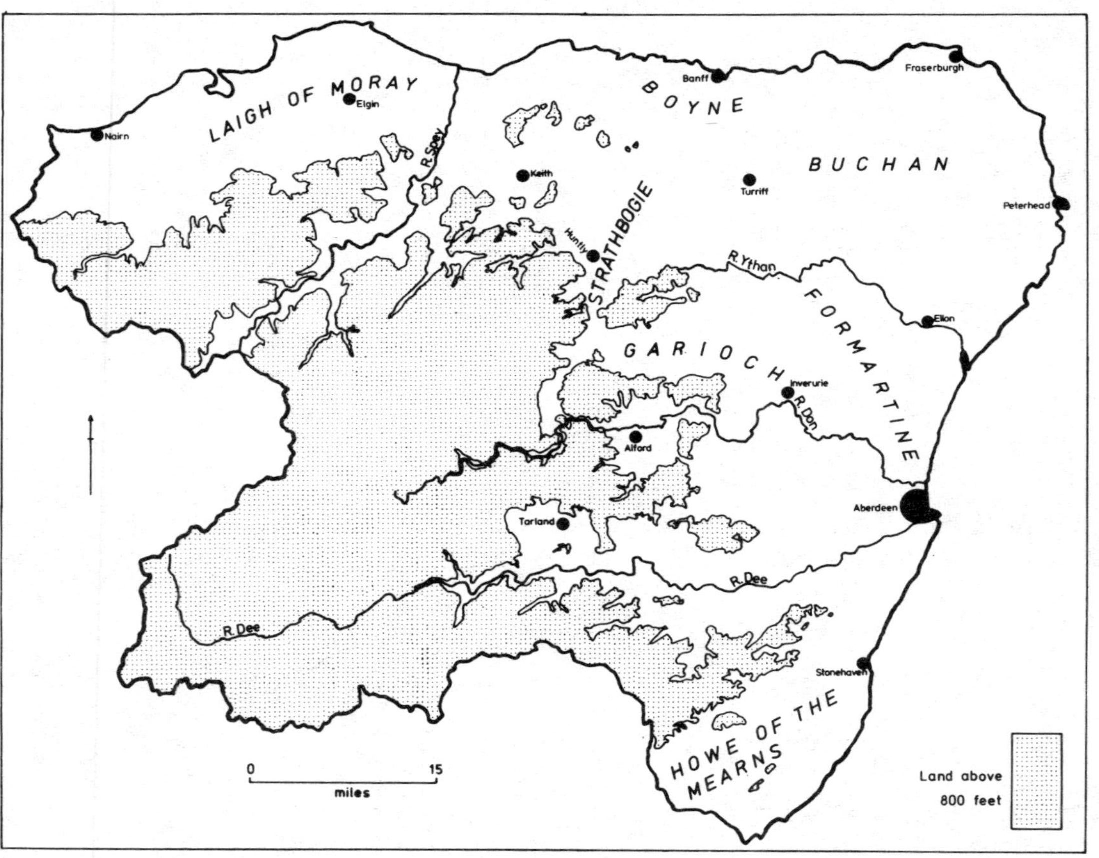

The Northeast, upland and lowland: major settlements and districts.

Introduction

IT was the minister of Rayne, 'the girnal of the Garioch', who wrote of 'Aberdeenshire, which has been sometimes called "the poor man's country" '. He meant the phrase to be a compliment: it pointed to what he regarded as the sound social economy of his parish in the years around 1840. In Rayne, as throughout northeast Scotland between 1840 and 1914, agricultural land was not monopolised by a few farmers with huge holdings:[1]

> One peculiarity to be noticed is the great variety in the size of the farms, from that of two horses labour to that of six horses; besides which, are numerous crofts for tradesmen keeping a cow, and other possessions, of eight, twelve, and twenty acres, occupied in lease by industrious tenants, labouring with their own hands, and usually tilling with a horse and ox yoked together. These multiplied subdivisions of the ground, into portions so small, may no doubt be adverse to the adopting of new and improved modes of culture, on a large and uniform scale; but this disadvantage has long appeared to the writer, to be counterbalanced by the powerful encouragement thereby afforded to the practice of honest industry and prudence, among the labouring classes of the community. In counties that are under a different management, and which have no gradation of possessions betwixt the cottar's acre and the grain farm of a hundred acres, or the sheep farm of a thousand acres, the man who begins life as a farm-servant, day-labourer, or tradesman, how diligent and economical soever he may be, is almost precluded from the hope of bettering his condition, by the occupancy of a small farm, suited to his means and industry, and must limit his views to the cottar's croft, realizing, in most instances, the English adage, 'once a hind, always a hind'.[2] But in Aberdeenshire, which has been sometimes called 'the poor man's country', a farm-servant or labourer, after having established his character by activity, temperance, and economy, has little difficulty in getting a possession proportioned to the amount of his savings, on which, by exertion and foresight, he may live comfortably, and bring up a family, in the like industrious, peaceable, and independent way. And, in proof of the efficiency of this stimulus, there are at present within the bounds of this small parish, many instances of persons who, from very humble beginnings, have gradually risen, by their own exertions, to be thriving and intelligent agriculturalists.[3]

Many points in this masterly account of Rayne's social economy will be embroidered in the following pages. But the major point — the beneficent social consequences of a very fine gradation in farm size — takes us back to the origin of this book, to the reasons why first I became interested in the historical sociology of farm life in northeast Scotland.

This book is the log of an unfinished journey — my attempt to understand the society in which I live. The journey began almost a decade ago, when first I came to live and work in northeast Scotland. Like most sociologists working in

Scottish universities, I had been born and bred in England. Indeed, prior to my appointment to a post in Aberdeen University, I had never visited the city, nor the region which it dominates — the five counties of Aberdeen, Banff, Kincardine, Moray and Nairn, now largely comprised in the Grampian Region. I found the culture of both city and hinterland accessible and friendly on one level; but at a deeper level the culture seemed to be mysterious and secret. Local people were wrapped in local concerns and, it seemed, long had been so wrapped. There are two classes of jokes about Aberdeen, both usually told against themselves by Aberdonians. One set concentrates on Aberdeen's fabled thriftiness[4] — like the dolorous occasion on which a taxi crashed in Union Street and all ninety-six occupants were killed. The second set concerns the remarkable ability of northeast folk to interpret national and international events through their effect on the northeast. The famous joke here is the apocryphal headline in a local newspaper in 1912 — 'Aberdeen Man Dies in Atlantic: Titanic Sinks'. In 1968, as in 1912, northeast folk seemed to share an unusually widespread agreement about what the social world looked like. My attempt to understand the social roots of this cultural self-sufficiency was the germ from which this book has grown.

To outsiders, and particularly to the condescending Olympians who swarm in Edinburgh's New Town, this cultural self-sufficiency usually appeared to be the merest parochialism — the result of the northeast's isolation from civilisation. Civilisation for such people meant — and means — the New Town, of course. This attitude blights attempts to understand northeast social life;[5] but it never could have been squared with the facts. In the nineteenth century, which still casts a long shadow over Scottish social life, the northeast was one of the most literate regions in a highly literate country. Newspapers were read widely and with care. Political questions were conned with particular care, and the conclusions drawn were usually rather radical. The northeast was a Chartist bastion in the 1840s.[6] At the end of the century Aberdeen city was a stronghold of Hyndman's Social Democratic Federation[7] and had an active, radical Trades Council.[8] Nor was this awareness of national and international issues limited to 'the Toon': country areas also had a powerful radical leaven.[9] I find it difficult to square this kind of evidence with accusations of parochialism. Radicalism was not introduced to the northeast by immigrants either: Aberdeen is unique among major Scottish cities in having suffered no large-scale immigration from outwith its region, until the recent oil boom at least. In the nineteenth century 'the Toon' grew almost exclusively at the expense of its hinterland. Northeast radicalism, like northeast cultural self-sufficiency, was home grown.

Were both culture and radicalism rooted in social class? Did northeast Scotland share common features with northeast England, both having a strong regional identity rooted in a working class culture generated by the dominant local industry?[10] At first sight the answer to these questions seemed to be a clear negative. One of the oddest features of northeast Scottish cultural self-sufficiency was the manner it which it cut across class lines. This was no working class culture, as in County Durham. But could the dominant local industry still have generated the culture? It was worth a look. The dominant local industry in northeast Scotland was agriculture, so I began to look for good modern local agrarian social history. I am still looking: it does not exist. Nor, to a large extent, can one find a corresponding economic history. One main purpose of this book is to begin to remedy this deficiency.

Thus the culture shock of being an Englishman in northeast Scotland started me on the road to doing local agrarian social history. My research started as a hobby: over the years it has deepened into an obsession and, to my continuing surprise, has become steadily more sociological. My first interest lay in studying the life and labour of farm servants and, more particularly, in examining the relationship between farm service and bothy ballads — the famous (and unique) northeast folk songs about farm life. As I worked so my puzzlement grew. An influential study tells us that bothy ballads got their name because they were sung in bothies, where most northeast male farm servants were housed.[11] But I knew that most of these servants had been lodged not in the bothy but in the chaumer.[12] Further, it soon became clear that if one plotted on a map the spatial distribution of bothies on the one hand and of bothy ballads on the other, then the two distributions would show almost no overlap. Put crudely, in Aberdeenshire, Banffshire and north Kincardine one had ballads but no bothies, while in Moray, Nairn and south Kincardine one had bothies but no ballads. It was clear that the argument that bothy ballads were written to be sung in bothies was a remarkably inadequate explanation of these songs' genesis. More importantly, however, the intermeshing of these distributions suggested that both were generated by a more fundamental, hidden factor: a conclusion that was reinforced by the fact that other important features of northeast agrarian structure also divided along the same line. The most important of these features concerned farm size. We shall see that average farm size was much smaller in Aberdeenshire, Banffshire and north Kincardine than in other districts,[13] and the finely graded farm size distribution that aroused the enthusiasm of Rayne's minister was found very much more often in these central districts. The hidden factor that underlay all these spatial distributions was the relative strength in different districts of two linked but analytically distinct forms of agricultural production. One form, called locally 'crofting' and 'small farming', was peasant production. The other — 'muckle farming' or 'large farming' — was capitalist agriculture.

The distinction between peasant farming and capitalist agriculture, between two modes of production, provided the key to unlock the intricacies of northeast agriculture's social history. The argument of this book is built around an analysis of the shifting combinations, the alliances and conflicts, of capitalist farmers and peasant farmers under the benevolent tutelage — in their own eyes at least — of the small group of men who monopolised the ownership of land, the crucial means of production. The first chapter sets the scene, showing that the social organisation of northeast agriculture in 1840, together with the crops grown in different districts, can be understood as the outcome of a complex interaction between the northeast's geology and climate, the manner in which the region was incorporated into the national economy, and the particular local form of the shift to capitalist agricultural production in the agricultural revolution. Chapters two and three examine technical innovation and adaptation in northeast agriculture, and the social consequences of technical change, in two very different periods. In the first period, from 1840 to 1870, firm commodity prices gave strong encouragement to capitalist production. In the second period, from 1870 to 1914, commodity prices slid in 'the great depression', giving severe difficulties to some class fractions, but presenting other groups — notably peasant fractions — with new but seductively dangerous opportunities. Chapters four and five concentrate on farm labour. Chapter four considers the numbers of different kinds of agricultural workers in the northeast between 1841 and 1911, together with their diet and living conditions, their housing and working conditions. The next chapter examines typical patterns of social interaction between farmers and their workers. In all of these chapters I stress that in trying to understand the social organisation of northeast agricultural production it is most important that we realise that although capitalism was the dominant mode of production after 1840, peasant production — pre-capitalist, that is — remained important. The continuing strength of the northeast peasantry gave a firm basis for bothy ballads, the Horseman's Society, and similar institutions: cultural productions that set the nineteenth century rural northeast apart as its own place and, in a highly attenuated form, still made the northeast seem a place apart to a raw southern immigrant in 1968. But the material base for this culture had been destroyed by 1914, with the final penetration of the local peasantry. Chapter six examines the peasantry's unavailing self-defence in the nineteenth century, and finds reasons for the failure of that defence in peasants' failure to recognise their own class interest sufficiently clearly, and in their consequent failure to organise an adequate political defence of that interest.

Thus an alternative title for this book might be *The Breaking of a Scottish Peasantry.* The word 'peasant' is not a word that one would apply to one's friends in everyday conversation. It is important to stress that I use the term in no pejorative sense.[14] I follow the usual academic usage in defining a peasant as a farmer working his holding with family labour as far as possible, growing his family's subsistence food crop as his highest priority, but with a subsidiary cash crop for the market being grown alongside.[15] Thus defined, the peasantry is very widely distributed in space and time: as a class (or, as we shall see below,[16] as a congerie of different class fractions) it was and is inevitably involved in production for the market to some extent, but enjoyed the invaluable ability to retreat somewhat into subsistence production when market conditions were particularly unfavourable.[17] Its firm grounding in subsistence production has always made the peasantry deeply unpopular with those concerned to maximise commodity production at all costs. I do not share this view; the peasant farmer is the doomed hero of my story, not simply a member of 'the awkward class.'[18]

Peasant farmers made the northeast land. But they also made and carried the region's distinctive culture: the most powerful folk song tradition in lowland Britain, the supple and resourceful Doric dialect (particularly rich in vituperation), the witchcraft beliefs that surface in the Horseman mystery. These cultural elements were used as levelling devices to try to block social differentiation among farmers, to try to prevent capitalist farmers from defining themselves as a class apart from other farmers. Thus the distinctive northeast rural culture does have a class base, but the fact that this base is a dead peasantry means that today the culture appears to cut across class lines. This is for two reasons. The first is theoretical. The peasantry does not fit comfortably within the usual vocabulary of class description. It was not a bourgeois class because its position did not rest on the extraction of surplus value from formally free hired workers. But nor was it proletarian, because it had not been separated from the material means of its maintenance and reproduction.[19] The peasantry was a transitional class, incompletely separated from control of land and seeking to remain independent of the labour market. Thus it is not surprising that a peasant culture appears to cut across class lines when we try to describe it in a vocabulary developed to describe clarified class relations. The second reason for this phenomenon is more concrete. Peasant opposition to social differentiation required a strong ideological emphasis on the 'kindly relations' that ought to hold between a capitalist farmer, his peasant neighbours and his hired farm workers. Thus a systematic blurring of class lines was a central element of peasant defensive tactics, and hence an important element in the culture generated by that peasantry. This blurring has been exacerbated by the subsequent romanticisation of northeast peasant life — the Bothy Nichts syndrome — and by individual social mobility. If you should find yourself pinioned in social conversation with an Aberdeen lawyer or surgeon, searching with increasing desperation for something to talk about, then I strongly recommend that you turn the conversation to the social history of agriculture. All of these urbane, sophisticated men seem to have had an auntie in Echt or a cousin in New Pitsligo. Aberdeen is a very rural city: its inhabitants' links with the surrounding countryside are deep and abiding. Those inhabitants can be guaranteed to wax lyrical about childhood days on the croft. Peasant life was like that: splendid for holidays, but less splendid if one had to suffer its hard, grinding routine day after day and year after year.

In seeing the northeast rural culture to have had a class base, I imply that the culture is best seen as a superstructure, a baroque edifice raised on economic foundations. This implies, in turn, a particular theoretical model: a model which finds its ultimate source in the writings of Karl Marx. This book uses a Marxist mode of analysis not for reasons of radical chic, but because that mode of analysis gives the greatest pay off. I have used other analytical schemes in the course of the research written up here, but I have been driven to the conclusion that no competing scheme has equivalent power in explaining the specific features of northeast farm life between 1840 and 1914. A Marxist methodology has the great advantage of forcing one to examine connections between economic life and social life, and provides both a vocabulary and an elaborated theory through which to pursue those connections. But it has one major difficulty: the vocabulary may not be familiar to many readers. In order to surmount this difficulty it is necessary to define the most important concepts that I will use; that done, I will try not to burden the book's argument with further jargon.

And so to definition.[20] I will be using two sets of concepts that operate at different levels of abstraction. The first set form part of a highly abstract theory: that is, they are used not to describe the northeast's concrete rural society directly, but to analyse the logic underlying agricultural production. The most important of these concepts is *mode of production* which refers, as the phrase suggests, to the abstract organisation of production. For Marx historical epochs — ancient society, feudal society, modern society — are defined through the dominance of a particular mode of production in that epoch. We will be concerned with two modes of production. One was capitalist in that it was, and is, based on the capitalist's extraction of surplus value from a formally free hired labour force. The other mode, peasant production using family labour that was not completely separated from the land and from other means of production, was pre-capitalist. Within any mode of production we may distinguish two separate elements — *productive forces* and *relations of production. Productive forces* comprise both *labour power,* the basis of all production for Marx, and the *means of production* — raw materials and semi-finished goods together with the tools (from a digging stick to a factory) and the infrastructure (roads, railways and so on) with which labour power transform raw materials. In agriculture the crucial means of production is land. The concept *relations of production* refers both to the relations holding between people in the productive process and to property relations. For Marx the growing lack of fit between productive forces and relations of production, as development in the productive forces is not matched by a corresponding change in relations of production, is the motor of history.

The second set of concepts is concrete rather than theoretical. That is, these concepts can be used to analyse the action and interaction of groups and individuals engaged in agricultural production. To describe the total structure of social groups in the rural northeast I shall use the term *social formation.* Marx tells us that we will always be able to perceive one dominant mode of production underlying any social formation, but that we will usually find one or more subordinate modes of production as well. So it was in the northeast between 1840 and 1914. At a level below the total social formation we will be looking at the interaction of different groups. Some of these groups were differentiated on religious criteria — adherents of the Church of Scotland against adherents of the Free Church, for example — or, like Liberals and Conservatives, on political criteria. But the groups with which we will be most concerned were differentiated on economic criteria — *social classes.* For Marx the class position of individuals and groups is defined by their relation to the means of production. In the pure case of capitalist production one class — the bourgeoisie — owns the means of production while the only other class (analytically at least) — the proletariat — owns nothing but its labour power, which it is forced to sell to the bourgeoisie in the market place in order to obtain wages upon which to live. Marx was aware that real life is much more complex than this, of course; that the clarity of the two-class model would be muddied in reality by the existence of intermediate strata, and that in analysing any social formation one would have to break down classes into smaller sections, or *fractions,* each with its own material interest to promote and defend. So it was in northeast Scottish agriculture. We will see that between 1840 and 1914 there was an agricultural proletariat in the northeast, albeit rather an odd one, in the shape of hired farm servants and farm labourers. But roughly as important (in numbers at least) as this agricultural proletariat were family workers on the farm, an unfree labouring class that belongs to a pre-capitalist mode of production. Within the bourgeoisie things get much more complicated. First we must distinguish between the three great bourgeois fractions: those whose class position rested on ownership of land, and who extracted surplus value in the form of rent (landlords); those whose class position rested on ownership of industrial capital, and who extracted surplus value in the form of profits (farmers and manufacturers); and those whose class position rested on ownership of the means of circulating capital, and who extracted surplus value in the form of interest (merchants and financiers). The fraction of industrial capitalists must be subdivided yet again. First, farmers must be divided into muckle (i.e. capitalist) farmers, middle peasants (small farmers), and poor peasants (crofters). The latter two groups' membership of the industrial capitalist class fraction was ambiguous, to say the least. Second, the industrial capitalist fraction contained groups other than farmers — groups like implement manufacturers who, while members of the same major class fraction, had material interests very different from those of farmers. An analysis based so firmly on social class may seem perverse to many northeast folk, for the nineteenth century northeast is usually seen in both lay and academic circles as a place where class was not a major organising principle of social life. There are reasons for this characteristic view and, as I hinted earlier, those reasons are themselves grounded in the social formation. We have a paradox: social class is an indispensable tool for analysing a situation where, on the face of it, class membership seemed not to be important.

I have received great kindness and assistance from many people while doing the research reported here. Some of my debts are acknowledged in notes scattered throughout the book. Some debts cannot be acknowledged because they came from discussion with people whose names I do not know in Extra-Mural lectures and W.E.A. classes scattered over the length and breadth of the northeast, at conferences, at meetings in many different departments of many English and Scottish universities, and on Auchenblae's bowling green. Some more specific acknowledgements can be made, however. I owe a particular debt to three Aberdeenshire men. It was hearing Malcolm Gray, of the Economic History department at Aberdeen University, talking about the class structure of nineteenth century Aberdeenshire agriculture that made me realise that in studying farm service I had to consider peasant life as well. And an Aberdeen loon exiled in London University, T. J. Byres, showed me that peasant life could only be understood fully in its relation to capitalist agriculture. Both men have been unstinting with advice and support: I thank them. Alexander Fenton of the National Museum of Antiquities in Edinburgh has given me great assistance too, both with advice and with photographs from his Country Life Archive. I gather that Sandy is none too happy at having his Auchterless forebears described as peasants: I trust that my (sincere) admiration for his great-uncle, Rev. Alexander Gray, will win him over! To my colleagues in the Aberdeen Sociology department I owe a deep debt. They have heard different parts of this book so many times, and have always managed at least to put on a show of being interested. It is invidious to single out individuals, but David Oldman has given me such careful and constructive advice on earlier drafts that I must record my particular obligation to him. To Kenneth Walton and his staff in the Aberdeen Geography department I give my thanks for providing me with base maps of the northeast.

Any work of this kind is impossible to do without good library facilities. In Aberdeen we are fortunate in having superb libraries. I record my deep gratitude to the University Librarian and his friendly, longsuffering and splendidly competent staff in King's College Library, the School of Agriculture Library and the Medical School Library for all their help. Likewise I thank the staff of the old Aberdeen City and Aberdeenshire County Libraries, the Mitchell Library in Glasgow, the National Library of Scotland in Edinburgh and — after I had managed to force my way in with dynamite — Edinburgh University Library. To the staff of the Old, New, and West Register Houses in Edinburgh I tender my thanks for their assistance with primary sources. I am grateful to Mrs Ramsay, Cairnbulg Castle, for letting me borrow the Philorth Steam Cultivation Company records; to Mr Troup, Inveressie, Rhynie, for allowing me to examine the Rhynie Mutual Instruction Class records; to Mrs Walker, Fintray, for lending me the Fintray Mutual Instruction Class minute book; and to the late Mr W. Cook, Little Meldrum, Tarves, for lending me documents and discussing his reminiscences of the late 1880s and 1890s. It is sad to realise that Mr Cook did not live to see the publication of this book, which his memories did so much to inspire. My final debt is to the dedicatees of this book, my wife and two daughters. They know how much I have depended on their interest and support during the time in which it was being researched and written. The only way in which I can express my gratitude is to say that but for them there would have been no point in writing this, or any, book.

Auchenblae, 1978.

1
A World Made New?

There is not perhaps an extensive corn country on the globe in which the farms in general are so small as in Aberdeenshire.[1]

NORTHEAST Scotland is a cold, hard land. The spring comes late and the autumn frosts come early. Over most of the region the predominant soils give little encouragement to the farmer. And yet these five counties — Aberdeen, Banff, Kincardine, Moray and Nairn — have a reputation for agricultural excellence. The basis of that reputation is high quality beef rearing and feeding: one of the great beef breeds, the Aberdeen-Angus, was created in the northeast. Morayshire barley has a fine reputation, as do seed potatoes and bulbs from Kincardine. But the excellence of northeast farming does not lie solely in the quality of cash crops sold out of the region. My grandmother, now dead, came from a Norfolk capitalist farming family. She remembered many occasions in her youth when she had gone to Attleborough Station with her father to collect truckloads of Aberdeenshire cattle for fattening on rich East Anglian pastures, but she had never been to the northeast. On her first visit she was amazed at the high quality of northeast husbandry: the clean crops, the trim steadings, the lack of weeds. Compared with Norfolk the whole region was, she said, more like a garden than a farming landscape. This twofold excellence, in cash crops and in husbandry, has deep roots. It goes back to the social formation of improved agriculture: to the structured relations between classes in the rural northeast at the end of the agricultural revolution of the late eighteenth and early nineteenth centuries. At bottom, then, the contemporary excellence of northeast farming is a social phenomenon.

Climate, Geology and Farming Systems

The nature of cash and subsistence crops grown in northeast Scotland between 1840 and 1914 was determined by a complex mixture of geological, climatic and political-economic[2] factors. Climate and geology formed the frame for political economy.

The northeast is Scotland's cold shoulder. Soil temperatures four inches below ground level at Craibstone, six miles northwest of Aberdeen city, do not reach 48°F (8.8°C) until about 6 May — one week later than at Boghall, Midlothian, and three weeks later than at Rothamsted, Hertfordshire.[3] The growing season is around 241 days on the coast at Aberdeen. Inland at Craibstone the figure falls to 222 and at Logie Coldstone, in the Howe of Cromar, to a mere 207 days.[4] The land slopes from sea coasts on the north and east to culminate in the Cairngorm plateau, the largest British land mass above 4,000 feet. The hills are penetrated by a number of river valleys: of these the Dee, Don and Bogie valleys have some agricultural importance. Lowland areas are protected from the prevailing wet southwest winds by the hills, but lie open to cold north and east winds. It follows that the region's general climate is cold and rather dry.

Geological factors reinforce these rather unfavourable climatic factors. The heartland of the northeast is the huge wedge of land that lies between the Laigh of Moray in the north and the Highland Boundary Fault that comes to the sea near Stonehaven. The rocks underlying this wedge — mostly Highland schists with igneous intrusions — give rise to rather poor soils unless, as in the Bogie valley and around Gamrie and Turriff, the farmer is fortunate to find folded-in Old Red Sandstone. Clays appear in some parts of Aberdeenshire and Banffshire: the most important location is a strip running along the Buchan coast through Slains to Fraserburgh.[5] Despite local advantages, then, the high quality of agriculture to be seen today in the broad swathe of land from Stonehaven to Fraserburgh and from Braemar to Peterhead is due more to skilful farming than to inherent advantages of soil or climate.[6]

Figure 1.1 White crops as a percentage of tilled acreage, northeast parishes, 1867.[7] Right-hand key, reading from top: (a) 45+; (b) 40-44.9; (c) 35-39.9; (d) 30-34.9; (e) 0-29.9.

Outside this great central wedge lie two districts where nature has been a little kinder. Moving south across the Highland Boundary Fault one comes to stony clays on the Bervie Braes and to clays and loams in the Howe of the Mearns. Both of these rather heavy soils are based on sandstone, and they are among the most fertile and most valuable farm lands in Scotland. Sandstone appears again at the other extremity of our region, in the Laigh of Moray and lowland Nairn. Here it gives a fertile light soil whose advantages, compounded by a remarkably warm climate for so northerly a latitude, are partly removed by a tendency to dry out too quickly in summer.[8]

The influence of these climatic and geological factors may be traced in Figure 1.1. The figure is based on the Board of Agriculture's manuscript parish totals for 1867 — the first year for which fairly reliable figures are available. The Board destroyed the original survey schedules to preserve confidentiality: hence these parish totals are the lowest level of analysis available to us. In this case they show that if we take the proportion of the tilled acreage under white (i.e. grain) crops[9] to be a measure of the degree of concentration on arable husbandry within a parish, then we can see that arable intensivity varied very little over the central section of the northeast. Only in Crathie/Braemar, Glenbuchat, and the Cabrach — all buried in the depths of the hills — was less than thirty per cent of the tilled acreage under white crops. The percentage rose above forty only in the Strathbogie parish of Drumblade, a strip of parishes along the sheltered Moray Firth coast, and three parishes near Aberdeen city — Kinellar, Nigg and Banchory Devenick. Over most of Aberdeenshire, Banffshire and north Kincardine arable intensivity was remarkably consistent at between thirty-five and forty per cent. But we can see also the considerable advantages of the sandstone districts. In south Kincardine six parishes had more than forty per cent of their tilled acreage under white crops and in two parishes — Bervie and St Cyrus — the figure rose above forty-five per cent. The Moray and Nairn lowlands present a more complicated picture. In general, advantages of soil and climate are reflected in the large number of parishes with more than forty per cent of tilled acreage under white crops, with the percentage exceeding forty-five in Elgin parish; but three parishes — Nairn, Auldearn and Bellie — show much lower figures. These paradoxical cases apart, however, the picture is clear. Climatic and geological advantages meant the possibility of a relatively heavy emphasis on arable production in the favoured sandstone districts, while elsewhere in the lowlands arable intensivity was very stable.

It would be a mistake to assume that the distribution of arable intensivity was a simple function of climate and soil. There is a crucial intervening variable: differences in farming systems. Figure 1.2 shows the northeast's farming systems in the early 1940s, but it can stand just as well for the period between 1840 and 1914.

The figure shows that as one moved from the agriculturally unproductive high tops toward the sea coasts on the north and east one came first to hill

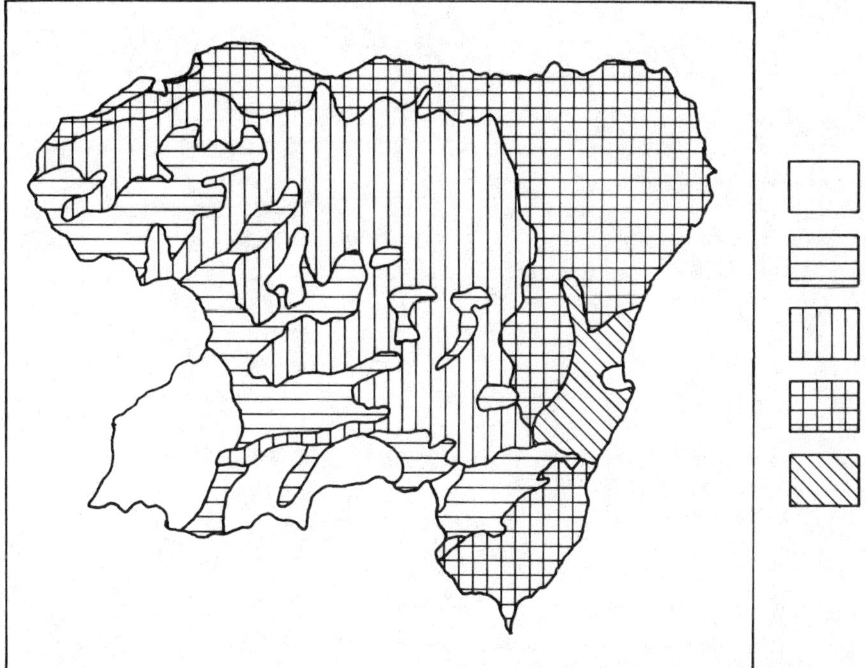

Figure 1.2 Farming systems in northeast Scotland about 1940.[10] Right-hand key, reading from top: (a) agriculturally unproductive; (b) hill sheep; (c) livestock rearing with arable; (d) arable with livestock feeding; (e) dairying with arable.

sheep areas; and then to areas where farmers specialised in rearing livestock, with arable production on the side. And then one came to the arable lowlands — indeed, to the largest single tract of arable land in Scotland — where arable production with subsidiary livestock feeding was the dominant farming system. This pattern was disturbed around Aberdeen city by a belt of specialised dairy production.[11]

These data seem wholly unsurprising. Who would expect other than that Braemar farmers were mostly raising cattle and hill sheep, while their St Cyrus brethren — on much better land and with a kindlier climate — were concentrating on growing corn crops and feeding cattle? But common sense is often a dangerous guide to interpretation. There is a complicating factor. All five northeast counties were numbered in the eleven Scottish 'corn counties' — the counties with land well suited for grain crops[12] — and yet all had rather high cattle stocking ratios.

The data expressed in Figure 1.3 show that in 1867 the number of cattle and followers per hundred tilled acres varied from 48.8 in the Cabrach to 12.8 in Drainie and Duffus. The cattle stocking ratio is high in upland parishes, as we should expect. But a broad band of rather high ratios spreads from the Garioch right across Formartine and Buchan to encompass the whole area between

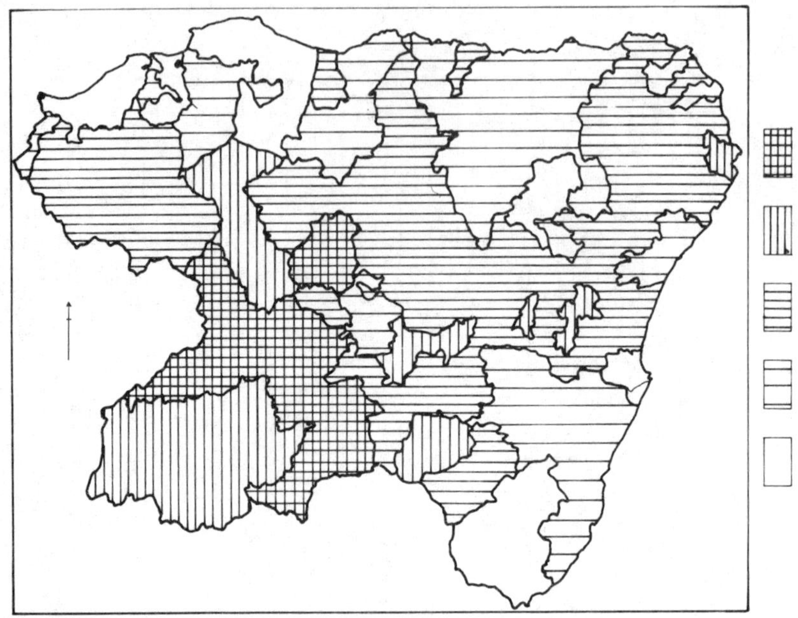

Figure 1.3 Cattle stocking ratios, northeast parishes, 1867.[13] Right-hand key, reading from top: (a) 35+; (b) 30-34.9; (c) 25-29.9; (d) 20-24.9; (e) 0-19.9.

Aberdeen and Fraserburgh. A narrower band of high ratios extends northwards from the hills through Strathbogie to the sea at Cullen. These lowland districts with high ratios show the importance of cattle feeding in lowland parts of the northeast's central wedge by 1867. The rather lower ratios of the sandstone districts reflect the stronger arable base in those areas; but the cattle stocking ratios in the Laigh of Moray and south Kincardine are higher than the climatic and geological endowment would lead us to expect. Throughout the northeast, a southern visitor observed in 1871, 'all the operations of husbandry are subordinate to the requirements of the byre'.[14] Political economy had modified the impact of physical elements. To understand how this came to be we must first retreat in time, and consider the manner in which northeast agriculture came to be 'improved'.

The Agricultural Revolution

It is not easy to make precise statements about northeast agriculture before the eighteenth century. Writers of the Improvement period buried prior arrangements under a heap of imprecations: thus one of the most perceptive nineteenth century commentators, speaking of the early eighteenth century, asserted that 'the method of tillage . . . had seen no improvement from time immemorial'.[15] That is too strong. The pace of change may have been slow, but it is clear that technical change was under way in the northeast, as elsewhere in Scotland, before the agricultural revolution.[16]

That being said, however, it remains true that material productive forces were primitive until the eighteenth century. Arable land was usually to be found near the coast and in river valleys. It lay unenclosed, in small patches dotted among tracts of bog and stony heather moor. The main arable land, the 'inbye land', was worked in runrig — the Scottish term for the ridge and furrow cultivation that had characterised the agriculture of almost all northern and western Europe. It was heavily manured and bore corn crops year after year without benefit of rotation. The corn crops grown were oats and bere — a primitive form of barley. With the inbye land never rested under fallow or grass and never cleaned with a turnip break, yields were low and weeds choked the growing crops. Arable production was extended beyond the limits of inbye land through sectoral fallowing, a primitive form of rotation. Sections of 'outbye land' were brought into cultivation from the waste, cropped for a few years until the land's natural fertility was exhausted, and then allowed to revert to waste in order to regenerate. Rough grazing between specks of arable was used to pasture animals — sheep, goats and the 'Buchan hummlie' — the native small black cow. There was plenty of grazing in the summer, but a farm's carry — particularly of cattle — was severely limited by an acute shortage of winter fodder.[17]

Farming implements were equally primitive. Ploughs were made of wood with very little metal work, and were drawn by up to twelve oxen — an arrangement defended by one traditionally minded eighteenth century Aberdeenshire laird on the ground that it allowed some animals to rest while the others were doing the work.[18] Threshing was accomplished with the flail, reaping with the sickle. Steadings were made of turf or rough stone, thatched with heather. Ropes were twisted from heather or horse hair. Roads scarcely existed, so neither did carts; loads were carried in baskets strapped on garrons, the small but sturdy local breed of horse.

These rather primitive material forces gave rise to a social formation comprising landlords on the one hand and a stratified peasantry on the other. In 1696 a poll tax was imposed throughout Scotland by the chronically impecunious government. The Poll Book for Aberdeenshire survives, and was published by the antiquarian Spalding Club in 1844.[19] It gives us a matchless view of the social formation in the difficult 'seven ill years' at the end of the seventeenth century. Although it is limited to Aberdeenshire, there is no reason to think that other northeast counties would have looked much different.

The Poll Book depicts a society where almost all land was held on tenancy. Landowners were surprisingly numerous, and since the arable acreage at this time was rather small we may conclude that the average laird's rent roll was also small. The laird let a piece of land on written or verbal lease to a single tenant or to a group of tenants who undertook to pay a joint rent and cooperated in working the farm. Each tenant probably had subtenants, and a subtenant might himself have subtenants — cottars and grassmen. Even the gangrel bodies enumerated on so many Aberdeenshire farms in 1696 — 'ane peer man', 'ane widow' — probably had access to some land on which to grow subsistence crops. Only unmarried farm servants had no access to land; their subsistence was provided by the farmer as part of the 'fee' (wages).

Thus the social organisation of the fermtoun was structured around access to land under tenancy and subtenancy.[20] The low level of productive forces compelled co-operation on many farms: joint tenants were obliged to combine their work oxen to construct a plough team for the 'twal owsen ploo', for instance. Production was predicated on such co-operation, hence social institutions were developed to protect it. On joint farms rigs of inbye and outbye land could periodically be reallocated to equalise access to good and bad land. Tensions and disagreements among tenants were defused, in theory at least, by the arbitration of the birleyman.

These strong co-operative elements would lead later generations to see in the pre-improvement social formation a lost Merrie Scotland, a 'kindly society' where social harmony reigned both among tenants and between tenants and lairds. That image was to prove a powerful political weapon, but it was not well grounded in fact. Rents exacted by lairds from tenants and from subtenants by tenants were heavy, and pressed insistently on the household's subsistence:

> Most of the farmers in those days, be it observed, did not think themselves *'well set down'* unless they could sublet as much as paid the greater part of their rent, and yet leave themselves a comfortable holding besides; and in some cases they even contrived to have something over for gathering it from their crofters and carrying it to the laird. While those farmers paid but little rent, they also paid but little wages to servants. They generally hired their (day) labourers from among their own crofters, on much their own terms; for the crofters could seldom afford to say them nay, being under heavy bondages of labour and perquisites to the laird or to *the muckle farmer*.[21]

It is evident that the peasantry had its own internal stratification. The 1696 Poll Book shows many rich peasants in Aberdeenshire, men whose holdings were so large that they could not be worked solely with labour drawn from the peasant's household. Additional labour came in two forms. One form was hired farm servants — invariably poor class peasant children whose paternal holdings had a labour surplus — who sold their labour power for six, nine or twelve months in return for board and wages. An equally important source of additional labour, however — as the passage quoted above makes clear — was the multitude of poor peasants who sublet part of the rich peasant's holding. Poor peasants had to find an additional source of income to eke out the proportion of the household's subsistence that could be wrung from their tiny parcels of land, to pay any money element in their rent, and to buy in commodities not made on the farm. But as casual or part-time wage labourers they had a weak bargaining position against the rich peasant from whom they sublet; very often the rich peasant had a monopsony position in the local labour market.[22]

Rent was exacted in a complex mixture of money, produce ('kind' or 'perquisites') and labour dues.[23] Neither the rent level nor, indeed, rural population density could have been sustained from agricultural production alone. But it was not until the early nineteenth century that the union between agriculture and artisan production was broken. Until that time the peasant household's income was supplemented by a whole range of non-agricultural occupations. One set of such occupations largely would survive until the mid-nineteenth century: the multitude of personal and country crafts — tailor, soutar (shoemaker), sievewright, millwright, blacksmith, mason, joiner, miller, and so on — that were integrated more or less closely with agriculture. Even today the Ordnance Survey maps are speckled with Smiths Crofts, Millers Crofts and Wrights Crofts.

Other handicrafts would not survive the onset of capitalist production in town and country. By 1840 three major northeast handicraft industries would be destroyed or would no longer be integrated with agricultural production — stocking knitting, spinning and hand-loom weaving, and distilling and smuggling illicit spirits. Chief among these was stocking knitting. The northeast had a European reputation for knitted hose,[24] and as early as 1680 an observer noted that it was knitting 'which bringeth money to the commons: other ways of getting it they have not'.[25] The high rate of women's wages in late eighteenth century Aberdeenshire was attributed '. . . to the extensive manufactory of stockings at Aberdeen, which has taught all of them to knit; and so industrious they are, that, in travelling the high road, they knit as busily as at home'.[26]

This widespread and important craft was organised and controlled by urban merchants on the 'putting-out' system: they supplied the yarn, took back the knitted stockings, and pocketed most of the profit. Spinning and hand-loom weaving was organised on similar lines:

> There was little produce to sell off such a croft, and the great source of revenue was the money earned by the women by spinning lint. At that time country merchants made a trade of giving out dressed lint to be hand-spun, the women spinning it into thread and rolling it into cuts. It was spun into so many cuts the lb., according to the fineness of the thread required. The spinner often had her work portioned out into so many hasps per day, or so many spindles per week. Much of the spinning was done in the winter evenings, the women sitting with their wheels between them by a blazing peat fire, which was their only light . . . Every kind of cloth, both lint and woollen, was home carded, spun and woven.[27]

The linked activities of illicitly distilling and smuggling spirits were the last great artisanal buttress of peasant production. Distillation is a peerless way of storing the exchange value of perishable corn crops.[28] This fact was not lost on northeast folk:

> . . . There was an illicit still on almost every farm, and on many farms as many as half a dozen . . . The great illicit distillers were the crofters and cottars.[29]

Thus, in Glenbuchat, 'every house had its hiding-place for the still and its produce'.[30] In the Garioch, as in many parts of the northeast, illicit distilling was 'very often the means of bringing in the rent'.[31] The same was true of the business of smuggling the whisky to consumers in Aberdeen city or further south. In many upland parishes smuggling made an essential contribution to the household budget at the risk (sometimes courted for revenge or excitement) of an occasional battle with the detested gaugers.[32] On sea coasts this domestic smuggling could be augmented with an unofficial trade in foreign spirits,[33] but wherever it went on it made a useful adjunct to peasant agricultural production:

> Smuggling was common in Buchan and throughout the whole country. In fact, the country folk had no other means of raising money with which to pay their rents, and the lairds were quite alive to that fact.[34]

In smuggling and distilling, as in knitting, spinning and weaving, much of the money earned was creamed by the laird or superior tenant in the form of rent.

The distinction between rich peasants (muckle farmers) on the one hand and middle peasants (small farmers) — who needed neither to hire servants nor sell their own labour power — and poor peasants (crofters) on the other was clear enough by 1696 to allow us to speak of them as two separate class fractions. Both fractions were contained within the peasantry in that both muckle farmer and crofter produced subsistence crops alongside cash crops: but their opposed interest in the labour market and in tenancy arrangements set one class fraction apart from the other. The separation grew over time. The 1696 Aberdeenshire Poll Book shows that joint tenancy was more common in upland districts and among smaller tenants at that date. Rich peasants, particularly those in more favoured lowland areas, were more likely to hold their land in a single tenancy. This shift to single tenancy reflected and deepened the social differentiation of the peasantry, preparing the ground for the later transformation of rich peasants into capitalist farmers. By the early eighteenth century differentiation was sufficiently marked to show in the level of productive forces: middle and poor peasants still yoked the Buchan hummlie to the plough, while rich peasants imported heavy work oxen from the Lothians.[35]

It was not just productive forces that were developing. Relations of production were changing too, and taking a form that would facilitate the triumph of the capitalist mode of production in the agricultural revolution. We noted earlier that by 1600 lowland rents were paid in a mixture of money, kind and labour dues. These labour dues were not light — tenants would be bound to work for a specified number of days in the year for the laird, to cut and carry a set number of loads of peat to his house, to maintain his mill and grind their grain there, and so on. Labour dues were probably even heavier for a subtenant, because it was in the superior tenant's interest to maintain the largest possible part of his subrent as labour. These labour dues, seeming to assert that personal dependence was the major element in the relation between a superior and his inferior clients, might make social relations before the agricultural revolution seem classically feudal. As late as the last decade of the eighteenth century one outraged progressive thundered that 'there is not in this island, such a compleat remain of feudal despotism, as in the practice respecting (thirlage to) mills in Aberdeenshire'.[36] But this view was misleading. Land tenure was still nominally feudal, but by the seventeenth century in lowland districts the classic Scottish feudalism — wardholding, with its obligation of an inferior to support his superior in warfare — had given way to feuferme. Under feuferme an inferior's obligations were (and are) economic; he merely had to pay a stated feu-duty to his superior. This feu-duty originally was fixed at an economic rent. Feuferme tenure was a commercialised, if not yet a capitalist, social relation. The fact was masked by the slow attrition of labour dues, but the shift to feuferme — a shift completed in the northeast lowlands a couple of centuries before the agricultural revolution and completed by force in upland districts after the '45 — had made the cash nexus the principal structure mediating the relationship between laird and tenant. Landlords had not yet come to see the main potential of their estates to be rent that could be transformed into capital, but the road to that blinding vision had largely been cleared.

More clearance work was done by the Scots Parliament. A series of Acts between 1660 and 1695 encouraged landlords to enclose (that is, to fence) their land and laid down a simple procedure for dividing common lands among neighbouring proprietors.[37] Scottish landlords were spared the expense, inconvenience and potential popular odium suffered by English landlords in having to go to Parliament for permission to enclose. So assiduously did Scots lairds pursue this advantage that by 1828 the Lord Advocate could report that

> There is very little property in Scotland that is now common. A Scottish Statute having authorised the division of all common property among the adjoining proprietors, there now exist few common rights.[38]

The way was clear: property relations offered no check to the radical development of productive forces that we call the agricultural revolution.

Technical aspects of the agricultural revolution need not detain us here. They have been chronicled so lovingly by generations of Scottish economic historians that the story will be familiar to all readers.[39] Social elements of the agricultural revolution are less familiar. Central to these social elements is the transformation of rich peasants into capitalist farmers.

The roots of this transformation lie in the mid-eighteenth century. A handful of northeast landowners began to transform agricultural production on their estates through enclosure, crop rotation and improved implements. The famous names are the Earls of Moray and Fife in Moray, the Earl of Findlater in Banffshire, Barclay of Ury, Ramsay of Balmain, Lord Gardenstone and Lord Monboddo in Kincardine, and — most famous of all because so heavily documented — Sir Archibald Grant of Monymusk in Aberdeenshire.[40] Grant consolidated previously scattered runrig holdings and thus destroyed the basis of existing tenancy forms. By limiting subtenancy as far as possible he tried to build a new social formation in which all tenants, large and small, held directly from the laird. His customarily autocratic methods sometimes generated opposition;[41] but no eighteenth century Scottish laird needed to fear the opposition of his peasant tenants. Grant pressed on regardless. His single-minded commitment to scientific agriculture under the capitalist mode of production has earned him the uncritical respect of Scottish economic historians. Yet it is important to note that Grant's efforts were premature. After his death his improvements stagnated under the half-hearted attention of his son, who 'had been long in the army (and had) no notion of bestowing his whole time upon husbandry'.[42] The material base was not yet sufficiently mature for Grant's initiative to spark off a continuous revolution in productive methods. Monymusk, in common with the rest of the northeast, was not yet ready for capitalist agriculture.

This does not mean that northeast farmers did not produce some cash crops for the market. The trade in black cattle for the English market grew considerably during the eighteenth century. But lean cattle for this trade could be produced within the existing mode of production, a sideline subsidiary to the peasant's primary concern to assure the household's subsistence grain supply. Thus we are told that most cattle driven south from the eighteenth century northeast were superannuated plough oxen aged from seven to seventeen years[43] — and tough eating they must have made. Aberdeen, unlike Edinburgh, was not of a size to stimulate a significant cattle feeding industry. Surplus grain was marketed, but the appallingly bad roads generally prevented the growth of large-scale capitalist arable production on the model of East Lothian, where the narrow belt of rich arable land lies along the coast. In the mid-eighteenth century, East Lothian farmers moved quickly from cattle raising to specialised arable production.[44] In the northeast at the same time, what specialised arable production there was similarly was concentrated within five miles of the coast.[45] This gave opportunities for specialisation in grain to farmers in the Laigh of Moray — long famous as a grain area — but elsewhere things were less favourable. Thus 'the girnal of Aberdeenshire' — the Garioch — lies more than twenty miles from the sea. Transport difficulties could have been overcome if commodity prices had been high enough to tempt rich peasants to take the plunge into capitalist production. In the mid-eighteenth century northeast this was not the case.

By the end of that century things were very different. Between 1780 and 1840 rich peasants throughout the northeast moved into full production for the market as capitalism matured to be the dominant mode of agricultural production in the region. This radical transfornation had two causes, one operating close to Aberdeen city, the other in districts removed from 'the Toon'. Around Aberdeen the stimulus came from a strong internal market. The growing textile and quarrying industries in the lower Don valley, together with growing trade at the city's port, produced a sharp increase in Aberdeen's population, leading in turn to a strong urban demand for milk and vegetables. The demand for milk was satisfied by the rapid development of specialised dairy farms around the city.[46] This specialisation lasted throughout the nineteenth century. In the 1880s, within ten miles of the city 'almost all the farms and a good many crofts are devoted to producing milk, butter and eggs for Aberdeen'.[47] The demand for vegetables induced the equally rapid growth of an intensive market gardening sector in the suburbs. The acreage of each market garden seems to have been rather small, but the intensity of production — using spade cultivation — meant that many market gardeners were capitalists, relying on hired labour to work the holding.[48] This flowering of dairying and market gardening near the city was all the more remarkable in that the land was naturally barren. A wild, stony, heather moor stretched west and south from Aberdeen. One visitor thought it was just as well that late eighteenth century Aberdonians were enthusiastic farmers, for 'in no part of the known world is such enthusiasm more necessary than about the town of Aberdeen'.[49]

Away from 'the Toon' the stimulus to capitalist production came from an external, rather than an internal, source — the growth of the cattle industry, which we will review in greater detail in the next chapter. The increasing demand for beef — a demand which the Napoleonic wars sent rocketing — together with a strong demand for grain gave commodity prices which rich peasants found irresistible. In this they were strongly encouraged by their lairds' desire for larger rent-rolls. In the 1780s Andrew Wight had still found a number of northeast proprietors who clung to a seigneurial role: of the Earl of Aberdeen's failure to capitalise the vast Haddo estate, for example, he snorted that 'it is a great misfortune to be too rich; for it makes many men negligent as to the improvement of their estates'.[50] By 1840 all lairds had seen the error of that way. Northeast landed property was now thoroughly capitalist, its major function for the owner the generation of ground rent.

Who were the new capitalist farmers? In Aberdeen city's suburban market gardening sector they were urban merchants, tradesmen and professionals looking for a good investment.[51] Elsewhere in the region things were rather different. Writing during the Napoleonic wars, the crucial time for the transformation of rich peasants into capitalist farmers, Keith[52] has an intriguing account of divisions within the ranks of muckle farmers. They belonged, he asserted, 'to three distinct classes, who have each their discriminating qualities, or characters'. First came the 'ancient farmers' — unreconstructed rich peasants. These were old men, irascible and litigious, though also honest and sensible. They were simple in their manners and plain in their dress. Good judges of black cattle, they were 'indolent in the management of their farms', paying little attention to scientific husbandry. They drank heavily, relishing the 'crack' and dram of market days, and continued to follow their fathers' leisure pursuits — like shooting at the mark. The second fraction was the opposite of these 'ancient farmers'. This was the leaven of improvement, 'the class of farmers who have been induced to leave the southern counties, and to take leases of farms in Aberdeenshire'. A number of progressive northeast lairds had enticed skilled Lothian capitalist farmers north to act as exemplars to the local farmers — men like James Anderson with his lease on 1,130 acres at Monkshill, Udny, at 19-28d per acre for sixty-three years, and Robert Bookless, brought north as a farm overseer by Sir Archibald Grant and tenant of 490 acres in Monymusk by 1780.[53] Other lairds ranged even further: Sir Alexander Ramsay of Balmain, Kincardine, brought men from Norfolk.[54] These southern exemplars were insignificant numerically, but their influence was enormous. Keith tells us that they were adept at the new husbandry. Living comfortably and hospitably, they were made welcome at their lairds' tables. They formed and took the lead in agricultural societies. Pure capitalist farmers, the reproduction and increase of their capital was their sole concern: they did not regret leaving the Lothians for Aberdeenshire, 'for they are now generally worth ten times as much of capital as they had when they first came to this county'.[55] James Anderson, the most celebrated of these Lothian men, returned to Edinburgh after making his pile in Udny. Not for him the 'ancient farmers'' attachment to a piece of northeast land. The final muckle farmer fraction connected the first two groups. These were the sons of the 'ancient farmers' — young and middle-aged men who, unlike their fathers, recognised the value of the new methods. They criticised inappropriate innovations on the basis of detailed local knowledge, but on the whole their farming — and their lifestyle — followed the Lothian men's precedent. This final fraction held the future in its hand. By 1840 rich peasants had all been transformed into capitalist farmers, and the vast majority of these men were locally born and bred, the descendants of former rich peasants.[56]

By 1840 the northeast's agricultural revolution was complete. Runrig was on its last legs and hung on only in the depths of the hills at places like Coilnacreich on upper Deeside.[57] Virtually the whole tilled acreage was in consolidated fields worked on a rotation carefully calculated — within limits set by cropping restrictions in leases — to take the greatest advantage of local variations in soil, climate and market conditions. The New Statistical Account of the 1840s shows a considerable range in rotations, from a four-shift with only one grass break on strong lands in arable districts to a seven-shift with four grass breaks in more pastoral districts. Bare fallowing had almost disappeared from the northeast. Drainage and enclosure were making steady progress. Artificial fertilisers, first bonemeal and later guano, had recently been introduced to the area. These fertilisers were carried on the carts — often made by the famous firm of Simpson of Peterhead — that trundled along the new roads that spread like couch-grass in the early nineteenth century. The first northeast turnpike was opened between Stonehaven and Aberdeen in 1797; by 1850 there were more than 766 miles of turnpike in the five counties[58] and 2,815 miles of secondary, commutation road.[59] In 1805 these new roads were supplemented by the northeast's only important canal, the Aberdeenshire Canal, between Aberdeen Harbour and Port Elphinstone, near Inverurie.[60] Farm steadings were being improved greatly by 1840, too — at least on large farms. Improved implements were common: iron ploughs had consigned the wooden 'twal owsen ploo' to the museum.

These rapidly developing productive forces brought the capitalist mode of production to a dominant position in northeast agriculture. That dominance would never subsequently be challenged. The basis of the capitalist mode was the farmer's reliance on hired labour to produce marketable commodities and thus to reproduce and augment his capital. Production was geared to the market. Hence the demand for large farms — capitalist farms — was closely related to market prices for cash crops. The Napoleonic war boom attracted many men with capital into farming and drove up the rent level, but 'after the conclusion of the war adventurers and speculators were turned out of the field'.[61] The same thing happened in the Crimean war boom of the 1850s when wholesale butchers, merchants, railway promoters, meal millers, manure manufacturers and estate valuers — among many others — rushed into farming in the expectation of a higher return on capital than could be looked for in their other businesses.[62] Many of these men had a purely calculative attitude to farming. A. S. George took a nineteen-year lease of Auchangrieve, Rothiemay, in 1865. George was a Keith meal miller: he took Auchangrieve in a competitive letting simply because farm rents were very depressed in 1865 as a result of the great rinderpest epidemic among cattle. His decision whether or not to renew the lease, he told the Richmond Commission in 1881, would be determined solely by the rent which the Fife estate would demand.[63] Other large farmers followed the logic of their mode of production less closely, and allowed sentiment to interfere with financial calculation. One man bewailed his foolish readiness to pay more rent than the farm was worth: 'It has turned out to be a bad bargain, I am sorry to say, but it is the place that I was born upon, and I had made things handy and I was very unwilling to leave'.[64]

A corollary of the capitalist farmer's concentration on cash crop production was that he tended not to rely on his farm to provide his family's foodstuffs. Oats, potatoes and — to a decreasing extent as the nineteenth century wore on — milk were all produced on the large farm to feed the farm servants, but the farmer and his family ate different food. The minister of Udny reported as early as the 1840s that 'the (large) farmers take most of their groceries from Aberdeen'.[65] These groceries — wheaten flour, tea, coffee, sugar, French wines and spirits, butcher meat — contrasted starkly with the diet of the other classes. We shall see later that this contrast became a *Leitmotif* in bothy ballads pillorying exploitative farmers. But, once again, one finds cases of capitalist farmers not following the logic of their mode of production too closely, and taking an unusual amount of their foodstuffs from the farm:

> You provide your own milk, and probably your own oatmeal, and meat and eggs, and chickens and ducks? — Yes . . . I am content with a very small profit, £43 a year, and the keep of my family. I daresay merchants look for a much higher return.[66]

One's admiration for this large farmer's forbearance is somewhat tempered when one realises that he started calculating the profit on working his 170-acre farm only after paying all the living expenses for himself and his family and allowing himself a five per cent return on invested capital.

The New Social Formation

The triumph of capitalist production in the agrarian northeast, as throughout the Scottish lowlands, led many recent commentators to assume that a new social formation of lairds, capitalist farmers and landless labourers sprang fully armed from the ruins of earlier arrangements.[67] We will study the reasons for this dramatically misguided perception in chapter seven; here we need merely show how wrong it is.

Table 1.1

Land ownership, northeast counties, 1873[68]

	No. of owners of more than 1 acre	Acreage	Gross annual value (£)	No. of owners of more than 500 acres
Aberdeen	869	1,252,100	768,791	212
Banff	142	406,939	190,681	33
Kincardine	251	302,736	167,940	36
Moray	195	244,396	236,021	62
Nairn	70	120,636	34,450	14
Northeast counties	1,527	2,326,807	1,397,883	357

Lairds did remain an important class. Scottish land was concentrated in few hands in the nineteenth century.[69] In 1873 seven per cent of England and Wales was in the hands of owners with more than 20,000 acres apiece. The corresponding figure for Scotland was fifty-eight per cent. More than three-quarters of the land area of Scotland was owned by 580 people.[70] The northeast was no exception to this national picture. Table 1.1 shows that land ownership was highly concentrated in 1873; only 1,527 people owned more than one acre.

The population of the five counties in 1871 was 395,093. The last column shows that larger estates (those above 500 acres) were in the hands of a mere 357 people. Northeast land, the crucial means of agricultural production, was owned by many fewer people in 1873 than had been the case in 1696. Even the 1873 figures understate the grip of great landowners, for some lairds held land in more than one county and hence would have been counted more than once. The Earl (later Duke) of Fife, for example, owned 249,220 acres in Aberdeenshire, Banffshire, and Moray; the Duke of Richmond and Gordon owned 241,883 acres in the same counties.[71]

It follows from this that the northeast was a leasehold area. In 1887 — the first year for which this information is available — only thirteen out of the 147 northeast parishes had more than fifteen per cent of tilled acreage in owner occupation.[72] No parish had more than one-third of tilled acreage in owner occupation. The picture does not change when we turn from tilled acreage to numbers of holdings.

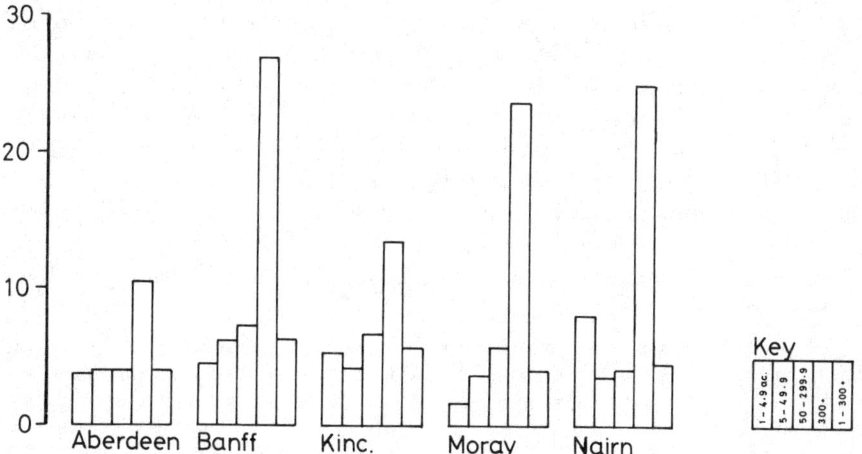

Figure 1.4 Percentage owner occupation of agricultural holdings by size of holding, northeast counties, 1912.[73]

The figure shows that even by 1912 the overwhelming majority of holdings were tenanted. It also shows that owner occupation was at all common only in the numerically insignificant category of huge farms (for the northeast) of more than 300 acres. On such owner-occupied big capitalist farms rentier capital and industrial capital, normally separately located in the landowning and muckle farming fractions of the bourgeoisie, were fused together. The same was true, of course, on farms which lairds had in hand.

Landowners were an important class in the social formation of agriculture, then: but their influence was disproportionately great when compared with their rather small numbers. The same is true of capitalist farmers. The point will be demonstrated with farm size data from the late nineteenth and early twentieth centuries, but first we need to make a few comments on the relationship between farm size and mode of production.

We have seen that the distinction between muckle farmers, small farmers, and crofters — that is, between capitalist farmers, middle peasants, and poor peasants — lay in the relation of each fraction to the labour market. Capitalist farmers always had to draw from the market a high proportion of the labour power needed to work their holdings. Peasant farmers, on the other hand, always sought to work their holdings with family labour, and hired labour only when absolutely forced to do so. Within the peasantry, middle peasant holdings were large enough both to support the farm household and to absorb all or most of the labour power of family members. Poor peasant holdings, on the other hand, could produce only a proportion of the household's subsistence: the crofter, and members of his family, were forced to take to casual, seasonal, or part-time wage work in order to eke out the subsistence that could be wrung from the croft. The relationship between a capitalist farmer and his workers was based on the cash nexus, while in peasant farming rights and obligations derived from common kinship cut across any attempt to ground relationships in money.[74] The family worker had claims on the farmer that were not open to the hired worker: in lean times the peasant holding did not lay off labour. This precapitalist mode of production was reflected in another thing too — the attitude to cash crop production. Like the capitalist farmer the peasant had to find the laird's rent, various kinds of rates for public authorities, and he had to generate a replacement fund for worn-out equipment. So a proportion of his production had to be for the market. But his dependence on the market was much slighter than in the case of the large farmer:

> Here the low price of grain does not affect the tenant, because his family require all that he can raise. His rent is paid from the produce of the poultry-yard and dairy, and work of his family in the moss, and a year old stirk makes up the balance, should there not be sufficient; and his own earnings go to provide clothing and such necessities or luxuries as he finds it requisite to purchase, or prudent to indulge in.[75]

This account of colonising crofters on the southern outskirts of Aberdeen city — hence the emphasis on dairying — makes it clear that the peasant household, and not the individual tenant, was the productive unit. Family members explored every niche of the local economy in an attempt to aggregate an adequate household income. Thus the peasant farmer, as unquestioned boss of his household's enterprise, was much less dependent on cash crop prices than was the capitalist farmer. This is one major reason why the demand for small farms and crofts was affected by changes in cash crop prices much more slowly, and much less deeply, than was the demand for large farms.

The division into large farms, small farms and crofts depended on a number of factors. The quality of land was important: on light land a pair of horse could plough up to twice the acreage that they could manage on heavy clay, and a given quantity of family labour hence could work a larger holding. The level of material forces was important, too — family labour using tractors and combines on today's northeast farms can manage acreages that would have needed a great squad of hired servants a century ago. But a third factor was more important for our purposes — the farm family's life cycle.[76] The smallest

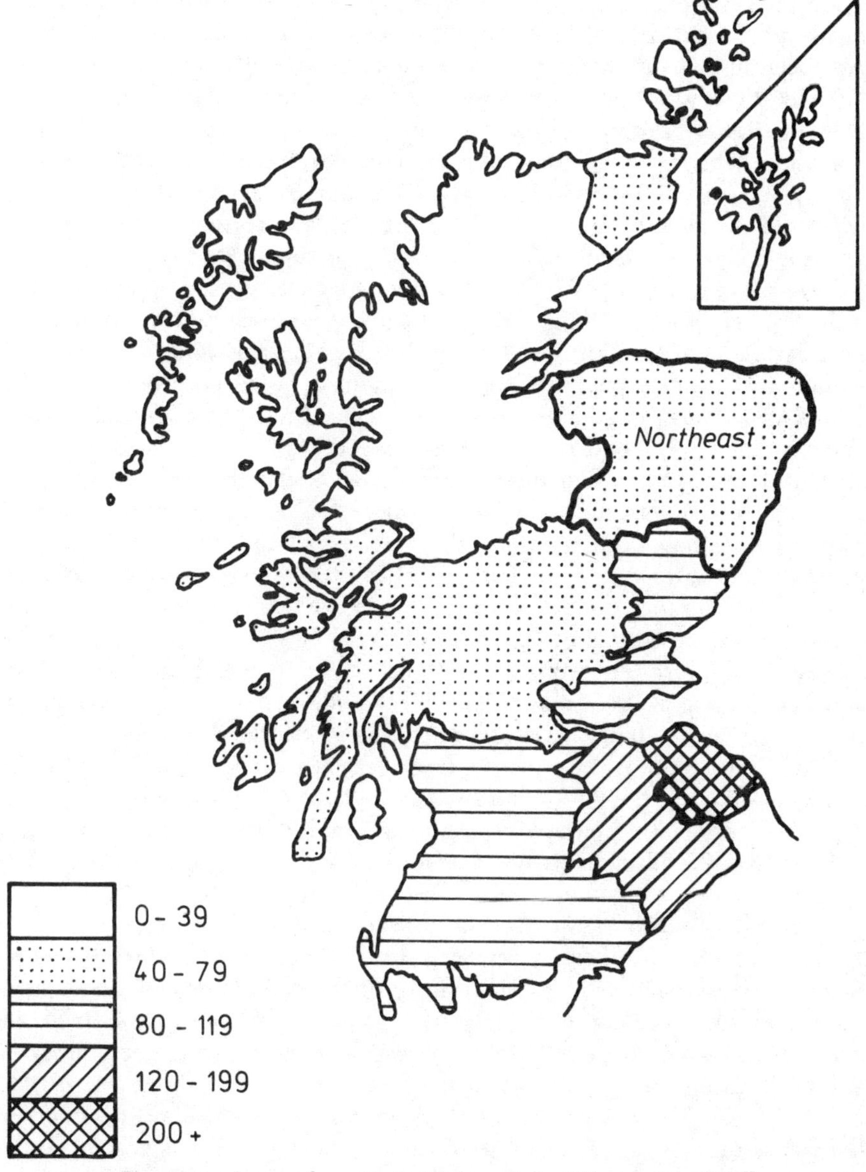

Figure 1.5 Average farm size (in tilled acres), Scottish counties, 1895.[77]

farm likely to prove capable of providing full-time work for the peasant household varied from twenty to fifty acres, depending on local circumstances.[78] But when the farmer was recently married, his children were young or his wife proved barren, then hired labour would be needed even on such a small place. Two literary examples make the point. In *Sunset Song* Blawearie, a Kincardine middle peasant holding formerly worked entirely with family labour, needs a 'fee'd loon' (hired male farm servant) when the farm household breaks up.[79] Gushetneuk, in William Alexander's magnificent novel of central Aberdeenshire, is once again a middle peasant farm: but Johnny Gibb always has a fee'd loon on the place because Johnny's marriage has proved childless.[80] Once his family began to grow up, then a peasant farmer might find his holding in labour surplus until all his children had left the paternal holding. Only when some of his children were old enough to work but they had not all left could the ideal balance between production and consumption within the household be maintained. At the peak of labour supply, and given good luck — several sons, for instance — even a two-pair farm[81] could be worked with little hired labour for a time. That time could not be long, however; thus we may assume that any farm of 100 tilled acres or more would rely on hired labour and hence be worked on the capitalist mode of production. The boundary between middle and poor peasant holdings is much fuzzier. I will assume that it lay at fifty tilled acres since this fits the categories used in statistical compilation, but this probably understates the size of the middle peasantry and overstates that of the poor peasantry. Using these cut-off points, we can now begin to look at the distribution of northeast farm size.

Figure 1.5 shows that the average farm size of northeast counties was small in 1895. Despite the counties' enumeration in the Scottish 'corn counties' the average farm size throughout the region was below eighty acres, far below the average for the strongly capitalist southeast region (in particular Berwickshire and East Lothian, so beloved of Scottish economic historians) and even below the average for the dairying region of southwest Scotland. If we go back ten years in time and look at the distribution of farm size within counties, then we will begin to see how insignificant, in numbers at least, were northeast capitalist farmers. Comparable figures are given for East Lothian to show how different was the social formation in that county: the East Lothian figures will form the basis for a polemic in chapter seven.

Table 1.2 shows that poor peasant farms formed much the largest group of holdings in each northeast county in 1885. Even if we ignore the many holdings of less than one acre, where agriculture could not make a very significant contribution to household income (except in the limited case of market gardening), then poor peasants were at least as numerous as middle peasants and capitalist farmers combined. Taking capitalist farmers alone, we see that only in Kincardine was one in four occupants of land a capitalist farmer. In Banffshire muckle farmers numbered only twelve per cent — one farmer in eight. East Lothian makes a stark contrast: there well over half of all holdings

Table 1.2

Percentage size distribution of agricultural holdings, in tilled acres, northeast counties and East Lothian, 1885[82]

	1-4	5-49	50-99	100+	Total
Aberdeen	15.7	48.9	18.0	17.4	100.0
Banff	24.1	49.9	13.7	12.3	100.0
Kincardine	15.3	41.1	18.2	25.5	100.1
Moray	24.0	44.0	15.6	16.5	100.1
Nairn	11.8	43.1	22.7	22.5	100.1
Northeast counties	18.2	47.9	17.0	17.0	100.1
East Lothian	12.6	23.0	6.5	57.9	100.0

were capitalist farms. Clearly the social formations of East Lothian and of the northeast were radically different. Equally clearly, numbers of northeast capitalist farmers do not suggest that the capitalist mode of production was dominant in the region.

But is the *number* of capitalist farmers and of middle and poor peasants the only way of measuring the relative strength of capitalist agriculture and peasant agriculture? Certainly the fact that capitalist farmers were outnumbered so heavily in the northeast had a profound effect on social relations in agriculture, as we shall see. But a better measure of the strength of each type of agriculture might be the tilled acreage worked under each mode of production. Table 1.3 presents data on this matter which can be compared directly with the data on numbers of holdings in Table 1.2. Table 1.3 reveals an intriguing situation. Northeast capitalist farmers may have represented only about one farmer in six in 1885, but that one sixth held well over half the tilled acreage. In fact their position was even stronger for, as we shall see in more detail below, capitalist farmers invariably occupied the best land in any

Table 1.3

Percentage of tilled acreage by farm size, northeast counties and East Lothian, 1885[83]

	1-4	5-49	50-99	100+	Total
Aberdeen	1.1	17.8	24.4	56.7	100.0
Banff	2.0	23.1	23.7	51.2	100.0
Kincardine	0.8	13.8	19.0	69.2	100.1
Moray	1.5	16.8	21.4	60.4	100.1
Nairn	0.7	13.7	23.9	61.8	100.1
Northeast counties	1.3	17.6	23.4	57.7	100.0
East Lothian	0.2	1.9	2.1	95.7	99.9

given area. These acreage figures do show the dominance of the capitalist mode of production in northeast agriculture. In East Lothian, with ninety-five per cent of the tilled acreage in capitalist farms, that dominance becomes an unshakable monopoly.

Table 1.3 hints at important variations within the northeast. The three counties that contain the rich sandstone districts — Kincardine, Moray and Nairn — show a higher proportion of their tilled acreage in capitalist farms than do Aberdeenshire and Banffshire. The 1885 data do not allow us to go below the county level to examine these variations, but data from the very end of our period do allow us so to do.

Table 1.4

Average size, and size distribution, of agricultural holdings by counties and districts of counties, northeast Scotland, 1912[84]

	Average size (acres under crops & grass)	%age distribution of holdings by size			
		1-4	5-49	50-99	100+
Aberdeenshire	57.3	12.4	48.2	20.5	18.7
Aberdeen	53.1	11.2	48.8	23.2	16.8
Alford	55.5	10.8	46.9	24.2	17.9
Deer	53.8	14.5	50.1	17.3	17.5
Deeside	45.3	16.2	48.6	23.8	11.2
Ellon	68.8	8.6	49.3	19.0	23.0
Garioch	58.8	14.2	42.2	23.7	19.9
Huntly	63.3	15.7	44.1	18.6	21.5
Turriff	63.8	7.2	53.2	17.1	22.4
Banffshire	47.3	17.8	49.9	18.1	14.2
Banff	54.2	12.3	51.1	18.6	17.7
Keith	40.7	23.0	48.6	17.5	10.7
Kincardine	75.3	10.7	40.8	21.1	27.3
Laurencekirk	104.1	9.6	35.8	15.0	39.6
Lower Deeside	50.1	13.0	43.8	31.6	11.5
St Cyrus	100.9	9.3	34.1	14.3	42.1
Stonehaven	72.3	8.0	43.0	22.9	26.2
Upper Deeside	53.3	14.7	45.4	20.8	19.1
Moray	57.7	20.1	44.0	17.3	18.6
Nairn	73.0	10.7	40.1	25.4	24.0

Table 1.4 shows that the average farm size in northeast counties remained small. The highest average, in Kincardine, was only seventy-five tilled acres. In East Lothian, by contrast, the average was 202 tilled acres. Comparison of Tables 1.2 and 1.4 shows a slow attrition of dwarf holdings — those below five acres — and a slight increase in the proportion of capitalist farms in all counties between 1885 and 1912. Middle and poor peasant holdings maintain their position remarkably well, however. Figures for districts of counties in 1912 show some variation. In Aberdeenshire the more strongly arable districts

of Huntly, Ellon and Turriff had a marginally higher average size than the other districts. Lower Banffshire had a less miniscule average size than the upper, more pastoral, district. The two Kincardine sandstone districts — Laurencekirk and St Cyrus — had an average farm size much larger than that of other parts of the county. Moray would have shown a similar pattern if figures for the Laigh of Moray had been disaggregated from the county figure.[85] Thus some relationship between farm size and physical endowment, mediated through the arrangement of predominant farming systems shown in Figure 1.2, can be seen.

Important as these differences are, they should not be overstated. The size distribution of holdings in Table 1.4 shows that difference in average farm size between counties and districts of counties represented diversity set upon a fundamental similarity in agrarian structure. The distribution does show considerable variation from the most southerly district — St Cyrus — where 56.6 per cent of holdings were more than fifty acres in extent, to upper Banffshire — the Keith district — where a mere 28.4 per cent of holdings were of this size. Yet the figures also show that only in southern Kincardine does the mode of the distribution fall outside the 5-49 tilled acres category. Capitalist agriculture may have been stronger in the sandstone districts than elsewhere, but in no northeast district did its dominance, undisputed though that dominance was in every district, approach the monopoly of the East Lothian muckle farmer. Peasant production, and more particularly the numbers of peasant farmers, remained a significant factor throughout the northeast.

Thus the agricultural revolution did not destroy the northeast peasantry. The older social formation was broken, but when the dust settled the new formation looked remarkably similar.[86] Subtenancy was almost dead by 1840 and with it, one might have thought, had gone the poor peasant's dependence on his neighbouring muckle farmer. Not so. The poor peasant was no longer the muckle farmer's subtenant, it is true, and now held his croft direct from the laird. But we shall see that the older relationship between rich peasant and poor peasant was reproduced in the nineteenth century in the relationship between capitalist farmer and crofter. This fact does not reflect benevolence on the part of lairds and muckle farmers in not pushing to the limit the logic of capitalist development and finally destroying the peasantry. The continued vitality of a peasant sector in northeast Scotland reflected the immaturity of capitalist production. Once capitalist production had matured to a point where it no longer needed peasant production, then the peasantry would finally be penetrated. The northeast no longer would be the poor man's country.

The northeast was the poor man's country in a social sense. We have seen that the physical endowment of the areas outwith the sandstone districts was not particularly generous either. But we must not make the error of assuming that this meant that nineteenth century northeast agricultural production was of little account.

Table 1.5

Percentage of Scottish acreage under various crops, and of Scottish cattle total, northeast counties and East Lothian, 1867[87]

	All crops	White (corn) crops	Green (root) crops	Clovers and rotation grass	Cattle
Aberdeen	13.6	15.2	15.3	18.1	14.9
Banff	3.6	4.4	4.2	4.6	4.0
Kincardine	2.6	3.3	3.3	3.3	2.4
Moray	2.3	2.9	2.8	2.7	2.1
Nairn	0.6	0.6	0.7	0.7	0.5
Northeast counties	22.7	26.4	26.4	29.4	24.0
East Lothian	2.5	3.1	3.6	2.1	0.8

Table 1.5 shows that in 1867, the first year for which we have adequate figures,[88] the northeast had 22.7 per cent of Scotland's total tilled acreage, 26.4 per cent of her corn crops, a similar proportion of her green crops (mostly in the form of turnips and, to a lesser extent, potatoes), and almost thirty per cent of her rotational grass. The northeast also had a quarter of Scotland's cattle stocks. Not an area of little account in terms of agricultural production, particularly when compared with the puny contribution of East Lothian about which economic historians wax so lyrical.

The point can be made more strongly by comparing county figures. Table 1.5 is dominated by the figures for Aberdeenshire, the northeast's giant county with eighty-one out of the region's 147 rural parishes. Big as it is, in total land area Aberdeenshire lies only sixth in the rank order of Scottish counties. In terms of agricultural production things are rather different. Its tilled acreage in 1867 — 612,724 acres — was 59.6 per cent greater than that of its nearest rival, Perthshire, with 347,723 acres. Aberdeenshire had 102.3 per cent more land under corn crops than any other county, and 188.9 per cent more land under turnips. Ayrshire, with its intensive dairying industry tailored to the rapidly expanding Clydeside market, had 79,840 cows in 1867. Only one county had more: Aberdeenshire, with 146,297—83.2 per cent more than Ayrshire. Only in the number of sheep did Aberdeenshire fall down the rank order of Scottish counties, coming thirteenth out of thirty-three. When we talk about agriculture in Aberdeenshire, then, and even more strongly when we talk about agriculture in the five northeast counties, we are not talking about a place of little account. The poor man's country was, financially if not geologically, a rich land. But which groups derived the greatest benefit from these riches?

2

Material Forces and Social Formation, 1840–1870

> To those who are acquainted with the north of Scotland, particularly the counties of Kincardine, Aberdeen, and Banff, it will be unnecessary to announce that the country in its natural state is either bogs or stone-covered muirs; but to those who have not visited that part of Scotland, it should be made known that no ground has by nature a more poor and sterile-looking surface, or one more seemingly unfit for the purpose of agriculture; and yet such as have gone from Edinburgh to Aberdeen by the mail-coach road during the last twenty years, must have remarked what skill and industry can do in effecting a change in so unpropitious looking a subject.[1]

1840 is an appropriate date at which to start an examination of the interlarding of capitalist and pre-capitalist modes of production in northeast agriculture. By 1840, we have seen, the agricultural revolution was complete: the decisive shift to 'modern', 'improved' methods of agricultural production had taken place. But history did not stop at this point. Mid-nineteenth century developments in material forces reinforced the northeast's existing specialisation in cattle production and tied its fortunes ever more closely to major southern markets, especially the great London cattle and meat markets. This dependent development was a mixed blessing. After 1870 the fact that northeast farmers 'are all ruled by the London market'[2] came to be something of an embarrassment, but in the years between 1840 and 1870 dependent development benefited farmers, particularly large farmers, and generated considerable further growth in productive forces. This chapter will examine this change of gear within capitalist agriculture and look at its consequences for the northeast's social formation.

Communications and Commodity Prices

The cattle trade was the engine that drove forward the development of material forces in northeast agriculture. We saw in the last chapter that in the late eighteenth and early nineteenth centuries, in districts removed from Aberdeen city, this trade had been the spur to the transformation of rich peasants into capitalist farmers. Things did not stop there, however.

At the turn of the nineteenth century almost all cattle not intended for home consumption were sold lean to drovers who took them, via local cattle trysts at Aikey Brae, Lowrin Fair, Paldy Fair and the rest, to the great central tryst at Falkirk.[3] From Falkirk they wended their way south, mostly to East Anglia, to be fattened for the London market or for the Navy victualling yards. All the value added processes — fattening, salting, and so on — went on outwith the northeast and generally outwith Scotland.[4]

In 1810, at the peak of the Napoleonic war demand for beef, Aberdeenshire held some 110,000 cattle. In that year some 12,000 cattle were sold to drovers for transport to the south, while another 10,000 were killed locally — mostly for home consumption.[5] This trade did not increase significantly during the next two decades, but the significance of the trade is shown by the fact that in 1831 grain exports from the arable district of Buchan were worth some £26,000, while exported cattle were worth more than £50,000.[6]

In the late 1820s transport improvements opened the door to a massive increase in the cattle trade and to the transformation of the nature of local cattle production. Some live cattle already were being sent from the northeast to London markets by sailing vessels, but the journey time was so unpredictable that only lean cattle could thus be sent. The breakthrough in the late 1820s was the introduction of regular steamship communication with London:

> Now, steam navigation has greatly altered the nature of the cattle trade in Scotland. All the superfluous fat cattle are shipped for London. The fat cattle (sic) and sheep which used to spend weeks on the hot and dusty roads are now transported, in the course of a few hours, to the metropolitan market . . . This trade, first begun at Leith, has extended itself to Dundee, Berwick, Montrose, Aberdeen, Inverness, for the London; and from the Solway Firth for the Liverpool market.[7]

This anonymous author provides figures, based on returns from the collectors of shore dues, of the quantity of live cattle and of beef carried from different ports in one year.

Table 2.1

Exports of live cattle and beef by steam vessels from selected east coast Scottish ports, June 1836 to May 1837[8]

	Cattle (head)	Beef (barrels)
Aberdeen	7,443	1,483
Dundee	1,800	940
Inverness	111	400
Leith	252	8,798

The table shows that by 1837 Aberdeen was already pre-eminent among east coast ports for the export of live cattle. But the dead meat trade was less fully developed — Aberdeen came a very poor second to Leith in the number of barrels of beef exported by steamship.

The trade in both cattle and beef saw a considerable growth in the next decade. In 1847, 15,634 cattle left Aberdeen for the south by sea, together with 750 tons of dead meat (representing about 1,800 cattle slaughtered in Aberdeen). A further 2,000 cattle were despatched from the smaller ports of Peterhead, Fraserburgh, Macduff, Banff and Portsoy.[9] It is clear that the lion's share of the northeast cattle and beef trade was channelled through Aberdeen city by the late 1840s. The arrival of the railway from the south at the end of that decade[10] reinforced Aberdeen's position and stimulated a dramatic growth in the city's dead meat trade. In 1865, 13,589 cattle and 10,135 tons of dead meat left Aberdeen for the London market.[11] A few years later it was calculated that in 1870 something over 65,000 cattle went through the Aberdeen markets. Of these some 26,000 beasts, mostly of inferior quality, went for local consumption. Another 11,224 went south as fat cattle by rail or sea, and the carcases of the remainder — over 28,100 animals — constituted the 8,040 tons of beef consigned south by wholesale butchers.[12] About half of these 65,000 cattle had been reared and fed in Aberdeenshire, while a further quarter had been fed in other northeast counties and slaughtered in Aberdeen. The final quarter were animals bought in as stores, mostly from Orkney and Shetland, Ireland, and Canada, to be fed in Aberdeenshire.[13] The scale of this trade in imported stores increased rapidly in the last decades of the century, allowing the trade in fat cattle and dead meat to increase to levels that never could have been sustained from home-produced stores alone. In 1880 the carcases of 104,000 cattle were sent to London by Aberdeen butchers. A further 20,000 cattle went to London on the hoof, and 5,000 live cattle went to other English markets.[14] By this time it was claimed of Kincardine that scarcely ten per cent of the cattle fattened in the county had been raised there.[15]

By 1870 beef from northeast Scotland carried the highest premium in London markets, and so great was the supply that it was said to regulate the Newgate market.[16] Part of the reason for the high premium was the skill of Aberdeen wholesale butchers: a London beef salesman gave evidence to a Commons committee that 'there are no others that know the beasts for the London market equal to the Aberdeen butchers, and from no other place does it arrive in the same condition'.[17] But all this skill would have been useless if the raw materials had not been of the highest quality, the result of decades of selective cattle breeding.

A few northeast lairds had been tinkering with selective breeding since the middle of the eighteenth century, but serious work began only in 1827 (the coincidence of the date with the arrival of steamships is not fortuitous), when Barclay of Ury and Hay, Shethin (Tarves), bought shorthorn cattle in East Lothian.[18] This stock formed the foundation on which skilled breeders, with the Quaker Cruikshank brothers who farmed Sittyton (Fintray) the most famous example, 'strove to provide a type of bull that would cross well with the native cows to produce the kind of animal most suitable for fattening for the London market'.[19] While the Cruikshanks, Hay and others were busy breeding shorthorns into the local stock, William McCombie, the largest tenant farmer in the five counties, was breeding the Buchan hummlie into the lordly pedigree Aberdeen-Angus on his 1,100-acre Donside farm at Tillyfour.[20] McCombie gave the breed a worldwide reputation, and his work was consolidated later by a Banffshire laird, Sir George Macpherson Grant of Ballindalloch. Improvements in cattle stocks diffused rapidly from these centres of excellence. The speed of diffusion was due in part to encouragement by landlords, both indirectly through laird-supported farmer clubs and more directly through efforts like that of the Duke of Richmond and Gordon — one of the northeast's largest and most benevolent lairds — who established model pedigree herds at Gordon Castle and exhibited them each year at his own show in order that his tenants might compare their stock with his.[21]

But a much more important spur to innovation was the greater profitability of improved over unimproved stock. This profitability in turn was the result of the massive switch to fat cattle production made possible by improvements in communication. The New Statistical Account is full of accounts by ministers of the new horizons opened in the 1830s and early 1840s to the farmers in their parishes by the arrival of steamships. In Fordoun, for example,

> The practice, now becoming common, of sending fat cattle to London by steam vessels, has materially influenced the cattle trade in this district. Instead of the greater part of the parish being bought up by dealers in spring or mid-summer markets and carried up to England to be grazed and fed off, many of the farmers now feed all the cattle they rear.[22]

The new northeast cattle feeding industry gave a decisive impetus to selective breeding. Pedigree breeders sought to improve cattle both in quality and in size. They also tried to breed cattle that would mature earlier, and thus lower the farmer's costs and allow him to turn over his capital more quickly. In 1770 few Aberdeenshire cattle sold off the farm for consumption were less than eight or ten years old.[23] By 1880 most fat cattle were sent to market at two or three years of age.[24]

The investment in stock improvement could be sustained only if underlying price trends for commodities sold off the farm — crucially fat cattle and grain — gave the capitalist farmer an acceptable return on invested capital. In the period between 1840 and 1870 this was the case.

I have been unable to trace time series data for the period before the 1860s, but Figure 2.1 shows that between 1866 and 1874 beef in London usually fetched prices above five shillings per eight pounds for first quality meat and four shillings per eight pounds for inferior meat. These data refer both to British and to foreign meat: the latter usually commanded rather lower prices. This fact, and the fact that northeast beef had the highest premiums in the market, means that northeast meat probably commanded prices at the upper end of the first quality range, providing a very acceptable return to the feeder even after the Aberdeen butchers had taken their not inconsiderable profit.

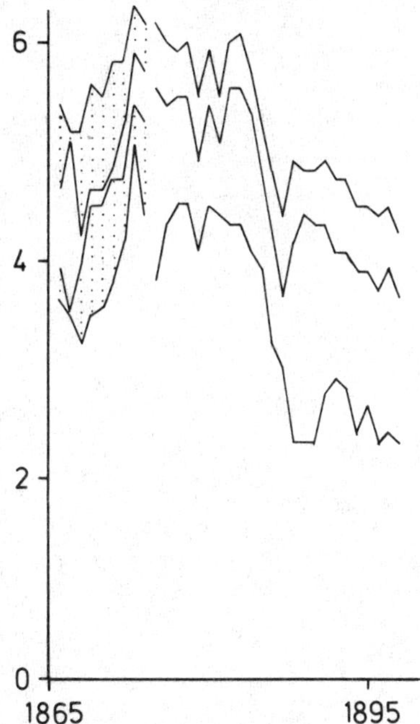

Figure 2.1 Price of beef (in shillings per 8 lbs sinking the offal) at the Metropolitan Cattle Market, London, 1866-1898.[25]

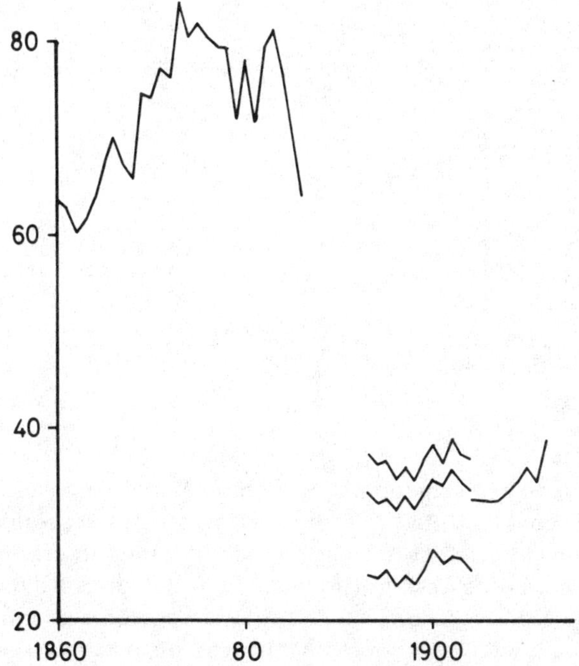

Figure 2.2 Prices, in shillings per pound, of fat cattle at Aberdeen markets, 1860-1912.[26]

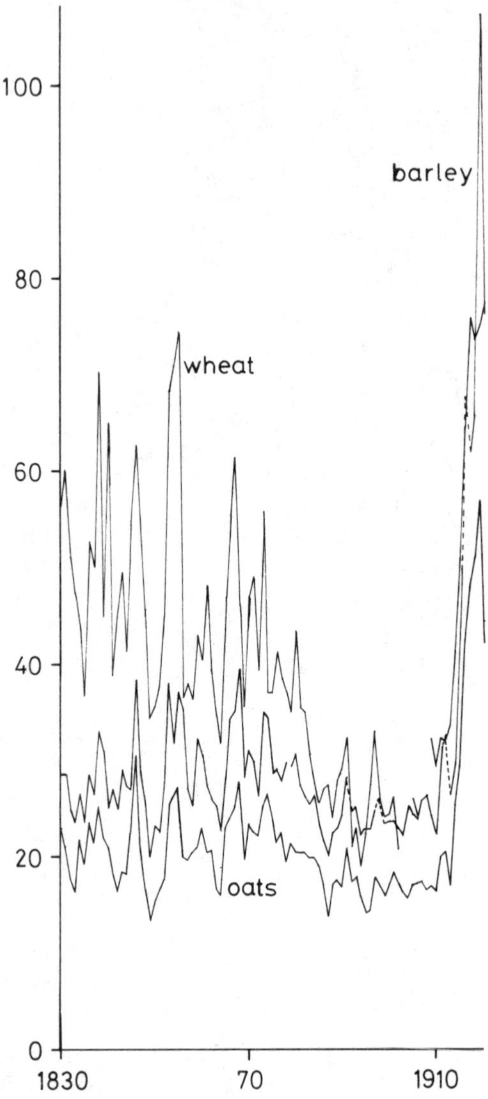

Figure 2.3 Fiars prices for wheat (Kincardine) and oats and barley (Aberdeenshire), in shillings per bushel, 1830-1920.[27]

After 1875 this happy state of affairs continued until the mid 1880s, with the price for top quality British beef fluctuating around six shillings per eight pounds. This picture is confirmed by the rather shorter time series for fat cattle at Aberdeen markets shown in Figure 2.2. It is not clear if the price refers to live weight or dead weight. The figure shows a price consistently above sixty shillings per hundred weight for top quality cattle, and above seventy shillings for most of the period. It is evident that cattle prices were buoyant between

1866 and 1885, certainly by the standards of the general run of prices after 1885.

This is not to say that northeast cattle breeders and feeders were without their problems. The area suffered outbreaks of different cattle diseases between 1840 and 1870. The most serious outbreak — the rinderpest epidemic which reached its peak in 1865 before being stamped out by a rigorous slaughter policy — ravaged local herds.[28] This epidemic gave a brief but serious check to farmers' confidence — rents offered for vacant capitalist farms fell sharply[29] — but the underlying trend of cattle prices was strong throughout the years until 1885 and gave a strong stimulus to improved breeding.

Prices of grain crops gave a good return, too. Figure 2.3 shows the Fiars prices for oats and barley in Aberdeenshire and for wheat in Kincardine between 1830 and 1920. The wheat figures are taken from Kincardine because a fiar for Aberdeenshire wheat was struck so rarely after 1876.[30] Figure 2.3 shows generally good prices for oats and barley from 1830 to 1880 interrupted

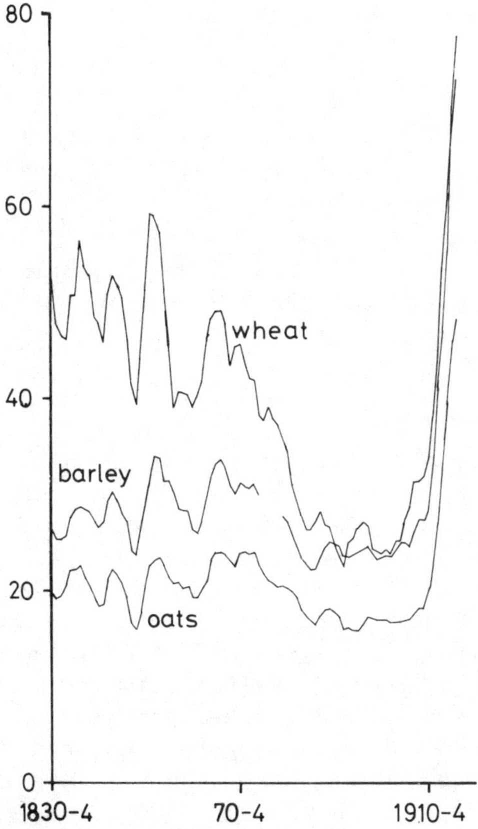

Figure 2.4 Five-year moving average of prices, in shillings per bushel, for wheat (Kincardine) and oats and barley (Aberdeenshire), 1830-1920.[31]

by a number of troughs. Wheat prices show violent fluctuations over the same period. We can see the underlying trend more clearly if we take a moving average. This also helps us to understand the farmer's viewpoint better, since he would make investment decisions not on the basis of a single year's prices, but on price runs for a few years. Figure 2.4 shows a five-year moving average based on the data expressed in Figure 2.3. For the years between 1840 and 1870 Figure 2.4 shows a close correspondence in the general shape of the graphs, with wheat prices moving within wider limits than prices for oats and barley. It also shows generally good prices: for most of the time before 1870 the average price of oats is above twenty shillings per bushel, barley above twenty-five shillings and wheat above forty shillings.

As with cattle prices, grain prices were not always profitable for the northeast farmer before 1870. The most serious trough in grain prices followed the repeal of the Corn Laws in 1846. Its effect was exacerbated in that it coincided with a period of low prices for cattle. The northeast's archetypal capitalist farmer, William McCombie, Tillyfour, remembered the serious consequences of this inconvenient conjuncture:

> I was one of those who passed through that great ordeal when Sir Robert Peel's Corn Law Bill was passed, and when foreign cattle were introduced. The little capital I had at that time was reduced by two-fifths, if not one-half; and for two or three years after that, I could not make above the half of what I was making before; we never got a farthing of recompense . . . There was two-fifths of my capital swept away at one blow, and thousands and thousands of tenant-farmers went to the wall at that time.[32]

This distressing situation was remedied in the early 1850s with the happy arrival of the Crimean War. The boom in grain and cattle prices generated by this war gave a head of steam that launched northeast agriculture into the golden summer of mid-Victorian high farming.

Technical Innovation

The middle decades of the nineteenth century were a profitable time for northeast farmers, then — as for farmers elsewhere in Britain.[33] High commodity prices made it worthwhile for capitalist farmers to invest their own capital in pushing forward the material forces of production. The high rents which farmers were able to offer in these decades meant that landlords similarly were willing to sink capital in the farm particularly if, as with Government drainage loans, they could borrow the capital at subsidised interest rates. The material forces developed rapidly between 1840 and 1870. The most dramatic development was the improvement in cattle stocks, consequent on the growth of a cattle feeding industry, that we reviewed earlier. But this development brought in its train improvements in working the land.

(a) *Rotations, manuring, draining, enclosure and steadings*

Rotations were organised around the needs of the cattle stocks — needs which varied according to the requirements of a particular farming system. We saw in the last chapter that by 1840 northeast farmers had a flexible and empirical attitude to rotation, adjusting the number of shifts — within limits permitted by lease restrictions — to take account of market conditions and local variations in soil and climate.

Grass breaks gave summer pasture for the nowt, and the turnip break provided the basis of the winter feeding regime. The introduction of a turnip break had been a crucial innovation in improved agriculture: winter feed long had been the limiting factor determining a farm's stocking capacity.[34] The introduction of artificial fertilisers increased the yield of the turnip break at the precise time when more turnips were needed to sustain the higher carry following from the growth of cattle feeding.[35] The increasing amounts of cattle cake fed to stock as farmers sought to bring fat cattle to marketable condition in a shorter period produced richer dung for the turnip break.[36] White crops served a dual purpose. Oats were fed to horses and formed the basis of the diet of peasant farmers and farm servants; any surplus grain could be marketed. Barley found a ready market in local distilleries and breweries. Straw was put through the cattle stock and returned to the land as dung. Rotation of white crops, green crops and temporary grass was a finely tuned mechanism making the most of the rather meagre physical resources of northeast agriculture. As decades of bought-in artificial fertilisers and evacuated cattle cake built up the fertility of the soil, so those physical resources grew steadily less meagre.[37]

Rotations tended to shorten between 1840 and 1870. Farmers were farming higher as they invested more capital per acre, and many were willing to substitute cattle cake for grass in order to bring cattle to a marketable condition more quickly. A shorter rotation meant heavier labour costs as the labour-intensive white and green crops formed a higher proportion of the tilled acreage, but these higher labour costs were outweighed by the increased income from more cattle and surplus grain selling at high prices.

Some people suggested that farmers would benefit from allowing some land to go out of rotation. A considerable increase in the minute acreage under permanent pasture[38] would be useful, they argued, for the ryegrasses that formed the largest part of the usual temporary leys ran to seed early in the season and red clover generally failed in the northeast. It followed that grazing was very short by the late summer, and 'it not infrequently happens that cattle sell for less after being grazed than they would have brought when put out to grass'.[39] But for technical, economic and social reasons permanent pasture remained a small part of the northeast's tilled acreage. The characteristic light soils of most of the region were ill-adapted to permanent pasture,[40] and laying down such a pasture cost a lot of money. Further, it was usual for tenants' leases to bind them to keep all their land under rotation.[41] The problem of the failure of red clover was solved on the eve of the First World War by the successful introduction of wild white clover to Scotland by James Cruikshank, Cairnhill, Turriff.[42]

The need for drainage varied widely according to the nature of the soil: heavy clays needed a great deal of draining while the light, sandy soils of the Laigh of Moray had much less need. Drainage was in train in the northeast from the early years of the nineteenth century.[43] Most drains were constructed with stones at this time,[44] but in some districts a shortage of fieldstone made this impossible and other materials had to be used.[45] Tile drains slowly replaced stone as the prosperous state of agriculture up to 1870 stimulated draining and subsoil ploughing. Another stimulus came from the central government: in 1846 Peel compensated landowners for the repeal of the Corn Laws by making two million pounds available as drainage loans at low rates of interest. Scottish lairds were very quick to take advantage of this subsidy from their class brothers in the Westminster parliament: when the first application list closed at the end of January 1847 they had applied for 168 loans worth £803,805. Northeast lairds were surprisingly tardy in this first phase, only twenty-one applications for a total of £67,869 — 8.4 per cent of the Scottish total — being on the books. But in the next three weeks northeast lairds applied for a further 69 loans, worth £308,803:[46] not for them the missed opportunity of a fast buck. This first scheme was very successful, and a further two million pounds were disbursed by the Treasury in 1850. Nearly half of the total four millions went to Scottish lairds,[47] and northeast lairds got their share. For example, one south Kincardine laird — Mrs Nicholson of Glenbervie — alone borrowed £4,500 under the Drainage Loan Act before 1855 and laid out ninety miles of subsoil drains on her small estate.[48] The government drainage money was equally important elsewhere in the northeast.[49] A parish survey of Aberdeenshire in the early 1870s showed evidence of considerable draining and redraining of newly cultivated or old arable land; but complaints of drainage still being insufficient came from widely scattered parishes, from Kildrummy and Towie in the west to Fraserburgh, St Fergus and Dyce in the east.[50] A comment from Towie makes it clear that the reason for this insufficiency lay in the policies of particular estates; that is, in the relations of production:

> No allowance is made for improving waste land, or for draining and fencing; consequently, fewer permanent improvements have been carried out than otherwise probably would have been had substantial assistance been given.[51]

Enclosure, whether by fences, stone dykes or hedges, had long been a problem in the northeast. Minister after minister in the New Statistical Account lamented the lack of adequate enclosure in his parish. Thorn hedges seemed not to grow well in the area. Where fieldstone was abundant it could be used to build dykes; in many places it was superabundant and huge 'consumption dykes' had to be built to hold the surplus:

> We have seen fields in (north) Kincardine, after trenching, whose surface presented a complete skin of blocks — a perfect Arabia Petraea on a small scale; and, if we mistake

not, there is to be found, in the classic neighbourhood of Drumthwacket, a spot which has been christened Gibraltar, from the formidable ramparts of stone fences erected out of the trenching.[52]

But in many districts fieldstone simply was not available for dyking, as in the sandstone areas, or there was not enough of it to enclose the land completely. Thus while Deeside was completely enclosed by 1880 with strong stone dykes,[53] large parts of the Buchan plain were inadequately enclosed. The arrival of wire fences after the mid-century greatly eased the problem[54] — and had important consequences for the many children who had been employed as herds for part of the year and could now be put into the compulsory education system that was established in 1872. But while wire fences divided one park from another, they gave no shelter to stock, and in windswept and treeless Buchan a dyke was valued as much for shelter as for division.

The years from 1840 to 1870 saw a great improvement in farm steadings, too. Improvement had been in train before 1840: by 1810 architect-designed stone and lime steadings with slated roofs were becoming common on capitalist farms.[55] Indeed, the Board of Agriculture's reporter for Kincardine, himself a highly competent capitalist farmer and freelance valuer in the south of the county, complained that

. . . The rage for building farm houses and offices, in a shewy style and of great extent, has been in several instances carried too far. That the farmer should inhabit a commodious lodging, and that his offices (i.e. his steading) should comprehend whatever is necessary for the rearing and feeding of his cattle, and the preservation of his corn and implements of husbandry, is not meant to be controverted. But, for a proprietor to be laying out from four to six years rent upon a farm-steading, as in several cases is done: this is certainly spending money very freely, and with little consideration.[56]

By 1840, then, the lairds who offended George Robertson's thrifty instincts had fine steadings on their estates' large farms, models of the efficient use of labour in the farming system for which they were designed. By 1870 tardy estates had caught up: Smith's survey of Aberdeenshire shows a consistent pattern of good steadings on large farms. Steadings were particularly fine in the sandstone districts.[57] Cattle courts began to be covered from about 1850 in order to preserve the value of the trodden dung:[58] once again the sandstone districts took the lead.[59] But even in 1881 relatively few farms outside these districts had covered courts.[60] One reason for their slow spread was feeders' prejudices: McCombie, Tillyfour, declared somewhat crustily in 1867 that he would buy no cattle wintered in covered courts.[61]

(b) *Implements*

The sight of the 'twal owsen ploo' — the old Scots wooden plough drawn by a team of up to a dozen oxen — at work in Culsalmond during Napoleon's time was rare enough to draw comment.[62] Agricultural historians tend to consign ox ploughing to the dustbin of pre-improvement practices, but one

Laurencekirk capitalist farmer found it economical to plough with oxen in the 1840's,[63] and 'Drumdelgie' records a time when the largest farm in Cairnie — a farm not even created until the large-scale reorganisation of the Gordon Castle estate in the early 1840s — was worked by both horse and ox:

> There's sax o' you'll gae to the ploo,
> And twa will ca' the neeps,
> And the owsen they'll be aifter you,
> Wi' strae raips roun' their queets.[64]

After 1850 plough oxen became much less common on large farms, although they could still be found at Auchlossan, Lumphanan, in the 1870s, working on soft land reclaimed by draining a loch.[65] And the idiosyncratic McCombie, Tillyfour, often yoked valuable pedigree Aberdeen-Angus cattle if they proved shy of breeding. But these were rare instances. The rapid substitution of horse for ox as the main source of draught power is shown by the history of ploughing matches sponsored by the Garioch Farmer Club. At the match in 1809 eleven ploughs competed. All were drawn by oxen. In 1816 twenty-nine ploughs competed, and all but one were horse-drawn. In the 1818 match horse teams ruled unchallenged no ox team took the field.[66] By 1850 the horse reigned supreme as the plough animal on capitalist farms. The small but sturdy garron gave way to the magnificently powerful oats-devouring Clydesdale. To begin with these splendid animals were imported from Lanarkshire, but as the staiger on his pony leading the Clydesdale stallion became a more familiar sight in the northeast, they were bred on many local farms, where they gave the farmer a useful additional income.[67]

By 1840 the wooden plough had been a memory for a generation. Iron ploughs held the field, first modelled on Small's plough and then, from the 1850s, on Wilkie's high-crested (or high-cutting) plough.[68] The wooden ploughs and iron copies of Small's plough had been made by country wrights and blacksmiths: the 1850s saw the eclipse of these craftsmen (as manufacturers if not as repairers) with the rise of the great specialist plough firms[69] — Sellar of Huntly, Banff Foundry, and the others from southern Scotland and England whose implements found their way to the northeast. Late in the nineteenth century high-crested iron ploughs were superseded in their turn by chilled steel ploughs, originating in America but soon copied in Britain. Other implements saw a corresponding improvement. A commentator noted in 1881 that

> The most improved implements of all kinds are in general use where good husbandry is carried on. Within the last twenty-five years the reaping machine has been introduced and is now almost universally employed, and so are grain sowing machines, broad-cast and drill. Steam cultivation has likewise been carried on in several districts. The introduction of the improved double-furrow plough about fifteen years ago

seemed to promise a considerable saving in the cost of cultivation, but this implement has not been adopted in the extent that its merits would have led us to expect . . . Improved cultivators, single ploughs, horse-rakes, harrows and land-rollers, potato-diggers, etc etc are likewise employed generally; a large proportion of the light implements of a farm, such as forks, hoes and graips are of American manufacture.[70]

Technical innovation between 1840 and 1870 reduced the labour needed in two activities that previously had absorbed a vast amount of labour on the farm — harvesting and threshing the corn crops. The spread of thorough draining gave flat fields that allowed, for the first time, the hairst to be taken by machine. From about 1850 the sickle and scythe began to give way to the machine reaper.[71] By 1870 reapers were common in the northeast:[72]

I hae seen the hairst o' Rettie,
Ay, and twa-three on the throne;
I've heard for sax and seven weeks
The hairsters girn and groan.
But a covie Willie Rae,
In a monthie and a day,
Mak's a' the jolly hairster lads
Gae singing down the brae.

A monthie and a day, my lads,
The like was never seen;
It beats to sticks the fastest strips
O' Victory's new machine.
A Speedwell now brings up the rear,
A Victory clears the way;
And twenty acres daily falls
Nor stands to Willie Rae.[73]

In threshing, as in cutting, handwork gave way to machines. Machine threshing was pioneered in southeast Scotland in the second half of the eighteenth century, and then it spread much more quickly in Scotland than in England.[74] By 1840 fixed threshing mills, driven by water, by horse or — in a few cases — by steam were ubiquitous on northeast large farms.[75] These machines used the slow and cumbersome beater drum: after 1860 some farmers tried the more efficient peg drum but found that it tore the straw. The problem was solved by the arrival of English portable steam-powered high speed rubbing drum threshers. Some of the largest farmers built such machines into their steadings, but most relied on the travelling 'Big Mull'.[76] By the 1870s 'numerous portable steam threshing mills patrol the country in every direction, and are extensively employed'.[77]

Social Formation

The shift to fat cattle production gave birth to a higher level of capitalist production. This, in turn, had important effects on the northeast's social formation. One of these effects was to strengthen the bourgeois fraction that extracted surplus value through the circulation of commodities: the owners of commercial capital. This was not a new class fraction, of course. Aberdeen city had had a flourishing mercantile bourgeoisie for centuries,[78] and we have seen that Aberdeen merchants put out materials for stocking knitting, for spinning and for weaving before the agricultural revolution. But this trade affected only the handicrafts buttressing peasant agricultural production: what was new in the nineteenth century was the deep penetration of agricultural production itself by commercial capital:

> I have been asked whether the amount of capital which is applied to the land is not very much greater in Aberdeenshire than it was thirty or forty years ago. I believe that it is very much greater; but the amount applied yearly is out of sight and out of comparison. I can remember the introduction of extraneous manures. I remember the first bones which were brought into the county. I am too old not to remember the first guano;[79] and the amount of capital which the tenant now puts into the land yearly is so much beyond what it was then, that there is no comparison whatever.[80]

These opinions, from a highly competent witness, date from the late 1860s — the height of the golden summer of high farming. But this did not mark the high water mark of commercial penetration of agriculture. A generation later an equally competent observer noted that the farmer's dealings with the manure merchant and the implement maker had grown to be of even greater scale and importance. Further, finance capital was making its mark on agriculture: at least a quarter of all capital in agriculture was borrowed by 1881, and the proportion had risen steeply since 1870.[81]

The penetration of commercial capital may be seen through the growth of the northeast's manure merchants. This growth was contingent on improvements in communication. The rather small trade from Aberdeen city in artificial manures before 1837 was focussed on the Aberdeenshire Canal: in that year cut-throat competition between the three major companies using the canal to transport lime and artificial manures forced them into an arrangement — legally a partnership, actually a cartel — to keep prices up and share trade.[82] But the trade on the Aberdeenshire Canal was small beer compared with what was to come. The manure companies' real opportunity arrived with the railways. Figure 2.5 shows that only the line from the south through Stonehaven to Aberdeen was built by 1850. But in the next two decades the framework of a remarkably comprehensive rail network was laid in the northeast. The Moray and Banff coasts were particularly well supplied with lines, the result of economically fatuous competition between two companies whose metals met at Keith — the Highland coming from the west and the Great North of Scotland from the east. After 1870 this bloodletting continued in the Laigh of Moray: elsewhere only the short St Combs branch and the line from Ellon to Boddam tapped new territory.

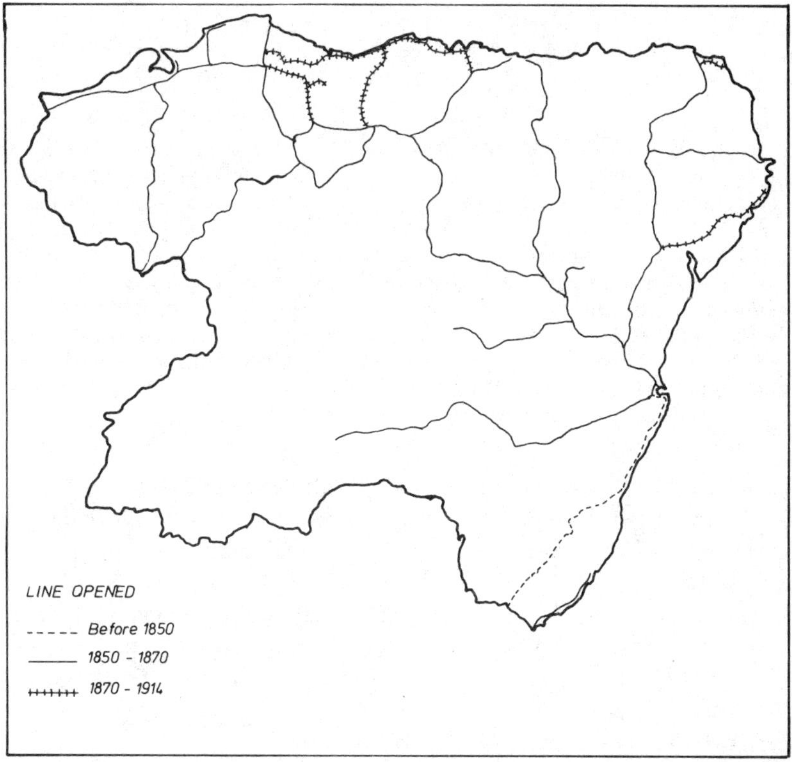

Figure 2.5 The railways of northeast Scotland.[83]

As the new railways spread through the lowland sections of the northeast — and many upland districts, too[84] — so the manure companies moved in. The Aberdeen Lime Company was capitalised at £7,500 in 1837. In 1847 they expanded into shipping, and by 1862 their share capital had increased to £42,056. In 1875 their share capital was increased again, to £70,000, specifically to allow the company to enter the lucrative business of manufacturing oilcake for cattle feed.[85] By 1865 the three big Aberdeen companies were selling a quarter of a million pounds' worth of artificial manures per year. One of them, the Aberdeen Commercial Company, alone had sales exceeding ninety thousand pounds per year. In 1862-64 an annual average of 7,241 tons of guano and 8,714 tons of bones were imported through Aberdeen Harbour.[86] The Aberdeen companies dominated the trade, but throughout the northeast one found other merchants, large and small, selling manure from railway yards to farmers. Thus when in 1923 the firm of G. & S. Kynoch, Morayshire Chemical Works, was transmogrified into the Banff and Moray Agricultural Co. Ltd., the new company took over stores and offices in railway stations at Keith, Aberlour, Auchindachy, Drummuir, Tochineal, Ballindalloch, Glenbarry, Dufftown and Mulben, as well as shed sites at Enzie, Rathven and

Aultmore, and offices at Keith Town, Huntly Mart and Cornhill Mart.[87] This company, like all its fellows, did more than sell manures: it also bought the farmer's grain:

> The purchases of oats by the Aberdeen Commercial Company (in the mid-1860s) amount to about 60,000 quarters a year; and taking oats, barley, bere and wheat, our purchases will represent over £60,000. No part of that grain is purchased in a bulk or stock market — there is no such market in Aberdeenshire; and very little of it is purchased by sample. Our system of purchase is this:— We have agents at all the principal railway stations in Aberdeenshire, about thirty in number. These agents receive the grain brought to them there, and pay the current price of the day for it. We ourselves seldom see the farmer. He sends the grain with his servant to the station, our agent receives it and gives a receipt for the quantity, and the settlement is often made in cash at the time, or it is passed to the farmer's credit in our books, and they receive the credit when they call at our premises.[88]

This arrangement meant that even quite small merchants could cover a wide territory: one man who combined business as a grain merchant in Inverurie with peasant farming on the Kintore estate had twenty-eight agents at different railway stations.[89]

The railways had a similar effect on the trade that dwarfed even that in grain and manure — the cattle trade. In 1800 'the cattle dealers were the great men to these counties'.[90] The dealer collected a drove of lean beasts from farms and local trysts, took them to the great Falkirk tryst, and there sold them to southern drovers. His livelihood was precarious:

> The short-lived peace that was patched up in October 1801, occasioned a temporary fall of twenty-five per cent in the price of cattle: and for *the third time* in the present Reign, *ruined most of the cattle dealers.*[91]

But given good luck and good judgement, the profits of dealing could accumulate. One of William Alexander's short stories is the superficially simple tale of the rise of a rural craftman's son, a witless youth with an eye for a good beast and a talent for haggling, to fame, fortune, and the tenancy of a large farm.[92] Beneath the surface the story is less simple, with Alexander casting his usual leery eye on the pretensions of capitalist farmers as part of his lifelong defence of peasant interests: but that is not the point. The rise of Sandy Mutch, however unmerited that rise, is not too far removed from the rise of 'the Grazier King', William McCombie, Tillyfour — the cousin of Alexander's own patron.[93] Successful dealers handled huge sums of money — one of the 'Stately Williamsons', a famous family of Aberdeen dealers, heard the bells of Perth ringing out the news of the victory of Waterloo and complained that the peace would cost him £4,000 on one drove[94] — but their business methods were slapdash in the extreme.[95]

All that had changed by 1870. Railways had destroyed the droving trade and with it the power of the dealers. 'The only real representatives of the cattle-dealers of the earlier half of the present century that now remain are the Cabrach and Glenlivet men who still do business very largely in the droving trade':[96] and those men continued to drive cattle simply because their district was so far from the railway network. The great northeast trysts degenerated into funfairs, if they survived at all.[97] The 'great men' of the rural northeast were now the wholesale butchers. They bought many of their fat cattle on the farm, as the old dealers had done;[98] but the opening of the first cattle market in Aberdeen city, in 1850,[99] simplified purchasing for them. By 1900 there would be four cattle markets in the city. The Aberdeen markets were, taken together, much the largest in the northeast, but by 1880 additional markets had grown up at nodes on the railway network from Nairn to Laurencekirk.[100] To begin with, these markets simply formed a regular setting in which farmer and butcher could make private bargains: the butchers had an extremely strong position in such haggling, and exploited it to the full. Things evened up a little in 1868 with the opening of the first auction market for cattle in Aberdeen city, and others followed quickly. The butchers did not like auction markets, not surprisingly; a cartel of big Aberdeen wholesale butchers tried and failed to break the pioneer market. Recovering from this setback, the butchers developed backward linkages that gave them control over short-term fluctuations and put them once again at a systematic advantage against farmers selling fat cattle:

> To assist in keeping their supply regular, several of the butchers have lately adopted a new plan. They take from the farmers turnips, straw and byres — sometimes all that the farms gives; at other times only part. They buy cattle extensively, put them in and feed them, and then, when they have difficulty in buying the quantity they require for market, they fall back on their own stocks.[101]

This buffer stock ensured that, whoever else suffered, the wholesale butchers were assured of their comfortable profit. Their subtle manipulation of the market was a long way from the hunches and slapdash accounting of the old dealers. In the rise of the wholesale butchers, a rise underpinned by the massive increase in the dead meat trade that we reviewed earlier, we see the rise of a fully capitalist big merchant class fraction: the final triumph of double-entry bookkeeping.

Things were happening in the sphere of production as well as circulation. Figure 2.6 shows that the rental of the Haddo estate — one the the three largest in the northeast and an estate with an unparalleled reputation for treating its tenants fairly — rose steadily from the early 1840s right through to the mid-1880s. We should be cautious in taking these figures as a direct measure of the profitability of Haddo, since the ubiquity of nineteen-year leases on capitalist farms and middle peasant holdings meant that the estate rental was very slow to follow the changes in commodity prices. But the steady increase in Haddo's

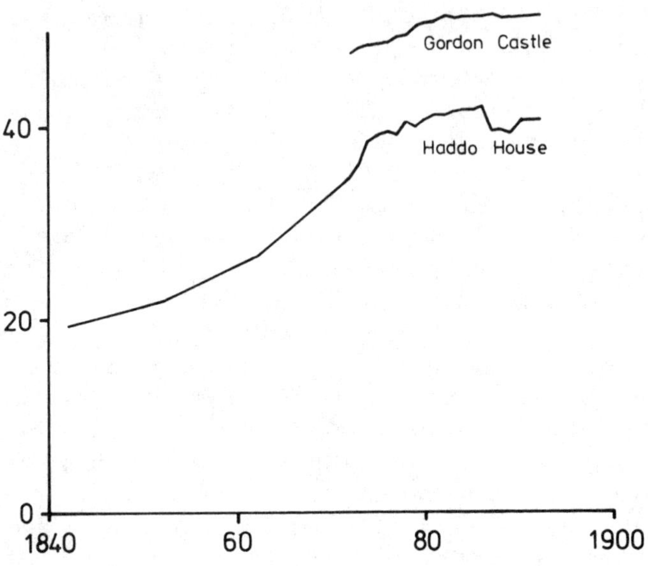

Figure 2.6 The rental (in thousands of pounds) of the Haddo House estate 1842-1892, and of the Gordon Castle estate 1872-1892.[102]

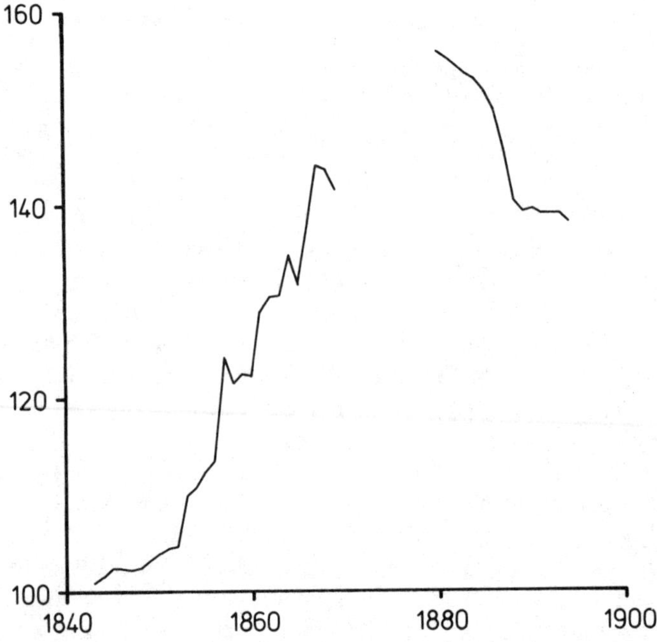

Figure 2.7 Index of changes in farmer's profits, northeast counties, 1842-43 to 1894-95, 1842-43=100.[103]

rental reflects the buoyancy of northeast agriculture up to 1870: a buoyancy which encouraged lairds to invest heavily in pushing forward the productive forces on their estates. Often they borrowed much of the money — the government's subsidised drainage loans that we have looked at already, state and private funds for building steadings.[104] The fact that money borrowed thus at six and a half per cent interest could be lent to tenants who would repay at eight per cent was particularly interesting to owners of the northeast's entailed estates;[105] from the laird's viewpoint there was no good reason why he should put his own money into such an estate.

Figure 2.7 shows that the trend of farmers' profits floated upwards during the 1840s and then rose sharply from the early 1850s. The sharp rise continued, with occasional hiccups, until the time series is broken in the late 1860s — but the high level at which the series starts again in 1880-81 shows that the rise must have continued through at least part of the 1870s. As with the previous figure, we should not place too precise a meaning on the data in Figure 2.7. Thus, for example, we see clearly that the Crimean war boom primed the pump for mid-Victorian high farming, but there is little evidence of the desperate slump after 1846 that McCombie, Tillyfour, described so feelingly. The reason is not that the slump never happened, but that the Inland Revenue calculated farmers' profits by means of a formula laid on each county's agricultural valuation. Since that valuation was related to estate rentals, which we have seen changed rather slowly, it follows that sharp but temporary reverses like the consequences of the Corn Laws repeal and the 1865 rinderpest epidemic are understated in these data. That being said, the rapid rise in the graph after 1852 shows the markedly increased profitability of farming after the mid-century. This high profitability stimulated a strong demand for vacant capitalist farms and encouraged capitalist tenants to sink their own capital in improving the farm. Over the whole period from 1840 to 1870, but more particularly after 1850, there was a fundamental congruence between the material interests of capitalist farmers and of landlords. Both would benefit — the one fraction through increased profits, the other through increased rent — from the fullest possible development of productive forces.

The development of material forces in these decades was, in two senses, wonderful. But we must recognise that this development was very uneven, coming first and most completely to capitalist farms and then slowly spreading down to smaller farms. McCombie, Tillyfour, wrote in 1867 that 'there is no doubt that in the north, and especially in Aberdeenshire, there is a rage for fine cattle':[106] but it was a rage that could be sustained by the purses of landowners and capitalist farmers alone. Pedigree breeding stock from the famous herds was selling, even before 1850, for sums counted in hundreds of guineas. Serious selective breeding needed reserves of capital far beyond the peasant farmer's competence.

Draught oxen effectively had disappeared from capitalist farms by 1850, but they could still be seen ploughing on some peasant holdings, often with an ox and a garron yoked together, in the 1930s. One Inverurie crofter was still threshing with the flail in 1947, more than a century after machine threshing had largely extirpated hand threshing on capitalist farms.[107] Field drainage came first to large farms. However patchy enclosure might have been in some northeast districts, it was always better on capitalist farms than on smaller places.[108] Steadings on large farms were uniformly good by 1875, 'but those on many of the smaller farms and crofts have only thatched roofs, and the buildings are of an inferior description'.[109] Improved implements came later to small farms than to large farms. In part this may have been the result of an understandable caution on the part of small farmers who wanted to see that some new kind of machine would work before buying one,[110] but it also reflects the large capital outlay needed for new implements. A common solution for the small farmer and crofter in the northeast, as elsewhere,[111] was to buy secondhand machines discarded by larger farmers for more modern models. Even today there are some northeast small farmers — no longer peasants since their holdings provide such a small proportion of the household's subsistence foodstuffs — who take it as a point of honour never to buy a new implement.

We have looked at the effect of higher productive forces in bringing into being a new class fraction — big merchant capitalists controlling the circulation of commodities into and out of agriculture — and in strengthening the position of landlords and capitalist farmers, the other two major fractions of the bourgeoisie in the rural northeast. But here we come to a paradox. We have seen that productive forces were less highly developed on peasant holdings, but we saw in the last chapter that in 1885 peasant farmers still outnumbered capitalist farmers by six to one. Why did northeast lairds not pursue the apparent logic of their material interest and make a Lothian-like social landscape by destroying the peasantry?

(a) *Engrossment and reclamation*

In 1838 Lord Cockburn, the celebrated Edinburgh lawyer and wit, wrote in his diary that

> I know no part of Scotland so much and so visibly improved within thirty years as Aberdeenshire. At the beginning of that time the country between Keith and Stonehaven was little else than a hopeless region of stones and moss. There were pieces of many miles where literally there was nothing but large white stones, of from half a ton to ten tons weight, to be seen. A stranger to the character of the people would have supposed that despair would have held back their hands from even attempting to remove them. However, they began, and year after year have been going on, making dykes and drains, and filling up holes with these materials till at last they have created a country which, when the rain happens to cease and the sun shines, is really very endurable.[112]

A characteristic Edinburgh comment, both in the tinge of contempt for outlandish Aberdeenshire and in the tendency to exaggeration. Cockburn was right in pointing to a massive increase in the county's tilled acreage, but the increase was not contained wholly within the period after 1808. Improving lairds had added something like thirty thousand acres to Aberdeenshire's tilled acreage in the second half of the eighteenth century.[113] But that was merely scratching the surface: the pace of expansion increased rapidly in the early nineteenth century. In 1811, after the very considerable increase in tillage caused by the French wars, Aberdeenshire's tilled acreage was estimated at 475,500[114] — an estimate which William Alexander later thought was too high.[115] By 1866, when the Board of Agriculture took its first agricultural census, the tilled acreage had risen above 550,000. The acreage peaked in 1901 at 631,015 tilled acres: a thirty-two per cent increase on the inflated figure for 1811.

For Kincardine we can trace the increase in tilled acreage at the parish level. In the course of his county report for the Board of Agriculture, George Robertson gave the tilled acreage of each parish in 1807. Robertson was a scrupulously competent observer, as well as having a valuing business that took him to every part of the county: thus we need not fear the accuracy of his data. Table 2.2 uses these data as a baseline against which to compare the tilled acreage of each parish in 1867, 1887 and 1911. Parishes are ranked in order of increase in tilled acreage between 1807 and 1887 — Kincardine's acreage peaked in the late 1880's. We see that six parishes more than doubled their tilled acreage between 1807 and 1887, and a further six had increases of more

Table 2.2

Index of changes in tilled acreage, Kincardine parishes, 1807-1911. 1807=100[116]

Parish	1867	1887	1911
Durris	407.6	408.4	408.5
Maryculter	338.9	373.7	379.4
Banchory Ternan	290.0	306.4	308.2
Banchory Devenick	270.8	299.8	227.8
Nigg	206.5	216.1	196.1
Garvock	220.8	208.2	195.8
Fettercairn	181.9	196.2	204.3
Bervie	152.8	166.0	168.1
Glenbervie	153.9	165.3	154.9
Marykirk	135.9	163.8	161.5
Fetteresso	139.9	154.9	155.6
Kinneff	144.3	151.3	144.4
St Cyrus	132.6	143.1	144.1
Fordoun	126.6	137.6	131.5
Dunnottar	134.0	137.4	135.1
Arbuthnott	127.4	134.9	131.0
Strachan	104.6	116.9	118.9
Benholm	110.4	113.2	110.3
Laurencekirk	100.0	106.9	101.6

than fifty per cent. The acreage of the whole county rose by just over seventy per cent over that period. But the increase had a marked geographical distribution: with the exception of Strachan, the rank order distinguishes neatly between north Kincardine parishes, which head the list, and the parishes in the richer sandstone districts of the county's southern half. We saw in Table 1.4 that in 1912 the average farm size in these southern districts was much higher than in the northern parishes. Table 2.2 suggests that this larger size was the result not simply of the better soils of the district. It arose because the southern parishes were brought under the plough earlier, allowing a longer time for engrossment to take place:

> Then our men, you know, have a great desire to get at the land; our saving ploughmen, who have got probably £200 or £300 in the bank, all want to get a little croft or holding; that, I am sorry to say, they can scarcely get now; we, the large farmers, have swallowed them all up.[117]

Engrossment took place outwith the sandstone districts as well, of course. The early census reports frequently attributed population decline in particular parishes to the throwing of small farms into larger ones. There were some spectacular examples: Cultercullen, Foveran, was said to have swallowed twenty-two peasant farms between 1824 and 1884.[118] John Wilken lived in Ellon until 1853, and remembered that 'When I was at school I could count more than forty children, mostly crofters' children, within one mile of Broomfield, and on my return from abroad in 1912, both the crofts and the children had gone.'[119] In the years around 1840 engrossment was particularly strongly encouraged by two factors. One was the highly profitable new opportunities opened up to the capitalist farmers by the shift to fat cattle production. The other was the possibility that lairds would have to carry the rate burden of supporting paupers in their parishes under the threatened new Poor Law. This second factor, in particular, clarified lairds' minds wonderfully: we have accounts of small tenants and subtenants being evicted to avoid a heavy poor law assessment from Huntly, Kincardine O'Neil, Keig, Forglen, Cruden, Clatt, Towie, Kennethmont, Coull, Banchory Ternan, Aboyne and Lonmay.[120] Doubtless the same thing happened in other parishes, too.

These twin spurs of larger potential rents and a larger potential poor rate assessment pushed a number of estates, from Invercauld in the southwest[121] to Strichen in the northeast, into large-scale reorganisation of tenures. The Lovat family sold the Strichen estate to a certain Mr Baird, who moved quickly to promote capitalist production. He lent thousands of pounds at four per cent interest to his capitalist tenants and evicted 120 crofters from Mormond Hill. Asked by the local minister what was to happen to the evicted crofters, the laird replied, 'They may go to hell for me.' The minister is alleged to have replied, 'If you really want to put them permanently out of your way I think you had better send them in the opposite direction.'[122] But even events on the Strichen estate pale into insignificance when compared with the reorganisation of the vast Gordon Castle estate, owned by the Duke of Richmond and Gordon, in the early 1840s:

> When the farms on his Grace's princely domain in Scotland were let about six years ago, a large number of the smaller holders were compelled to an immediate surrender of their possessions, to make way for the annexation of these to the larger adjacent farms. These smaller tenantry were composed partly of those who held immediately of the Duke, and partly of those who held of the tenant, commonly known in Scotland by the name of subtenants. A considerable number of the smaller holders were allowed to retain their little farms in the meantime, but were refused, almost without exception, a renewal of their leases. The class of subtenants the heritor did not feel himself obliged to recognise at all, and in no case were they allowed to retain occupation of their acres.[123]

It is from this reorganisation that Drumdelgie, Cairnie — later to be stigmatised in one of the most famous bothy ballads — took its character as the largest farm in Strathbogie. Another Cairnie farm, Newton, swallowed the previous peasant holdings of Clashbrae, Thorntree, Gateside, Bushwarnie, Cairnwhelp, Corse and Midtown.[124] The Duke of Richmond and Gordon's manifest intention of extirpating subtenancy was common to almost all lairds by the 1840s. I can find examples of a few capitalist farmers being allowed to sublet only in two places — the Vale of Alford and Strachan parish.[125] By contrast, in the mid-1840s one finds statements that subletting was prohibited from parishes spread throughout the length and breadth of the northeast.

Events on the Gordon Castle estate were merely the most dramatic example of a general tendency. The policies pursued on particular estates determined the rate of engrossment, but between 1840 and 1870 all northeast lairds pushed forward the consolidation of peasant holdings in capitalist farms. And yet only in the sandstone districts did this engrossment mean an absolute increase in the proportion of farmers working the capitalist mode of production.

Table 2.3
Distribution of agricultural holdings by rateable value, Tarves, 1859-60 to 1912-13[126]

	4-	20-	50-	100-	200-	300+	Total
1859-60	139	41	30	12	5	4	231
1892-93	132	40	35	19	8	10	244
1912-13	126	47	34	21	7	10	245

Table 2.3 shows the distribution of holdings by rateable value in Tarves, a lowland Aberdeenshire parish contained within the Haddo estate, in 1859-60, 1892-93 and 1912-13. Other parishes from Aberdeenshire, Banffshire and north Kincardine show a similar picture. Assuming that one pound of rateable value equals one tilled acre, then the table shows a remarkable stability in the numerical balance between capitalist, middle peasant and poor peasant holdings. This stability in numbers while engrossment was under way can only

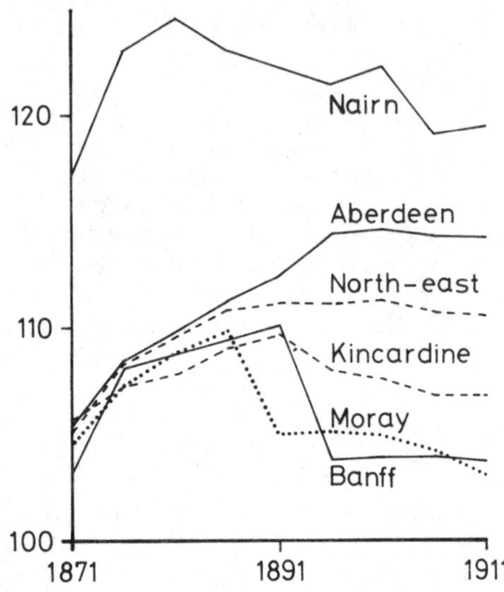

Figure 2.8 Index of changes in tilled acreage, northeast counties, 1866-1911. 1866=100.[127]

be explained by an increase in tilled acreage. Figure 2.8 shows that the tilled acreage was increasing in all northeast counties up to 1870.

Even though much new land had been brought into cultivation in all northeast counties before 1866, Figure 2.8 shows that the tilled acreage of each county continued to rise thereafter. The maximum tilled acreage for Aberdeenshire was reached in 1901, for Banffshire and Kincardine in 1891, for Moray in 1886 and for Nairn in 1881. As is usual, the maximum for the five counties combined follows fairly closely the figure for the northeast's giant county, Aberdeenshire. The sharp drop in Banffshire's figure between 1891 and 1896 was the result of boundary changes.

Who brought this new land into cultivation? In the late eighteenth century the high rents that lairds could demand from graziers and market gardeners for land close to Aberdeen city had meant that the high labour cost of reclaiming difficult land — up to twenty pounds sterling per acre in 1780[128] — could be borne. Away from 'the Toon' things were very different, although even after 1840 one still can find a rare case of a laird hiring labourers to cut new land from the waste.[129] One also finds a laird employing hired labour to tidy up his estate by reclaiming unimproved land between patches of new arable ground cut out by colonising crofters.[130] Hired labour was also used by capitalist farmers to reclaim land on occasions, either by improving waste among old arable while enclosing a former runrig farm[131] or by adding new arable land to an already enclosed capitalist farm.[132] Very rarely, one also finds a capitalist farmer employing hired labour to cut a complete large farm from the waste, as in the draining of the Deeside Loch of Auchlossan after

1860.[133] But both lairds and capitalist farmers pale into insignificance as land reclaimers when compared with peasant farmers — the men who rarely wrote essays for Highland Society prizes, yet were, in every parish, the real makers of the northeast land.[134]

What the northeast lairds did was to harness the peasant's mode of production to the laird's own ends. The peasant farmer wanted land on which to produce his household's subsistence. The laird wanted the tilled acreage of his estate increased. In the short and medium term these interests meshed in the improving lease. The laird leased a patch of moor to an intending peasant farmer for a number of years — usually nineteen, though sometimes fewer and occasionally more. For the first few years, while he was cutting his holding from the waste, the tenant paid a nominal rent or no rent at all. During these years the tenant also constructed his own dwelling house and steading, and built dykes on his holding: typically the estate gave no help whatsoever in these tasks. After this initial period of 'riving in' the land, the rent rose steadily until, during the last full rotation under lease, the tenant was paying the full market price for his holding. Landlords used improving leases to bring into cultivation waste land lying between existing farms and thus connect the previously isolated specks of arable land. But they also promoted large-scale cultivation of waste land at the same time: while many estates were ejecting peasant tenants in the 1840s for fear of a heavy poor rate assessment, other estates were recruiting colonising crofters to tackle the reclamation of large tracts of inhospitable land.[135] These major crofting colonies typically were found on interfluvial ridges, near peat mosses — the Rora crofts near Peterhead are perhaps the most famous example — and on the higher slopes of valley sides above the level of previous cultivation.[136] In the last case cultivation sometimes spilled on to the high and exposed summit surfaces: in upper Banffshire, for example,

> On the estate of the Earl of Fife, in Aberlour and Mortlach, a large level tract of country called the Bechach, on the north-west side of Benrinnes and south-west of the Convals, grew only heather, rushes, and bent; but now, by a system of colonisation, it has been almost wholly reclaimed, and studded over with substantial dwelling-houses, and small steadings, without costing the proprietor a penny. The plan adopted was this:— almost every one who applied for it got permission to build a house there, and bring into cultivation as much land as he was able. The factor saw that the new settlements were arranged so as not to interfere with each other, but for a long time there were not even marches set. The holdings were at first mere specs (sic) of cultivated land in the midst of the great waste. But by-and-by the extent of cultivation broadened, and new places were given off after a time with great rapidity. No rent was to be charged for many years, and it was not till very recently that small sums were put upon the holdings, some of which extend now to a considerable number of acres and have good houses put upon them. A great part of the heathy expanse may now be said to be a closely cultivated country.
>
> The same thing has been done on a very extensive scale on Lord Fife's property, in the hill of Newmill, to the north of Keith, and also in Bogmuchals, the property of the Earl of Seafield, lying to the north of the Knock hill. In both of these places new

colonies have become so important that they require schools, merchants, carriers, smiths, shoemakers, tailors — all the machinery which the greater and older communities call into existence among them.[137]

It was necessary for some peasant farmers to use some hired day labour to help in trenching and dyking waste land,[138] but this was the case only when family labour was insufficient for the task. In keeping with the peasant's pre-capitalist mode of production, as much labour power as possible was squeezed from the farm household. Sons were called back from farm service for a part of the year to help their father rive in new land.[139] The central part played by the family in mobilising labour power in colonisation, and its continuing importance in the organisation of production thereafter, is shown in the following account of an exemplary tenant. The account was written in the early 1850s by Alexander Thomson of Banchory, a north Kincardine laird and an important contemporary social reformer:

J. R. took five acres of barren land in 1823. He had a wife and a numerous family, a very few pounds of money, and a most excellent character for industry, sobriety and honesty. In 1828 he took five acres more, and, having improved these ten, he got another lot of five. He transferred one of his lots to his eldest son, who married and built a house. The father took two or three small additional lots, and afterwards purchased up a larger lot of about twenty acres from an adjoining tenant, on which occasion the usual practice of making all the leases run out together was abandoned, and he got a new lease of his purchase; and the conclusion of his labours is, that he now occupies 48 acres of arable land, with a thrashing-mill erected by himself, and has three sons settled, with their wives and families, on portions of the ground he improved, and in houses erected by themselves with a little assistance from the proprietor; and now the family, the father and his three sons, occupy nearly 100 acres of arable land, extending about a mile along the southern boundary of the estate, where not a blade of grass grew when the father first settled upon it.[140]

His unquestioned command of the household's labour power was the peasant farmer's trump card: his children would work at what he wanted for as long as he wanted, and would expect in return only board, lodging and clothes. This command of family labour gave the peasant farmer that independence which he valued so highly, but his independence was bought at the cost of servitude for his wife and children. John Milne was still at school when his father took the unexpired five years of a lease on a run-down middle peasant farm — Atherb, New Deer — in 1836. This was not colonising crofting in the strict sense since much of the farm was nominally arable, but getting the land back into condition and extending the tilled acreage was still very hard work indeed. The passage illustrates vividly the superexploitation of family labour that underpinned the peasant's mode of production:

. . . A struggle for bare existence began. Economy had to be practised; we had to be content with the most frugal food and clothes. I can remember my father and mother taking but one cup of tea, and that only in the morning, sweetening it with treacle because that was cheaper than sugar. The children never got tea, excepting one cup on Sabbath morning, while tobacco was a luxury not to be thought of. When (oat) meal got scarce before harvest, we had, Irish-like, to fall back on potatoes. Everything had to give place to rent and manure. Being the only boy, I had to work as soon as I was able — and indeed, before I was able — and 'tis with sadness that I look back on those early years. My education was curtailed and interrupted, partly because I could not be spared, and partly because there was no money to pay school fees. Even when at school in winter, I had to work morning and evening, plying the flail when I should have been at lessons. My father began his improvements by draining the bogs with stone drains. Part of my first work was to fill the stones into a barrow when the ground was too soft to carry carts, or to hand them to my father as he built the drains. During the (five year) lease we put in about 4000 yards of these stone drains. The labour and the quantity of stones required — a load to a yard — were immense, but at that time we were glad to be rid of the stones. Though labour was cheap, I don't think these drains could have been put in for less than threepence per yard — about £50 in all. Some of the neighbouring farmers also carted away our spare stones, a thing which I afterwards regretted when we began to build dykes. We broke up some of the hard land every year, spade-trenching the parts which were too stony to plough. We had to spade two acres of moss which was too soft to carry horses.[141]

Not that the peasant farmer drove himself any less hard than his children. George Carr took a twenty-one year improving lease on thirty acres of barren heath at Westhill of Park, Drumoak, in 1863. He had a wife and family, but his children were too young to help him with the heavy work of riving in the land. He did it himself: a herculean labour that astonished William Alexander — a man well used to the rigours of peasant agriculture — when he visited Carr in 1886:

The dykes which surround the Westhill croft measure in their own length some 1,900 yards; they are from 5 ft. to 15 ft. in width, and from 5 ft. to 8 ft. in height. The stones, some of which, as we have said, are of great weight, were nearly all lifted, or sledged, into their present position by the tenant himself. No proper idea could, however, be formed of the magnitude of the labour involved without visiting the place itself. The dykes are more like a military rampart than anything else. And the visitor is disposed to be incredulous when he is told that they were all built by one man who, with the aid of his tough and hardy 'horsie', that seemed to get nearly so well accustomed to the work as himself, had actually lifted the whole material of these huge fences off the land, and no limited part of it after a stiff 'pilget' with pick and pinch to get the individual boulders out of their earth-fast beds. Yet such was the case. Under the conditions of tenancy it was important, of course, that the reclamation should be accomplished as early as possible, and the whole place was actually brought under cultivation by the end of the first seven years.[142]

No wonder that the expenditure of so much labour power generated a fierce attachment to the land — 'those rigs curling away, only half-inanimate, into the night', in Leslie Mitchell's memorable phrase.[143] Northeast literature's archetypal peasant farmer, Johnny Gibb, expresses this attachment most exquisitely in musing on his lifetime spent on Gushetneuk — a farm which he himself cut from the waste many years before:

Takin' 't as it is, there's been grun made oot o' fat wasna grun ava; an' there it is, growin' craps for the eese o' man an' beast — Ou ay, aw ken we've made weel aneuch oot upon't; but its nae i' the naitur' o' man to gyang on year aifter year plewin', an' del'in', an' earin', an' shearin' the bits o' howes an' knowes, seein' the vera yird, obaidient till's care, takin' shape, an' sen'in' up the bonny caller blade in its sizzon, an' aifter that the fu' corn i' the ear, as the Scriptur' says, onbeen a kin' o' thirl't to the vera rigs.[144]

But this attachment could not, as among owner-occupying peasant farmers in west Clare, take the form of attachment to a particular piece of family land.[145] The northeast was a leasehold area, and hence the peasant farmer could cleave only to the generalised idea of holding land. This did not weaken his attachment to the notion, however.

(b) *Stirks and peasant children*

Landlords did not seek the destruction of the northeast peasantry, then — except in limited parts of the sandstone districts — because that peasantry could be used to increase the tilled acreage of lairds' estates at no cost to the lairds themselves. But why did capitalist farmers not seek to destroy the peasantry? In the northwest Highlands at this time, we are told, capitalist sheep farmers energetically sought — and often achieved — the attachment of contiguous crofts to their own holdings.[146] These sheep farmers employed some crofters as casual labour when sheep were to be smeared, but their extensive pastoralism meant that they needed to hire no permanent labour from their neighbouring crofters: the few shepherds that they employed usually were not local men. Further, crofters were a nuisance to Highland sheep farmers. There was always the danger that a crofter's weedy tup might inseminate some of the farmer's highly bred ewes, and in hungry times some of those ewes found their way into the crofter's cauldron. For their part crofters knew that within living memory the richest and lushest pastures of that barren land had borne the arable crops of their peasant ancestors — the cultivation ridges still were plain to see — and now they found themselves crowded together on bogs and rocky outcrops, unable to produce their household's subsistence. In this bifurcated agrarian structure the capitalist farmer faced the poor peasant in mutual hatred and enmity. The bridging group — the middle peasantry — had been utterly destroyed in the clearances.[147]

Things were different in the northeast. Not only was the middle peasantry still numerous,[148] but the articulation between capitalist farmers and peasant households was deep and abiding. Northeast muckle farmers were relatively heavily specialised in cattle feeding by the mid-century,[149] and they all needed to hire labour to work their holdings. Thus they needed an assured and high quality supply of two means of production — lean cattle for fattening and labour power. The peasantry gave them both.

When new land was cut from waste in the nineteenth century its quality rarely could be compared with existing arable. Northeast farmers had a canny appreciation of where the best land lay, and had been careful to bring it into cultivation first.[150] The consequences of centuries of engrossment, as McCombie, Tillyfour, noted, was that the best land was monopolised by capitalist farmers, with peasant farmers being pushed on to inferior land.[151] This meant that peasant farmers' land usually was not good enough to fatten cattle, even if the high cost and high return economy of the feeder had been less out of tune with the peasant's overwhelming priority to assure his household's subsistence. Cattle breeding fitted very well into the peasant's mode of production, and cattle feeding meshed equally well in the capitalist farmer's mode. Thus, when, after 1840, capitalist farmers moved rapidly to a heavy emphasis on cattle feeding, peasant farmers stayed as specialised breeders.[152] As his breeding stock was improved through the diffusion of improved animals, so the peasant's stirk became the basis on which was raised the northeast feeder's worldwide reputation for top quality beef. The capitalist feeder was spared the lengthy business of raising his own cattle for feeding. He could circulate his capital much more rapidly — and increase his profits — by passing on the reproduction of an essential means of production, lean cattle, to his peasant neighbours.

The same was true of labour power. In the Lothians, with the local peasantry effectively destroyed, the capitalist farmer had to bear the full cost of reproducing his permanent labour force. The married hind had to be given money wages and perquisites sufficient to allow him to bring up a family of children to take his place in the farm's permanent labour team.[153] The Lothian muckle farmer had also to rely on migrant casual labour to take his corn harvest — a critical dependence in the heavily arable southeast.[154] The northeast muckle farmer was more fortunate. As we shall see in greater detail in chapter four, the vast majority of northeast farm servants were unmarried, the children of peasant farmers whose own holdings were in labour surplus. A shortage of farm servants in the sandstone districts, where the peasantry had been penetrated more thoroughly, could be met from the unfailing reservoir of peasant children in the northeast's central wedge. Thus the capitalist farmer passed to his peasant neighbours the task of reproducing that means of production which underlay his whole productive mode — full-time hired labour power.

He was more fortunate than his Lothian compeer in the matter of casual labour, too. Poor peasants needed wage work in order to eke out subsistence production on the croft, and after 1840 that wage work had to be found more and more in casual labour for capitalist farmers. By that date the development of capitalism in town and country had broken the age-old combination of artisan work and peasant agriculture. The effects of the Illicit Distillation (Scotland) Act of 1822 and the 1823 Excise Act had destroyed distilling and smuggling as a major cottage industry, to the great delight of local ministers:

> Previous to 1827 there was a great deal of illicit distillation. On my becoming minister that year, I assisted in taking measures to put it down. It was subsequently

completely suppressed, and those who had previously been engaged in it, after having for a while lived upon their friends, thought their best plan would be to emigrate.[155]

By 1840 linen spinning and weaving likewise had been separated from peasant agriculture:

> At a former period, not yet beyond the recollection of people alive, there was carried on, in this quarter, an extensive domestic manufacture of linen, which was commonly known in the markets by the name of 'Mearns linen', and the spinning of the yarn, and manufacturing of the cloth, afforded employment to many hands in the families both of tenants and of crofters. The system is now entirely done away: at the old markets which used to be held several days in succession, the day formerly appropriated for the sale of linen is a blank; all those employed in weaving have, with scarcely an exception, gone to the villages, and there, at least in Laurencekirk, by far the greater part work, not at home, but in public weaving-shops.[156]

Most serious of all, lost markets, poor quality control and the growth of factory production meant that by 1840 stocking knitting — long the strongest industrial buttress of the northeast peasantry — had dwindled almost to nothing. By working far into the night pauper women could earn a mere one penny per day from knitting.[157]

Thus poor peasants were forced to find an increasing proportion of their subsidiary wage work in agriculture. This was not an altogether new experience. As early as 1780 Andrew Wight had noted with approval that day labourers in central Buchan were all crofters: this arrangement had the particular virtue of being 'the only way to keep down the hire of labourers, it being always in the landlord's power to raise the rent upon the labourer, in proportion to the advance of hire'.[158] One of a landlord's major concerns in laying off waste ground for colonising crofters always had been to assure an adequate supply of casual labour for the convenience of his capitalist tenants. In Cluny, for example,

> The first allotments were let to married men, in the situation of labourers, whose former dwellings stood in the way of improvement upon newly improved farms. Those preferred were young married men, brought up on the property, well recommended, who would hire themselves as useful labourers to farmers during the busy seasons, but always employing part of their time in the improvement of their crofts.[159]

This kind of arrangement could be found throughout the nineteenth century. Even in the Laigh of Moray in the 1890s James Black, Sheriffston, St Andrews asserted that

> I am in the happy position of having a colony of about a dozen crofters in my immediate neighbourhood. They have families and they are most advantageous to us for a supply of labour. They get good wages from us and steady employment, and they are all comfortable and contented.[160]

Black would have treated his crofter labourers as gently as any capitalist farmer. A peasant son from the Moray glens, he had written a strongly pro-peasant Highland Society essay while factor on the Ellon estate,[161] and retained his liberal beliefs after his subsequent career in journalism left him proprietor of the *Elgin Courier,* Provost of Elgin, Secretary of the Morayshire Farmers Club, and owner-occupier of Sheriffston. But it would be interesting to have his version of his relation with the Balmuckity crofters confirmed from peasant lips. The decline of non-agricultural work in the countryside had given capitalist farmers a stronger bargaining position with crofter-labourers, particularly when — as seems to have been the case with James Black — the muckle farmer was almost a monopoly buyer of his local crofter labour.

In some cases poor peasants moved beyond day labouring to fee as farm servants, cultivating their crofts with the labour of their female relatives and what little spare time they themselves had.[162] In such a case the crofter's plight was desperate. He had lost that independence which was the justification of the crofting life's rigours — for the crofter himself, if not for his family — and yet he lacked the sanction available to other farm servants, particularly the 'nomadic' single men, of moving to another farm. This degree of integration with the muckle farm remained rare, however: most crofters relied on day labouring — trenching, dyking — and wage work in times of peaked labour demand in agriculture to eke out their crofting subsistence. The most important of these times of peaked labour demand was the corn harvest.

Apart from some very localised districts in the Moray lowlands,[163] the northeast was unique among Scottish lowland areas in having no need for migrant hairst labour.[164] Some of the northeast's hairst labour came from rural tradesmen and craftsmen — blacksmiths, millers, soutars, tailors and (very important in the earlier decades of the century) hand-loom weavers[165] — who took a hairst fee in August and September. Another group, overlapping with the first, was urban craftsmen: one year weavers from the Angus and Kincardine towns were not allowed to go to the hairst, and in those counties 'many a field of corn stood uncut, till a high wind shook a great proportion of the crop'.[166] The families of married farm servants found themselves pressed into service in the harvest fields. But all over the northeast one important source of hairst labour was the crofter and his family. In Cairnie, for instance,

> The sickle was used on small holdings for shearing all kinds of grain crops after the scythe was used on the larger holdings. The reason for this was that many small crofters were engaged in reaping the farmers' crops with the scythe, while their wives, with the assistance of old people at home, harvested their small patches with the sickle.[167]

The hairst fee provided crofters with an invaluable supplementary income, and it could be augmented by seasonal migration to the great arable districts of southeast Scotland where the hairst came earlier than in the northeast:

On August twelfth from Aberdeen
We sailed upon the Prince,
And landed safe at Clifford's fields,
Our harvest to commence.

For six lang weeks the country roun'
Frae toon to toon we went,
And I took richt weel wi' the Lothian fare
And aye was weel content.[168]

The mechanisation of the hairst sharply limited opportunities for crofters, as for other casual hairst workers. In the late 1850s machine reaping in southern Scotland brought a reduction in labour per acre of more than sixty per cent compared with sickle harvesting, and thirty per cent compared with scythe harvesting.[169] Labour economies grew even greater, of course, as self-binders replaced reapers. One six hundred acre lowland Aberdeenshire farm needed twenty-seven people to secure the harvest with reapers in 1880. In 1933 the hairst on that farm needed eight men.[170] In 1900 one Buchan capitalist farmer paid £12 in casual hairst wages, against an annual wage bill for permanent labour of £345.[171]

Poor peasants were driven more and more insistently into wage work for capitalist farmers after 1840. They, and their middle peasant brethren, preserved their precapitalist mode of production centred on the use of family labour to assure the household's subsistence: but they preserved that mode of production at the cost of tailoring their production more and more closely to the needs of capitalist farmers. The tight integration of capitalist and peasant farmers through labour and commodity markets boded ill for the northeast peasantry should capitalist production mature to the point where the peasant's stirk and his children were no longer indispensable to the profitability of capitalist agriculture. But in 1870 that gloomy time still lay ahead.

Relations of Production

The relationship between capitalist farmer on the one hand, and peasant children fee'd as farm servants and crofters employed as day labourers and hairst workers on the other, reproduced much of the earlier arrangement between rich peasants and poor peasants from pre-improvement days. The crofter now held his land from the laird, of course, and not as the rich peasant's sub-tenant. But that apart, the agricultural revolution had caused remarkably little change in the relations between capitalist farmers and various peasant fractions. The same was not true of other elements in the social relations of agricultural production.

As landlords came to see land simply as another commodity to be bought and sold, so estates changed hands more frequently. This was not the case with the three giant estates that dominated the northeast — the Gordon Castle, Fife, and Haddo House estates had been built up in the eighteenth century and saw little change until the end of the nineteenth century. But smaller estates, if not entailed, saw a considerable turnover. Since the owner's concern was, through rent, to maximise his return on invested capital, it is not surprising that — as with capitalist farms — the estate market was brightest when capitalist agriculture was booming. The point was not lost on some northeast farmers of a radical turn of mind:

> I look on a landlord simply as a capitalist. In my own neighbourhood there are two or three properties, which have been bought within the last few years by men who have been the architects of their own fortune. They formerly had their money invested in hazardous mercantile speculations, bank stock, railways, etc., and they had no security there for their interests.[172]

Since the northeast was a leasehold area, relations between peasant farmers seeking their household's subsistence and lairds seeking to maximise the surplus which they extracted as rent turned on the conditions of leasehold tenure. The same was true of the relations between the capitalist farmer and his landlord, each seeking to maximise his share of surplus value as profit or rent.

Long leases had been a major reason for the fast pace of agricultural improvement in lowland Scotland from the late eighteenth century: given security of tenure for the period of his lease, the Scottish farmer had been more willing than his English counterpart to invest his own capital in pushing forward the material forces of production.[173] By 1840 the written nineteen-year lease was ubiquitous among northeast capitalist farmers and middle peasants as older forms of lease — some as long as three lives — died out.[174] Many crofters held nineteen-year leases too; but the laird's usual view of colonising crofters as merely 'the pioneers of cultivation, the outpost of advancing agriculture'[175] meant that many crofters were not granted long leases that might block a profitable reorganisation of the estate at a later date. It was common, therefore, for crofters to hold shorter leases than small farmers,[176] to hold from year to year,[177] or to have no leases at all and sit as tenants at will.[178] At this point crofters shade into the class below, squatters.[179] Squatters colonised land unclaimed by any estate. The most celebrated colony was the Commonty of Bennachie in central Aberdeenshire, which existed, to the profound annoyance of neighbouring lairds, until the hill was divided among the surrounding estates in 1859.[180] Long after the division Bennachie remained a symbol of a lost sanctuary from lairdly power: even today the reverence in which many Aberdeenshire country people hold the hill is an echo of the squatter colony of more than a century ago. Squatters settled on other unclaimed commons as well: the forest of Correnie in Aberdeenshire and the Commonty of Cowie near Stonehaven, for instance.[181] All came to an end with the division of the commons.

The written lease symbolised the mediation through the cash nexus of the relations between laird and tenant. By 1840 labour dues had long been dead. Payment of part of the rent in kind lasted rather longer, but by 1860 this too was on its last legs.[182] The tenant contracted to pay his laird a stipulated money rent for the next nineteen years. His lease laid down the crop rotation to be followed, and debarred the tenant from selling certain crops — hay, for instance — off the farm. That apart, as long as he paid his rent, the farmer had the usufruct of his land for the period of his lease and the laird could not interfere. Conflict arose, if at all, at the end of the lease. The grounds for conflict with his laird differed for the peasant farmer and for the capitalist farmer. Thus we have to analyse the two cases separately.

(a) *Capitalist farmers*

Between 1840 and 1870 landlords and capitalist farmers shared a common interest in pushing forward the material forces of production as fast as possible. This shared interest is shown in the agricultural societies that spread across the northeast in the nineteenth century. We have seen[183] that the moving spirits in starting these societies were the Lothian capitalist farmers attracted north by improving lairds in the late eighteenth century: in the following century these societies brought together lairds and muckle farmers in amity, mutual congratulation and whisky. The Fettercairn Club, for instance — the premier society in southern Kincardine — consisted of 'about 86 members, from among the proprietors and principal tenants of the neighbourhood'.[184] The very old Buchan and Boyn Farmer Society was much the same.[185] The Garioch Farmer Club was started in 1808 by local lairds who then invited selected farmers to join — only farmers occupying more than fifty arable acres were eligible.[186] The Aberdeenshire Agricultural Association at its foundation in 1819 had a committee composed of fifteen lairds, three large tenant farmers, and two military gentlemen. This big society was organised in districts based on the Commutation Act: each district had its own committee of lairds and capitalist farmers.[187] The societies' activities show a marked proclivity towards the interests of capitalist production. They stimulated mechanisation, tried to improve techniques of cultivation, and encouraged selective breeding: the cattle classes in the Garioch Farmer Club's show were limited to peasant farmers between 1845 and 1853, and in 1839 the Club held a special bull and seed show 'in consequence of a deficiency of good bulls being found to exist among small farmers and crofters in the district'.[188] Not altogether disinterested: this was the time when capitalist farmers were moving rapidly to specialised cattle feeding, and it was very much in their interest to improve the quality of young cattle being supplied to them by peasant farmers for feeding off. One major concern of all these societies was to improve the quality of work from farm servants by giving prizes at ploughing and hoeing matches. They tried to inhibit the movement of farm servants — an important card for the servant in his dealings with the muckle farmer — by offering prizes for 'long and faithful service'.[189] But their most pervasive effect was to assert and demonstrate the community of interest between laird and capitalist farmer, to tie the head of the farmers to the tail of the gentry:

> They have raised his general standard in the management of a farm, by bestowing due honour and commendation on the active, industrious, economical and neat-handed farmer. They have been the means of introducing better stock, better seed, better implements of husbandry, and better modes of culture. And they have contributed not a little to rub off that rusticity which might leave us fit for a market or fair, or for bearing a prominently ridiculous part in a picture of 'The Rent Day'; but which completely unfitted us for general society.[190]

The community of interest in pressing forward material forces of production was only one, though one of the most important, of the threads in the rope binding together lairds and capitalist farmers. Another thread was public administration: a thread that bound these class fractions much closer in Scotland than in England:

> For a long period the Scotch landowners have been compelled to look into the management of their property in a different manner from those of England. Upon them the liability was directly placed of finding the money for the public establishments of their counties, the churches, prisons, and police. They had the determination of questions of road-making; and having to contribute directly a large part of the county expenditure, they took an active part in its administration. This brought them into closer business contact with the farmers; and recent legislation has tended to increase this connection by the principle of imposing all county rates in certain proportion directly on landowners and farmers, and giving to both a representation in the same county or parish board. There is thus a better fusion of the two interests than in England, and a readier appreciation on the part of the landowner of the outlays requisite on his part to enable his tenant to make the most of the land he farms.[191]

This fusion of interest was evident in other spheres of influence, too. One of these was the Kirk. Maclaren shows that Kirk elders in Aberdeen city — in both Church of Scotland and Free Church congregations — were recruited from 'men of substance'.[192] In the country 'men of substance' meant capitalist farmers.[193] In the Auld Kirk at least the link between heritors and elders was a strong link between lairds and capitalist farmers. The 1843 Disruption of the Church of Scotland weakened this bond to some extent, but since many large farmers stayed in the Auld Kirk while several northeast lairds came 'out', the damage was less serious than it might have been. Yet another link was forged by the volunteer Yeomanry raised by many northeast lairds in the 1859 war scare and maintained thereafter. Capitalist farmers and their sons gained a social cachet by joining these elegant ranks — which required that one could provide one's own riding horse and hence excluded peasant farmers.[194] These many strands of common interest overlay each other to form a strong cord. The point is best appreciated through biography. Mr G. Johnson died in April 1856, a capitalist farmer whose main holding — Overton, New Deer — had been leased by members of his family for more than two centuries. In his later years he added to this a lease of Aquhorthies, Inverurie. His obituary makes it clear that Johnson was, as well as being an enterprising farmer, very active outside farming. He was the first chairman of the New Deer school board, and sat on the Inverurie school board for six years. He enlisted in the Methlick volunteer company in 1859 and rose to command it. He was also a zealous temperance campaigner, an office-bearer in the Free Church for many years and a keen, if moderate, Liberal. Johnson would have come into contact with his lairds in many of these roles, spinning a close web of mutual dependence and common interest.

But even before 1870 there were some ravelled threads in this web. Three main sources of conflict between capitalist farmers and lairds were the game laws, the laird's privileged access to a struggling tenant's capital through the Hypothec law, and tenant right — compensation at the lease end for permanent or unexhausted improvements carried out by the tenant. All three originated in, or at least were greatly exacerbated as a result of, the more rigorously capitalist attitude to land use in the period after 1840.

Conflict over the game question arose as landowners sought to maximise the sporting potential of their estates. Earlier in the century northeast lairds or their sporting tenants had blasted off with murderous intent at whatever small birds and large hairy animals were unwise enough actually to dwell on the property. By 1870 game was being developed systematically: many estates were raising pheasants for subsequent sporting slaughter.[195] Lairds could cash in not only from increased sporting rents but also from carcase sales. In 1864, for example, Sir Archibald Grant sold the carcases of 15,700 rabbits off his small Monymusk estate: in 1865 the figure was 15,900. Calculating at sixpence per carcase, Grant was clearing £400 per annum from his rabbit crop[196] — a sum that could not be looked for in rent from any but the largest and finest capitalist farms in the parish.

The drawback to all this lairdly enterprise, from the farmer's point of view, was that the birds and animals were growing fat on his crops. Nor did it stop there. The capitalist tenant of Aquhorthies, a Mr Lumsden, 'complains most bitterly of the destruction done by pheasants to his crops before harvest; that his loss has grown to such an extent that it is perfectly intolerable; that he can neither keep cat nor dog but what are killed by the gamekeepers, and, as a consequence, his house, farmsteading, and stock yard, are overrun with vermin, and that the loss to his corn-stack is incalculable'.[197] Agitation over game erupted in the northeast in 1865 with local anti-game law committees springing up throughout the five counties, and rumbled on until a Select Committee was appointed to enquire into the subject in the early 1870s. As part of this agitation an Aberdeen Game Conference was called in 1871, which elected a joint committee of lairds and capitalist farmers. This committee sent out a questionnaire to all Aberdeenshire landowners whose annual rental exceeded £500 and to all tenants paying more than £14 in annual rent. The replies showed that game was reserved to the proprietor on sixty-nine large estates in Aberdeenshire. This meant that tenant farmers on these estates were (officially at least) powerless to protect their crops from the laird's pheasants, grouse, hares, rabbits and deer. On only sixteen estates was game not mentioned in the lease.[198] The replies also showed that 3,817 tenants — eighty three per cent of those that returned their schedule — claimed to have suffered damaged crops from ground game (rabbits and hares) or from game birds.[199] It was clear, then, that the interests of lairds and tenants were opposed over the game question — and capitalist tenants had more crops to lose, of course. But what was remarkable about this agitation was its amicable nature. One laird — Leslie of Warthill — grew somewhat crusty and had to be cooled out. That apart, the joint committee moved forward smoothly to a conclusion with which the Select Committee later would concur: that tenants should have the right to protect their crops from ground game. Agriculture was so much more important an element in estate finances than was sport — except in the depths of the hills — that lairds dared not risk rupturing their wider shared interest with capitalist farmers on the narrow point of game.

Hypothec was a different matter. Scottish statutes gave the laird a hypothec in the soil: this meant that if a tenant fell behind with his rent, the laird could safely put a process of sequestration in train. The creditors then lined up. First to be met were Crown claims, then any feu duties owing to the superior, then farm servants' wages, then creditors for funeral expenses.[200] None of these claims would be expected to make too great a dent in the tenant's capital. The next in line was the landlord. He had the right to take the full rent arrears due to him before any other creditor saw a penny. Hypothec was long established, but

> The law under which the landlord's right of hypothec exists does not appear to have attracted public attention as a law supposed to require amendment until a comparatively recent period.

This was attributed

> . . . to the fact, that the successful cultivation of the soil now depends very much on classes of persons, such as the manure merchant and mechanical engineer, whose capital and labour only a few years ago contributed but little to the ordinary operations of agriculture.[201]

Thus the hypothec controversy was the child of capitalist agricultural development. The main thrust of the controversy was between two bourgeois fractions — the landlords and the merchants. Landlords' hypothec put the latter group at a distinct disadvantage when a tenant failed. But hypothec also had another, much more subtle, effect. William McCombie, Tillyfour, in arguing for its abolition, asserted that

> I think the law of hypothec is much worse than the game laws, because the game laws only affect the game-preserving properties; whereas the law of hypothec affects

the whole of the tenants in Scotland, and also the manure merchants, implement makers, seed merchants and tradesmen; I think that the law of hypothec is the greatest grievance which we have in Scotland.[202]

Now McCombie was quite right in his claim that hypothec affected every Scottish tenant farmer. But the point is that it affected capitalist farmers differently from peasant farmers. The general effect of hypothec was to allow a laird to gamble when letting a farm: to accept a tenant without farming experience, or a tenant who was undercapitalised, if that man offered a fancy rent for the farm. The laird knew that he would get his rent whatever happened: the problems of manure merchants were not his business. The extent to which lairds pursued this exclusive interest varied from district to district — in Kincardine there were fifty-nine sequestrations in three years in the mid-1860s, while East Lothian, with a similar tilled acreage, saw only three or four[203] — but in all districts the laird's ability to gamble when letting a farm exposed existing large farmers to considerable competition from merchants and other urban capitalists. Not surprisingly, since this competition forced up the general rent level, large farmers detested hypothec almost to a man.[204] Peasant farmers, on the other hand, generally supported the existing law. The laird's freedom to select undercapitalised tenants allowed him to give croft leases to farm servants whose life savings, scraped together through remorseless thrift and sobriety, still did not run to the eight or ten pounds per acre needed in the mid-1860s to stock the croft.[205] In similar fashion it allowed a successful crofter to move up to a larger holding at the end of what lease he had.

Thus the controversy over hypothec was, in Garland, Cairton's words, 'a question very much between the large and the small farmers'.[206] The hypothec controversy generated a peculiar set of alliances: landlords and peasant farmers against capitalist farmers, urban merchants and manufacturers. Like the game law controversy, the controversy over hypothec erupted in 1865 in a rash of local protest committees organised by capitalist farmers:[207] like the game question, hypothec was still a grievance between laird and muckle farmer in 1870.

Controversy over tenant right was, as with hypothec, born of the more rigorously capitalist production of the years after 1840. The capitalist mode of production required a heavy investment in dykes, buildings, drainage, and so on — permanent improvements. If the laird would not provide this investment, then the muckle farmer was forced to do so. The muckle farmer also needed to put a lot of animal and artificial manure in the land — an investment that was referred to by the less malodorous name of 'unexhausted improvements'. Conflict between laird and muckle farmer could arise at the end of the lease, when the tenant asked for compensation for his permanent or unexhausted improvements.

Conflict over permanent improvements was more likely to arise on entailed estates: large farmers complained that the owners of such estates were less willing to invest money in improvements to their farms, and were more tardy in doing repairs.[208] It was more likely, too, on estates that treated large and small farmers alike in requiring the tenant to do all draining and building: on the Netherdale estate near Turriff, for instance, one capitalist farmer claimed that the estate had paid not one penny for permanent improvements or drainage on his farm between 1754 and 1881.[209] Not all parsimonious estates were small, like Netherdale: the huge Fife estate, it was claimed, did no building or drainage before 1886.[210]

Compensation for unexhausted improvement was difficult to calculate — so difficult, in fact, that northeast capitalist farmers sought, like their counterparts elsewhere in Scotland, to avoid the problem:

> The Scotch farmer, when he enters on a farm, has a problem to solve which does not often present itself to the mind of the occupier in England. He has made a strictly commercial bargain with his landlord and, as a man of business, he immediately sets himself to work to make the most of it. The landlord does the same; and this is one reason why the game question is such a sore point across the Border. But this is by the way. The farmer finds his land in as poor a condition as his predecessor could possibly reduce it to, having due regard to the conditions of his lease. His experience has taught him that the most profitable thing to be done is to put 'condition' into his land as fast as he can do it without endangering any crops, and then to keep up that condition until the commencement of his last shift of five or six years, as the case may be, when he steadily and scientifically devotes himself to the task of taking as much out of the land as he dare, in the face of the restrictive covenants of his lease. It is not that he has any particular desire to rob the land, but he wishes both to recoup his own outlay, in view of the contingency of his lease not being renewed, and also to reduce as much as possible the compensation for his farm.[211]

In summary, we can see that between 1840 and 1870 there was an inherent conflict of interest between landlords and capitalist farmers only in the matter of hypothec — which assumed major importance only in times like the Crimean war boom when the returns to be looked for in agriculture outstripped those in other branches of capitalist production. The game question could strain relations, but few lairds were willing to allow it to imperil social relations in agriculture. Tenant right could prove difficult, too, but before 1870 it did not form the major problem that it was to be in the difficult 1880s. All of these difficulties were pinpricks in the generally harmonious relations between lairds and muckle farmers up to 1870, as both groups sought the fullest possible development of productive forces for their own ends. The relationship between peasant farmers and their lairds was less harmonious.

(b) *Peasant farmers*

The capitalist farmer, in the pure case at least, produced only for the market. The peasant farmer produced two crops — one for the market and one for the farm family's subsistence. His need to gear some production to the market in order to meet demands for rent, rates and a replacement fund for worn-out equipment gave the peasant farmer some community of interest with capitalist farmers in the matter of tenant right. Indeed, with regard to compensation for permanent improvements, the peasant's grievance often was more profound. Before 1870 scarcely any northeast lairds built steadings for their peasant tenants.[212] The reason is not far to seek: in 1909, after changed conditions had compelled estates to build on peasant holdings, it cost the Haddo House estate £9 18s per acre to build a suitable steading on a fifty-acre holding, while a much larger steading on a three hundred acre farm cost only five guineas per acre.[213] It is not surprising that peasant tenants, forced to do their own building, did not join in 'the rage for building farm houses and offices in a shewy style and of great extent' that had infuriated George Robertson at the beginning of the nineteenth century.[214] John Milne's description of the steading on Atherb in the 1880s shows the miracles that could be achieved with old wood and binder twine:

> I was told when I renewed my lease that five roods of mason work was all the building the proprietor would pay for — half the cost when finished and the other half at removal; I could build whatever else I liked, but I was made to understand I would not be paid for it. I built one half of a barn; the other half still stands in the condition in which it was when built in the end of the last century. Even then it had been roofed with old wood. This roof is a good museum in its way, containing as it does pieces of rafters from an older roof, along with pieces of farm implements of a hundred years ago, contrasting strangely with the steam engine and other agricultural machinery of the present day only a few feet distant, under slate and iron roofs. As the byres built during the prior lease could not contain the cattle kept on the enlarged holding, I put up wooden houses to hold the extra stock. As I did not wish to have large sums lying out on farm houses, I erected a wooden house and roofed it with peats, for carts and implements. The dwelling-house is as old as the barn, part of the walls being turf . . . It cannot be said that extravagance has ruined the Buchan farmers.[215]

Peasant farmers had seen the dramatic increases in productivity — and profit — that development of the material forces had brought to capitalist farmers between 1840 and 1870. They tried their damnedest to follow that example, but they had a critical problem — a lack of capital. In some ways the peasant could substitute labour for capital: he could use family labour in land reclamation, draining and dyking, for instance, while the capitalist farmer was forced to hire day labourers for these tasks. But elsewhere this substitution was not possible, and capital had to be accumulated slowly from the meagre resources of the holding:

> About this time we sold three stirks to a dealer who failed. Well can I remember the bitterness of that disappointment, not so much for the money as for having to thresh with the flails for another year. In 1856, however, we were able to put in a threshing mill. This was our first great start, as it allowed more time for other work . . . Great efforts were made to raise this mill, and the first money that could be spared always went for that purpose.[216]

Who could be surprised that the laird's ability to expropriate so much blood, sweat, toil and tears at the end of the lease was bitterly resented by peasant farmers, who slowly came to contrast their own productive labour with the unproductive labour of their lairds as the century took its course?[217]

The peasant farmer's need to produce a marketable surplus gave him some common interest with capitalist farmers over tenant right, then. But this common interest was overridden by conflict between the two groups over hypothec and by the consequences of the peasant's predominant concern to assure his household's subsistence. In pursuing this goal his interests came into direct conflict with those of both lairds and muckle farmers. We can see the point clearly if we look at the peasant's twin nightmares — rack-renting and engrossment.

It is not surprising that we should have many complaints about rack-renting from northeast peasant farmers. In the years of good prices before 1870, competition from large farmers looking for more land and from men trying to get into farming forced up the general rent level for peasant holdings, and thus peasants found that they had to offer a higher rent for the next lease. The rise in the general rent level was accelerated by two other factors unconnected with the demand for peasant holdings. The first concerned improving leases. The essence of an improving lease was an artificially low rent per acre, a rent that would attract tenants to rive in waste land in the hope of making an adequate living from the holding in the last few years of the lease. Once that lease was exhausted, the laird could ask a significantly higher rent for the next one. Secondly, the fact that so few estates built houses and steadings on peasant farms before 1870 meant that any building had to be done by the tenant. In theory the crofter or small farmer then paid a rather lower rent than would have been the case if the estate had provided buildings. However determined the peasant was to leave his house and steading in a ramshackle condition at the lease end in order to minimise the permanent improvements that his laird could expropriate, the peasant's unaided efforts at building, dyking and draining would make his holding worth more rent for the next lease.

Allowing these caveats, however, it remains true that between 1840 and 1870 peasants paid a higher rent per acre than capitalist farmers, and for inferior land. Landlords could exploit the peasant's dogged commitment to maintain his household's subsistence, and cream as rent a large proportion of the household's money income. On some estates this meant simply charging what the traffic would bear. On other estates — usually small lawyer-factored estates — the laird or his representative went far beyond this to a scandalous super-exploitation of the peasantry. At Lenabo on the Aden estate, to take one example from many,

> A character came from ——, a carter or something sic like, and bade for a croft. His bid was so very good that the factor saw he was to be a useful man. A number of crofts were out at the same time, and were advertised. When this man applied for one

of the crofts (the rent was then £12) he offered £27 or £28 for it. The factor told him to offer for 'the puckle' and he might get one of them. Some of the houses were miserable shielings . . . Take one of the crofters in the lot referred to, B—— say. He has 23 acres of ground, and he entered upon it forty years ago, when it was a wilderness of gorse and heather. He paid £11 of rent, and put up houses for himself. The man was naturally anxious to better his position in the world, if he could. At the end of the first nineteen years he had it all under the plough and got his lease renewed, the rent being fixed at £18, with the land in fair working order. He goes on his weary pilgrimage, till the close of the second nineteen years, when this interloping old carter comes on the carpet, and bids £28 for the croft. And this follows — The factor, having got similarly exorbitant bids, in the way indicated, for over half a dozen of the crofts, goes round the poor characters and says to one after another, 'Now I've been bidden such and such for your place; I would not like to see you shift, but you could not expect that I could let it at less money than I have been bidden. Will you give me £1 more than the offer I have mentioned?' The result of what on the factor's part it would need one or two profane words properly to describe was that, rather than flit, the crofters gave rents out of all proportion to their bits of land; that they lost all the little money they had made, and have never since been able to hold their heads above water. B——, whom I have mentioned, bade £23 for his placie, but the factor says, 'I would like to be fair with you, Jeems, so if you will split the difference, and say £25 10s 0d, you will get it.' James, after a great deal of deliberation, come up to £25. 'It's cheap, Jeems,' says the factor, 'and you'll manage the other ten shillings.' And that ten shillings James B—— had to pay, and does to this day. The man is 76 years of age, and during fifty years has continued in a course of the hardest industry and perseverance, bringing his land under the plough, and continuously cultivating it — practically making the place — for which he pays twenty-two shillings an acre. It was, I need hardly say, a lawyer factor; a man weel kent in Buchan and its capital in mair capacities than one. 'Pawky'! aye, wasna he pawky: but, oh, man, it was damnably cruel — as cruel as maist that even the Highland crafter ever thol't, only that it was thol't wi' greater helpfu'ness an' faculty.[218]

Bitterly though peasants complained of rack-renting, it was the desire for tenurial security that lay at the heart of the conflict of interest between peasants and their lairds between 1840 and 1870. When the leases of crofts and small farms fell in, they were in danger of being engrossed in larger holdings. A few crofts were consolidated into a small farm, or 'bittie places' were added to a neighbouring capitalist farm as the northeast's land frontier rolled up the hillsides. The displaced tenant then had to find a new piece of blasted heath to cultivate under the benevolent eye of the laird and his factor.[219] This process could be repeated several times. For example, Donald Jack cut three crofts in succession from waste land in Udny and Belhelvie. He held the first two without a written lease: in each case he was evicted and saw his laboriously improved arable land engrossed. His third croft he held on a nineteen-year lease, but his laird gave him no assistance in building or draining and the rent was set at a level which gave Jack 'the barest of livings'.[220] A farmer remembered 'the bitter feelings engendered in the bosoms of our hard-working peasantry by such proceedings, but what of that?'[221] What indeed? In the years between 1840 and 1870 the lairds' interest lay in promoting capitalist agriculture through engrossment — as long as land reclamation ensured a continuing supply of stirks and peasant children — and they had irresistible power with which to pursue that interest.

The extent to which estates followed this grim logic differed considerably. In part the difference turned on estate size. Big estates tended to be gentler with peasant tenants.[222] On the Haddo House estate eviction was unknown. The Gordon Castle estate was as benevolent, once its draconian reorganisation of the 1840s had been digested, in its effective recognition of peasant farmers' desire for security and heritability of tenure:

> . . . When a farm is out of lease on the death of a tenant, they take every pain and trouble that they can to find a relative of the last tenant, just as though it was an heritable estate, and give it to him in preference to anyone else.[223]

On these large estates the customary expectation that a tenant would be offered another lease, or that his nominee would be given first refusal, was met more often. Holdings were let on professional valuation. Resident factors with a practical knowledge of agriculture sought to get good tenants rather than simply to maximise the rental.

Things tended to be different on smaller estates:

> When ye gang to our petty lairds
> Your dwelling-place to crave,
> And if you give the worth three-fold,
> Your asking you may have.
>
> Gin you fall in their arrears,
> I tell you what they'll do:
> They will not leave you horse nor mare,
> Your sheep nor yet your cow.
>
> First, they'll empty your barn walls,
> The next, they'll empty your byre;
> They'll thirdly tirr your back and bed,
> And last, put out your fire.[224]

Small estates did not have resident factors. They were administered by capitalist farmers, by freelance valuers or — most commonly — by lawyer factors, the principal devil in the peasant farmer's demonology.[225] The factor's concern on many small estates was simply to maximise the estate rental: these estates not infrequently were owned by companies or trusts interested simply in their return on invested capital. Holdings sometimes were let on valuation, but most small estate factors let through open competition. This meant that the existing tenant or his assignee had no advantage over competitors. The interests of peasant farmers and landlords were incompatible on all estates; but that incompatibility would become obvious, and have more radical political consequences, on small estates when peasant farmers began to develop a consciousness of their common class interest as the glow of mid-Victorian high farming darkened into the gloom of the 1880s.

3

Depression and Adjustment, 1870-1914

> Nae won'er tho' the times mak's us a' discontented,
> For faith the puir fairmers they've cause to complain;
> The meal is cheap sellin', their fairms high rentit,
> And sma' is their profit, when sellin' their grain.
>
> Some one thing, some other, likewise the bad weather,
> The craps torn doon wi' the torrents o' rain;
> The cattle that's parket will no tak' the market,
> We'll jist tak' them in for a twalmonth again.[1]

THE future of northeast agriculture and its social formation would have seemed clear to any keen-eyed observer in 1870. The capitalist mode of production would continue its relentless spread, with a consequent growth of large farms at the expense of small farms and crofts. But quantitative changes would soon force a qualitative change. We have seen that the early cultivation of the sandstone-based clays and loams of southern Kincardine had led, through engrossment, to a much higher average farm size than in other parts of the northeast outside the Laigh of Moray. Peasant agriculture was much more attenuated in southern Kincardine than in most other districts. In 1870 it seemed that peasant agriculture quickly would go into a similar decline in the heartland of the northeast: for the reserve of improvable land, the internal frontier which had allowed the reproduction of peasant agriculture throughout the first three-quarters of the century, was beginning to be exhausted. Reports from parishes spread right across lowland Aberdeenshire — from Dyce, Huntly, Newhills, Old Deer, Peterculter, Slains and Tough — suggested that the limit of reclaimable land had been reached or was about to be reached.[2]

Peasant farming was not engulfed by a rising tide of capitalist agriculture, however. It was granted a stay of execution. The high prices for cash crops which had carried capitalist farmers through three profitable decades began to fall, and large farmers were the chief sufferers in 'the great depression'[3] from the late 1870s until 1914. Henry Hamilton gives an account of these bleak years in Banffshire:

> The last quarter of the century . . . saw a reversal of fortunes, and agriculture in the county, as in other parts of the country, passed through a trying time. The wholesale

general price level fell on the average by forty per cent; prices of oats and barley fell by about this amount, beef and mutton by twenty-nine per cent, and wool by fifty per cent. To make matters worse the livestock industry was severely hit by the import of frozen beef which had come to this country in 1880. In addition to these depressing factors there was a series of five bad harvests, in 1873, 1875, 1876, 1877 and 1879, the latter being the worst experienced in the nineteenth century. In parts of upper Banffshire the protracted harvest carried on until winter. The inhabitants of Glenlivet district still talk of the heartrending task of trying to save some of the crop, most of which was frozen to the ground. This long continued adversity left an enduring mark on the spirit, outlook and enterprise of farmers. Much of the arable land in the county, brought under cultivation in the prosperous years, reverted to grass. Many farmers faced bankruptcy, and only those who had capital and could adapt their farming to the new conditions survived. Some of them were able to take over additional farms cheaply. The land suffered most; cornlands became sheepruns, and grazings were stocked by the livestock of speculators who exhausted the pastures without expending any capital on their rehabilitation.[4]

A gloomy picture indeed: but one that owes more to the traditional view of the hardships endured by British farmers between 1875 and 1914 than to what actually happened in the northeast. In this chapter we will look at Hamilton's assertions against the backcloth of what actually did happen in these years. We will divide the problem into three parts. First we will look at the difficulties which bad seasons, changed price runs and external competition presented to northeast farmers as a whole. We will then consider how the farmers adapted to these difficulties. Finally we will examine the effect of all these changes on the social formation of northeast agriculture.

Harvests and Prices

Hamilton is quite correct in emphasising that the lower cash crop prices of these years formed one of the major problems facing farmers in the northeast. We saw in Figure 2.4 that in the years from 1850 to 1875 the moving average price for oats, barley and wheat generally stayed comfortably above twenty, twenty-five and forty shillings per quarter respectively. Looking at the right side of the figure, we can see that the last quarter of the century was a less happy time for the farmer selling corn crops. The price of oats slid throughout the 1880s, to bottom out at around sixteen shillings a quarter and stay there until the end of the first decade of the twentieth century. Barley prices show a similar trajectory, falling through the eighties to a low point of about twenty-three shillings and bumping along at that level for two decades. But the really spectacular fall is in wheat prices: from above forty shillings per quarter in the prosperous years to around twenty-five shillings in the years before 1910, a level which was held until the war boom after 1914 made prices as spectacularly high and profitable as those between 1880 and 1910 had been low and unprofitable. In percentage terms the average price for oats between 1890 and 1899 was 26 per cent lower than the average price between 1870 and 1879.

Barley prices fell by 18 per cent over the same period. Wheat prices fell by 40 per cent.

Cattle prices were at least as important as corn prices for northeast farmers. Figure 2.2 gives two time series for fat cattle at Aberdeen markets. One series is for top quality cattle between 1860 and 1886 and shows generally high prices for the feeder until the beginning of a big slide in the mid-1880s. The second series is based on data collected under the Markets and Fairs (Weighing of Cattle) Act 1891. It shows that by 1893 prices for fat cattle had settled to much lower levels, and stayed there until about 1910. The two time series are not directly comparable, since it is not clear if the first series is based on dead weight or live weight; but the general picture is clear — the farmer got good returns from fat cattle until the early 1880s and much less good returns thereafter. This picture is confirmed by Figure 2.1, which shows a serious drop in the price of British cattle at the Metropolitan market after 1886.

Hamilton is correct also in ascribing some of the problems in the early years of 'the great depression' to the series of bad harvests in the later 1870s. These harvests were recognised at the time to be a contributing factor to the farmers' difficulties;[5] but their effect was so serious only because the small quantity and low quality of the crop was not counterbalanced by high market prices. The opening of the American prairies, yielding hard wheat to compete with home-grown soft wheat, and maize to compete as animal feed with home-grown oats, buffered the urban consumer against supply fluctuations at the expense of denying the farmer windfall profits in years of bad harvests. The importation from the early 1880s of chilled and frozen beef and mutton had similarly severe implications for the livestock producer. In the prosperous decades before 1870 developments in the material forces made it profitable for northeast farmers to tailor their production ever more closely to the needs of the southern market. But the relationship between metropolis and satellite was asymmetrical: the northeast needed the London market more than London needed the northeast. When alternative supplies bcame available, the interests of northeast producers and southern consumers ceased to mesh. The developments in material forces which gave the region a comparative advantage in cattle production in the 1830s and laid the basis of the prosperity of the years to 1870 removed that advantage when further developments in means of communication allowed foreign competition to challenge the market position of northeast producers. The difficulties of the years after 1870 were not fortuitous; they were the logical outcome of the further development of capitalism on a world scale.[6]

It is clear, then, that the fall in cash crop prices between 1870 and 1914 hit northeast farmers hard. But it is important to recognise that they suffered less than farmers in some other parts of Britain. The fall in wheat prices affected farmers in the heavy clay lands of southern England much more than those in northeast Scotland, where wheat was an insignificant crop. The grain crops that mattered in the northeast were oats and barley, and their prices fell much less severely. Again, the fall in cattle prices was less serious than it might have been. Figure 2.1 shows that it was the price of inferior quality fat cattle that suffered most from the importation of foreign beef. But the northeast specialised in producing high quality fat cattle, and the price for good quality animals held up much better. This is not to say that local farmers did not have problems between 1870 and 1914, merely that those problems were less severe than those faced by farmers in some other parts of Britain.

Adjustment to Depression

How did northeast farmers face up to these problems? Hamilton asserted that a great deal of arable land in Banffshire went out of cultivation in the years after 1870, and that a great deal more was laid down to permanent pasture. If this had been true of Banffshire, then the same tendencies would have been even more marked in counties with more intensive farming systems. Unfortunately for his argument, however, there is very little evidence of arable land going back or land in rotation being put down to permanent pasture.

We saw in Figure 2.8 that the tilled acreage in the northeast as a whole increased sharply from 1866 to 1886. It then levelled out until 1901 and dropped slightly over the next decade. The patterns for individual counties show a sharper decline from the 1880s for those counties with a higher proportion of good arable land — Nairn, Kincardine and Moray — and a very slight decrease indeed after 1901 for Aberdeenshire. The dramatic decrease in

Figure 3.1 Change in tilled acreage, northeast parishes: 1911 as a percentage of 1867.[7] Right-hand key, reading from top: (a) 150+; (b) 130-149.9; (c) 110-129.9; (d) 90-109.9; (e) 70-89.9; (f) 0-69.9.

the tilled acreage of Banffshire between 1891 and 1896 might appear to support Hamilton's argument, but this period saw the transfer of one whole parish — St Fergus — and some smaller pendicles from Banffshire to Aberdeenshire: boundary changes which explain the fall in the Banffshire tilled acreage after 1891. Figure 3.1 shows changes in tilled acreage at the parish level between 1867 and 1911. It shows a general pattern of no change or of modest increase spread right across the area. Increases of more than a half are found in the tilled acreage of two upland parishes — Cabrach and Cromdale — and of Newmachar and Strichen in the Aberdeenshire lowlands. Increases of about a third appear in two further upland parishes — Edinkillie and Towie — and in the lowland parishes of Elgin, Tyrie and Peterculter. The effect of 'the great depression' is shown in the string of coastal parishes, from Garvock in the south to Kinloss and Duffus in the Moray lowlands, showing a decline of more than ten per cent in tilled acreage. The fall in the inland parish of Tarland is explained by the transfer of a detached pendicle to Strathdon. In summary, then, Hamilton's assertion of a serious decline in tilled acreage between 1870 and 1914 can be sustained neither for Banffshire nor for any other northeast county. The tilled acreage did fall in a few parishes, but this decline was more than balanced by increase in other parishes. Certainly there is no evidence of arable land going back to grazings for sheep: not surprising, when wool prices collapsed much more completely than did prices for the northeast's major grain crops.

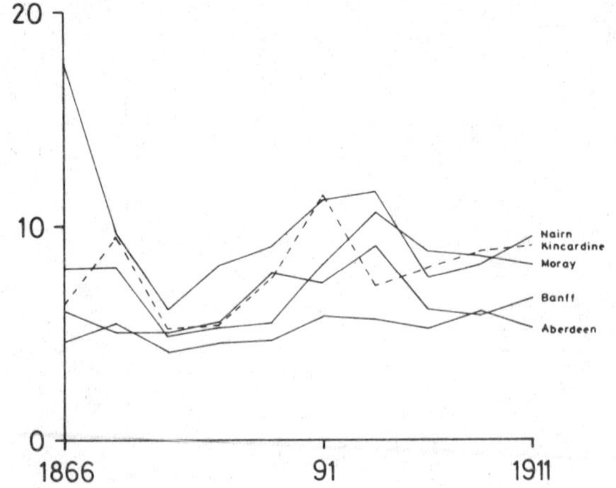

Figure 3.2 Permanent grass as a percentage of tilled acreage, 1866-1911[8]

What about the acreage under permanent pasture? Hamilton asserts a massive increase in Banffshire's permanent grass: but we saw in the last chapter that any attempt to increase the extent of such pastures faced technical and social obstacles.[9] These obstacles did not disappear after 1870. Figure 3.2 shows that the proportion of tilled acreage under permanent grass rose in all northeast counties between 1876 and 1891, and then began to fall.[10] But the important point is that the proportion moved within very narrow limits, the figure for all northeast counties varying only between 4.5 per cent and 7.1 per cent. Apart from the rogue figure for Nairn in 1866, no county had more than twelve per cent of tilled acreage under permanent pasture in any year. In Oxfordshire, by contrast, permanent pasture increased dramatically — by 41 per cent between 1874 and 1900.[11] The situation in Oxfordshire is the traditional academic view of the effect of 'the great depression', and Hamilton followed that tradition. It simply has no relevance to what happened in northeast Scotland.

The fall in cash crop prices did have important effects on the crops grown by local farmers. Figure 3.3 shows that the proportion of the tilled acreage given over to white (corn) crops and to green crops drifted lower over the whole period from 1866 to 1911, while that given over to grass slowly increased.

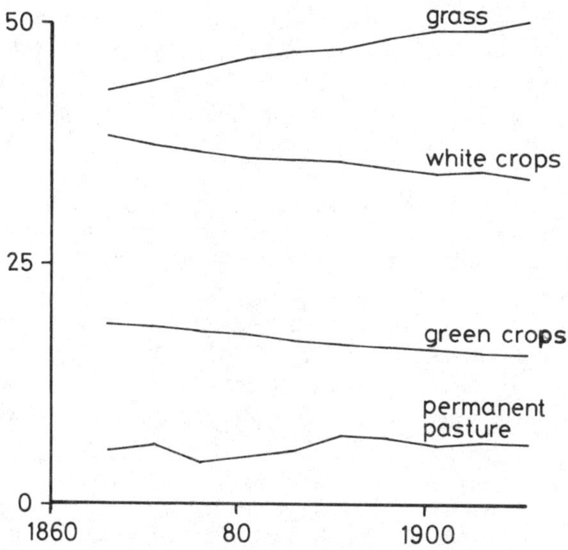

Figure 3.3 Changes in the percentage of tilled acreage under grass, white (corn) crops, green (root) crops and permanent pasture, northeast counties, 1866-1911[12]

Two points are important. Firstly, the changes were slight; the proportion under white crops in 1911 was only 4.2 per cent less than it had been in 1866. Second, the increase in the proportion under grass was an increase in temporary leys. The vast majority of tilled acres in the region remained in rotation; they did not — to repeat — go down to permanent pasture. The changes shown in Figure 3.3 were the result of changing rotations. There is evidence that rotations were tending to grow shorter between 1840 and 1870 as farmers sought, within the limitations imposed by their leases, to increase arable intensivity. This trend was reversed in the last quarter of the century. Rotations lengthened,[13] with more grass breaks being added both because cattle prices held up better than grain prices — in the early part of 'the great depression' at least — and because more grass breaks gave significant labour economies. Some farmers now found that improvements in the material forces of production carried out in previous decades inhibited a flexible response to new market conditions; a large farmer on the Durris estate wanted to change from a five to a six-shift rotation, but his farm was laid out in five shifts with excellent — and strong — stone dykes which prevented him from following his inclination.[14]

Farmers did show considerable flexibility when they could, however. His lease bound the farmer to keep a certain proportion of his farm under corn crops, but it did not specify which grain he was to grow.

Figure 3.4 shows that the collapse of wheat prices from the mid-1870s led immediately to a corresponding collapse of the wheat acreage in the northeast as a whole and in individual counties. Wheat always had been a gambler's crop in the region: it could return a profit only in favoured locations and in times when prices were very firm.[15] Thus the northeast's wheat acreage had melted away on previous occasions — when the high prices of the Napoleonic war period disappeared, for example.[16] The Crimean War caused a brief stampede in marginally suitable locations: the wheat acreage of Kincardine in 1856 was double that of 1855,

> . . . the famine prices of the Crimean War causing a rush to this cereal, for which neither soil nor climate was suitable; but 80s. a quarter was a considerable temptation, and as usual with most risky speculations, a smart lesson was taught.[17]

The flight from wheat after 1875 was hastened by falling yields and rust disease, but it was caused by falling prices. Those farmers who had been growing it fled to barley, the price of which was underpinned by a buoyant demand from local distilleries.[18] Aided by developments in material forces, the lowland gambler turned to potatoes:

> This is the most speculative crop of any which the farmer grows. It may either give him a very handsome profit, or no profit at all. In the course of a single season, it may be selling at £1 and £5 a ton . . . This crop is grown to the greatest extent within fair carting distance of railway stations or shipping ports; but these advantages are being neutralised a good deal by the system of traction engines, which are now [1881] becoming so common. During the past few years, by bagging them up, they can be conveyed in waggons to stations eight or ten miles distant by the traction engine for 3s. or 4s. a ton. The area of their cultivation is therefore extending . . .[19]

Disease was as serious a problem to farmers growing potatoes as were unpredictable price runs; but given reasonable luck, the humble tattie would give a good return on a heavy investment in muck and labour. It is worth noting that the reason why the Kincardine wheat acreage held up better than that in other counties was that Mearns farmers needed the straw to thatch potato pits. Their interest in the grain was distinctly secondary.

Turning from crops to stock, it is clear that the central role of cattle breeding and feeding in the productive arrangements of northeast agriculture was not disturbed.[20] Indeed, the scale of the trade in fat cattle and dead meat from the northeast to southern markets continued to expand throughout 'the great depression'. In the early 1870s some 39,000 cattle had left Aberdeen city for the south as fat cattle or beef.[21] By 1900 the figure for cattle exported from Aberdeenshire and Banffshire alone had passed 60,000. These cattle had a value for the farmer of some £1,500,000 — roughly double the agricultural rental of the two counties.[22]

This increasing trade did not bring uniform advantages to all northeast farmers. Those transport improvements that had precipitated the low prices for grain and for beef that caused difficulties to all northeast farmers also came to the aid of the specialised cattle feeder by allowing the importation of store cattle from abroad. Some of these came from Canada until the diagnosis of pleuro-pneumonia in a cargo landed at Dundee in 1893 compelled the state to order Canadian cattle, like American cattle, to be slaughtered at the port of debarkation. But the number of Canadian stores imported to Britain — 345,428 in 1893 — dwindles almost to nothing against the 2,253,200 Irish stores imported in the same year.[23] These massive imports had a profound effect on northeast breeding and feeding. For example, Lawson wrote in 1881 of southern Kincardine, largely a feeding district, that

> As early as the beginning of the present century, the half of the cattle that were fed were imported from the northern counties.[24] This practice continued down till about twenty five or thirty years ago, when a good many English cattle, and latterly large

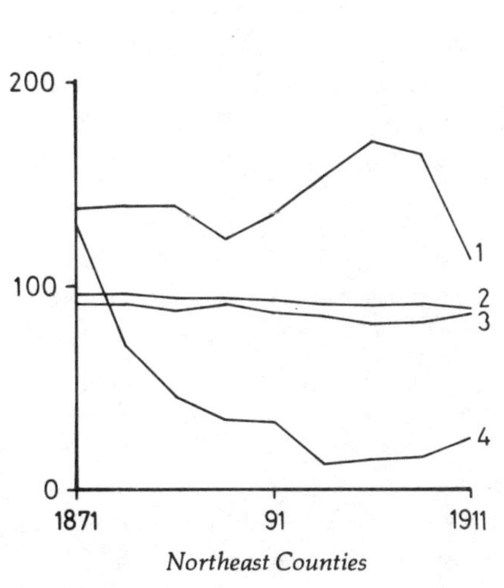

Northeast Counties

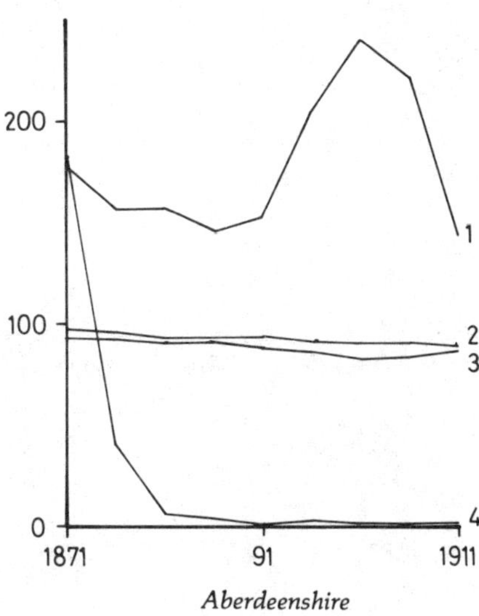

Aberdeenshire

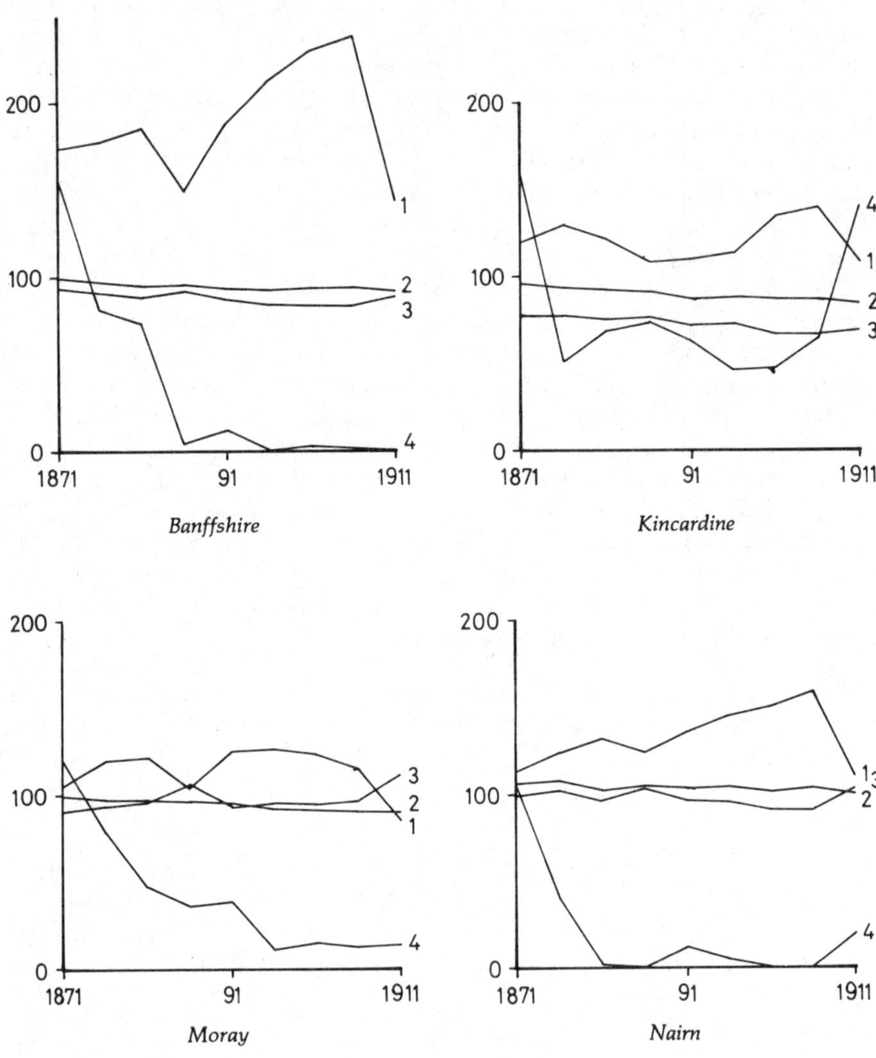

Figure 3.4 Index of changes in acreage under corn crops, controlled for changes in tilled acreage, 1866-1911.[25] Key: 1=Barley; 2=All White Crops; 3=Oats; 4=Wheat.

numbers of Irish stores, were imported. So great have these importations become, that at the present time barely one-tenth of the cattle fattened are bred [in the district]. Farmers now depend almost entirely on Ireland for their supply of stores, which they get of all ages, from newly weaned calves to three year olds. During the past year a great many Canadian stores have found their way into the counties, and have thriven very well.[26]

These imported stores usually went for local consumption after fattening, or were sent fat to second-class markets in the south.[27] The top quality beef for the London market mostly still came from cattle reared by northeast peasant farmers; but Irish competition steadily eroded the peasant's indispensibility for the capitalist feeder.

These years saw a slight absolute decline in northeast cattle breeding as peasants sought desperately to benefit from the added value of cattle feeding,[28] but their land often was not good enough. Other difficulties faced the peasant breeder, too:

The steady decline in prices which began after 1884 caused greater difficulties for breeders than for feeders, since it was not so easy for the farmers to make adjustments in their cattle enterprises to meet falling prices. On many of the breeding and rearing farms the major items of farm expenditure, were fixed, and occupiers often felt themselves to be at the mercy of the feeders, who were able to pass back to producers of store cattle almost all the expected reductions in prices and stabilise their own 'feeders' margin'.[29]

The increase of feeding at the expense of breeding might appear to lend credence to Hamilton's assertion that speculators overstocked grazings and mined the fertility of the soil. This seems not to have been the case, however. One certainly can find witnesses arguing that farmers were responding to the problems of 'the great depression' by economising on the artificial manures bill,[30] but evidence on yields of white crops tends to deny this conclusion. In 1855 yields, in bushels per acre, of wheat, barley and oats in Aberdeenshire were 27.3, 32.2 and 31.2 respectively. The corresponding average figures for the decade 1900-09 were 31.6, 32.9 and 35.5.[31] These figures underestimate the increase in yields between 1855 and 1909, for the 1855 figures exclude holdings with a rateable value below ten pounds sterling per annum — a large group of holdings in Aberdeenshire, and one on which yields tended to be lower than on larger farms.[32]

The Spatial Distribution of Depression

'The great depression' varied considerably in its geographical incidence. Figure 3.1, with its evidence of a significant fall between 1867 and 1911 in the tilled acreage of Garvock, Nigg, Fraserburgh, Duffus, Kinloss and Rothes might lead us to suppose that arable areas suffered disproportionately. Other evidence denies this conclusion. For example, there seems little argument that the Laigh of Moray escaped relatively lightly.[33] The areas which suffered most were those remote from communications, and those with a heavy soil needing a heavier investment per acre in horsepower and labour power than areas with lighter soils.[34] In such areas matters were indeed serious. A Banffshire capitalist farmer on the Earl of Fife's estate gave evidence to the Cobham Commission in the 1890s. He had taken his farm in 1876, when the whole area around his farm — all heavy clay land — was being broken out of the waste on improving leases. By the 1890s reclamation had come to a dead stop. Fourteen farms of 150 acres or above on the Banffshire sector of the Fife and Richmond estates had changed hands between 1878 and 1893. Six of the outgoing fourteen tenants had been bankrupt.[35] Those fourteen farms had paid £3,743 in rent in 1878; by 1894 the rental was £2,477.[36] This seems to have been an acutely depressed district, however: despite assertions that Aberdeenshire and Banffshire were particularly severely hit by the depression,[37] the assistant commissioner of the Commission, James Hope, could find no evidence of an abnormal number of tenancies changing hands, or of an unusually large number of farms being left unoccupied.[38]

The Social Formation

For our purpose the spatial distribution of depression is less important than its social distribution. Which groups suffered most severely from 'the great depression', and in which ways did they suffer? How were the social relations between lairds, capitalist farmers, and middle and poor peasants affected by the fall in cash crop prices and by attempts to adjust to that fall?

We will consider the position of hired workers in greater detail later.[39] Here we need to note merely that while the real wages of all British farm workers remained fairly stable between 1870 and 1900, the real wages of northeast farm servants rose by thirty per cent over the same period.[40] Whoever suffered from the great depression, then, one peasant fraction[41] — hired farm workers — did rather well in these years.

The same was not true of landowners. As rents offered for capitalist farms slumped, so did lairds' fortunes. The extent to which a particular laird suffered depended partly on his estate's location and on the soil which underlay it — proximity to railways and markets, and a light soil, giving a definite advantage — but prior estate policies also played a part. There is a comforting irony in the fact that those small lawyer-factored estates which had been most single-minded in pushing up the general rent level before 1870 were the places whose owners were in deepest trouble after 1880.[42] The Earl of Aberdeen, by contrast, reaped the reward of a century of fair dealing with large and small tenants: rent arrears on the Haddo House estate were insignificant throughout the deepest trough of 'the great depression'. The same was true of the north-east's other benevolently managed great estate, centred on Gordon Castle.[43]

Elsewhere things were different. A harbinger of things to come a generation later was the Fife estate's attempt in the 1890s to turn its finances round by selling many holdings to sitting tenants.[44] This attempt was a complete failure: peasant tenants were not interested in owning their land, and no sane capitalist farmer would sink more of his own capital in the land than was absolutely necessary. The proportion of the northeast's tilled acreage owned by the ocupier in 1912 was almost identical to the proportion in 1887, when data on the matter were first collected. The northeast remained a leasehold area. So what of the relative advantage of capitalist tenants and peasant tenants in the difficult years?

(a) *Capitalist farmers*

In the course of his exhaustive account of the agriculture of Moray and Nairn, one of the Macdonald brothers — both protégés of their journalist uncle James Black, Sherriffston — asserted that

> . . . On very stiffly rented farms, as well as on badly drained, indifferently managed farms, more especially where working capital has been inadequate, there have been rather heavy losses in recent years.[45]

Leaving aside the matter of rent for the moment, this seems to suggest that the capitalist mode of production was best able to tackle the problems of depression: a conclusion with which Henry Hamilton agreed.[46] Other observers concurred:

> They explained that a man with a large holding had much better organisation for carrying on the work of the farm; that he could employ all the most modern labour-saving machinery and was better able to develop to the utmost the resources of the soil. The prevailing view was, that in some districts, small farms did well enough, but that, as regards money making, the large farmer was in a much better position than the small one, as he could produce proportionately much heavier crops, raise and feed more stock per acre, and generally cultivate the land, and sell the produce to much better advantage.[47]

It is clear that large farmers could derive some advantage by pushing forward the material forces of production to make more efficient use of increasingly expensive hired labour. A Strathbogie large farmer complained in 1886 that 'we farmers have been outlaying so freely in order to make the labour of the farm efficient and easy, that some of our workers are beginning to think that they ought not to draw sweat in themselves from one year's end to the other, in "hairst or harrowin' time".'[48] Labour economies were most significant in the hairst, when demand for farm labour was strongly peaked. The replacement of reaping machines by self-binders meant that by the time of the hairst feeing market in St Sair's Fair (Aberdeenshire) in 1891, 'there was hardly such a thing as scythesmen, binders and gatherers required'.[49] Other factors helped the large farmer, too. The greater profitability of cattle feeding over breeding was to his advantage, and lairds' rapid discovery of how difficult capitalist farms would be to let while cash crop prices languished gave the muckle farmer a strong bargaining position.

Against this one has evidence that large farms were much less profitable after 1880. The history of steam ploughing is instructive in this context. We first hear of a steam plough in the northeast in 1858, on Torry, Nigg.[50] The first major breakthrough comes eight years later, however, with the formation on 8 February 1866 of the Kincardineshire Steam Ploughing Company (Limited).[51] The leading light and major shareholder in this company was George Greig, Harvieston, a Kinneff large farmer, and the brother of John Fowler's principal assistant and successor at Fowler's Leeds factory. Greig ran a contracting business from Harvieston with steam traction engines, and acted as Fowler & Co.'s agent in the northeast; the Kincardine company always worked Fowler double-engine steam tackle. The first set was purchased in 1866, and so eager were southern Kincardine farmers to hire the tackle that the company had made enough profit by 1871 to pay a five per cent dividend. In 1872 they purchased a second set of tackle.

The future for steam ploughing seemed bright. Its supporters made extravagant claims. In a paper read in 1865 to the Institute of Mechanical Engineers in London, David Greig — Greig, Harvieston's brother — looked forward to the time when steam traction engines would replace horses completely on the farm. Within ten years, he predicted, two thirds of farm cartage would be done by steam.[52] George Greig and fellow enthusiasts made similar noises in the northeast. Sir Alexander Anderson, who squeezed in time to be Lord Philorth's chamberlain on his Fraserburgh estate among other careers as lawyer, businessman (he was chairman of the Great North of Scotland Railway Company among much else) and Lord Provost of Aberdeen, asserted to a meeting of the Philorth tenantry convened on 27 December 1871 to discuss founding a steam cultivation company that 'it would be an excellent thing for the Philorth tenantry to be the first to introduce into Aberdeenshire a system of cultivation by steam, which, before long, must become universal'.[53] His language was even more extragavant a few months later at a dinner held to celebrate the first experiments with steam ploughing in Aberdeenshire.[54] Anderson's railway interest might be thought to have made him uncritically enthusiastic about the future of steam ploughing, but he seemed to have ample evidence for this conclusion. Steam traction engines had revolutionised threshing, and were making inroads on the carting trade. The Kincardine steam ploughing company had enjoyed six successful years. A private set of tackle was at work somewhere in Morayshire,[55] and another private set — using the single engine roundabout system — was working Tochineal, Cullen.[56] A committee of Philorth capitalist tenants had seen Greig, Harvieston blasting waste land into his newly leased large out-farm of Banffhill, Arbuthnott by means of his private set of Fowler double-engine steam tackle.[57]

Steam ploughing was first seen in Aberdeenshire at Brownhill, Slains in April 1872.[58] The tackle belonged to the Scottish Steam Cultivation and Traction Company, based in Edinburgh;[59] it consisted of two twelve horse power Fowler engines with winding drums, a four-cut balance plough, a nine-tine cultivator and a large set of harrows.[60] After one season in the Buchan clays this tackle returned south, but this was not the end of steam ploughing in Aberdeenshire. The Philorth Company took delivery of its own set of Fowler double-engine tackle in October 1872, and quickly built up a heavy order book for ploughing and cultivation.

For a few years things seemed to be going well. The Kincardine company's purchase of a second set of steam tackle in 1872 had proved too ambitious, but they managed to lease this second set to Greig, Harvieston for five years from 1873. This allowed the company to declare a dividend in 1875, 1876, 1877, and 1878.[61] The Philorth company made a fifteen per cent operating profit in its first full year of work (1872-3), having ploughed 814 acres and hauled 178 fishing boats to winter stations during the year.[62] This company declared a five per cent dividend in 1875 and 1876. But income from ploughing fell from above £500 per annum in the years from 1872 to 1876 to £182 in 1879-80. The directors tried to sell the tackle back to Greig, Harvieston; but he declined the poisoned chalice.[63] For by this time the Kincardine company was in even deeper trouble. It declared no dividend after 1878 and was wound up on 26 January 1885.[64] The Philorth company struggled on after 1880, kept barely afloat by revenue from hauling fishing boats — originally a minor sideline of its operations — and by hiring out its engines to break stones, saw wood and bark nets. But it now faced competition from a Port Errol brickmaker for the boat-hauling business, and the engines were deteriorating rapidly. The Philorth company went into liquidation on 6 April 1888. Mechanical ploughing would not be seen again in Aberdeenshire until the arrival of the first Ivel tractor in 1906,[65] although people in the Howe of the Mearns still remember steam tackle working on Whitefield, Arbuthnott before 1914.

Steam ploughing never could have replaced horse ploughing in the north-east. The large number of earth-fast boulders in the soil of many districts presented severe problems, and the optimal kind of field for steam ploughing — flat, rectangular, about twenty acres in extent[66] — was rarely found among the northeast's small and lumpy parks. But it was feasible and profitable under certain conditions; notably on large farms growing wheat on a heavy soil.[67] The reasons why its penetration was halted were not technical but economic. Steam ploughing offered big increases in productivity; on the Buchan clays a pair of horses would plough rather less than one acre in a ten-hour yoking, while the Philorth tackle could plough up to seven acres per day. This was valuable when wheat was being grown, since the long growing season needed for this crop meant that early preparation of the soil was of paramount importance. The fall in wheat prices removed this stimulus to early cultivation, however, and under depressed market prices the economics of steam ploughing made no sense. The necessary capital investment was heavy: the Philorth tackle cost £1,460 in 1872. But an investment in steam tackle promised no labour economies to compare with those of the self-binder. The labour team was large — 'two engine drivers, one ploughman, one foreman, three men and two horses with box cart and water cart carting coals and water for the engines.[68] As labour costs held up while wheat prices fell, steam ploughing became insufferably expensive. A major development of the material forces of production that a decade before had seemed very likely to cause a further unfolding of the potential inherent in capitalist agricultural production[69] had, of necessity, been abandoned — a significant event.

More direct evidence of the acute difficulties of capitalist farmers in 'the great depression' comes from data on rents offered for vacant large farms. We have seen that the rent level was a sensitive indicator of the profitability of capitalist agriculture.[70] Thus it is significant that between 1878 and 1894 the rents of large farms in the Banffshire sector of the Fife and Richmond estates fell by between 33 and 36 per cent in money terms.[71] In Moray, rents of large farms fell by at least twenty-five per cent, those of largeish middle peasant farms by up to ten per cent. Smaller middle peasant farms and crofts, by contrast, held their money rents.[72]

The difficulties of capitalist farmers were eased somewhat by changes in social relations. Political pressure, mostly through the Liberal party, gradually forced legislative redress of many grievances that bore heavily on the northeast large farmer. The farmer got the right to protect his crops from the depredations of rabbits and hares, if not from winged game, under the 1880 Ground Game Act. His landlord's privileged access to the capital of a struggling tenant, with all its complex social implications, disappeared with the abolition of rural hypothec in 1881: some of the more paranoid northeast capitalist farmers expected lairds to bounce back by dusting off the ancient Act of Sederunt[73] — which would have had much the same effect as landlord's hypothec — but their fears proved groundless. The difficulty of letting large farms in a time when cash crop prices stubbornly stayed on the floor gave the capitalist farmer some leverage on his laird. Not only could he press for a temporary rent remission in particularly bad years but, as leases contracted in the good years ran out, he could also get his farm at a lower rent for the next lease and force the proprietor to spend money on building or repairing the house and steading. It is significant that it was in these decades, when income on many estates was seriously depressed, that the majority of cottar houses in the great central wedge of the northeast were built.[74]

The muckle farmer did not get it all his own way, however. Tenant right had been a controversial element in the social relations of capitalist landlord and capitalist farmer before 1870, but 'the great depression' gave the controversy added vigour. Northeast farmer witnesses before the Richmond Commission — all large farmers, of course — were unanimous in demanding better compensation for permanent improvements.[75] Compensation for unexhausted improvements — manure, bones and lime in the ground — was a more difficult matter. There is evidence that some northeast farmers sought to minimise the problem by letting down the farm's condition as far as they dared.[76] Some farmers thought it impossible to calculate the value of unexhausted improvements,[77] despite the fact that such calculations had become routine in England and Wales under the 1875 Agricultural Holdings Act. Those northeast farmers who drew the obvious conclusion and pressed for compensation to be extended to Scotland[78] were vilified by lairds' representatives. One correspondent to the Tory *Aberdeen Journal* saw this demand as the thin end of a very thick wedge:

> The real parties whose ends are forwarded by the stirring of these questions, are the Socialists, and the Anarchists, among whom we live, and whose aim is to destroy all property. At present the chief raid is upon the land, but the aim is at all realised property.[79]

Bonamy Price had a similarly inflamed imagination: he accused J. W. Barclay, Liberal M.P. and Aberdeenshire capitalist farmer, of 'the socialistic principle, which is held by people of communistic tendencies, that the landlord finds the land better at the end of the period; that betterness was because it was well cultivated, and the communist farmer is to have a portion of that'.[80]

For such folk Armaggedon arrived in 1883, when the 1875 Agricultural Holdings Act was extended to Scotland and its provisions made mandatory.[81] This Act was not the solution which northeast farmers had sought, however: it offered lairds too many loopholes. Thus one ingenious laird allowed a Peterhead crofter hard pressed by the low prices of the mid-1880s to sit rent-free for one year. At the end of his lease the crofter found that he had lost his right to a claim under the Agricultural Holdings Act. The laird had given up £4 in rent, but had avoided the need to pay compensation for the steading built by the crofter and for unexhausted improvements — quite a bargain.[82]

This was not the principal loophole, however. The major defect in the 1883 Act was the wide scope which it allowed to the laird for a counter-claim. A farmer's lease bound him to a crop rotation and prevented him from selling certain produce off the farm. Many leases simply repeated the clauses of earlier leases; this was particularly true of lawyer-factored estates, where it was common for the lawyers to 'adhere most tenaciously to the old forms of leases, and repeat clauses in new leases without having any practical knowledge of the hardship they are thereby imposing on the tenant'.[83] As farmers came under increasing pressure from low cash crop prices, many estates tacitly relaxed the strict cropping clauses in their leases, allowing tenants to lengthen rotations, for example.[84] But after 1883 some tenants found that the estate's forbearance in looking the other way when the tenant broke the letter of a cropping clause had given the estate grounds for a counter-claim under the Agricultural Holdings Act. The expenses of arbitration under the Act not infrequently dwarfed the amount originally claimed by the tenant.[85] This problem was finally solved in 1908, when legal freedom of cropping came at last. Until that date, however, the tenant knew that his laird had the right to lodge a counter-claim for a penal rent, even if he chose not to exercise that right. The lack of adequate machinery for giving a tenant compensation for unexhausted improvements led to a significant innovation. The nineteen-year lease remained standard throughout the northeast, but by the mid-1890s new leases always allowed for breaks, by laird or tenant, every five years. This new arrangement allowed the capitalist tenant to cut his losses, and reduced problems about compensation; but it brought new problems. By reducing the farmer's security of tenure from nineteen years to five, it took away some of the advantages which long leases had given to northeast farmers. The problem was not terribly serious for large farmers, however, since demand for such farms was depressed right up to 1914; but even here the capitalist farmer might face severe competition, if a break came when stock prices were low, from 'adventurers' speculating on higher prices five years thence.[86] In summary, then, the years from 1870 to 1914 saw the end of the harmonious shared interest between laird and capitalist farmer that had marked the period between 1840 and 1870. The two groups struggled over the proportion of surplus value that was to be expropriated by the laird as rent or by the muckle farmer as profit. But the market still mediated relations between these two fractions in a way that, at the most general level, satisfied them both. Pressure points in social relations were relieved through the political mobilisation of northeast capitalist farmers, along with their fellows elsewhere in Britain, in the Liberal party. Peasant farmers were less fortunate.

(b) *Peasant farmers*

The undeniable fact that money rents for peasant holdings held up very much better in 'the great depression' than did rents for capitalist farms suggests strongly that peasants had a particular advantage in these years — especially since an unchanged money rent meant one that had increased significantly in real terms as the wholesale price level fell. What was the peasant's advantage? Was it his household's combination of artisan and agricultural production that allowed the peasant to pay a higher real rent from the proceeds of domestic industry?[87] This cannot be the answer: we have seen[88] that these sources of non-agricultural income were drying up in the first half of the nineteenth century as first rural domestic industry — spinning, weaving, knitting, distilling — and later craft work were destroyed by competition from large-scale capitalist production in the towns. In 'the great depression', opportunities for casual and part-time wage work in agriculture contracted too, with the mechanisation of the hairst on large farms and a reduced demand for day labourers to build dykes and dig drains.

What makes the situation even more difficult to understand is the fact that the small farmer and crofter faced many of the problems that daunted the large farmer. The fall in cash crop prices affected the peasant's stirk as well as the large farmer's fat bullock. The peasant also had financial obligations to meet — rent, road rate, school rate, poor rate. Indeed, as with the decline in rents for large farms vis-a-vis small farms and crofts, we can see ways in which the peasant was particularly pressed. His relative specialisation in cattle breeding made him particularly vulnerable to the importation of Irish and Canadian stores for feeding in the northeast. Again, when many lairds gave temporary rent remissions to their tenants in particularly disastrous years during the 1880s, it was not uncommon for crofters to be excluded from the remission — as on the Durris estate — despite the fact that the crofters already paid a rent per acre above that of the larger tenants.[89]

Peasant farmers did hold one trump card, however. The thing that made their mode of production pre-capitalist gave them a decisive advantage over large farmers; they worked their holdings with labour drawn almost exclusively from the household:

> Can they make a living at the old rents? — In some cases they can perhaps with their own labour and the labour of their families. A man with two or three young sons and some small daughters doing all his work for him, saving his labour bills, may, in spite of the bad times.[90]

James Hope found this perception widespread among northeast peasant farmers but he also found that not having to pay wages to hired workers was only part of their advantage. Almost equally important was the unlimited labour commitment expected from, and given by, family workers:

> . . . I found a disposition on the part of some witnesses to hold that the smaller farmer had more successfully met the bad times than the large one. Those who held this view, however, were chiefly farmers holding from sixty to one hundred and twenty acres, who not only worked hard themselves, but who employed their families to do the entire work of the farm and so were able to manage their holdings without hired labour. I put it to these witnesses whether they allowed the members of their families the same wage as they would have had to provide if strangers had been employed for the farm labour, and I was almost invariably told that fixed wages, as between the farmer and his family, were never thought of, and that all the family expected to get was their board and a reasonable allowance for clothing.
>
> I was generally told that the rent of these small farms was usually at a higher rate per acre than that of the larger farms, and it was generally admitted by the smaller farmers themselves that, with the rents which they had to pay, they would not be able to get along at all if they were also obliged to pay fair market value for the labour of their families. Indeed, several of the farmers of this class stated that neither they nor their families observed any working hours at all, but that they worked on from daylight to dark, and that even by doing so it was with the utmost difficulty that they got both ends to meet.[91]

This reliance on family labour raised its own problems. The peasant's mode of production had always held a contradiction deep within itself: a contradiction between family independence and family discipline. Independence, 'being your own man', always had been the great attraction of a crofting or small farming life. But this independence was for the peasant farmer alone — it was predicated on unquestioning obedience from other family members. John Milne left school when his father needed his help on the farm, regretting his lost education.[92] Alex. Mitchell oscillated between farm service and work on his father's croft according to the labour needs of the croft.[93] William Alexander's articles on the Aberdeenshire crofter show innumerable similar examples.[94] Children accepted their lowly position in this patriarchal system because they hoped to be patriarchs themselves one day. A farmer was expected to try to set up his children when he retired. Daughters would be given a tocher to attract a match with a farmer. One son would inherit the lease of the paternal holding. Other sons would be placed in other holdings or given a share of the paternal inheritance. At least one son would be sponsored through university and into one of the learned professions — law, medicine or (above all) the Kirk; the enhanced status of the professional son would cast a radiance of social respectability on the farm family.[95] The crofter's son who stayed on the land might hope to climb some way up the farming ladder. His chances were not very good after the middle of the nineteenth century — it is clear that relatively few peasant farmers made it in these years into the ranks of the large farmers[96] — but the ideology of the lad o' pairts asserted the opposite and moulded the aspirations of peasant children. Thus peasant agriculture could be reproduced because of the unfailing supply of men and women willing to make an unlimited labour commitment in order to be independent at some future date.

This situation began to change in the later decades of the nineteenth century. Opportunities for colonising crofters to rive in new land on the margins of cultivation were reduced radically. The old common lands had long been divided among neighbouring lairds. Those lairds no longer sought to extend the tilled acreage of their estates — even though improvable land was still to be found in some places.[97] The northeast's internal frontier had been closed; and it had been closed at a time when other factors were pressing with a new insistence on peasant farmers. The contradiction between independence and discipline deepened as the rents for peasant holdings held up much better than rents for large farms: 'The result of the competition for small farms is that it takes the farmer all his time, even with the free labour of his children, to hold his own against the present times.'[98] Labour had never been light for family workers, but in 'the great depression', with rents for small places holding up while cash crop prices fell, the peasant farmer had to screw even more labour power out of his family, to make 'the whole of his family, his sons and his daughters, and his wife and himself, work like slaves'.[99] This intensified exploitation put a heavier burden on peasant children; in many cases the burden became unbearable.

The contradiction between independence and discipline slowly dissolved in the years between 1880 and 1914. On one level the dissolution came simply through a changed attitude to emigration. A condition of the successful continuation of peasant agriculture under impartible land tenure always had been the emigration of children who could not be settled on the land.[100] But these emigrants had left with regret; the typical ambition of a peasant son had been to get his 'wee bit placie'. In the later nineteenth century the situation was very different. The first group to leave peasant agriculture in large numbers from choice was, as always,[101] young women — for whom there was no hope of ever replacing domestic servitude with the independence of the peasant farmer. By the 1890s the trickle of young women out of northeast peasant agriculture had become a flood: 'They seem to be running away from the land', 'Our girls about the country are all getting an education and finding their ways into shops as cashiers, and bookkeepers, and into business'.[102] By 1910 it was claimed — and it is difficult to credit — that 'Many mistresses, because of the scarcity of girls to do kitchen work, fear to correct their servants' faults.'[103] Peasant sons were not far behind their sisters in leaving the land. Farmers complained throughout our period of a shortage of male farm servants — which drove up the price — but by the 1890s they were beginning to complain that the shortage was structural. Crofts and small farms, the great nurseries of northeast farm servants, no longer supplied enough skilled men; some farmers were now forced to hire inferior servants from the towns.[104] This reduction in the supply of peasant sons willing to fee as farm servants reinforced tendencies to proletarianisation among farm servants. As fewer and fewer unmarried men fee'd, so large farmers pressed their lairds to build more cottar houses. In 1914 the factor of the Haddo House estate, James Cobban, attributed the estate's recent efforts in building cottar houses — they had built seventy new farm cottages since 1900 and had renewed another ninety — to the exteme scarcity of unmarried male farm servants, which forced the estate to provide more accommodation for married servants on its capitalist farms.[105] The character of the hired labour force began to change, even in the northeast's central wedge, towards the proletarianised hinding arrangement typical of southeast Scotland.

The usual explanation of the changed attitude to emigration among peasant children is the effect of education. Two novels of the crisis of the (by now highly marginal) peasantry of south Kincardine at the time of the First World War concentrate on the consciousness of peasant children caught between two modes of apprehending the world, one rooted in the family farm and the other in the school.[106] It is difficult to see the *existence* of education as the prime cause of the changed attitude to emigration, however; Scotland had had a parish education system since the Reformation. This older system was well adapted to the educational needs of an aspiring peasant farmer — Alexander gives us a picture of an education centred on the Shorter Catechism, 'coontin'', and ground measurement.[107] The compulsory system of the 1870s was very different; highly centralised, with a strong urban and bourgeois bias, the new system had been devised with an eye to the increasing demand for skilled manpower in an urban, industrialised, capitalist society. It should not surprise us that this new education system helped to destructure peasant agriculture in the northeast after 1870, any more than it should surprise us that the same system continues to undermine a residual peasantry in Highland crofting areas today. The changed attitude of northeast peasant children to emigration after 1870 is thus the result not simply of education, but of varied aspects of the final incorporation of the peasantry within the capitalist world.

By 1880 the northeast peasantry was in crisis. There was no longer any need for new land to be cut from the waste: indeed lairds were having great difficulty in letting their existing capitalist farms. Irish and Canadian stores had greatly supplemented the northeast peasant's stirk as raw materials for the capitalist cattle feeder. Peasant production no longer underpinned a rapidly maturing capitalist agriculture and thus, inevitably, the northeast peasantry finally was penetrated. The number of small farms and crofts did not change radically between 1880 and 1914, but the nature of their occupants did change. In 1914 a Turriff laird commented that 'in recent years most of my crofts of five or ten acres have been taken by men of advanced age, who have retired from steady labour and are receiving the old-age pension, and not as formerly by a young couple starting in life'.[108] Peasant agriculture could no longer reproduce itself. Men were no longer willing to drive a plough up the hillside in the pursuit of a barely adequate combination of subsistence and cash crops. Girls were no longer willing to sign themselves away to a lifetime of drudgery as a peasant's wife. The northeast had many small farms after 1920 — it has many small farms today. Some of these farms continued to rely on family labour, and to produce subsistence crops alongside cash crops. But that was no longer true of small farmers and crofters *as a class* — it was no longer a defining characteristic of their mode of production. The characteristic Janus-face of peasant farming, growing crops for subsistence and for the market, became increasingly rare as the older generation of peasant farmers died out. Smaller farmers produced more and more for the market, buying food from shops in towns and villages or from the ubiquitous travelling vans.[109] After the First World War one no longer can speak properly of peasant agriculture and capitalist agriculture, but merely of capitalist production on larger or smaller farms.

Between 1880 and 1914, then, the northeast peasantry stood at the classic crossroads of a commodity-producing peasantry in lean times. They had either to increase household production or to reduce household consumption. The first choice meant abandoning their peasant mode of production, transforming the holding into a minute capitalist enterprise. The second choice meant saving that mode of production at the cost of a yet more relentless exploitation of family labour. It was a cruel dilemma. In the early years of 'the great depression' the northeast peasantry mostly chose to reduce consumption: but the super-exploitation of family labour that this involved as rents for peasant holdings held up all too well could not be maintained for long — peasant children would not (and did not) stand for it. Thus northeast peasants rapidly came into conflict with their lairds over the matter of rack-renting and security of tenure. This conflict erupted into large-scale peasant land agitation in 1881 and culminated in an attempt to have the northeast counties included in the area covered by the 1886 Crofters Holdings Act.[110] The success of this attempt would have meant an end to rack-renting — eviction for engrossment had become a thing of the past with the collapse of capitalist farmers' comparative advantage — and would have saved the peasant class for a time. Its failure meant the death-knell for the peasantry. With the possibility of legally assured security and heritability of tenure with rents set by a Land Court finally dead, the northeast peasantry reversed its earlier policy and tried to expand production. Cattle breeders tried to feed a couple of bullocks — to the extent that their usually poor land allowed. More and more of the holding was given over to cash crops, less and less to subsistence crops. The peasantry was abandoning its mode of production and was withering internally. The commodity boom of the First World War would blow away its empty husk.

4
Bothy Lads an' Plooman Chiels

> And how patient and genial and ingenuously foul-mouthed and dourly wary and kindly they are, those selfless aristos of Scotland. They endure a life of mean and bitter poverty, an order sneered upon by the little folk of the towns, their gait is a mockery in city streets, you see little waitresses stare haughtily at their great red, suncreased hands, plump professors in spectacles and pimples enunciate theses on their mortality and morality, their habits of breeding and their shiftlessness — and they endure it all! They endure the chatter of the city salons, the plannings of this and that war and blockade, they endure the pretensions of every social class but their own to be the mainspring and base of human society — they, the masters, who feed the world![1]

WHO were the people who obeyed northeast farmers' orders, who did the productive work in agriculture? In this chapter, to avoid accusations of pimpledom, we will not be concerned with northeast farm workers' mortality and morality. We will look instead at their numbers — with which we begin — and at their hours and working conditions, their diet and living conditions.

Numbers

To begin with we must consider not just the numbers of hired and family workers but — for reasons which will become clear later — the number of *chefs d'entreprise*[2] as well. It might appear a simple task to lay out a clear account of how many farm workers of different kinds there were in the northeast between 1840 and 1914, and how many *chefs d'entreprise:* after all, each decennial census from 1841 to 1911 has information on the occupational structure of agriculture. This is the material on which we must base our account, but we shall see that its interpretation is less simple than might be thought.

Let us start with the total numbers involved in agriculture. Figure 4.1 shows the total number of farmers, farmers' relatives, hired farm servants and farm labourers enumerated at each census between 1841 and 1911. The upper line shows that the number of men counted as being engaged in agriculture in the northeast increased by over six and a half thousand between 1841 and 1851 — a rise of more than sixteen per cent — and then shot up a further thirteen thousand — twenty-eight per cent — between 1861 and 1871. The numbers

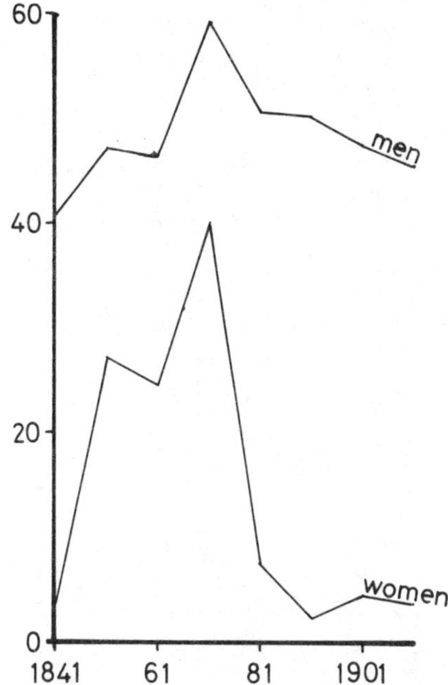

Figure 4.1 Total farm labour force (in thousands), northeast counties, 1841-1911[3]

then tumble by thirty-two per cent to 1881 and drift lower over the rest of the period. The lower line shows yet more dramatic movements for women; the figure in 1881 was a mere eighteen per cent of the figure ten years before. What was happening? Is Figure 4.1 a true reflection of the number of people in agriculture?

The answer, quite obviously, must be 'no'. The graphs are affected seriously by changes in census categories. The 1841 census understated the number in agriculture; one finds a very bald set of categories — which are not even consistent between counties — and family labour, apart from the *chef d'entreprise* himself, is ignored. The 1851 census was much better; family labour was included. In 1861, because of contemporary agitation over the living conditions of farm servants, one finds a highly refined set of categories dividing up the hired labour force. In the 1871 census these categories have been collapsed somewhat, but family labour is still included. Indeed, in this year all children were counted as part of the farm labour team, even those below five years of age. This is one main reason for the dramatic peak in both the male and the female figures in 1871. An attempt was made in the 1881 report to allow for this difficulty by including only children of fifteen years and over in the figures. This procedure had limitations too, for — as the 1901 census was to show — many children of less than fifteen years worked on the family farm. The categories used in 1881 were open to more serious objection, however. Only *male* relatives of fifteen and above were counted as being engaged in agriculture. Farmers' wives, daughters, granddaughters and nieces

Table 4.1

Percentage distribution by counties of northeast farm labour force (including chefs d'entreprise), *1841-1911*[4]

Men	1841	1851	1861	1871	1881	1891	1901	1911
Aberdeen	56.8	57.4	59.0	60.2	59.7	60.5	60.5	60.4
Banff	16.4	16.9	16.3	17.0	16.3	16.8	16.3	16.2
Kincardine	12.6	11.7	11.2	10.1	11.0	10.6	11.0	11.0
Moray	10.9	10.8	11.1	10.3	10.8	9.6	9.6	9.9
Nairn	3.2	3.2	2.4	2.3	2.2	2.5	2.6	2.6
Total	99.9	100.0	100.0	99.9	100.0	100.0	100.0	100.1
No.	40,728	47,254	46,242	59,230	40,715	40,137	37,367	35,447

Women	1841	1851	1861	1871	1881	1891	1901	1911
Aberdeen	42.3	53.2	58.1	62.0	38.0	52.3	50.4	56.9
Banff	21.6	20.1	16.7	18.0	34.6	18.1	18.8	18.9
Kincardine	15.4	10.1	8.9	8.4	8.9	6.8	12.6	8.8
Moray	13.7	12.6	14.1	9.9	16.8	19.1	15.8	12.7
Nairn	7.0	4.0	2.2	1.8	1.7	3.7	2.5	2.7
Total	100.0	100.0	100.0	100.1	100.0	100.0	100.1	100.0
No.	3,615	27,157	24,485	40,057	7,355	2,290	4,333	3,484

were not so counted — a most inaccurate reflection of what actually happened, and one that partly explains the dramatic slump in the lower line from 1871 to 1881. The categories of the 1881 census were used again in 1891. The 1901 report continued to ignore farmers' wives, but included male and female relatives 'assisting in the Work of the Farm' — a great improvement on the previous assumptions about age-sets. The 1911 report repeated the categories of its predecessor, except that it included an interesting breakdown of family labour on 'farms' and on 'crofts'. Sadly, this breakdown was not extended to hired labour.

It is difficult, then, to talk about the 'real' trend in numbers between 1841 and 1911. The 1841 report clearly understated numbers and, equally clearly, the 1871 report inflated them. We are probably not far wrong if we assume that the number of men engaged in agriculture in the northeast rose somewhat to 1851 and then fell, at a faster or slower rate, over the rest of the period. Even here, however, we have problems. How were crofters enumerated, for example: as farmers or in terms of subsidiary occupations? Were different enumerators consistent in their categorisations of crofters? Was each enumerator consistent over time? We can never know — but we can see that the problems involved in categorising men were as nothing compared with the problems presented by women. Table 4.1 shows the distribution of the entire labour force (including *chefs d'entreprise*) by counties at each census. The data for male labour show an astonishing consistency from one census to the next. Stability does not guarantee validity, but one might argue that the problems of categorisation are not all that serious for male labour.

The same cannot be said of women. Table 4.1 shows extravagant changes in the distribution of the female labour force — in 1871 the figure for Banffshire is less than a third of that for Aberdeenshire, while in 1881 the figures are not far from equality. One could argue that the wild changes in census categories had an effect here, although it is difficult to sustain this argument when the 1881 and 1891 distributions rest on the same categories yet are so different. It is true, of course, that there is a systematic ambiguity about whether the many girls working in farm houses were to be counted as domestic servants or farm servants;[5] but it is far from clear why this ambiguity should operate with such different weight in different counties. We know so little about female agricultural workers[6] that it is most unfortunate that census data about this group should be hopelessly unreliable. We have to fall back on less systematic sources to get any idea of changes in the size and nature of the female farm labour-force.

At the beginning of our period in 1840 many farms had an 'outworker' or two — female farm servants who did field work alongside the male servants:

> Janet Barron is oor oot-woman,
> She is on the roll, oh-ty,
> She has to work the ootdoor wark,
> And help to milk the kye.[7]

Most of the female farm servants were not outworkers, however, but maids in the farmhouse. On larger farms they would be specialised as dairymaids, kitchen maids or housemaids; on smaller places one maid — or 'deem' — would combine these roles. In the middle decades of the nineteenth century maids were often required to work 'baith oot an' in' — in the fields or the house — according to the farm's labour needs. The female relatives of the *chef d'entreprise* replicated this pattern of partial specialisation between outworkers and deems. We have no extended account of female labour in the northeast, but here is an account of the life of hired women from Perthshire in the 1850s which is probably very close to what was happening in the northeast at the mid-century. The only possible difference lies in carting; the cultural prescription against women working with horses was absolute in the northeast:

> On most farms where two or more servants are kept, one of them is generally engaged to act as housemaid, her duty being to attend to indoor matters; and the others

are engaged to work on the farm — that is, to labour at almost anything the men are employed at, with the exception of holding the plough. These latter work on the dunghill, at filling, mixing and spreading in the fields; in the thrashing-mill, in loosing, riddling or bundling straw; besides they drive carts, roller and brake, or pull and cart turnips in all sorts of weather in the winter time; and on farms where only one is kept, she must try her hand at all kinds of labour, outside as well as inside.[8]

What about change over time in the form and extent of female farm labour? It is exceedingly difficult to discover anything about family labour under this heading, but for hired servants we have the major source of the Royal Commission on the Employment of Women and Children in Agriculture. The report, and supporting evidence, of the Assistant Commissioner for the northeast counties, F. H. Norman, shows that in the late 1860s many women were employed as day labourers in times of peak labour demand — harvest, potato lifting, hoeing and cleaning turnips. These workers were usually widows, or the wives of married farm servants.[9] In the case of female farm servants, there was general agreement that women were less frequently seen as outworkers than had been the case a generation before,[10] though a number of witnesses reported that outworkers were still to be found in their districts.[11] It seems that they were to be found only on farms of 100 acres and above, however — on capitalist farms, that is — since a smaller place would not provide enough work to keep an outworker busy for a six-month fee.[12] Deems were still often required to work out and in, but this requirement seemed to be rather less common than before.[13]

In the decades after 1870 the number of hired women in agriculture dropped steadily. Improvements in the material forces — machine reaping, for instance — seem to have affected the demand for female workers more seriously than for men,[14] but the number of farmers that one finds complaining about a changed attitude to farm work among girls in the 1890s[15] suggests that the reduction in job opportunities for female day-labourers and outworkers was probably less marked than the fall in the number of women willing to do such work. This conclusion is supported by the fact that wages for women fell less sharply from the peak of the mid-1870s than was the case for male farm servants.[16] Whatever the reason, however, it is indubitable that fewer and fewer women did do field work in the northeast,[17] and that deems were less frequently required to work 'out and in' in 1910 — except in the hairst — than had been the case in 1860 as the supply of girls willing to be deems also fell.[18]

If we now turn to male farm labour, then we can return to census data and start to break down the total numbers in agriculture into discrete groups. Figure 4.2 shows a simple breakdown between male family labour, including *chefs d'entreprise,*[19] and hired labour in the northeast. The figure shows that the difficulties in the enumeration of male workers that we discussed earlier are limited to family labour. Hired farm labour is capable of unambiguous definition — except, perhaps, in the case of crofters feeing as farm servants — and we can place credence in the data for hired workers in Figure 4.2. These

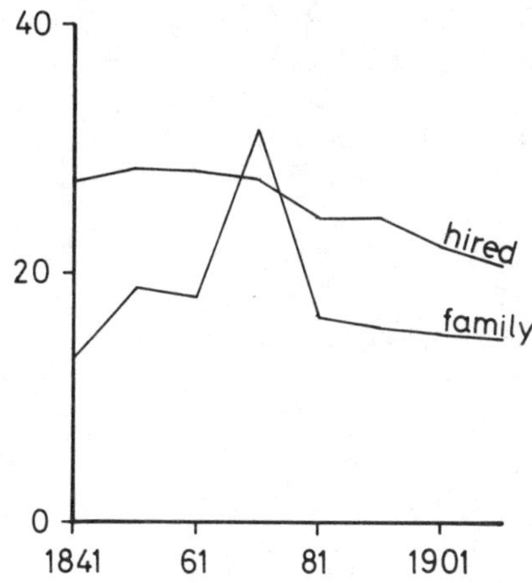

Figure 4.2 Number of hired male workers and male family workers (including *chefs d'entreprise)*, in thousands, northeast counties, 1841-1911[20]

data show a slight increase in numbers between 1841 and 1851, followed by a decline to 1911 that was halted only between 1881 and 1891. The figure for 1911 was twenty-seven per cent below that for 1851. Figure 4.2 is interesting in the context of our earlier discussion. We saw in Figure 2.8 that the tilled acreage of the northeast reached its maximum extent in 1901. We saw also that engrossment of holdings was going on at a quite rapid rate until 1880 and at a slower rate thereafter. Yet Figure 4.2 shows that the hired labour force needed to work the increasing area under the capitalist mode of production was falling in size over the half-century after 1851. This shows clearly the effect of improvements in the material forces of production — improvements which had as one major purpose significant labour economies. The hiccup in the graph between 1881 and 1891 may reflect the decisions of farmers in the early stages of 'the great depression', squeezed between low returns on invested capital and buoyant labour costs, not to invest yet more capital in machinery. It may also reflect, in part, reduced opportunities for men to move out of farm service born of the commercial depression of the 1880s.[21]

Table 4.2 allows us to move below the level of the five northeast counties combined and to look at the balance between family labour and hired labour in each county. The figures for female labour show the same wild fluctuations that we noted above,[22] and for the same reasons. The figures for men show the deflation of numbers in family labour in 1841, and the inflation of those numbers in 1871, that we considered earlier;[23] but it also shows two interesting new points. Firstly, it shows that male family labour in Kincardine, Moray and Nairn consistently lies a few percentage points below the level for Aberdeenshire and Banffshire. This reflects the rather stronger hold of capitalist agriculture in the sandstone districts.[24] The second point is more important. We saw in Tables 1.2 and 1.4 that large farms working the capitalist mode of production were heavily outnumbered by small farms and crofts in all parts of

Table 4.2

Family labour as a percentage of all labour in agriculture, northeast counties, 1841-1911[25]

Men	1841	1851	1861	1871	1881	1891	1901	1911
Aberdeen	35.0	40.8	40.1	55.2	41.2	39.9	43.1	43.5
Banff	34.6	42.5	41.7	57.5	44.4	42.9	42.8	45.3
Kincardine	24.0	34.8	33.0	46.3	34.7	31.3	32.5	34.6
Moray	31.4	39.2	37.3	46.3	36.2	36.1	36.0	35.8
Nairn	29.3	36.3	35.0	34.5	35.9	34.5	32.0	32.0

Women	1841	1851	1861	1871	1881	1891	1901	1911
Aberdeen	38.4	70.3	89.9	78.8	36.4	75.9	83.1	87.1
Banff	31.0	63.1	82.6	83.9	13.6	68.7	73.9	73.0
Kincardine	17.5	66.2	78.4	91.1	17.7	56.8	88.3	64.7
Moray	18.6	58.2	60.5	80.3	12.6	35.6	67.1	65.1
Nairn	2.8	48.0	64.2	82.1	25.8	31.8	72.0	73.7

the northeast. But Table 4.2 shows that, with the exception of the inflated figure for 1871, hired agricultural workers outnumbered family workers throughout the area and throughout our period — even when farmers are included in the family labour category. This complex situation is important in the analysis of the social relations of agricultural production.

What does census material tell us about the integration of family and hired workers? The inadequacy of data on women means that we must walk very circumspectly, but we can discover some rather interesting things. Let us look at family labour first. The 1911 census gives us an interesting breakdown of family labour on crofts as against farms. Tables 4.3, 4.4 and 4.5 are calculated from this material. Table 4.3 shows that crofts consistently had a higher proportion of female *chefs d'entreprise* than had farms. This should not surprise us: it was quite common for a farmer to retire to a croft from a larger farm,[26] and age-specific mortality rates for the two sexes, plus the fact that northeast farmers were often considerably older than their wives, would lead us to expect that the proportion of female *chefs* would be higher on crofts. There is little reason to think that problems about the enumeration of female labour are significant in Table 4.3. The same is not true of the two other tables. Table 4.4 shows the percentage of family labour inputs supplied by the *chef d'entreprise* in different counties. As we might expect, it shows that family labour additional to the lessee himself was more common on larger holdings than on crofts. Table 4.5 shows the sex distribution of this additional family labour. It shows a marked feminisation of family labour on crofts when compared with farms. Problems about female labour affect both of these tables rather seriously. In particular, farmers' wives are not included in the labour team. Thus Table 4.4 overstates the percentage of family labour inputs provided by the *chef d'entreprise* and Table 4.5 seriously understates the feminisation of family labour. This latter table is particularly interesting, for if we allow for the understatement of female labour, then it suggests that family labour on crofts was almost entirely female apart from the crofter — except in those cases when the crofter was a widow and a son remained on the croft to help her.[27] This suggests in turn that poor peasant holdings had a surplus of male labour much earlier in the life cycle of the farm family than they had a surplus of female labour. Sons went to farm service more or less as soon as they were able, while daughters were more likely to stay longer on the croft and help their parents. We may speculate that despite the decline of female-employing subsidiary cottage industries like stocking knitting, crofts continued to be able to absorb more female than male family labour in difficult times. Middle peasant and capitalist farms, by contrast, seem to have been able to absorb a higher proportion of male family labour — as the need for a greater number of cattlemen and horsemen on such holdings would lead us to expect.

What about hired labour? We must first of all make a crucial distinction between farm servants, who were hired on long engagements, and farm labourers hired by the day or the week. Census figures do not always allow us to separate these categories; hence the collapsing of all categories of farm

Table 4.3

Sex distribution of chefs d'entreprise, *distinguishing farms from crofts, northeast counties, 1911*[28]

	Farms		Crofts	
	No. *chefs*	% Male	No. *chefs*	% Male
Aberdeen	5,770	92.7	2,135	81.8
Banff	1,575	91.6	656	79.3
Kincardine	878	93.2	232	84.5
Moray	808	90.7	287	72.8
Nairn	209	87.1	57	80.4

Table 4.4

Percentage of family labour inputs supplied by chefs d'entreprise on farms and crofts, northeast counties, 1911[29]

	Farms		Crofts	
	%	No. *chefs*	%	No. *chefs*
Aberdeen	67.7	5,770	85.2	2,135
Banff	68.4	1,575	83.9	656
Kincardine	69.3	878	83.2	232
Moray	66.9	808	84.9	287
Nairn	72.3	209	80.0	56

Table 4.5

Percentage of family labour inputs (excluding chefs d'entreprise) *on farms and crofts coming from male relatives, northeast counties, 1911*[30]

	Family labour (farms)			Family labour (crofts)		
	M	F	%age Male	M	F	%age Male
Aberdeen	2,035	716	74.0	172	198	46.5
Banff	577	150	79.4	64	62	51.2
Kincardine	312	77	80.2	22	25	46.8
Moray	292	107	73.2	22	29	43.1
Nairn	56	24	70.0	6	8	42.9

labour in Figures 4.1 and 4.2 and Tables 4.1 and 4.2. When we can divide servants from labourers, however, we find that labourers were a relatively small part of the hired labour force. In Nairn in 1871 only sixteen per cent of male agricultural workers were labourers. Comparable figures for other counties were Moray 24 per cent, Banff 25 per cent, Aberdeen 22 per cent and Kincardine 28 per cent. These figures probably are close to the peak of the male labouring population, since job opportunities in reclaiming land, building dykes and digging drains peaked in the 1860s and 1870s. Much day labour came from crofters.[31] Despite this reservoir, however, capitalist farmers complained again and again of a shortage of day-labourers in the latter decades of the century. In the 1890s, for example, one Banffshire muckle farmer complained that the shortage was so acute that he was forced to hire his day-labourers by the half-year, like unmarried farm servants.[32] This arrangement was very agreeable for the day-labourers concerned, of course, since it guaranteed them wages in broken time.

Table 4.6 is calculated from the 1881 census material. Recognising the difficulties inherent in female labour figures and that the data do not distinguish farm servants from labourers, we can see that hired labour in northeast agri-

Table 4.6
Hired labour in agriculture by farm size, northeast counties, 1881 [33]

Farm size (tilled acres)	Number of farmers	Hired labour				Total hired labour
		Men	Boys	Women	Girls	
0-49	6,952	787	491	378	645	2,301
50-99	2,943	2,846	1,384	764	1,353	6,447
100-299	2,956	8,283	1,878	1,275	2,142	13,578
300+	450	2,760	277	478	323	3,838

culture was heavily concentrated on farms between fifty and three hundred tilled acres; that is, on farms working the capitalist mode of production (those above 100 acres) and, to a lesser extent, on middle peasant farms. We can see the same thing if we go somewhat deeper into the same material and consider the percentage distribution of hired men by farm size and by labour squad size in Table 4.7. The table shows a concentration of hired men on holdings between fifty and three hundred acres, as in Table 4.6. It is evident both that the large number of crofts in the northeast used little hired labour, as we should expect, and that the small number of giant farms (in northeast terms)

Table 4.7
Percentage distribution of hired men in agriculture by farm size and labour squad size, northeast counties, 1881 [34]

Farm size (tilled acres)	Number of men in labour squad				
	1-2	3-5	6-9	10+	Total
0-49	11.6	0.1			11.7
50-99	33.3	1.7			35.0
100-299	19.7	23.1	3.4	0.1	46.3
300+	1.1	1.7	2.8	1.4	7.0
Total	65.7	26.6	6.2	1.5	100.0

over three hundred tilled acres employed a small proportion of the total of hired men at any one time. This point is important: it suggests that servants' conceptions of appropriate social relations between a farmer and his farm servants were based on their experience of family farms and smaller capitalist farms, although we must remember that the frequent shifting of farm servants at terms gave most an experience of working on a very large farm at some time. This impression is confirmed by the data on labour squad size. These show that in 1881 only some eight per cent of northeast hired men worked in labour squads that contained more than six hired men. We must not make the mistake of assuming that this was the entire labour team — boys and women were also hired, and family workers were an important part of the labour squad, especially at the lower end of the farm size hierarchy. Even with these qualifications, however, we can conclude that hired farm workers usually found themselves in small labour squads, particularly when compared with the huge squads of the enormous capitalist farms of south-eastern Scotland.[35] The consequences of this fact for the social relations of agricultural production will concern us in the next chapter.

Table 4.8

Percentage distribution of male farm servants by occupational specialisation, northeast counties, 1861[36]

	Horsemen	Cattlemen	Shepherds	Orramen	Grieves	Total	No.
Aberdeen	51.6	18.6	2.5	23.9	3.4	100.0	12,647
Banff	53.8	19.2	3.1	20.6	3.3	100.0	3,260
Kincardine	54.4	14.3	4.2	23.0	4.1	100.0	2,488
Moray	56.7	18.4	6.4	13.9	4.6	100.0	2,426
Nairn	49.9	21.7	9.5	12.9	6.0	100.0	599

It is impossible to get any reasonable impression of occupational specialisation among family workers from census data. One can get evidence about such specialisation among farm servants, however. Table 4.8 presents such evidence for each northeast county in 1861. The table shows that roughly half of all the male farm servants in each county were horsemen (ploughmen), and another fifth were specialised cattlemen. A further fifth were orramen — skilled servants who could turn their hand to any task on the farm and fill in if a specialised servant was ill. Shepherds were few in number. Grieves — the managing servant on a large farm — represented about one farm servant in twenty-seven. They were recruited from the ranks of horsemen. On smaller farms the grieve's responsibilities in controlling other farm servants and representing their interests to the farmer were exercised by the senior horseman, the foreman.

Tables 4.9 and 4.10 show the age distribution of the male labour force on Aberdeenshire farms in 1851 and 1901. The tables raise some slight problems — the very large number of agricultural labourers in Table 4.9 seems to be the result of counting day-labourers and married farm servants in one category, for example — but some points come out rather clearly. First, the similarity in distributions derived from censuses half a century apart reflects the underlying stability of the age distribution of those men involved in Aberdeenshire farming. Secondly, the tables graphically illustrate Joe Duncan's sardonic jibe

Table 4.9

Percentage distribution by age of male farmers, family labour and hired agricultural labour, Aberdeenshire, 1851[37]

	5-	15-	20-	25-	35-	45-	55-	65+	Total	No.
Farmers		0.2	1.4	10.8	20.0	24.8	19.7	23.1	100.0	7,855
Farmers' relatives		32.5	27.5	27.4	8.9	2.6	0.9	0.3	100.1	3,209
Grieves			4.5	39.3	32.2	15.1	6.4	2.5	100.0	311
Shepherds	10.4	18.1	22.2	20.1	14.6	8.3	3.5	2.8	100.0	144
Other farm servants	16.9	34.5	22.5	16.8	5.3	2.5	0.9	0.6	100.0	7,328
Farm labourers	3.9	11.7	15.0	26.7	16.6	12.2	7.0	6.9	100.0	8,273

Table 4.10

Percentage distribution by age of male farmers, family labour and hired agricultural labour, Aberdeenshire, 1901[38]

	10-	15-	20-	25-	35-	45-	55-	65+	Total	No.
Farmers			0.7	9.8	19.9	24.1	22.1	23.4	100.0	7,022
Farmers' relatives	6.8	31.3	21.2	26.7	10.0	2.8	0.6	0.6	100.0	2,720
Grieves and foremen			3.9	25.4	32.6	23.2	9.8	5.1	100.0	692
Horsemen	1.1	30.2	25.9	25.2	10.1	4.9	2.2	0.5	100.1	5,361
Cattlemen	11.7	36.4	11.2	15.3	11.5	7.8	4.3	1.8	100.0	3,173
Shepherds	3.5	6.8	8.7	23.6	23.4	16.6	10.7	6.8	100.1	458
Other workers	10.7	28.6	10.9	15.4	11.2	8.4	7.5	7.3	100.0	3,185

that 'agriculture is run by adolescent labour and senile management'.[39] The figures for farmers rise with increasing age, while figures for family labour and for hired workers — apart from supervisory servants — peak at an early age and then fall away. Figures for grieves and foremen show a peak at a rather later age than other farm servants, as we should expect.

This evidence about age distributions shows something of the greatest importance for an understanding of farm life in northeast Scotland: for most men farm service was not a career in itself but a stage in a career that started outside farm service and would finish outside. Some male farm servants were themselves the sons of cottars — married farm servants. But evidence suggests that in most parts of the northeast such men were in a minority.[40] Most of the male farm servants were the sons of crofters and small farmers — again and again one finds the northeast peasant sector described as a nursery for farm servants. A son would work at home, learning the skills of farm work, until the paternal croft or small farm was in labour surplus. Then, if conditions in the labour market were at all favourable, he would go to farm service. Alex. Mitchell had left his Bennachie croft home for farm service at the age of twelve in 1855:[41] by 1870 boys went to the farms at thirteen or fourteen.[42] A loon would spend one or two six-month fees as a herd laddie — a job rendered necessary by the typical inadequacy of fencing, particularly on smaller farms. The next stage in his career was promotion from herd to coo baillie — cattleman. The servant now had a choice. He could continue as a specialised cattleman, enjoying the relative freedom that the job brought — unless he was a dairy cattleman, in which case the milking routine gave rise to a rigid work discipline.[43] Cattlemen earned wages which were not far below those of specialised horsemen, and a very skilled beef cattleman who could bring pedigree beasts to show condition and present them to advantage would get high wages and considerable prestige. A surer route to prestige was to leave the ranks of the coo baillies and join those of the horsemen. After one or two years as a cattleman most lads took a fee as a 'halflin' working the 'orra beast' (the odd horse), or as the most junior horseman working a pair of horse. They would now get 'the Horseman's grippin' Word' and henceforth scrupulously deny any knowledge of cattle; for the internal status structure of farm service placed work with horses above 'coo wark'. The new horseman, if skilful, would move through the ranks of horsemen until he became a foreman or even a grieve. If he stayed a horseman, then his declining physical strength in middle age would mean that he could no longer manage the demanding regime of specialised horse work, and he would become an orraman, able to turn his hand to any task on the farm. Many men would not take this route, however. Many farm servants left the northeast for the colonies — Canada, Australia, New Zealand — and for the United States. Local newspapers were full of accounts by émigrés of the delights of prairie farming. Other men left the northeast to try farm work further south. Others went to the towns:

I've often thocht I'd like tae be
A bobby on the force,
Or maybe I'll get on the trams
Tae drive a pair o' horse.
But fitiver it's my lot tae be,
The bobbies or the trams,
I'll niver forget the happy days
I wore my Nicky Tams.

But many men left farm service to return to peasant agriculture, either by taking over the lease of the family holding on the death or retirement of their fathers or by leasing a colonising croft or an established croft. Thus farm service and peasant agriculture were intimately and intricately articulated. Indeed, so close was this articulation that peasant farmers, farm servants and day labourers are best seen as fractions of a single class. Individual peasants circulated through family labour, farm service, day labouring and peasant farming in the course of a life's work: in so doing they bound together the three fractions that, in the desiccated social anatomy of the census report, seemed to share no common features.

Hours of work and specialisation

The deeper penetration of the capitalist mode of production extended the division of labour among northeast farm servants and family labour. A very old former farm servant remembered the low division of labour on a large Moray farm in the late eighteenth century:

> Fan I was a loon I gied to ma gran' uncle's at Tulloch to work for them — herdin' nowte or sheep or any kin' o' a job that I was ordered to dae. It was a big fairm, an' they hed a great scringe o' kwintra for pastur'.[44]

This probably understates the degree of specialisation at the time; the Board of Agriculture reports of the 1790s take for granted categories like 'ordinary ploughman'. This notwithstanding, however, the fairly precise division of labour between horsemen, cattlemen and orramen that was evident by 1840 was a new phenomenon.

The period between 1840 and 1914 saw a steady movement towards the limitation of a farm servant's labour commitment, but the possibility of farm servants reducing the number of hours that they were required to work was limited by the logic of capitalist production. Peter Laing remembered a time, in the late eighteenth century, when the labour commitment was effectively unlimited:

> *What did you do after you got up in the winter time?*
> We got up aboot three or four o'clock, an' fat ither wud we dee but jist start the flail. We thun'ert an' whippit awa' till aboot daylicht in the mornin', an' syne we gaed an' meated an' muckit the horse an' nowte. Aifter oor brakfast we startit awa' wi' oor horse to work, an' in the short winter day we had to work on till it was dark afore we got onything mair to eat. In the simmer time we aye got dinner.
>
> *And was your work finished when you got your supper?*
> Nae fears o' that; for we hed to gang oot to the barn, an' aifter reddin' it up we dressed the corn. Deil a muckle dressin' did it get, however, for there was nae fanners in that days, an' we jist open twa doors, an' fan it fell oot o' the sieve the win' blew awa' the cauff. In the early mornin's an' at nicht fan we were at wark we wrocht wi' the licht o' a fir stick. Feint a muckle did it gie sometimes, fan there was little rozzit in the sticks. It wud hae been aucht o'clock at nicht afore we war deen. Man, fowk dinna ken fat wark is noo-a-days. If they wrocht as hard as we did in my young days they wud be glaid to gang to their beds seener at nicht. Faith, fan we war hard wrocht about the sawin' time an' hairst we were geyan willin' to crawl into oor beds gin nine o'clock at nicht.[45]

A horseman's labour commitment was much the same in 1840 as it had been half a century before. Alexander Gray was born at Craigie, Tarves in 1822. By the age of 20 he was a champion ploughman with a name famous throughout Aberdeenshire. At 22 he went back to school, fought his way with great success through university and Divinity Hall, and ended his days as the respected Auld Kirk minister of Auchterless.[46] From his extreme old age he remembered his years as a horseman. Were the horsemen of 1906 exploited, he asked, in having to work some twelve hours a day on field and in stable?

> In my farm-servant days we wrought longer time. We had no interval of two hours at mid-day, as you have now. We were at it from five till seven o'clock. We took no fixed time for breakfast and dinner; we just ate our meal, picked out teeth, and at it again. And during turnip seed we began work at five o'clock, so that, what with getting the horses ready in the morning, and settling up things at night, we were engaged from four a.m. till seven p.m., making for us a day of fifteen hours.[47]

Gray's statement that there were no fixed times for meals in the 1840s is hard to credit — on grounds of efficient working of the farm kitchen if no other — but certainly hours of work had been longer at that time. Taking just the hours when the horses were yoked, horsemen in the Turriff district and in Cairnie worked eleven hours in 1843-4, ten hours in 1881.[48] This reduction in the yoking time was a consequence of the increased division of labour brought about by the intensified capitalisation of agriculture in the middle decades of the nineteenth century; ten hours yoked was the rule throughout the northeast by 1870, and so remained until 1914.[49] This remarkable stability in the horseman's formal labour commitment over a half century when hours at work outside agriculture were tumbling needs explanation. The explanation lies in the capitalist mode of production. Horses were expensive pieces of capital equipment. Hence, as the capitalist mode unfolded, the daily life of horsemen came to be linked more closely to the need to use horses in the most efficient possible manner.[50] We are told — and it is difficult to believe — that in Moray in the 1790s horses were worked in the long summer days only for two three-hour yokings.[51] This under-utilisation of capital equipment had disappeared by the middle of the following century. Experiment and observation had shown that two five-hour yokings — from six to eleven in the morning and from one to six in the afternoon — was the most efficient manner of working a pair of horse; this therefore became the basis of the horseman's routine.

This does not mean that hours of work were not a matter of negotiation between farmer and farm servant. The horseman's ten hours were his formal labour commitment; around this there revolved an additional labour commitment that was open to negotiation. Figure 4.3 shows the daily timetable of horsemen and beef cattlemen in the summer term on the 500-acre farm of Tipperty, Logie Buchan, in 1871. The figure shows the usual ten-hour yokings for horsemen. But they also had to put in another three and a quarter hours per day cleaning, feeding and grooming their horses. The horseman's day stretched from 4.45 a.m. to 8 p.m., with a total of two hours for meal breaks.

Cattlemen worked a ten and a half hour day, spread over the time between 5.30 a.m. and 8 p.m.

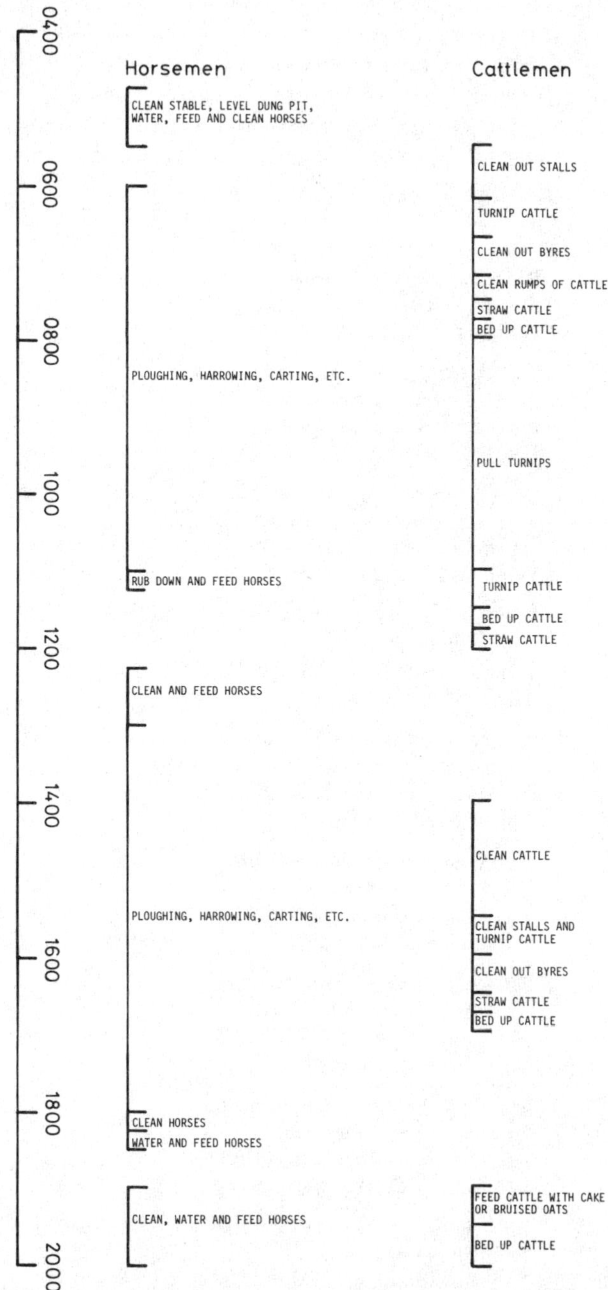

Figure 4.3 Daily timetable for horsemen and cattlemen on Tipperty, Logie Buchan, c. 1870[52]

We must remember that Figure 4.3 shows the maximum number of hours worked by male farm servants on specialised tasks under normal conditions. In the hairst — and to a lesser extent at seed-time — all limitations on hours worked were put in abeyance. Against this, however, at other seasons the men had to spend less time on specialised work. In the short winter days yokings were shorter; for horses, unlike tractors, were not fitted with headlights. At these times, and in broken weather, horsemen turned their hands to barnwork and other odd jobs. 'Drumdelgie' is an account of a horseman's life in the winter term on the largest farm in Cairnie:

O ken ye o' Drumdelgie's toon,
Where a' the crack lads go?
Stra'bogie braw in a' her bounds
A bigger cannot show.

At five o'clock we quickly rise,
And hurry doon the stair,
It's there to corn oor horses,
Likewise to straik their hair.

Syne after workin' half an hour,
To the kitchen each one goes;
It's there to get oor breakfast,
Which is generally brose.

We've scarcely got oor brose weel supt,
And gi'en oor pints a tie,
When the foreman cries, 'Hullo, my lads!
The hour is drawin' nigh.'

At sax o'clock the mull's put on,
To gie us a' strait wark;
It tak's four o' us to mak' to her,
Till we could wring oor sark.

And when the water is put aff,
We hurry doon the stair,
To get some quarters through the fan,
Till daylicht does appear.

When daylicht it begins to peep,
And the sky begins to clear,
The foreman he cries oot, 'My lads
Ye'll stay nae longer here!

There's sax o' you'll gae to the ploo,
And twa can ca' the neeps;
And the owsen they'll be aifter you,
Wi' strae raips roun their queets.'

But when that we were gyaun furth,
An turnin' oot to yoke,
The snaw dang on sae thick and fast
That we were like to choke.

The frost had been so very hard,
The ploo she widna go;
And sae oor cairtin' days commenced
Among the frost and snow.[53]

At such times, when the ground was frozen, all cultivation came to a dead stop. Some horses were used for carting neeps for cattle food, but most were exercised but not worked.[54] The horsemen took to doing repairs, odd jobs and barnwork — hashing neeps, or threshing with the mill. In summer horses were put out to grass for about three months and thus no stable cleaning and no evening suppering of horses were needed. Cattlemen needed to spend much less time in the byre in summer, when the nowt were in the fields.[55] In early summer one could see the farm's whole labour team at work singling neeps, the organisation of the squad on the field carefully reflecting the status hierarchy within the labour team. Horsemen often resented having to do tasks unrelated to 'horse wark';[56] but they had no choice. In times of slack work for horses or of broken weather, the horseman had to make up his labour commitment with other work. The only thing that no farmer would ask his horsemen to do was to work in the byre[57] — to work with cattle meant ritual defilement for a horseman who had left his days as a 'coo baillie' behind him.

The existence of this 'informal' labour commitment — in the case of horsemen hours spent tending their horses outside the standard yoking, and general work about the farm — gave considerable room for negotiation with the farmer. The demands of local branches of the nascent farm servants' union in Aberdeenshire in 1886 included demands for a ten — or even nine — hours' day and a half-holiday on a Saturday afternoon once a month: reductions in the formal labour commitment. Other demands concerned improvements in housing and diet. But the demands which seem to have sparked off the agitation of 1886 were about the informal labour commitment: that travel to and from the fields should be included in the yoking, and that horsemen should carry plough irons to the smithy for repair in the farmer's time and not their own.[58] This informal commitment was very sensitive to changes in labour market conditions; the evidence to the Royal Commission on Labour in the early 1890s — a time of farm labour shortage in the northeast — shows that the union had not been entirely unsuccessful. The informal labour commitment of horsemen had shrunk; plough irons now went to the smithy in the farmer's time, and the hours required in cleaning, grooming and feeding horses had been reduced.[59]

Wages

Family workers expected no more payment for their labour than board, clothes, and pocket money. Because they did not sell their labour, we have little idea of how family labour costs changed in the years between 1840 and 1914. But farm servants were usually hired in the feeing market,[60] and local newspapers gave good coverage of the markets. Hence we should be able to make clear and unambiguous statements about the movement of farm servants' wages. Two caveats must be entered, however. Firstly, newspapers could only report the 'ruling prices' of a particular market. Each farmer and farm servant negotiated a particular bargain — based on the reputations of the parties, the time of day, and other factors — within the range of wages being offered for that class of servant at that market.[61] Secondly, money wages — which were all that were reported in the newspapers — formed only one part of a servant's fee; the servant was also boarded by the farmer or given customarily defined amounts of basic foodstuffs in lieu of board. Thus his total wage depended on the bargain that he made with the farmer in the feeing market, and the current market price of his perquisites. Bearing these points in mind, we can make some statements about the movement of farm servants' wages.

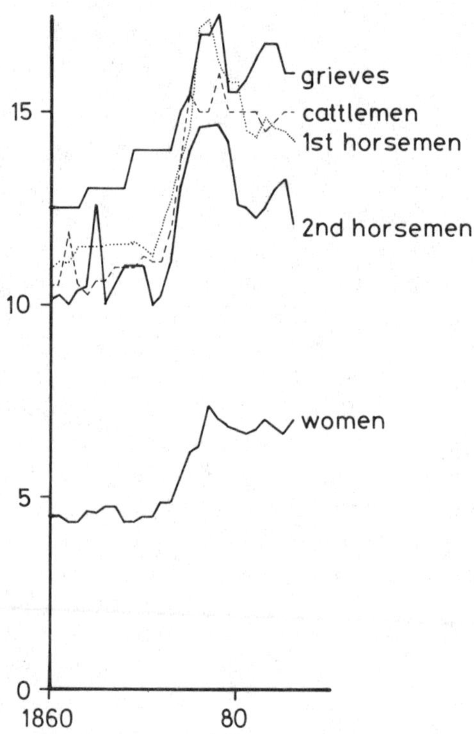

Figure 4.4 Price of labour, in pounds per annum, on two Aberdeenshire capitalist farms, 1860-1886[62]

Figure 4.4 shows the price of labour on two Aberdeenshire capitalist farms between 1860 and 1886. That is, it shows not simply the money wages paid by the two farmers to their servants, but the total annual cost to them of different categories of farm servant.[63] It shows a dramatic increase in labour costs after 1870. It also shows very clearly the weak market position of female farm servants: a reflection not of a market flooded with girls and women seeking fees but of plain straightforward sexism among employers. But Figure 4.4 also shows graphically the effect of the separate bargain made between each servant and the farmer in the feeing market: the difference in the cost of first and second horsemen varies from ten shillings in 1868 to fifty-five shillings in 1877. In 1865 we have the extraordinary circumstance that second horsemen cost twenty shillings more than foremen, and in 1866 and 1867 foremen cost more than grieves.[64]

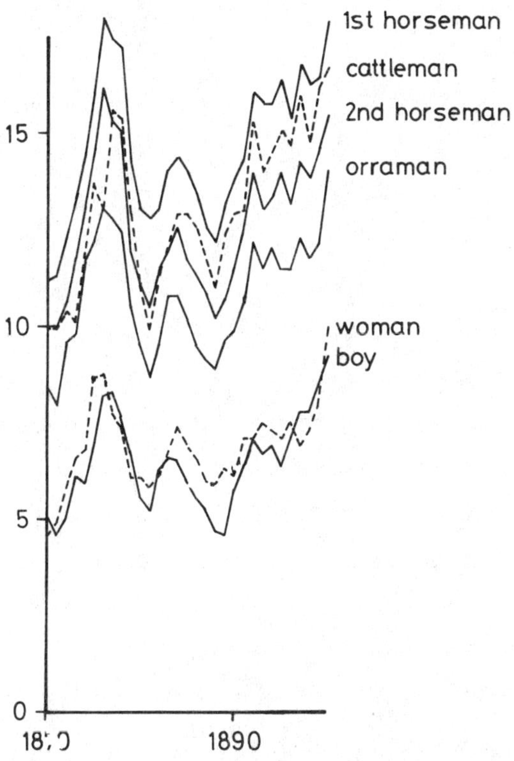

Figure 4.5 Average cash wage, in pounds, of farm servants at northeast spring feeing markets, 1870-1900[65]

Figure 4.5 shows average money wages for a six-month fee (therefore for unmarried servants alone) at spring feeing markets in the northeast. Cash wages for the autumn term generally were a few shillings lower. The figure shows a sharp peak for all categories of farm servant in the late 1870s, as in Figure 4.4. This peak was followed by a slump in the 1880s, but after 1887 wage rates slowly climbed to higher ground and stayed there until the end of

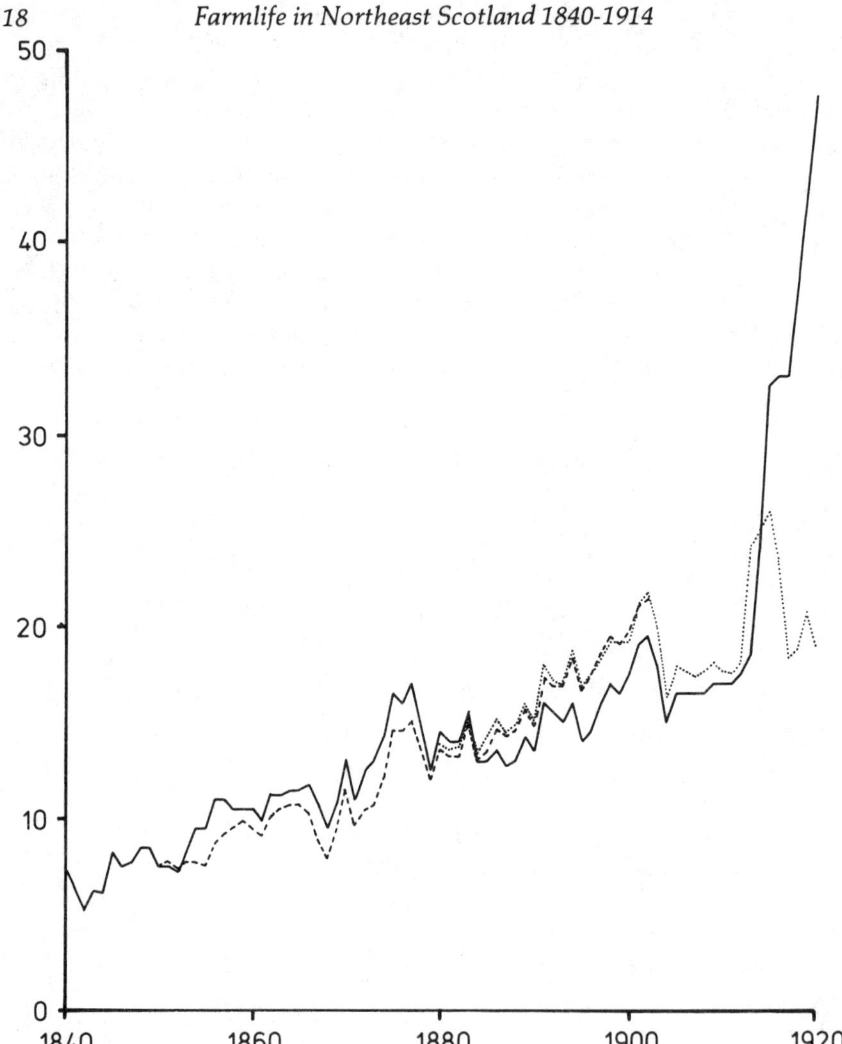

Figure 4.6 Average cash wage (solid line) and real wage (broken line), in pounds, paid to first horsemen at the Aberdeen autumn feeing market, 1840-1920[66]

the century. Figure 4.5 shows us one other interesting feature which links up with the preceding figure. Adult male wage rates were closely clustered, while rates for women (and, in Figure 4.5, for boys) were very much lower.

Figure 4.6 shows the average cash wage paid to first horsemen (foremen) at the Aberdeen autumn feeing market between 1840 and 1920. It shows a steady rise in money wages from 1840 to the First World War, interrupted after 1877 by a long trough. It also shows that the First World War boom — and associated inflation — sent money wage rates soaring. But the particularly interesting feature of Figure 4.6 is the broken line — the trend of real wages. This shows that the slump in money wages after 1877 affected farm servants less severely than might have been supposed, since the cost of living also fell.

From 1880 real wages rose inexorably until 1902. Thereafter real wages for foremen fell back rather sharply until the war years with their erratic movements; but even in the years after 1902 real wages were well above the level of any period apart from the years from 1891 to 1902.

What conclusions can we draw from this evidence? The most important conclusion is that the continued mechanisation of agriculture in the years of poor cash crop prices between 1880 and 1914 — a mechanisation that contributed largely to the growing problems of peasant farmers in that period — was a consequence, not a cause, of the fall in the numbers of hired farm servants shown in Figure 4.2. Farmers always complained that wages were too high (the Rice-Davis principle would lead us to be surprised if it were otherwise), but the wail of anguish from capitalist farmers in evidence to the Royal Commission on Labour in the 1890s seems to have been justified in their eyes if not in those of their servants. Faced with falling cash crop prices, these farmers had to pay wages that were rising in both cash and real terms. The explanation of this situation lies in emigration, of course: emigration to urban areas or to the colonies.[67] It is significant that regional variations in cash wages within Scotland were more marked for some categories of farm servant than others; the pull of lowland industrial areas was stronger for horsemen and orramen than for cattlemen, and hence led to higher wage rates for horsemen and orramen in counties closer to industrial centres,[68] because they — unlike cattlemen — had marketable skills. Driving a horse tram was not very different from driving a farm cart. We may conclude, then, that farm servants in north-east Scotland had a strong market situation throughout our period. The mode of hiring through feeing markets allowed them to exploit that advantage to the full.[69]

Housing

Housing is a large and complex topic; and one which raised fierce controversy throughout our period. It is necessary, then, to discuss it in some detail.

(a) Female farm servants

We may disregard the question of how outworkers were housed, since these women were almost invariably related to, and lived with, farm labourers or married farm servants. Maids in the farmhouse were a different matter. Whether employed in the house, the kitchen or the dairy, they invariably were lodged in the farm house.[70] The house on a large farm usually had a warren of tiny bedrooms — often little bigger than closets — for the maids in the attic. On smaller places the deem slept in the kitchen while the farmer and his wife slept 'ben the hoose'. Wherever the maids were lodged, however, the male servants found them, tapping at the window or clambering over the roof with priapic intent:[71]

The maids — by which I mean the long succession of magdalens and half-wits that did the heavy work about the house — lived in one of the back (attic) rooms. Of course it was not considered necessary to give a kitchen wench a decent room — she wasn't accustomed to it and wouldn't have known what to do with it. A creaky bed, a cracked mirror, and a rickety table were all she deserved and all she usually got . . . a hole into which she could creep at night and from which she could emerge at half-past four, eager for another day's work. Now my grandmother was not of that school of thought, but she was not a revolutionary either and, though the maid's room had some amenities such as a wardrobe and a chest of drawers, it was by no means a Paradise in which a lonely girl might be soothed to sweet slumbers. It was long and narrow with a skylight opening on the north. The walls were distempered a cold blue. There the domestics spent their dreary nights diversified with spasms of bucolic love at the week-ends.[72]

(b) Unmarried men

This was the really controversial issue in the nineteenth century, as a result of James Begg's moral crusade of the late 1850s and early 1860s to explain the scandalously high illegitimacy ratios of northeast counties — first revealed to a horrified local and national bourgeoisie in 1855 — as a function of the mode of housing unmarried male farm servants.[73] Begg was wrong, as it happens, but his arguments had immense influence.

Unmarried male farm servants outnumbered married servants in all northeast counties, but the preponderance of unmarried men was more marked in some areas than in others. Under the spur of Begg's agitation the 1861 Census tried to measure the balance between the two groups by distinguishing 'indoor servants' — that is, those who were boarded by the farmer — from 'outdoor servants'. Unfortunately the latter category did not distinguish between married servants and unmarried bothymen[74] — a failing that vitiated the whole attempt. Comments from observers throughout our period make it clear, however, that married servants were particularly uncommon in the northeast's central wedge but rather more common in the sandstone districts.

One may distinguish three ways of housing unmarried male farm servants in the northeast: the bothy system, the chaumer (the farm kitchen system), and boarding the loons with a married servant or with a crofter. The latter system was not common; it was found only in very local areas and was always combined with some other arrangement.[75] It is possible to hold conceptual distinctions between these three methods of housing unmarried male servants but, as we shall see, the distinctions were less clear in the real world.

In the farm kitchen system the men were boarded; as a part of their fee the farmer undertook to have their meals cooked for them. They ate these meals in the farm kitchen, and had the customary right to sit by the kitchen fire until nine o'clock at night,[76] when they went to bed in the chaumer, a room in the farm steading. Chaumers were remarkably uniform structures until the late nineteenth century. Here is an account of a typical one from the Midmar doctor in 1891:

> A part of a loft above a stable, to get to which you have to pass along the stable, behind the heels of half-a-dozen horses, and then up by a rickety stair or ladder. Inside the room are two or more beds,[77] according to the size of the farm; and if any space is left, it is nearly all taken up with trunks, which also serve as seats. Soiled clothes, bits of harness, etc., are lying about. The floor is often not very clean. There is no fireplace of any description. The place is lighted by a sky-light, with one or two panes broken, perhaps, and filled up with straw or a pair of trousers, which is, perhaps, of excellent use for ventilation. Such, with variations, are the sleeping apartments I have visited in the course of my practice during the last three years.[78]

This account of the roughness of most chaumers is not overdrawn. Farm servants remembered worse places; on one farm in the 1860s the men had 'to acquire the habit, in the morning, of refraining from opening our eyes until first we shook our heads face downwards over the bedside to clear the dust which fell overnight from the rats upon our eyelids'.[79] Another farm servant, who wisely chose to publish his essay anonymously, remembered one particular chaumer in west Aberdeenshire:

> Two of the men invited me to go along with them; the other two followed close after. It is hardly necessary to state, that the sleeping apartments were, as is customary, in the loft, over the stable. We passed the entry to the cart-shed, stable door, and round to the east end of the building, resting against which stood a ladder, up which we were to ascend to the chamber. Before we had got to the ladder, the two male companions that we had left in the kitchen later than us appeared at the loft door looking on us below. By this circumstance, I fancied that the bedroom behoved to be a strange sort of place, when a person can drop into his bedroom from any end. But I should soon see and unravel the mystery; so getting up to the loft, I could discover that the stable wall, bordering on the cart-shed, was of no greater height than the level of the floor; so that the men could step upon the cart, and by another step, stand on the floor. The servants' chests stood arranged on the north side. On the other three beds were boxed in below the legs of the couples, the front of them not reaching to the middle of the floor. In going to repose in these singular sort of beds, it required no little amount of ingenuity, and the greatest stock of caution, in a stranger to get safely into a position of going to sleep, to prevent the head or the knees from being broken, getting up in the morning, or through a fit of somnambulism, as the legs of the couples were so close, that the occupant at the back-side required to lie down edgeways. By this judicious arrangement of the chests on one side, and the beds on the other, the centre of the loft was left perfectly clear, where any ordinary sized man could have paraded with his head all safe, provided he held in the middle. There was no window in the place, and as little use for it. The whole gable was entirely open above the level of the floor, and the east gable door was never closed by day or by night during the whole summer six months, from the circumstance that one of the iron bands broke away, and that rascal procrastination never allowed it to be mended. There was no complaint for want of proper ventilation here, as both ends of the apartment were ever open . . . There was plenty of light too, although not admitted in a very scientific manner.[80]

Chaumers improved slowly in the later nineteenth century under the spur of public controversy over the moral consequences of inadequate farm servant accommodation. It became increasingly common for the kitchie deem to include sweeping out the chaumer and making the men's beds among her manifold other duties — and if the bawdy rural underground is to be believed, then she had to be careful not to be caught by any of the men while doing so. The advent of county Medical Officers of Health in the 1890s gave authoritative muscle to the previous merely exhortatory denunciation of bad farm servant accommodation that stemmed from Begg's moral crusade; the new M.O.H.s took farm servant accommodation as one of their pressing problems and the more scandalous chaumers were quickly closed and replaced with buildings physically separate from the farm steading. Despite these improvements, however, the chaumer remained a cheerless place. John R. Allan gives an account of an improved chaumer — which he calls a bothy, although it is clear that the men did not cook and eat their food in this place. The chaumer was built apart from the steading. It had a cement floor, a fireplace and wood-lined walls. What is striking about it, however — apart from the advent of the bicycle, which was so important in making a farm servant's life more bearable by increasing his mobility — is the slight improvement in material conditions for the chaumered servant of 1914 over his compeer of a half century earlier:

They lived in the bothy, a one-roomed house across the yard from the cart-shed. Unlike most of its kind this bothy was pleasant enough, for its back window looked west to the valleys and the hills. The furniture was of the simplest — two big double beds filled with chaff, a wide open fireplace for burning peats, a tin basin to wash in and a roller towel behind the door, and a spotty mirror in one of the windows. Pitch-pine walls and a cement floor looked almost as cold as they were, but they had the necessary merit of being clean. Cold and clean but never a home, you might have said if you had seen it at Whitsunday weekend when the old men had left and the new ones were not yet home, and after Sally had spent a day in scrubbing it out with soap, soda and ammonia. If you had seen it a fortnight later, when the new boys had moved in, you would have found it neither cold nor clean nor any more like home. The farm servant in those days . . . had only two possessions — a kist and a bicycle. So, if you had looked into the bothy, you would see the kists set out against the walls and the bicycles in a recess at the foot of the bed. Sunday suits, shirts and long woollen drawers hung from nails on either side of the windows, each man having a bit of the wall for wardrobe. Boots, ranging from stylish browns for Sunday to great tacketty boots all glaur and dung, huddled beneath the beds where they had been lightly thrown off their owner's feet. A strange collection of things littered every shelf — bits and pieces mostly broken, collar studs, screw nails, Jews' harps, cogs, flints, gas burners, ball bearings, old knives, corkscrews, cartridges, bicycle clips — everything for which you might find a use if you kept it seven years. Anything they really valued they kept locked in their kists. But you must not think that they left only rubbish about or that they made no attempt at decoration. Most of them had photographs nailed up beside their beds — photographs of relations, very self-conscious in Sunday blacks or white elbow-length cotton gloves, photographs of horses in gala trim on the way to a show or a ploughing match; or photographs of ample ladies in a state of frilly déshabillé who must have been left over from the Gay Nineties. These last were real art and treasured as such.[81]

Plate 1. Peasant Ingenuity. A crofter near Rothienorman, Fyvie, ploughing with a horse and an ox yoked together. Later nineteenth century.

Plate 2. Peasant Respectability. George Smith, the tenant of Lintmill Croft, Hythie, Mintlaw with his wife and family about 1904. Note the neatly thatched roof and the fieldstone walls of the crofthouse: George Smith and the previous tenants of Lintmill Croft, like their great literary exemplar Johnny Gibb, have evidently made the croft with their own labour and with no assistance from the laird or his architect.

Plate 3. The 'Big Mull' working on a farm near Insch, late nineteenth century. Note the large labour team needed for steam threshing: a labour team accumulated through mutual aid arrangements with neighbouring farmers and crofters. The necessity for mutual aid generated novel cultural forms: the farmer whose stacks were being threshed provided a slap-up meal for his helpers. Thus the arrival of the 'Big Mull' in the district is still remembered as one of the social highlights of the year.

Plate 4. The horsemen on Guise, Tough, early twentieth century.

I gaed to the stable,
My pairie for to view,
And, fegs, they were a dandy pair,
A chestnut and a blue.

The horsemen on Guise o' Tough ranked in strict array from right to left: foreman, second, third, and orra loon. The strict hierarchy and rigid discipline among horsemen determined every aspect of their working lives, and a good part of their scant leisure time (see pp. 138–42). Note how beautifully groomed are the horses: each horseman took an intense pride in the appearance of his pair.

Plate 5. The Made Horseman. This photograph comes from Kirriemuir, Angus in 1926; thus it is, strictly speaking, out of our area and our period. But it summarises so much about the Horseman mystery that it is worth its place. Note the calm assurance with which the horseman sits below a ton of Clydesdale, secure in his total control of 'horse beasts'. The framing of the horse in the doorway had a secret significance—perhaps a reference to the usual name for the Horseman's Word initiation ceremony, 'gangin' thru' the c'affhoose door'? (See pp. 154–6). The placing of the horse against a gable end gives the picture a strong triangular composition that echoes the characteristic structure of paintings of the Crucifixion. This may be accidental but, given that the Horseman mystery inverted Christian ritual and iconography at every possible opportunity, it may well be a calculated effect.

Plate 6. The farm servants on Minmore, early twentieth century. Itinerant photographers to thousands of photographs like this in the northeast: the whole hired labour squad on a farm, from foreman down to the kitchie deem and farm cat, arranged behind the painted nameboard fr the farm cart. These photographs often contain gallows humour about food—a loaf of br being cut with a saw, for example. Here the humour appears in the loon at the left-hand end the back row stirring his brose with an enormous spurtle, and the man at the right-hand enc the back row making his brose in an enamelled basin. The containers ranged along the fron the group are labelled, from left to right, 'eggs', 'tattie soup', 'Minmore', and 'the Glenl whiskey'.

Plate 7. Porter Fair in 1871.

Beware of going to Swaggers,
For he'll be in Porter Fair...

Porter Fair was the autumn feeing market in Turriff, and the largest feeing market in the northeast. This splendid early photograph shows clearly how a big market could take over the town or village in which it was held, to the profound disgruntlement of respectable folk (see pp. 145–6).

Plate 8. The Turra Coo. The decorated heroine of Paterson, Lendrum's tragi-comic campaign in 1913 against Lloyd George's Insurance Act (see pp. 172–3).

The comfortless nature of the chaumer might be excused to some extent by the convention that its occupants could sit by the kitchen fire after supper until nine o'clock and then return to the chaumer merely to sleep. The same was not true of the bothy, in which the unmarried men not only slept but cooked the foodstuffs allowed by the farmer in lieu of board. To the usual clutter of the chaumer was added the detritus of men tired, and frequently wet, cooking for themselves. First-hand accounts of bothy life in the northeast are exceedingly rare;[82] the most celebrated account of a 'roch' bothy by one who had stayed in it is by Hugh Miller and refers to Easter Ross. This essay was much more influential in its time than Cobbett's account of a Dunfermline bothy which is now so widely quoted[83] — for Miller's essay first appeared in the *Witness* and formed the basis for Begg's assault on the moral consequences of bothying:

> Some twenty or thirty years before it had been a barn; for it had formed part of an older steading, of which all the other buildings had been pulled down, to make way for the more modern erection. It was a dingy, low, thatched building, bulged in the side-walls in a dozen different places, and green atop with chickenweed and stone-crop. One long apartment without partition or ceiling, occupied the interior from gable to gable. A row of undressed deal-beds ran along the sides. There was a fire at each gable, or rather a place at which fires might be lighted, for there were no chimneys; the narrow slits in the walls were crammed with turf; the roof leaked in a dozen different places; and along the ridge the sky might be seen from end to end of the apartment. We learned to know what o'clock it was, when we awoke in the night-time, by the stars which we saw glimmering through the opening.
>
> It was, in truth, a comfortless habitation for human creatures in a wet and gusty November, and the inmates were as rugged as their dwelling-place was rude.[84]

There were reasons particular to the farm and its tenant why this bothy was so bad, as Miller makes clear in his essay; but the accounts of bourgeois explorers who penetrated the mysteries of bothy life at the mid-century show that conditions were rough enough in the general run of bothies:

> The walls are rough, bare and dingy. There are three beds, six chests, belonging to the men, which contain their clothing, and six barrels to hold the oatmeal which is supplied every four weeks, at the rate of half a boll to each man. The only furniture supplied by the master, in addition to the beds, consists of a pot or kettle for boiling water, six wooden *cappies* or bowls, six spoons, and a short form or seat. There is no chair on which the weary man may rest, and no table. Inasmuch as the form, a seat without a back, can accommodate only four persons, two must seat themselves on the top of their chests or meal barrels. The ashes are never removed, nor the apartment swept and cleaned, except by the men themselves, nor are their beds made except once in six weeks, when change of sheets is supplied. Only two clean towels are given weekly for the use of six men, whose hands and faces would require frequent washing.[85]

Even more than is the case with the chaumer, moral controversy led to a great improvement in the condition of bothies. As early as the 1850s 'improved' bothies were being built with the cooking area separate from the sleeping area, and with single beds in cubicles.[86] These improvements started in the great bothy districts to the south of the northeast — Harry Stuart, minister of Oathlaw, Angus was a seminal figure in the movement — but they soon spread north. In the Moray lowlands, in particular, where bothying came very late, many bothies were of this improved kind,[87] and thus far removed from the one-room hovel that had so roused the anger of William Cobbett and Hugh Miller. Once again the advent of the county Medical Officers of Health hastened improvement. But there were frequent complaints from outside the ranks of farm servants that the men did not appreciate better conditions and continued to pig it as of old.[88] It is impossible to judge how much truth there was in this rural variant of the coals in the bath myth.

But it was not only the physical condition of bothies that changed between 1850 and 1914. The defining character of a bothy was that the men both ate and slept in the one building. But as the nineteenth century passed, it became less and less the rule that the men did the cooking themselves. As early as 1840 some farmers paid the wife of one of the married farm servants to cook the bothymen's food, and to sweep out and tidy the place.[89] By the 1890s this arrangement had become common in northeast bothying districts; the cooking and cleaning might be done by the wife of a farm servant, by the kitchen maid, or by a woman hired to take charge of the bothy full-time.[90] In an extreme example, a bothy was built on the Haddo estate in Aberdeenshire which consisted of two cottar houses separated by a large communal kitchen. One cottar house was the bothy, while the other was occupied by a married farm servant whose wife serviced the bothy.[91] Many bothies remained, of course, where the men had to do their own cooking; in these cases the men would sometimes pay the kitchen maid to cook their Sunday lunch. Despite the improvements after 1850 many bothies, like many chaumers, remained rough, hard, comfortless places. The first general secretary of the Scottish Farm Servants Union — a union which had its roots in the northeast — argued that even in 1914 bothies were generally dirtier and less inviting than chaumers.[92] The housing of unmarried male farm servants, in bothy or chaumer, was still no bed of roses.

We started out with a simple distinction between chaumer, bothy, and lodging with a married farm servant or crofter. We can now see that the situation was a good deal more complex than that. The Haddo bothy was midway between bothying and lodging with a married servant. Some observers still saw the situation where a cottar's wife or the kitchie deem came to cook and clean the bothy as 'the bothy system', while for others it was a new social institution — the 'out kitchen'.[93] The simple conceptual distinction between bothy and chaumer fails to capture the rich variety of modes of housing unmarried farm servants; yet it is a distinction which we have to use to examine the spatial distribution of different modes. That distribution was important ammunition in Begg's moral crusade, and it gives us clues about social relations of production.

In the eighteenth century the custom in all northeast counties had been for unmarried men to be lodged in the chaumer and boarded in the kitchen. But differences between districts within the northeast begin to appear in the 1790s. Bothying began to spread up Strathmore into southern Kincardine.[94] Over time it strengthened its hold in this area;[95] by the 1840s we can see from the New Statistical Account that the bothy was the dominant mode of housing unmarried men in the parishes of Garvock, Fordoun and Laurencekirk, and that bothying had penetrated to Nigg on the southern outskirts of Aberdeen city.[96] The minister of Garvock viewed its spread with a clerical distaste that was already common and would by 1865 be universal:

> That vile and demoralising system of banishing male servants from the *ha'board* to bothies, or apartments where they must eat as well as sleep by themselves, has unfortunately found its way into this sequestered parish. It may be advantageous in a *present* or economical point of view; but is most disadvantageous for moral, intellectual, and religious improvement. In fact, many of them are really hot-beds of irreligion, immorality and vice; and consequently, of mischief and ruin not only to the rising generation, but to society in general.[97]

By the late 1860's 'a bothy is to be found on almost every farm in the lowland district of Forfarshire and Kincardineshire';[98] a conclusion supported — for Kincardine — by evidence from Fettercairn, Kinneff, and Laurencekirk. The Deeside parish of Banchory Ternan, on the other hand, had few bothies.[99] This distinction between northern and southern Kincardine in the typical mode of housing unmarried men remained unchanged through the rest of our period — in the 1890s most men in Laurencekirk, Fetteresso and St. Cyrus were bothied, while in Banchory Devenick most men were chaumered.[100]

In the case of Aberdeenshire, bothying seems to have made no inroads until the 1830s.[101] But there is a hint in 1836 of some bothies north of the Dee,[102] and the Rev. James Cruickshank recorded in his account of Turriff in the New Statistical Account that

> It is a matter of regret that this very interesting portion of the population (farm servants) is by no means in a healthy state, and that a demoralising system, adopted, no doubt, for convenience and, perhaps, economy, has in several of our large agricultural establishments been introduced — we mean 'the bothy system', which, if not abandoned, or checked and placed under proper control, must eventually bring with it a train of evils alike prejudicial to the temporal interests of master and servant, and assuredly most injurious to the spiritual interests of the latter, a large and valuable class of the community.[103]

Where modes of housing can be identified in other parish reports, however, the chaumer still appeared to be unchallenged.[104] Bothying slowly permeated Aberdeenshire in the middle decades of the century. In 1849, 530 men were in bothies in the county; but this still represented a mere five per cent of the male farm servants — 10,953 of them in 1851.[105] The editor of the *North British*

Agriculturalist made a tour through the county some ten years later. He found that the proportion of men in bothies rose as one moved south-westwards from Buchan to Deeside, towards the 'bothy county' of Kincardine. Yet the proportion remained small. In northern Buchan it was zero; even on Deeside the bothy was less in evidence than the chaumer.[106] This was the high tide of bothying in Aberdeenshire. Ten years later the tide was ebbing. Evidence given to the Royal Commission on the Employment of Women and Children in Agriculture notes the existence of bothies in only two parishes — Ellon and Rayne — and then on an insignificant scale. By contrast, bothying was unknown in a large number of parishes spread right across Aberdeenshire.[107] The 1890s saw a mixed pattern, but the bothy seems not to have made any sort of comeback in the preceding two decades. Only in Tarves and Methlick was it claimed that bothies were increasing in number;[108] and these parishes were comprised in the Haddo estate which, as we have seen, had idiosyncratic notions about what constituted a bothy. The Rev. Cruickshank would have been relieved to know, if he was still alive, that bothying was dying out around Turriff.[109] The last three bothies in Insch closed in 1895.[110] The chaumer held sway in Clatt, Kincardine O'Neil, Turriff, on the Duke of Richmond's estate near Huntly, in King Edward, Alford, Tough, Leochel-Cushnie, Keig, Tullynessle, Auchterless, Kintore, Longside, New Deer, Methlick, Fintray, and Midmar.[111] If we except the preposterous suggestion that bothying was the predominant mode of housing unmarried men throughout Buchan[112] — probably the result of lax use of concepts — then the only area where bothying was stated to be important was Ellon.[113] By 1914 it could with truth be claimed that 'there are scarcely any bothies in Aberdeenshire';[114] a judgement supported by evidence from Monymusk, the extensive Haddo estates, Turriff, Strathdon, and Towie.[115]

The bothy seems to have penetrated Banffshire even less than Aberdeenshire. There is no mention of it in the New Statistical Account, nor in the evidence to the Royal Commission on the Employment of Women and Children in Agriculture.[116] It was claimed to be the typical mode of housing unmarried men in only one parish in the 1890s — and that, curiously enough, was the upland parish of Aberlour.[117] By contrast, the chaumer was stated to be typical of Banff, Botriphnie, Mortlach, Gamrie, Cullen and Boyndie.[118] Thus the general pattern for the counties of Aberdeen and Banff is a complete lack of bothies until 1830, then a slow increase to a peak around 1860. After this date — the date of Begg's moral crusade — bothying falls away.

The remaining area shows a curious pattern. In Moray and Nairn the chaumer was unchallenged until the second half of the nineteenth century.[119] But after 1860 farm servants were imported to the Moray lowlands from Ross-shire,[120] and they brought the bothy with them. By 1870 bothies were to be found in Drainie, Urquhart, Speymouth and Cawdor (but not in Spynie).[121] By the 1880s bothying was the typical mode of housing unmarried men in lowland parts of Moray and Nairn on all but the smallest farms.[122] In the 1890s, and afterwards, the bothy retained its predominance in Moray; but in Nairn bothying, while common, appeared to be on the wane. The chaumer was now the typical mode of housing unmarried men.[123]

The Royal Commission on Working Class Housing in Scotland reported in 1917 that the predominant mode of housing unmarried male farm servants in Kincardine was the bothy, in Aberdeenshire and Banffshire the chaumer, and in Moray and Nairn a mixture of the two.[124] They were of course quite correct. But we can see that such a bald statement needs qualification. Firstly, the identification of bothy and chaumer was not always the simple task that it might appear. Secondly, the balance between bothy and chaumer was not immutable. It could, and did, change radically over time in particular areas. So what determined the balance? The general opinion today is that it was simply a function of farm size. Small farms had a chaumer, big ones a bothy.[125] This idea has a superficial attraction; Aberdeen and Banff had a lower average farm size than Kincardine, so the preference for the bothy in Kincardine could be a function of farm size. But an eight-pair Banffshire farm had a chaumer[126] — albeit a rather grand chaumer — while bothies were the rule on two-pair farms in the Howe o' the Mearns. And how could a simple equation of farm size with mode of housing explain the upsurge of bothying in the Laigh of Moray after 1860? Clearly we need to look for an alternative explanation.

That explanation lies in the social relations of production. The strong growth of capitalist agriculture in southern Kincardine, not balanced by the creation of new peasant holdings, led to an assertion by large farmers of the desirability of relations of production unmediated by conceptions of 'kindly relations', and an early acceptance by farm servants of the bothy as part of these quintessentially capitalist relations of production. When Buchan farmers moved into the Howe of the Mearns after 1900 they tried to bring the chaumer with them; but the local farm servants resisted the loss of the independence of the bothy and the farmers gave in.[127] In Aberdeenshire and Banffshire, by contrast, capitalist agriculture had not yet transformed relations of production to the extent that farm servants would accept that bothying was preferable to being chaumered. The fact that Begg's moral crusade put the slow penetration of bothying in these counties into reverse gear, while it made no impact in southern Kincardine, shows the point very clearly. The really puzzling area remains to be discussed, however. Conditions in the Laigh of Moray appeared to be just as advantageous for the early development of typically capitalist relations of production as were those in southern Kincardine — and yet bothying made headway in the area only after the immigration of Ross-shire farm servants after 1860. This is a puzzle that needs detailed investigation; which we are unable to give it here.

(c) *Married men*

Married male farm servants occupied a cottage on the farm rent-free as a part of their fee. The cottage — or 'cottar house' — was rented to the farmer by his laird as part of the farm's fixed equipment. The farm servant was thus technically a tenant of the farmer. A few estates tried the experiment of the laird letting cottages direct to farm servants.[128] Evidence suggests that an expansion of this arrangement would have been popular with married servants: the reason usually advanced is that cottage repairs would be undertaken more speedily and conscientiously,[129] but there may be a deeper reason. For the servant to hold his cottage from the laird rather than the farmer would have removed the farmer's ability to use the tied cottage as a bargaining counter and would have transformed the married farm servant into something close to a crofter.

Table 4.11

Married farm servants' allotments, northeast counties, 1885[130]

	Percentage of male farm servants with		
	Potato ground	Cow's grass	Land
Aberdeen	9.9	2.9	0.1
Banff	9.0	1.9	0.0
Kincardine	9.0	1.6	1.3
Moray	23.0	2.6	0.0
Nairn	52.4	2.7	0.0
Northeast counties	12.0	2.6	0.2

The married farm servant received money wages (negotiated in the annual 'cottar market') and perquisites as well as his cottage. These perquisites comprised customarily defined amounts of staples — oatmeal, coal or peat and so on — together with the cottage garden, and milk and potatoes or rights to graze a cow and plant potatoes in the farmer's fields. Table 4.11 shows that these perquisites varied markedly between northeast counties.[131] Only some ten per cent of farm servants in Aberdeenshire, Banffshire and Kincardine had a right to plant potatoes in the farmers' fields as part of their fee, while twenty-three per cent of Moray cottars and a massive fifty-two per cent of Nairn cottars had this right. The difference partly reflects the smaller proportion of married servants in the northeast's central wedge, but not entirely: it is evident that in Moray and Nairn the right to plant a drill of tatties was more widespread than in other districts. In Aberdeenshire and Kincardine, on the other hand, a few cottars still sublet parcels of land from the farmer. Add to this the general fact that the cottage garden could range from a mere kailyard to something closer to a croft,[132] and we can see that the seemingly clear distinction between landless married farm servants and poor peasants evaporates. The two peasant fractions interpenetrated in terms of land occupation as well as being linked through the circulation of labour power between peasant and capitalist agriculture.

The nature and physical condition of the cottar house varied enormously. In the first half of the nineteenth century many of these houses previously had been the dwelling houses of engrossed crofts. James Black gives an account of the typical Buchan cottar house in 1850, and the description mirrors accounts of croft houses from other sources:[133]

The side walls are scarcely five feet in height. The door, at the one side of which are piled up irregular blocks of stone to form a buttress to the wall, and prevent it from falling, is so low, that an ordinary-sized person on entering requires to bend considerably to the ground; and the gables, considerably above the level of the side-walls. are built with turfs, and do not even at the apex exceed the height of the side-walls above four feet. The whole mason-work is composed of undressed surface-stone and mortar. An entire absence of every idea of comfort in the occupants is shown by the carelessness which has allowed the walls to be deprived to a great extent, through the influence of the draught and wind, of their cementing mortar, which at first gave them a degree of compactness, and a power of resistance to the weather; but they are now quite open, and almost permeable by the wind in every part.

The roof of the house is covered with turfs, which are overlaid with straw; and above all may be observed quantities of grass-weeds growing up through the straw, and forming, by their decomposition, a very convenient receptacle for the lodgement of the rain from heaven.

The floor is depressed below the level of the surrounding ground, and is exactly the same material as the subsoil of the surrounding area on which the structure is raised. It is full of inequalities, arising from the nature of its composition, from defective drainage, from heaps of circumjacent refuse, and from the slovenly habits of the inmates. It is therefore frequently damp, and thus serves to augment the general discomfort. There are two small windows in front, each containing four small panes of glass. There is no ceiling. You see immediately above you, from the floor, the rafters and turfs densely covered with soot, and, in damp and rainy weather, giving off to the furniture below a copious covering. Nor is any attempt made at separate apartments by regular partitions. One or two bedsteads, placed in the middle, divide the building into two portions, familiarly denominated a *but* and a *ben;* in the one of which, being used as a kitchen, and, for this reason, the more comfortable of the two, the whole family sit and eat, and converse together.

The internal arrangements of the building are as defective as its construction. An air of discomfort pervades its whole interior. No regard has been paid in its construction to the principles of ventilation; and both its external and internal economy bespeaks the want of all ideas of order, cleanliness, and personal comfort. Above and beneath the bedsteads are huddled various articles of clothing and of useless furniture, imparting by their decomposition a peculiarly offensive influence to the air, which is detrimental to health, and prolongs and aggravates disease.[134]

Cottage-building had lagged behind the erection of new steadings in quantity and in design — Robertson's 1811 survey of Kincardine has a plate showing a splendid new slated steading on a six-pair farm with a pair of rude stob-thatched cottages tucked away in a corner[135] — but the kind of ramshackle cottar houses described by Black was slowly replaced by something better. This replacement was in train in 1850,[136] when Black was writing, and the pace quickened thereafter. The activities of the Highland Society, the Cottage Association and similar bodies — and the related controversy over the moral consequences of farm servant accommodation — hastened improvement. The Haddo estate built fifty-six new cottages between July 1861 and March 1864 — less than three years.[137] The Duke of Richmond and Gordon was said never to have refused a request from a tenant farmer on his estate to build cottar houses.[138] Findlay of Aberlour bought his estate in the difficult years of the 1880s. In the next nine years he built thirty-five new cottages for farm servants and renovated twelve more, in addition to building twenty houses for labourers.[139] There were many estates whose owners pushed forward the construction of new cottages, then; but there were many others — and these not always small estates — where cottage building was neglected scandalously:

> The Duke of Fife had never such a thing as a workman's cottage on his property. The tenants were left to do as they liked; the Duke drew the rents. There was not a cottage formerly in the parish built by the landlord.[140]

Improved cottages were never palatial, even where they were built. It is instructive to compare cottage plans in successive editions of Stephens' *Book of the Farm,* the standard handbook for the young Scottish aspirant farmer. The first edition, published in 1844, had plans for model cottages based firmly on a translation into modern materials of the 'but and ben' pattern which had typified previous Scottish croft houses and cottar houses. The plans for farm houses — even for houses on large farms — showed a corresponding modesty of design and provision.[141] But as the years and the editions rolled by, designs for farm houses grew ever more ponderously ornate and pretentious. By contrast, even in the 1908 edition designs for cottages showed little change from those six decades before. The but and ben remained the model, and any rising expectations were satisfied by the provision of a separate bedroom under the stairs leading to the floored attic. In some of the 1908 plans the division of the cottage's interior space was still brought about by judiciously placed box beds.[142]

Thus the efforts of philanthropical individuals and organisations, and the torrent of plans of model cottages that poured out throughout the second half of the nineteenth century, had their most important effects not in increasing the living space available to the farm servant and his family, but in improving the fabric of his cottage. The architectural determinism so characteristic of that period gave moral force to improvements in design and construction. Cavity walls, casement windows, fireplaces, ashpits, privies, drainage — these and many other topics received detailed attention in pamphlets, essays and reports, thus (hopefully) ensuring that the new cottages presented fewer public health problems (and, by extension, moral problems) than those that they replaced. But the failure to build bigger cottages, while obviously related to the desire of landlords to build as cheaply as possible (a constraint on architects which is always present in the literature) has another origin as well.

Those benevolent proprietors who did try to give the farm servants on their estates more commodious cottages often found that their attempts were not appreciated. When two-storey cottages were erected, their inhabitants not infrequently refused to sleep upstairs.[143] The new cottages may have been healthier than the old thackit hooses; they were certainly more draughty. The increased cost of heating a larger, colder house meant that some rooms were not used. It also meant, on many occasions, a nostalgia for 'the warmth and peat reek of the auld house'.[144] This nostalgia could become a spur to action: '[They] put this preference to practical effect by flitting, when they have a chance, from the new to the old'.[145]

One can argue, then, that landlords are not to be blamed for building small cottar houses. But many nineteenth century commentators blamed lairds on other grounds. By 1870 most north-eastern cottar houses may have been of improved design and construction, but that did not mean that there were enough of them. It was asserted in the late 1860s that only in southern Kincardine was the supply of cottar houses adequate; elsewhere the supply was 'quite insufficient'.[146] Two decades later it was claimed that cottage accommodation in Aberdeenshire was adequate at Strichen, Kintore and Monymusk, and insufficient at Mintlaw, Alford, Auchterless, Turriff, Huntly and Methlick. In Kincardine, there were not enough cottar houses round Stonehaven. A general shortage of cottar houses was noted throughout Banffshire and in upland districts of Moray and Nairn.[147] The situation had not changed by 1914; there were enough cottar houses in Kincardine, but elsewhere there was a shortage.[148]

There are grounds for believing that in fact there was not a shortage of cottar houses in any part of the northeast. Analysis of Valuation Rolls shows many cottar houses standing empty and others occupied not by farm servants but by day-labourers or country craftsmen.[149] There were many complaints in the latter decades of the nineteenth century that a shortage of cottar houses drove married farm servants to lodge their wives and families in towns and villages and fee as single men;[150] but searches in the census enumerators' books for northeast villages have failed to find these alleged multitudes.[151] As with the distribution of modes of housing unmarried men, the pattern of many cottages relative to the farm servant population in southern Kincardine, rather fewer in the Moray lowlands, and many fewer elsewhere in the northeast makes sense in terms of the agrarian structure and social history of the area. Lawson makes the point in his 1881 account of cottages in Angus and Kincardine:

> There has been a great improvement in the condition of the ploughmen's cottages during the past twenty-five years. Many of them at that time contained only one big room, generally subdivided by the furniture, which then consisted of two box-beds, and a chest of drawers and cupboard combined, which piece of furniture went under the appellation of 'the press'. These articles all being of wood, and fully six feet high, formed the partition. There was no room behind this, but only the 'loom', and the time-

honoured 'pirn-wheel' — the one for weaving linen, the other for winding the bobbins. In many cases the room was too small for division. The floors were generally of earth or consolidated clay, unless in the pavement districts, where they were usually roughly-dressed flags. The stone and turf and clay walls, with thatched roof, were quite common during the last quarter of a century; but the cottages came in for their share in the general improvement. I will briefly state the reasons which led to the improvement of the cottages, and their late adoption in some parts of Angus and Mearns. Before steam was applied to the linen trade, the greater part of it was wrought by hand-loom, and there were many cottages sprinkled all over the interior districts of the counties, similar in construction to what I have described, which were inhabited by hand-loom weavers, who carried their work to and from the nearest town, village, or hamlet. These people could all be had for field labour when required, and the result was that neither farmers nor proprietors sought to build cottages for the ploughmen, whose wives and families were not necessarily required for out-door labour. But the application of steam to the linen trade, and its gradual development, rapidly drained the non-agricultural population to attend to the machinery in the manufacturing centres. So rapidly did the linen and jute trade grow, and so great did the demand become for labour, that even the ordinary workers of the farm could with difficulty be had, and it was only when these weavers removed that the Strathmore farmers especially felt the want of the cottage system . . . The coast district never suffered so much from the scarcity of labour. The farms there were more closely cropped, and required more regular field labour, and had, moreover, earlier adopted the cottage system, and thus did not feel the difficulty so much during press of work.[152]

Thus the distribution of farm cottages within the northeast is explicable in terms of the agrarian structure of different districts. South Kincardine — and, to a slightly lesser extent, the Moray lowlands — had an adequate supply of cottages because the attrition of the local peasantry had compelled capitalist farmers to rely more heavily on married servants for permanent labour and on specialised day-labourers for casual wage work. Farmers thus pressed lairds to build an adequate supply of cottar houses and of labourers' houses. In the northeast's central wedge, by contrast, farm service still was but one stage in a peasant child's agricultural career, and poor peasants still provided much of the capitalist farmer's casual labour. There was no need for as many cottages in these districts then — but when, after 1880, this peasantry moved into crisis, then cottar houses sprang up on farms throughout Aberdeenshire, Banffshire and north Kincardine. These new cottages did not reflect lairds' perceptions of a moral obligation to house farm workers adequately. They reflected a sea-change in the social formation of the central wedge: the northeast peasantry's growing inability to reproduce itself as a class. More evidence for this shift comes from changes in diet.

Diet

In the 1840s all peasant fractions shared a similar diet. In Leochel Cushnie, for instance

The usual food of the farm servants is porridge and milk for breakfast: for dinner, potatoes, bread and milk with perhaps oatmeal brose, made with greens, for supper.

They do not have beer, except when there is a deficiency of milk. In harvest time an allowance of beer is given then. The diet of the small crofters is much the same . . . The usual diet of paupers on the roll is much the same with that of the small crofters. They are generally furnished with a little milk from the nearest farmer.[153]

Peasants in parishes near sea-coasts ate some fish,[154] those in grazing parishes buried in the depths of the hills ate some flesh meat.[155] These apart, however, northeast peasants had a vegetarian diet produced on the peasant holding or on the larger farm where the farm servant was fee'd. A little food was being bought in by the 1840s: peasant farmers were beginning to catch their betters' addiction to tea, much to the scandalised distaste of ministers and other moralists. But peasant diets still were sharply differentiated from those typical of capitalist farmers. Butcher meat, wheaten bread, French wines and spirits already formed a significant part of muckle farming families' food; and peasants and capitalist farmers tended to buy food into the farm in a different manner. In Udny, for instance, 'the farmers take most of their groceries from Aberdeen. Many of the crofters and small tenants barter their butter and eggs with the country retailers, for groceries.'[156]

Table 4.12 shows the weekly menu for the farm servants on an Aberdeenshire capitalist farm which had a good reputation for feeding its servants. The table shows that even in 1880 oatmeal was the basis of the diet,[157] appearing in a bewildering variety of forms as brose, porridge, sowens, skirley, and oatcakes — the latter called bread locally. Oatmeal was displaced occasionally by broth, various prepared forms of potato, and fresh, dried or cured fish.[158] Fish played a larger part in peasant diets of the 1880s than had been the case four decades earlier. The reason was that the tentacles of the new railway network reached into many lowland areas, and allowed the fishwife with her creel to establish rounds among the country people.[159] Fish provided some protein, but most protein still came from milk. One looks in vain for butcher meat in Figure 4.12: the nearest that the servants came to eating meat was on Sunday, when the water in which the farm family's fowl or bit of beef had been boiled was used to make barley broth for the servants. Those servants' diet was still relentlessly monotonous, a procession of 'brose, broth, tatties and porridge, with cabbage, kale and chappit neeps (mashed turnips) as variants'.[160] The solid core of the diet, in two senses, was brose:

In the mornin' we got brose,
As mony's we could belly in;
Willie Buchan made the brose,
And, faith, he didna mak' them thin.[161]

This diet was still shared by all peasant fractions — by small farmers and crofters, by farm servants lodged in bothy or chaumer, and by day labourers. Despite its monotony, the diet was adequately nutritious,[162] apart from certain vitamin deficiencies which gave rise to a scurvy-like condition called 'Scotch fiddle'.[163]

Bothymen had to cook their own food, unless a woman was hired by the farmer to do it for them. The farmer provided firing and customarily defined amounts of basic foodstuffs — oatmeal (usually six and a half bolls per man for the six months' fee), milk and potatoes. With these ingredients alone bothy food would have been even more monotonous than that in the farm kitchen; but the bothymen had a reputation for eking out their meagre protein allow-

Table 4.12

Weekly menu in the kitchen of an Aberdeenshire capitalist farm, 1880[164]

	Breakfast	Dinner	Supper
Sunday	Porridge with sweet milk, fried salt or fresh herring, butter (liberal supply), oatmeal and skimmed milk.	Barley broth made with beef or fowl, potatoes, oatcakes and skimmed milk.	Drinking sowens, potatoes boiled in jackets, skimmed milk cheese, oatcakes and skimmed milk.
Monday	Brose, sweet milk, oatcakes and skimmed milk.	Yaval broth, potatoes, oatcakes and skimmed milk.	Milk or water porridge, oatcakes and skimmed milk.
Tuesday	Same.	Stoved potatoes, oatcakes and skimmed milk.	Turnip brose and mashed turnips, oatcakes and skimmed milk.
Wednesday	Same.	Milk broth made with barley, skimmed milk cheese, oatcakes and skimmed milk.	Mashed potatoes, oatcakes and skimmed milk.
Thursday	Same.	Mashed potatoes, skirley, oatcakes and skimmed milk.	Milk brose, oatcakes, and skimmed milk.
Friday	Same.	Kale or cabbage brose, kale or cabbage mashed with milk, oatcakes and skimmed milk.	Stoved potatoes, oatcakes and skimmed milk.
Saturday	Same.	Soup potatoes, oatcakes and skimmed milk.	Milk porridge, oatcakes and skimmed milk.

Note: Yaval broth is made with yaval oats, the second oat crop taken from a field after it was ploughed out of grass. They would be of inferior quality compared with the first year (ley) oats. Stoved potatoes (stovies) are potatoes simmered in a saucepan with salt and a little fat. Skirley is oatmeal fried in fat with — if available — a little onion. Sowens is a sourish gruel made with the fermented inner husks of oats that were returned by the miller separate from the sweet oatmeal.

ance by unofficial means. Both bothymen and married servants were great poachers of rabbits and hares,[165] and many men still have stories of fishing for the guidwife's chickens out of the bothy window while the farm family was at Kirk. Without these additions bothy food was as cheerless as the surroundings:

> Their breakfast and dinner consist of brose only . . At supper, when there is rather more time each man, acting as cook in his turn, makes strong well-boiled porridge. A Scotch pint of new milk is supplied to each man daily, to be used with his brose or porridge. If at any time they have potatoes to supper, these are poured on a sack, spread on the floor, instead of a table, and are eaten with salt. It must be borne in mind that there is no one to keep alive their fire, or see that water is boiling, so that the first thing necessary to be done by them when they come home from toil, often drenched and cold, hungry and weary, is to kindle their fire and prepare their hasty meal. In summer, when no fire is needed, they are permitted to go with their *cappie* and meal to the master's kitchen for boiling water. As this is sometimes supplied with a grudge, they content themselves with *cold steer,* which is made by using cold water instead of boiling water with their brose.[166]

The cottar, like the bothyman, received foodstuffs as part of his fee from the farmer. He eked out these staple supplies with eggs from his hens, poached rabbits and, perhaps, with a pig.[167] His garden gave him some vegetables — usually the unholy trinity of neeps, tatties and kale that still dominates northeast vegetable gardens and greengrocers' shops. Like his unmarried brethren, however, until the last few decades of the nineteenth century the cottar maintained his household largely without recourse to bought-in provisions.

But in the last decades of the century things did begin to change. In the decade from 1881 to 1890 an annual average of thirty-three quarters of oats left Cairnhill, Turriff — a progressive Aberdeenshire capitalist farm — to be milled for consumption on the farm. In the following decade the average dropped to twenty-seven quarters.[168] Part of the fall might be due to a slightly smaller squad born of attempts to handle 'the great depression' through labour economies; but there is no doubt that most of the fall came from dietary changes. Unmarried servants demanded more varied food in the farm kitchen. Jam, tea, and even butcher meat began to appear regularly — if not frequently — on the kitchen table. Where oatmeal was supplied as part of the bothyman's or cottar's fee, it became common for the servants to sell a proportion of the meal to the miller, and to use the money to buy wheaten bread, jam and other noxious delicacies.[169] The culinary skills of bothymen, in particular, were strained to the utmost by these new demands: Willie Buchan might have been an expert maker of glutinous brose, but with much of the food now being brought into the bothy he was lost:

> They bought fish, meat, and tins of fruit, but they were abominable cooks. They had to throw out a lot of stuff. Sometimes they had not time to cook it again, and they had just to eat it as it was.[170]

Table 4.13

An Aberdeenshire married farm servant's diet in the early twentieth century[171]

Breakfast (5.30 a.m. for father; 8 to 9 a.m. for rest of family). Brose (oatmeal and a little salt stirred up with boiling water and milk poured over), with some oatcakes or white bread and milk. Sometimes oatmeal porridge with tea and oatcakes; more often white bread with treacle, syrup, or jam.

Dinner (12 noon). Boiled potatoes, plain or mashed with chives (a small kind of onion, known as 'size' in some parts), sometimes potato soup or milk soup. Oatcakes or white bread, with milk or tea; seldom cheese. In season, cabbage, turnips, kale, or brose made with vegetables. On Sundays (from 1 to 2 p.m.) Scotch broth, with beef and potatoes, bread, milk, or tea.

Supper (6.30 p.m.). Tea, oatcakes, white bread, rolls or biscuits, sometimes fish (yellow haddocks) or cheese. Syrup or jam, seldom much butter. Home-made jam is used as much as possible.

This Aberdeenshire cottar's diet shows that oatmeal, potatoes, milk, turnips and kale remained important elements of the peasant's food in the new century. But the list of foodstuffs bought in has lengthened remarkably — tea, treacle, syrup, jam (even if this was home-made then sugar would have to be purchased), cheese, beef, biscuits, fish. The references to bread are particularly interesting. 'Bread' had always meant oatcakes in the northeast: the vast majority of local kitchens had no oven to cook leavened dough. Little wheat had been grown in the region, and that little had disappeared after 1870. Yet Table 4.13 shows wheaten bread making very considerable inroads in this cottar's diet. The decline in the proportion of the household's food that was provided from the peasant holding (or, in the case of farm servants, as perquisites from the farmer) — a decline dramatised by the replacement of oatcakes by white bread — shows that the peasantry was being transformed. In the sphere of consumption, as of production, peasant fractions were being drawn inexorably into the world of commodities. The characteristically ambiguous peasant attitude to the market, with cash crop production subordinate to the production of the household's subsistence, was giving way to more wholehearted production for the market. As the grocer's shop and travelling van slowly replaced the peasant's oat field and milk cow, so the peasant's mode of production was falling to pieces.

5

Mannie and Men: the Farmer and his Workers

There's some that sing o' Cromar Fair,
An' sound out an alarm,
But the best song that e'er was sung
It was about the term;
The term-time is drawing near
When we will a' win free,
An' wi' the weary farmers
Again we'll never fee.

Wi' broad-tail'd coats and quaker hats,
And whips below their arms,
They'll hawk and ca' the country roun'
Until they a' get farms;
Their boots a' glawr and glitterin',
Wi' spurs upon their heels;
An' though ye ca' the country roun'
Ye winna find such deils.

They'll tip you on the shoulder
And speir gin ye're to fee;
They'll tell you a fine story,
That's every word a lee;
They'll tell ye a fine story,
An' get ye to perform;
But, lads, when ye are under them
Ye'll stand the raging storm.[1]

BOTHY ballads are a unique cultural production of northeast Scotland. The three stanzas quoted above are from a particularly interesting song — 'The Weary Farmers'. What makes this song interesting is its class-consciousness — its identification of all farmers (or, to be more precise, of all capitalist farmers) as the class enemies of all farm servants. This attitude is very rare in the songs; we will see that the usual pattern is an attack on one farmer at one time. This absence of more general criticism suggests that the typical social relations of production holding between farmer and farm servants had not been fully transformed by the dominant capitalist mode of production. We will see in this chapter that this suggestion is true, but needs qualification. Let us begin by looking at the internal organisation of the farm labour squad.

The Organisation of the Labour Squad

In discussing the numbers of people involved in northeast agriculture we had, in the last chapter, to make a fundamental distinction between family labour and hired labour.[2] We will see that this distinction had some importance for relations of production. But in the work of the farm it was not very important. It mattered less in the fields that a man was the farmer's son or a farm servant than that he was second horseman, third coo baillie, or whatever. The labour squad had its own rigid internal structure, and whether the occupant of a particular position was a hired worker or a family worker was a secondary matter.

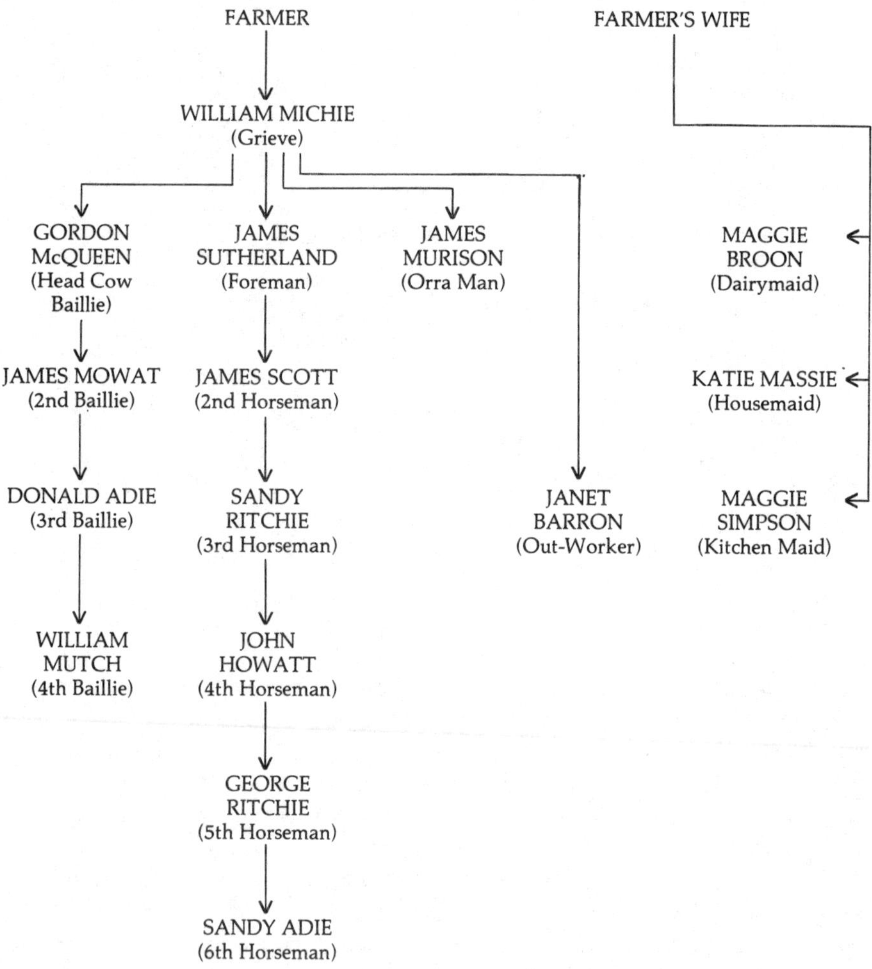

Figure 5.1 Chart of the formal organisation of Ardlaw, Longside, in 1880[3]

Figure 5.1 shows the organisation of labour on Ardlaw, Longside, in 1880. It shows a large labour squad — sixteen of them, excluding the farmer and his wife. Ardlaw had no family workers in 1880, as we would expect would be the case on such a large farm. The figure shows two main lines of command devolving from the grieve, marking the principal division of labour on all northeast holdings larger than a croft. One command line goes through the ranks of the horsemen, from the foreman — the most senior working ploughman — down to the halflin with the sixth pair. The other line goes down the cattlemen. These command lines were hierarchical but independent: a man low in either line would take orders from one higher in that line but a coo baillie would not take orders from a horseman[4] and a horseman would never take orders from a cattleman. The orraman's work brought him into both lines of command as his varied duties led him to work with horses one day, and with cattle the next. When working with neither horses nor cattle his orders — like those of the female outworker — came direct from the grieve. The deems (maids) stood outside this role structure. There was no clear hierarchy among deems, though it was quite common for the dairymaid to supervise the other maids. Another important factor separates maids from all other farm servants. The basic sexual division of labour on the farm made the steading the man's responsibility, the house the woman's. Thus maids, alone of farm servants, were hired, fired and controlled by the farmer's wife rather than the farmer.[5]

The functional division of labour shown in Figure 5.1 was only one facet of the internal organisation of the labour squad on every northeast farm in our period. Superimposed on this division of labour one found a status hierarchy. 'The Ardlaw Crew' makes the point neatly. Written by the head cattleman on the farm in 1880, Gordon McQueen, the song does not start, as one might expect, by singing the praises of coo baillies. The first man mentioned is the grieve, followed by the foreman and the junior horsemen in strict order of seniority. Next comes the orraman. Only at this point do we hear of the cattlemen, who again appear in strict seniority. The men accounted for, McQueen turns to the female servants. The dairymaid has her stanza, followed by the housemaid and the kitchen deem. The female outworker brings up the rear of the procession.[6] This order is not accidental; it is an accurate reflection of the status hierarchy within the labour team. Women had lower status than men, and female outworkers had lower status than maids in the house. Hence the successful pressure of maids in the latter half of the nineteenth century not to be required to work 'baith out and in'. Among male servants work with horses had higher status than 'coo wark'.[7] Hence the most prestigious position, the grieve (always filled by a former horseman) or foreman, was followed by the specialised ploughmen and then by the orraman who was called on occasionally to work horses. Only then does one come to the cattlemen.

This status hierarchy was independent of income. We saw earlier[8] that northeast cattlemen earned wages comparable with, and sometimes above, those of horsemen. Yet horsemen always outranked coo baillies in terms of status. The point was made symbolically at neep hoeing time, in the organisation of the hoe gang in the field. The usual status hierarchy was altered slightly; the women were put at the head of the line where their manual dexterity would set a cracking pace, and the grieve or working farmer hoed at the end of the line so that he could keep an eye on those pariahs, the junior cattlemen. These exceptions apart, the hoe gang showed to any passer-by the status hierarchy of the farm labour squad. Immediately behind the women came the foreman, followed by the horsemen in strict order, the orramen and the cattlemen.

Every aspect of the farm's daily life was permeated by this hierarchical organisation:

> The etiquette of the bothy and stable was equalled in rigidity only by that of the court of Louis XIV. Each man had his place and was taught to keep it. For the second horseman to have gone in to supper before the first horseman would have created as much indignation as an infringement of precedence at Versailles. The foreman was always the first to wash his face in the bothy at night; it was he who wound the alarm clock and set it for the morning, and so on, and so on. The order of seniority was as strictly observed between the second horseman and the third, while the halflin always got the tarry end of the stick . . . But the foreman had pride of place in everything. He slept at the front end of the first bed — that is, nearest the fire; he sat at the top of the table in the kitchen; he worked the best pair of horses; and he had the right to make the first pass at the kitchen maid.[9]

I am told[10] that at breakfast time the foreman alone, as most senior unmarried servant, was allowed to lift the sneck of the kitchen door. He walked in, followed by the rest of the male servants in strict order. He picked up his brose caup, put meal in it, a pinch of salt, and then poured in boiling water. He then sat, as John R. Allan tells us, at the head of the table. The other servants made their brose in their turn, and sat down. Until the foreman lifted his spoon no other servant could start to eat his brose. If the foreman chose not to speak to the kitchie deem then no other servant would dare speak to her. This may sound overdrawn, but other sources emphasise the enormous power and influence of the most senior male servant within the labour squad:

> . . . It depends entirely upon the character of the man who happens to be 'grieve' or 'foreman' upon the farm, what the behaviour and style of talk indulged in at meals, and during the leisure time after hours, amongst the company of lads and young women who assemble in the kitchen shall be. His influence may be for good; but it may also be for evil, and the master is practically helpless to find it out or check it.[11]

We will see below that the most senior male servant occupied a key role in the social relations of farmer and farm workers.

Different groups within the division of labour on the farm enjoyed different degrees of work autonomy. We saw in Figure 4.3 that beef cattlemen on

Tipperty, Logie Buchan, in 1870 worked a ten and a half hour day between 5.30 a.m. and 8 p.m. It was a long day, but the coo baillie had a great deal of autonomy. It was common for a cattleman to have a group of cattle to look after — perhaps all the cattle in one byre — and he was effectively left to his own devices as to how he organised his work. As long as the cattle in his charge were kept fed, watered, groomed and mucked out, then the farmer was satisfied. Dairy cattlemen in the belt of intensive dairy farms around Aberdeen city were exposed to a tighter work discipline born of the unrelenting routine of twice daily milking.[12] Orramen enjoyed a high degree of autonomy, from the nature of their work:

> James Murison is our orra man,
> He keeps ticht baith close and pens,
> And ony orra job like that,
> Siclike as muck the hens.[13]

But one group of male workers had very little autonomy: the horsemen.

We saw in the last chapter that the horseman's day revolved around maximising the efficiency of his pair.[14] The two-hour mid-day break was not to give the horseman a rest — he had to spend a large part of it feeding his horses and doing odd jobs about the steading — but to rest his pair. This constant pressure to make the best use of horse-power gave rise to an iron discipline among horsemen. They were expected to be skilled at their work, and lack of skill was punished simply but effectively:

> I remember one time bein' at a farm masel — ye ca'd oot muck wi' your pair at that time, ye used your pair at that time. The foreman went out first, and of course I was oot ahin', man; I happened til miss my hin'-sling, o' my cairt, like — and the horse gaed agley, dae ye see. He [the foreman] pulled me oot-ow'r the cairt and thrashed me wi' a back chain — richt ow'r the back wi' a back chain. An' the fairmer was passin' at the time, and never lookit near hand. I was aboot 14 or 15 year auld at that time.[15]

The horsemen left the steading to go to the fields in strict order, the foreman first, followed by the second, third and so on. If more than one pair was ploughing a particular field, then the same strict order was preserved — the foreman's pair was lined up next to the dyke, then the second man's, then the third horseman's. The foreman led the same procession back to the steading, and watered his horses first. To break these iron rules spelt trouble, even for an orraman like John Reid, who never worked as a specialised ploughman:

> I'd been working in a different field from the foreman, and trying to be home when he came home. But I was first home, just by mere chance, and I was at the horse-trough with the orra beast when he came in about. He gave me a swearing — he said I had no damn business to be there until he came with his pair. I was supposed to stand back. This is the sort of thing that went on. He started harnessing his horses first. You were not supposed to take a collar from a peg until he did it. And at the same time you were

supposed to be at his heels when he went out — you didn't have to fall behind just because of that. You had to be ready when he wanted you.[16]

We see this strict order among horsemen even in the photographs of the horsemen on a particular farm taken by travelling photographers (Plate 4).

Farm Servant Mobility and the Feeing Market

Observers from outside the farming industry inveighed against the nomadic habits of farm servants throughout our period. It is undeniable that unmarried male farm servants rarely stayed at any farm for more than one six-month fee. Married men stayed rather longer, but here again the roads would be crowded on the annual cottar term-day with farm-wagons carrying the cottar's belongings and families to new farms. But this frequent flitting did not mean, as many observers asserted, that farm servants put down no roots in the course of their wanderings. The most remarkable feature of farm servant mobility, apart from its frequency, was the narrowly circumscribed limits of that mobility. Figure 5.2 shows the travels of two farm servants in the Garioch in the mid-nineteenth century.

The first of the two careers shown is that of Alex. Mitchell. Born and raised in a poor peasant colony on the flank of Bennachie at Edingerrock, Premnay, he was on the farms between May 1855 and May 1863 — when he became a coachman. He left farm service in the winter term of 1861-2 to return to school and to help on the family croft; but the rest of this period he spent in service, beginning as a herd loon and ending as second horseman. Mitchell stayed on one farm — Johnston, Insch — for three terms, and graduated during that time from little loon to big loon. That apart, he never stayed more than one term on any farm during his career in farm service. Yet, as the map shows, after moving as far away from his birthplace as Fyvie while he was a herd loon, Mitchell eventually settled down in the upper Garioch and spent the rest of his time in farm service, crossing the Bennachie range every six months between the Garioch and the Vale of Alford.

Figure 5.2 also shows the movements of Mr Cook in the Garioch and upper Strathbogie between 1865 and 1896. His manuscript account of his career is incomplete before 1869, but from May 1869 to May 1871 he fee'd as a single man and moved at every term. In May 1871 he fee'd as a cottar and shifted at every annual term for the next four years. He spent two terms at Mains of Lesmoir, Rhynie, between 1875 and 1877, and then shifted in May 1878, 1880, 1882 and 1883. His first fee as a married man had been as an orraman, but a year later he fee'd as a foreman and two years after that — in 1874 — as a grieve. A grieve he remained. In May 1885 he went to Mains of Williamston, Culsalmond, as grieve and stayed there until 1896, when he took the tenancy of a small farm. Apart from his last two places — Mains of Williamston and, before that, Murriel, Insch — his entire farm servant career, eighteen years of it, had been spent in an area measuring eight miles by six miles in upper Strathbogie.

These careers seem not to have been at all unusual. A farm servant moved around until he found an area he liked, and then stayed there until he left farm service or decided to fee in another district. This latter decision might be made because a servant wanted to move to a bothying district, as many Aberdeen-

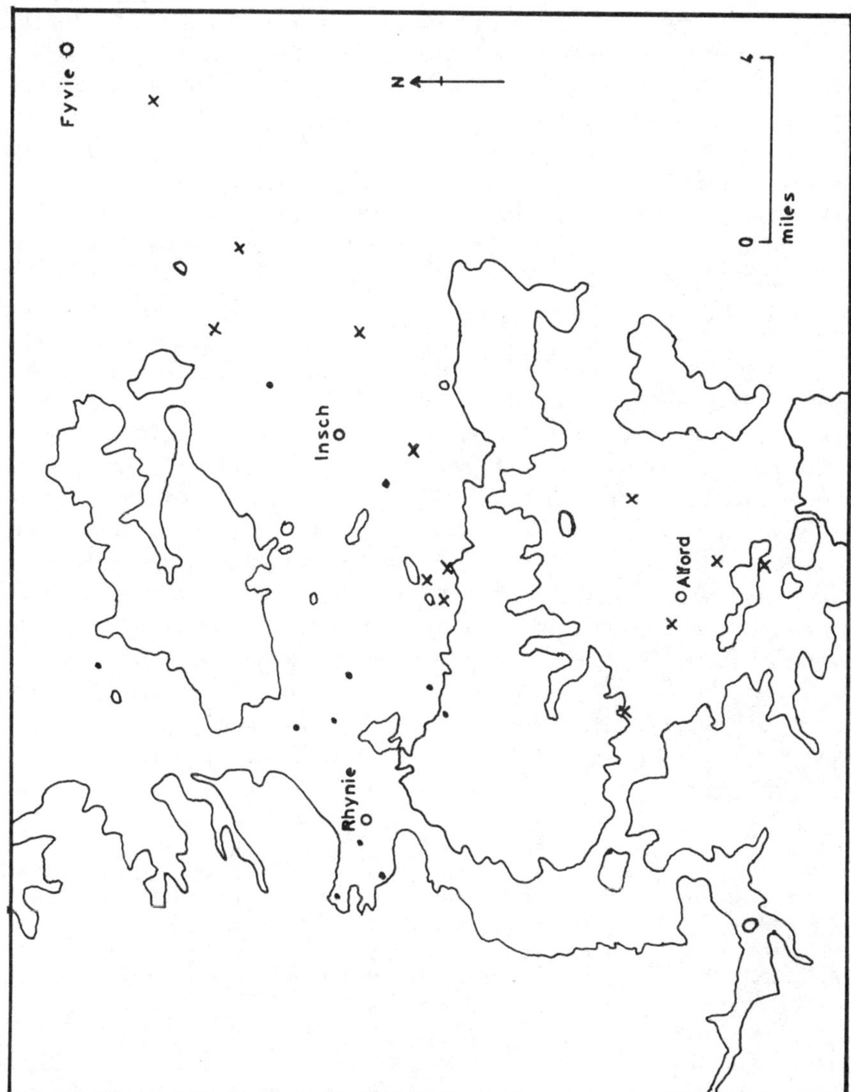

Figure 5.2 Two farm servant careers.[17]
Note: cross represents Mitchell, dot represents Cook. Circles are village settlements.

shire and Banffshire men did, or it might be precipitated by the fact that he had got the kitchen maid pregnant and did not want to marry her.[18]

The decision whether or not to stay on a farm for another term was not a decision for the farm servant to make. He had to wait for 'the speaking time', a couple of weeks before the local feeing market, to see if the farmer would ask him to stay. The farmer decided which servants he wished to keep and asked them 'Will ye bide?' Any servant not asked knew that he must take his chance in the market. If he was asked, then the servant would negotiate terms for the next six or twelve months just as if he and the farmer had met in the feeing market. This market was the cockpit in which social relations of farmers and servants stood out most sharply.

Some specialised feeing markets had a considerable antiquity. Insch village was created a burgh of barony under a charter granted in 1677. This charter allowed the new burgh to hold four hiring fairs in the year: from their timing the four seem to have been two markets for unmarried servants, a cottar market and a hairst market.[19] In many parts of the northeast these specialised feeing markets did not appear until the nineteenth century, however. Before that time farm servants were hired on a specified day during one of the local fairs — Aikey Brae, Lowrin Fair, St James Fair, Paldy Fair and so on; fairs which on other days were concerned with the sale of cattle, horses and linen rather than labour power.[20] But as competition from railways and urban markets slowly withered these fairs so, in the middle decades of the nineteenth century, specialised feeing markets were established at towns and villages throughout the northeast.[21] Thus the first feeing market at Forres was established in the mid-1830s.[22] By the mid-century the specialised feeing market had become much the most important setting for the hiring of permanent farm servants. A loon's first fee might be arranged privately between his father and a neighbouring farmer, and many maids were recruited privately by the farmer's wife: these apart, however, all farm servants were hired in the feeing market.

Negotiations in the feeing market were controlled by a rigid etiquette. Here is the farm servant's viewpoint:

> You never spoke first. You never approached the farmer. You always gave the farmer a chance, the initiative, to come and ask you, 'Are ye lookin' for a fee, laddie?' And if you were you said 'Aye'. 'And would ye like to come to me? I've a place —' wherever it was. Maybe you knew it and maybe you didn't. You thought about it. He told you what you'd have to do, and the wages were the last thing to be spoken about.[23]

And here is the farmer's view of the feeing market:

> Ye just went there and stood up, and the farm servants were standing there, very often in a boodich together, but ye just had to draw the attention of what ye thought was a likely person, and begin and bargain with him. Ye see, it wisna jist the wages —

there was ither things that they thought they would like to make a bargain about — when they would get a day off. Holidays. You see, there was no half day on Saturday, and they would sometimes stick up for an extra day at the term. 'When we get hame, the nicht o' the term, or the nicht efter, ye'll gie us anither day' — something like that. And some o' them would say, 'We'll get St Sair's Fair, and we'll get Lowrin' Fair, will we?' It just was there were certain things that they would request. And the bargain was made there — there was nae use speakin' about it after you were home, no, because that widna stand law.[24]

The bargain between farmer and servant was usually sealed with a dram at the farmer's expense and with the payment of arles — a token sum paid by the farmer to symbolise the bargain, and to pay the servant's expenses in moving his possessions (usually merely his kist) to the new farm at the term. Once made, however, the bargain was indeed binding:

> The farm worker is still a servant who enters into a contract of service of a binding nature and for a lengthy period . . . If he fails to fulfill his engagement, the farmer may confiscate any part of the wages that may be due to him, and may sue him for damages for breach of contract. If the farm servant deserts his master and another farmer employs him before the date of the expiry of his engagement, the first master may sue the second for 'harbouring a deserter'.[25]

Farmers often took advantage of their systematic advantage under this contract of service.[26] For example, in July 1891 six farm servants left Berryleys, Keith, because of their dissatisfaction with the food provided in the kitchen. Brought to Court,

> The whole of them gave evidence to the effect that the milk was sour and often stinking; some of them described the milk as being 'rotten', and that it curdled when it was poured on brose. The usual round of the daily diet was brose for breakfast, rice and milk for dinner, and porridge with skimmed milk for supper. They had got flesh meat once since Whitsunday, but they stated that on that occasion it was part of a sheep that had died.[27]

The evidence was not seriously challenged. Nevertheless, the farmer won his case on the simple point of desertion of service, and was awarded damages.

Throughout their existence feeing markets were regarded with profound distaste by observers from outside farming. When it was suggested in 1850 that the Aberdeen market be moved from the Poultry Market in Queen Street — a nice hole-in-the-corner situation — to the heart of bourgeois Aberdeen in Castle Street, Baillie Alexander Henderson opposed the proposal. In his opinion 'the feeing markets should by no means be encouraged, and . . . the citizens should not be called on to submit to any inconvenience on account of them'.[28] Big markets like Muckle Friday in Aberdeen and Porter Fair in Turriff — the largest of the lot; in 1882 more than 3,000 farmers and servants jammed the main street of Turra[29] — did cause inconvenience to the genteel sections of the towns and villages thus temporarily blighted, and the drinking and wenching that came with this rare holiday for the servants raised respectable folks' usual hackles against the lower orders enjoying themselves too noisily and visibly. Accounts of feeing markets by 'respectable' observers vary little; here is a typical account:

> . . . Nothing can be more calculated to lower the moral position of the agricultural labourer than these degrading exhibitions. Upon the hiring day, nearly the whole rural population flock to the 'market'. Great numbers give up their places for no other purpose than to obtain the holiday. Assembled in the county town, they crowd its principal street, packed up in one dense and promiscuous mass, and there remain, like the man in the parable, 'idle in the market-place, waiting to be hired'. No attempt is made to inquire into character, and the labourers who thus exhibit themselves like oxen, are judged like oxen by their physical appearance only. The long day done, the thoughtless lads and lassies compensate themselves for the tedium of the morning by evening orgies, which many of the women, at least, may have life-long cause to regret.[30]

Attempts were made to remove some of the more distasteful aspects of feeing markets, notably drunkenness. In 1859 the Huntly Temperance Society bought a Temperance Tent, with dining-room, which they took to local markets.[31] By 1891 this had become routine; the *Aberdeen Free Press* reported the riotous goings-on at Insch — 'The market was a comparatively small one. Temperance refreshments were served in the Public Hall, and were well patronised during the day. Some local young ladies supplied piano music.[32] Despite these attempts, feeing market days remained fairly wild occasions, however — particularly in the evening after the close of the market.

Drinking and wenching were only one facet of feeing markets that bourgeois observers found obnoxious. Another aspect, well expressed in the passage quoted above, was the belief that the markets were formless: that farmers hired servants simply by feeling their muscles, and that a good character and a reputation as a good workman counted for nothing.[33] It was this belief that underlay the persistent attempts to replace feeing markets with registers, on which a farm servant wishing to change farms could place his name after producing a certificate of good character and competence from his last employer. Such a register was established in Forres in 1838; by 1841 it contained 1,110 names,[34] but it seems to have folded soon afterwards. In 1849 we hear of an attempt by Sir John S. Forbes to found a similar register at New Pitsligo,[35] but this seems to have met with just as little success. Further attempts were made, however. The Aberdeenshire Central Labour Registration Association was founded in the mid-1860s, but by the time of its third annual meeting this organisation, too, was on its last legs: 'four of the Registrars have either done no business or neglected to report it, and other three or four offices have scarcely been patronised.'[36] In the following decade the Royal Northern Agricultural Society tried once more to get the registration bandwagon rolling.[37] For a time they seemed to be having more success: several societies, led by the Strathbogie Farmers' Club, had started registers.[38] By the early 1890s 'little loons' and maids for the farm house were almost all recruited through registers,[39] but this was scant reward for half a century's pressure to abolish feeing markets. In 1870 James Black wrote that 'Every attempt to put an end to [feeing markets] has resulted in failure. Neither register offices nor any other substitute that has been proposed has ever made any headway against them.'[40] A decade later Lawson reported that in Kincardine only a few grieves and foremen were recruited through press advertisements: the vast majority of male farm servants still were fee'd in the market.[41] So it remained to the First World War. A few male farm servants were fee'd privately or by advertisement in 1914, but the vast majority still went through the market.[42]

Why was this persistent pressure to abolish markets so unsuccessful? The principal reason is that the crusade against the markets was founded on a false premise. To an observer a feeing market seemed intoxicatedly incoherent. To farmers and servants in the market it seemed much less anarchic. Gordon quotes an imaginary conversation between a farmer and a servant in an upper Banffshire market, and then continues thus:

> . . . In order to appreciate the force of the foregoing conversation, it is necessary to understand that the farmer and the labourer *(sic)* are very well acquainted with each other's character, and in all probability had each mentally decided to come to terms . . . The farmers, of course, prefer to engage those men of whose capabilities they are previously cognizant, and the ploughmen and other hands naturally choose to be 'fee'ed' by persons of whose good treatment of their servants they are pretty well aware.[43]

Interview evidence supports the conclusion that many farmers and servants meeting in the market had a pretty accurate apprehension of the capabilities and proclivities of the other:

> *How did you know which man you wanted in the fair? Did you know anybody? Did you know any of the servants who were there?*
>
> Well, yes now, that's quite right. I'm glad ye've mentioned that. Ye'd maybe see someone that ye'd seen working at another place, or ye might see the son of somebody who was a good man, and a useful man, and ye'd think like father like son, and the son might be a bit like his father. I've had that quite often in my time — a young man following on and taking the job that his father had. Oh yes, yes.
>
> *So if a man had a good name, he'd have a better chance of getting a fee?*
>
> There's no doubt about that. A man's reputation goes before him, and it was perfectly true even in the feeing market days, because a man who had a good name, well, he began to be known among the farmers, and he had a far better chance, and would get a better wage.
>
> *And if a man had a bad name, he'd have trouble getting a fee?*
>
> Oh, there's no doubt about that, no doubt at all about that. And some of them, well, if there was anything against them, ye see, if men were plentiful and places scarce, they certainly would be unemployed. And no dole, or anything of that kind.[44]

A farmer looking for new servants would know many men in the market, then; and if he did not know a man in whom he was interested, then he probably could get his 'character' from somebody else in the market.[45] Alex. Mitchell mentioned three occasions when he got a fee at the Alford market on the recommendation of somebody in the market; on one occasion the recommendation came from a farmer with whom he had served before, while the other two recommendations came from former fellow servants.[46] But it was not only farm servants that had a character in the market:

> There's a story of a feeing market, that the farmer and the loon met, and argued for a while. The farmer said, 'Weel, I'll along an' get your character, laddie.' And of course he got the loon's character and went back to fee the loon. 'Ah!' the loon said, 'but I've got your een, an' I'm no' comin'!'[47]

The fact that many farmers and servants meeting in the feeing market were already well acquainted explains why the pressure for registers was so unsuccessful.[48] But that fact meant that the farmer — even a large farmer — had to maintain a good reputation in the market. This gave farm servants a strong card in their dealings with farmers, a card which they used to great effect.

Reputations

We have seen that the contract of service between a farmer and his farm servants gave systematic advantages to the farmer. Many farmers went to law when deserted by one or more servants; but a much greater number did not. Doubtless part of the reason was a profound distrust of the law and, more particularly, of lawyers — who often doubled as factors. But there was a more important reason for farmers' forbearance. As early as the 1790s the minister of Alford noted regretfully that '. . . The dislike of getting what they call a bad word, among servants, generally ties up the farmer from applying for that redress which the law affords.'[49] The 'bad word' was spread through gossip — facilitated by the frequent shifting of farm servants at the term — and by the northeast's own institutionalised form of gossip, the bothy ballads. Many ballads are not about the iniquities of farmers. Many rejoice in the deems' willingness to allow the farm lads in their beds:

> Jean McPherson maks my bed,
> She sleeps between me and the wa',
> And when I climb in ower at nicht,
> She says 'Buchan Geordie, ca' awa.'[50]

Other songs record pride in strength or occupational skill, like the many harvest songs, or the wistfully nostalgic 'Mill of Boyndie':

> When I was young and in my prime,
> Guid-fegs, like me there wisna mony;
> I was the best man in the Boyne,
> And foreman lang at Mullnabeeny.

When I engaged wi' Johnny Mull,
My fee was five pounds and a guinea.
It was to drive the foremost pair,
Ay, and lead the mennies o' Mullnabeeny.

I had a hat upon my heid,
It cost me mair than half-a-guinea,
Held a' the lasses in Brannan Fair
Gazing at the foremost man o' Mullnabeeny.[51]

But the most important group of bothy ballads for our purpose is that group that attacks a particular farmer. We saw in the last chapter that the view from outside farming saw housing to be the major problem facing northeast farm servants. It is at once surprising and very suggestive that the 'roch' conditions of chaumers, bothies and cottages go unremarked in bothy ballads. The complaints of farm servants lie elsewhere, in the diet provided in the farm kitchen and in the amount of work demanded by the farmer.

Recruiting sergeants were to be found in all the major feeing markets.[52] They knew that one of the surest ways of attracting loons to the colours was to compare army food with that of the farm kitchen:

It's awa' wi' your taties, your meal, and your kale,
Your ill-seyed sowens, and stinkin' ale,
Your soor-milk fye, and breid fired raw;
So list, bonnie laddie, and come awa'.[53]

We have seen that the typical diet of farm servants in our period was relentlessly monotonous; but it was generally accepted.[54] It was only when the food in the kitchen was much worse than usual that the servants objected. In extreme cases, like that of Berryleys, Keith quoted above, they might break their contracts and leave. It was more usual for them simply to bellyache about the food;[55] and their complaints often found their way into a song. Since feeding the servants was the farmer's wife's responsibility it was she who was the principal target in such songs. Here is part of one of the best songs about food, 'Newmill':

I hadna been a week come hame
When I could plainly see
The tables they were rather bare
And they did not suit me.

The breid was thick, the brose was thin,
The broth they were like bree;
I chased the barley roun' the plate
And a' I got was three.

So unsuccessful was my search,
My spoon I did throw doon;
The knife and fork were seldom seen
But in the carpet room.

Now farewell, Maister Langnecks,
And to your daughters three;
But the turkey-hen that lives her lane,
I think I'll lat her be.[56]

The other main ground for complaint in bothy songs is 'hashing' — the farmer driving his farm servants too hard. 'Drumdelgie' is a song of this kind; Henderson calls it 'The Hash o' Drumdelgie'.[57] This song was the model for many others which focus on the unusually harsh routine of work on a particular farm.[58]

A common pattern in all these songs is to compare the farmer's words in the feeing market with his actions on his farm. In 'Sleepytown', for example, the farmer is all reasonableness in the market:

If you and I agree, he says,
You'll have the fairest play,
For I never bid my servants work
Above ten hours a day.

But things are rather different when the servants are on the farm:

Do ye refuse what I command,
Ye scoundrels that ye are?
Ye bargained for ten hours a day,
Refuse them if ye daur.[59]

This contrast is not fortuitous. Those songs to do with bad food and working conditions on a particular farm were composed to be sung in the feeing market:

Come all you jolly ploughboys,
I pray you have a care,
Beware o' going to Swaggers,
For he'll be in Porter Fair.

He'll be aye lauch-lauchin',
He'll aye be lauchin' there;
And he'll hae on the blithest face
In a' Porter Fair.

Wi' his fine horse and harness
Sae weel's he'll gar ye true;
But when ye come tae Auchterless
Sae sair's he'll gar ye rue.[60]

The song might be written by a servant on the farm — like the 'Poet Clark' — or it might be written by a specialist;[61] but the purpose was the same. Potential servants in the market learnt that conditions on that farm were bad, and they could refuse to fee to the farmer or could demand a higher fee to compensate for the bad conditions. In extreme examples the farmer would be forced to go further away to recruit servants:

Sae he'll gang on some twenty miles,
Faur people disna him ken
And he'll engage some harvest hands
And bring them far frae hame.[62]

Thus the 'dislike of getting what they call a bad word, among servants' that so infuriated the Alford minister was a wise policy for a farmer to adopt. The chance of being attacked in a ballad restrained farmers from trying to screw the maximum amount of work out of their farm servants at minimum cost. The need to maintain a good reputation is the major reason why farmers did not always pursue their legal claim against defaulting servants: even when, in the latter decades of the nineteenth century, bargain-breaking had become so common that 'rascal fairs' had to be held a week after the term-day in major centres to allow deserted masters and servants who had not fancied the places that they had fee'd to work to make new bargains.[63] And of course the need to maintain a good name in the feeing market bore particularly heavily on capitalist farmers, since they had to hire a much larger proportion of the labour team on their farms than did peasant producers.

But it was not just farmers that needed a good reputation in the market. We saw earlier that a good 'character' would give a farm servant an advantage in the market. Reputation was of particular importance for a horseman, since 'horse wark' was both the route to the top positions in farm service and an essential skill for any man to learn who hoped later to take a farm. For these reasons, and also because of the strict work discipline among horsemen, relations within the ranks of ploughmen were fiercely competitive. This competition went on throughout the year — horsemen would tramp around on Sunday looking at the quality of other men's work in the fields — but it came to a head at ploughing matches. A horseman cashed in his reputation in the feeing market; but he made that reputation at the ploughing match:

> Nobody who knows anything of ploughmen at all can deny they are, after their own fashion, a vain community. By being vain we mean that there is a certain display about them, and an inherent wish to outstrip their fellows in the same rank of life. At ploughing matches and other agricultural competitions they can be seen throwing their whole souls into the contest, not so much for the pecuniary prizes as to have it said they were the victors.[64]

An important ploughing match would attract a large and knowledgeable audience — James Allan remembered a championship match at Balhaggarty, Inverurie, in 1872 at which nineteen thousand spectators paid for admission.[65] To win such a match would make a man's name over a wide area. The reputation of James Morrice — the most famous northeast ploughman of the earlier decades of the nineteenth century and William McCombie's foreman on Tillyfour, Tough, for many years — spread far beyond the five counties. The same was true of the young Alexander Gray[66] and, a couple of decades later, of 'the Aberdeenshire champions — the Beatons of Fyvie — whose fame has almost become national'.[67] Such a man's reputation would be spread in gossip and song; Ord's collection has a song, typical of many, which shows the making and breaking of reputations at the ploughing match, and also the strong cultural levelling tendencies that were so marked in the northeast's central wedge:

Willie Petrie he cam' frae New Deer,
To tak' the prize he had nae fear,
But he got, 'Hey, my mannie, here',
That day among the ploomen.

Jim Forbes thocht he'd tak' a prize,
A bonny lass is mair his size,
He'll stick to them if he is wise,
An' syne he'll be a plooman.

The champion plooman stood the test,
But young Jim Whyte cam' out the best;
And Davie Fife got some lang-faced
That day among the ploomen.

The judges cam' frae far an' near,
To put them richt they had nae fear,
But some wad sae their sicht was puir
That day among the ploomen.[68]

The Clean Toon

The need for a farm servant to maintain a good name underlies a curious feature of Northeast farm life, the 'clean toon'. This was the occasion when every hired servant on the farm left at one term day. Observers found it quite inexplicable.[69] Even Joe Duncan saw it as merely a spectacular example of the general unsettled habits of farm servants.[70] But consider these two stanzas from 'The Barns o' Beneuchies':

At the Barnyards o' Beneuchies he has lang been a grieve,
But come May the twenty-saxt he has to pad, I believe;
For he's seigned at his men till his maister's gien him's leave,
For he canna get them up in the mornin'.

But it's May the twenty-saxt will be here in a crack,
And we'll a' leave the Barns never mair to gang back,
We'll gang blithely doon the road like an ill-tongued pack,
Singin', Kempie he can follow in the mornin'.[71]

There is an implication here that the other servants have to leave the farm when the grieve leaves. That implication becomes explicit in 'The Ardlaw Crew':

By now our gaffer's leavin',
And nae langer can we bide,
So we'll gang to the hirin's,
Baith Strichen and Longside.[72]

Why should the fact that the most senior hired man was leaving cause a clean toon? John R. Allan, a radical farmer, suggests that it was the other servants' fear of what the next man might be like: 'He might be a bigger bastard than the last one.'[73] But this seems too simple an answer, for farm servants felt a very strong moral obligation to leave when a clean toon was declared:

What happened if the grieve didn't bide? Was there always a clean toon if the grieve left?
In the old days there was, yes. In the old days there was always a clean toon. I rejected this, because once I had to leave because of this, and I didn't want to leave. I think it was a foolish thing.
But you did leave?
Oh yes, you had to leave.
What would have happened if you hadn't left?
Well, it was an unwritten law. You had to leave.[74]

This unwritten law existed to protect the most senior hired man in his dealings with the farmer. The grieve or foreman occupied the crucial mediating position between farmer and farm servants:

A grieve is in the position of one who runs with the hare while keeping pace with the hounds . . . He has to get a fair deal for his fellow workers and at the same time get fair work for his employer.[75]

In most of the 'hasher' songs it was not the farmer himself who set too hard a pace for the farm servants, but the grieve or foreman — acting on the farmer's instructions.[76] If the most senior man proved incapable of maintaining that pace, then the hasher farmer would threaten him with the sack:

He'll say unto the foreman chiel,
'Keep aye the steady grind,
And dinna let the orra lads
Fa' idle back behind.'

'For I pay ye a' guid wages,
And sae ye maun get on,
And gin ye are not able,
There's anither when ye're done.'[77]

Clearly it was in the servants' interest to protect the grieve or foreman in this situation in order to block the farmer's attempt to screw too much work out of his servants. The clean toon was some defence. The farmer knew that if he did not ask the most senior man to bide, then he would have to replace the entire hired labour team. A farmer who repeatedly suffered a clean toon would find great difficulty in hiring new servants and would find it impossible to hire good servants.

But why did all the farm servants leave when a clean toon was called, those who did not wish to leave as well as those who had decided already to shift at the term? The answer lies in reputation. A servant who did not shift at a clean toon would lose his 'character'. In *Johnny Gibb* the Clinkstyle foreman, Tam Meerison, was not well thought of by his fellow servants because he had not stood up to 'the auld soo' — Mrs Birse — in a dispute over the food in the kitchen. But then

> A day or two before the feeing market day it had leaked out that Tam was bidin', and the fact considerably intensified the feeling of contempt which his fellow-servants had been in the habit of occasionally displaying towards him. They had hoped to leave Clinkstyle with a clean toon again, and they were angry at being disappointed.[78]

The Horseman's Word

A good name was a valuable asset for any northeast farm servant, but for one group it was of particular importance. The fierce competition for promoted posts in the ranks of horsemen, and the high prestige that went with those posts, made a good reputation even more important for a horseman than for other farm servants. If a man hoped to become foreman, then he had to have a name as a skilled ploughman. This required skilled control of horses, and this in turn gave a foundation for the Society of the Horseman's Word.

The Horseman's Society was a secret society.[79] Despite this fact it has generated a large, if scattered, literature. Folklore scholars trace the origins of the Society in the northeast — the epicentre of its distribution — back to witchcraft[80] or to a very old horse cult.[81] Oddly enough, however, contemporary observers saw its roots not in witchcraft and magic but in craft guilds — particularly freemasonry and a derived guild among meal millers.[82] The Miller's Word was a clear example of a guild concerned with restricting access to the craft — the miller's was a highly desirable position in pre-improvement days[83] — and cultural lumber lying around from days when witchcraft was widely practised in the northeast was used to restrict access. The candidate for admission was required not to go to church for three years, and in that time to read through the Bible backwards three times.[84] Such goings on would not pass unnoticed even in the latitudinarian northeast. As the Horseman's Society grew in the early nineteenth century — it was not until that time that the replacement of oxen by horses as the main draught animals on the farm gave a basis for the Society — so the new organisation among horsemen carried over many features of the older Millers' Society.[85] The initiation ceremony retained witchcraft elements. An initiate had to bring with him a blasphemous sacrament — a loaf of bread, a jar of jam and a bottle of whisky. The ceremony was conducted by a Minister of the Word, using an upended bushel of corn as an altar. The initiate had to answer a parodied Catechism. The climax of the ceremony came when he had to 'shak' the Aul Chiel's hand' — alternatively a stick, a heated spade or a stirk's foot smeared with phosphorus to make it glow in the dark — to the accompaniment of chains dragged along the floor. Great care was taken to cash in on the uncanny reputation of millers as well. To enter the Horseman's Society was to 'gang thru the c'aff hoose door'; the chaffhouse was part of the water-driven threshing mill to be found on very many northeast farms — a dangerous and, by association with milling, an uncanny place.

But there is one crucial difference between the Millers' Society and that of the Horsemen. The principal object of the millers was to restrict access to the craft; their guild was strongly exclusive. The Horseman's Society, on the other hand, was inclusive. The Word was not to be given to a loon under sixteen years of age, but this injunction was frequently broken.[86] It was not age that mattered, but occupational specialisation:

> First I got on for baillie loon,
> Syne I got on for third,[87]
> And syne of course I hid to get
> The Horseman's grippin' Word.
> A loaf of breid to be ma' piece,
> A bottle for drinkin' drams,
> Ye couldna get thru' the c'affhoose door
> Without yer Nicky Tams.[88]

This emphasis on inclusion meant that soon after a loon began to work with horses he would be approached to join the Society. Sometimes the approach would be made directly, by a fellow servant. On other occasions the local taste for the eerily dramatic effect led him to receive through the post an envelope containing a single horse hair. When he had stewed for a few days over the meaning of this cryptic message, then a made horseman would approach the loon directly. The Society tried to recruit every man working horses in the district. Few loons disdained its summons. In getting the Word he was promised, in theory at least, control of two sets of unruly creatures — horses and women.[89] If he did refuse the summons, then the loon faced the usual, and usually effective, northeast sanction — gossip:

> The man who has not got the Horseman's Word is looked upon as an 'ootlin' aboot the [farm] toon. He is made to feel uncomfortable at every turn. At kirk or market, marriage, kirsnin, ball, or raffle, the non-horseman is shunned, whispered about, pointed at, and otherwise made to feel uncomfortable. These doings have very seldom to be resorted to, as young ploughmen are as a rule eager to pass through the mysteries of horsemanship, so much so that they will endeavour to falsify their age if possible in

order that they may sooner attain the much coveted diploma. Like the rest I was anxious to be counted a man. Had I not driven the orra beast for twelve months at 'The Mains', and had now got charge of the second pair at 'Mossies'? Moreover, the lan' side horse was a biter, and the foreman could give me no information as to how to manage him because I was not a brother.[90]

This passage brings out well the limitation to members of the Society of knowledge about the skilled control of horses. The famous 'miracles' of the Horseman mystery — to reist a horse (to stop it in its tracks so that no man can make it move) and to make a horse move when no other man could — were open to a man who knew the medicinal tricks of the Society.[91] But the tips that made a loon just starting as a horseman into a skilled ploughman were generally less dramatic than that: 'That's the best secret; be kine to them, Johnnie, be kine to them, and they'll seen dee onything ye want them.'[92] Careful training and advice from a senior horseman soon made an apt pupil highly skilled; but that skill was often put down to supernatural causes:

I've heard that men who were really initiated in the Horseman's Word could make horses do almost anything. I've heard of a man coming out with two carts loaded with turnips, out of a very dubby field. And rather than wet his feet he walked out himself, threw his reins over the horses' backs, and they came out themselves.[93]

This degree of control over horses might seem uncanny to an outsider. But in the early nineteenth century George Robertson had noted of Kincardine horsemen that 'In the management of horses, the servants are dextrous to a fault; they govern them wholly by the tongue, and never use the hand-reins. It is astonishing to see the docility of the horse. He turns to the right or left, or goes forward, or follows his guide like a dog, just as he is bidden . . . Even at the plough, there are many young men who will not use [hand reins].'[94] It was skill, not magic, that the young made horseman was taught.

The Society of the Horseman's Word was an early, and remarkably successful, form of trade unionism among the largest group of northeast farm servants.[95] It served other purposes as well, however. It was an important prop supporting the rigid internal hierarchy among the horsemen on a farm. It was also a 'working-class hell-fire club'.[96] Lubricated by the whisky provided by the initiates, the horseman meeting often turned to the bawdry that was so vital a part of the rural underground in the northeast. The Society could also have a direct effect on relations upon a particular farm. The widespread belief, among farmers as well as farm servants, in the efficacy of even the more preposterous parts of the Horseman mystery could be turned to purposes very like those of critical bothy ballads:

. . . Though horsemen did not indulge in sit-down strikes or walk-outs, it was sometimes possible, by playing on the mystic power of the Word, backed up by a supernatural throwing of kail runts and clods, or nocturnal dirling of muck-barrows across the close, to persuade a farmer to improve living conditions, or his wife to diversify the diet.[97]

Relations of Production and Modes of Production

How were social relations between farmer and farm workers affected by differences in mode of production between farms? At first sight the mode of production appears not to have been important. The Horseman's Society was equally strong among ploughmen on large and on small farms. Bothy ballads attacked middle peasant farmers as well as capitalist farmers. But as one probes the evidence it slowly becomes clear that the mode of production did have an important effect on social relations. The effect was not mechanical: the cash nexus was not the only thing that mediated the relationship between a capitalist farmer and his servants. Rather one finds a complex interaction between the form of control exercised over servants on different kinds of farm — personal control by the middle peasant, bureaucratic control by the big capitalist farmer through his grieve[98] — and the cultural expectations that farm servants brought into the encounter with their 'mannie'.

We have seen that most farm servants were the children of peasant farmers. Their experience of the peasant's mode of production gave a deep colour to their expectations of 'proper' relations between farmers and farm servant. They did not complain of housing conditions which bourgeois observers found inexcusable, for conditions had been no better on their fathers' crofts. They did not find the rigidly hierarchical organisation of the labour squad irksome: it was a continuation of the tyrannical patriarchy of the family farm. When they did complain it was because expectations of equal treatment, derived from family farming, had been offended. These expectations usually were not offended. Where hired and family labour was mixed on one farm, then the male workers all slept in the bothy or chaumer. In the work of the farm it was one's position in the labour squad that determined one's status, not whether one was the farmer's son or a farm servant.

But there was one aspect of northeast farm life where family workers and hired workers were usually treated differently — the matter of food. Bothy ballads often record chaumered servants' grumbles about the quality of food served to them in the farm kitchen, but these grumbles were given added point by the servants' perception that the farm family was eating more palatable food 'ben the hoose' in 'the carpet room'.[99] For peasant children fee'd as farm servants this was a double insult. First, the different quality of food served to the farm family and to servants offended against the expectation, derived from peasant life, that the whole household should share a common diet: that they should, in the Russian peasant phrase, eat from the same bowl.[100] Second, the fact that the farm family was no longer eating in the kitchen with the servants — except for some peasant households — symbolised a growing gulf between the farmer and his servants. This decline in commensuality was traced to rising consumption expectations, particularly among capitalist farmers, which made farmers feel that it was socially demeaning to eat with one's servants.[101] This in turn threatened to destroy the 'kindly relations' that allegedly and ideally had held between a farmer and his servants, and to replace a quasi-family relationship with one based firmly and exclusively on the cash nexus. Thus farm servants' complaints about feeding arrangements were concerned with more than food alone: they formed one point of a multi-pronged attack by all peasant fractions on capitalist farmers' attempts to bring social relations of production into correspondence with the dominant capitalist mode of production.[102]

But farm servants had a more ambiguous attitude than other peasant fractions to classically capitalist social relations. The fact that social relations retained strong precapitalist elements while capitalism was the dominant mode of production allowed northeast farm servants to develop strategies against the farmer that were not open to their more proletarianised brethren in East Lothian or Norfolk. The fact that a farmer had to maintain a good reputation if he wanted to get good servants at a fair price gave northeast farm servants the opportunity to prevent what they thought were flagrant breaches of customary relations through the threat of gossip or, in extreme cases, the threat of having a critical ballad written to be sung in the feeing market. The need for a farm servant to maintain a good reputation allowed the development of the clean toon and the Horseman's Society — primitive forms of trade union activity that gave servants some degree of solidarity against the farmer without allowing farmers to identify, and possibly victimise, ringleaders. The 'nomadic' habits of farm servants — particularly unmarried men who, as we saw,[103] formed the great majority of northeast hired men — limited the hold that a farmer could get over his men. The fact that most unmarried men moved every six months[104] gave farm servants considerable independence from the farmer: an independence not dissimilar from that which was such a valued part of the life of another peasant fraction, poor and middle peasant farmers.

This does not mean that farm servants defended every element in the northeast's version of precapitalist social relations. They used an idealised image of social relations in peasant agriculture as a backcloth against which to criticise farmers who sought to push capitalist relations too intensively, but in some ways farm service provided an escape from family labour on peasant farms which, they were only too well aware, did have its drawbacks. Wage labour meant wages: family labour meant working for board, lodging and clothes. A farm servant negotiated his working hours with the farmer in the feeing market: the peasant son on the family holding had an unlimited labour commitment. Farm service gave a loon the chance to broaden his experience and sharpen his skill on farms of different size working different farming systems and modes of production, rather than ploughing and reaping the same small parks on the parental holding. As a class, farm servants adeptly exploited the ambiguities of the northeast's pervasive interpenetration of capitalist and precapitalist modes of production.

This conclusion needs two qualifications. One has to do with space, the other with time. In areas where capitalist production had taken over from peasant production most completely — the sandstone districts of south Kincardine and the Moray and Nairn lowlands — farm servants tended more readily to accept classically capitalist relations of production. These were the bothying districts, where the farmer's lack of interest in the way in which his servants spent their leisure time came to fullest flower. These districts generated no bothy ballads. 'Kindly relations' had little meaning or resonance in such a social landscape: hence in these districts, among this relatively proletarianised labour force with a higher proportion of married male farm servants, the defence of precapitalist social relations was incomprehensible. When immigrant Buchan farmers tried to reintroduce chaumering to the Howe o' the Mearns, after the bothy had been dominant for more than a century, the farm servants refused to play ball. They liked the bothy's freedom, the sense that neither the farmer nor his wife was overseeing their activities too closely. In the northeast's central wedge, by contrast James Begg's moral crusade of the 1860s was enough to roll back the slow penetration of the bothy into Aberdeenshire, Banffshire and north Kincardine.

This distinction between a relatively proletarianised hired labour force in the sandstone districts and a labour force still tightly integrated with other peasant fractions in the northeast's central wedge was a real distinction, though it must not be stressed too strongly. It was reinforced by selective migration. Districts where peasant farming had not been destroyed had a permanent labour surplus. The sandstone districts, where the peasantry was effectively gone by the later decades of the nineteenth century, had a permanent labour shortage. Hence the migration of Aberdeen and Banff farm servants into the sandstone districts,[105] a migration that could be demonstrated by mapping the distribution of the characteristic Aberdeen scythe, with its Y-shaped sned. But the men who left for the bothies of Angus and the Mearns were men who found the 'kindly relations' of the north stifling, who preferred the independence of the bothy to the social control — however tenuous — of the farm kitchen.

As the nineteenth century wore on, so proletarian tendencies began to develop even in the peasantry's heartland. Most bothy ballads seem to date from the four decades between 1830 and 1870: others were written after 1870, but the flow of song seemed to be drying up. The Horseman's Society changed its nature in the latter decades of the century too, as the first struggling attempts were made to establish open trade unions for farm servants. More cottar houses were built, and a higher proportion of men on the farms were now married. The later decades of the nineteenth century saw a slow attrition of farm servants as a peasant fraction, a slow growth of an agricultural working class, a rural proletariat. But the attrition of this peasant fraction was not an isolated phenomenon. It was part and parcel of the slow death of all northeast peasant fractions: the northeast peasantry was in its final crisis.

6
Death of a Peasantry

> With them we may say there died a thing older than themselves, these were the Last of the Peasants, the last of the Old Scots folk. A new generation comes up that will know them not, except as a memory in a song . . .[1]

WHAT killed the northeast peasantry? For Gibbon the answer is the commodity boom of the First World War, with its strong encouragement to capitalist agricultural production. The idea has some appeal: that war clearly marked the end of an era in northeast farming. But the boom in commodity prices merely formed the gale that blew away the withered husk of peasant agriculture. The northeast peasantry was destroyed more slowly, over the last three decades of the nineteenth century and the first of the twentieth: it was a long time a-dying.

John R. Allan gives another explanation in the course of his exquisite elegy for the northeast peasantry:

> As you walk across the lower slopes of the hills you may find a heap of stones that was once a house, and trace among the bracken the rectangle that was once a field. They are melancholy things, witnessing that courage, determination and all the ancient virtues are not enough to bring life out of a stone. A hunger for land drove the people there, and the insatiable hunger of the soil drove them away again. Those ruins are at the stony limit where a human tide spent itself before it began to ebb away.[2]

Once again this explanation has some appeal. It is true that the engrossment of old arable pushed peasant farmers on to ever more difficult and infertile land. But this in itself cannot explain the northeast peasantry's demise: after the clearances of the early nineteenth century the Highland peasantry was forced on to rocky outcrops and barren moor, yet they never lost their commitment to maintain their distinctive peasant mode of production and later mounted a remarkably successful counter-offensive against capitalist agriculture.[3]

The death of the northeast peasantry, like all major changes in social formation, must be explained through changes in the material base — in the intermingled modes of production that gave logical structure to peasant production and to capitalist production. We saw earlier[4] that after 1870 the peasantry's prior indispensibility for capitalist production disappeared as lairds no longer sought to expand the tilled acreage of their estates and as cattle feeders drew ever more of their lean cattle from Ireland. The need for an assured supply of farm servants — previously met from peasant children — was now met through the extensive construction of cottages for married farm servants. As the peasantry was gripped ever more tightly between high rents and low commodity prices, so the exploitation of family labour had to grow ever more systematic and profound. The new compulsory education system of the 1870s gave peasant children an escape hatch from super-exploitation on the family farm. As more and more of them took this route, so the contradiction between independence and discipline that was buried at the heart of the peasant's mode of production slowly dissolved, destroying the peasantry from within.

By 1912 the fact that the northeast peasantry was the mere husk of its former self was plain for all to see. In that year Alfred Russell visited Aberdeenshire for the *Times* newspaper. He gives a matchless account of the reasons for the demise of the doomed peasantry in this, the very heartland of lowland Scottish peasant life:

> This district is well provided with small holdings or crofts, some as small as ten acres, so that a hard-working labourer can work his way up from a croft to a considerable farm. But though many such cases can be cited, few men care to face the toil and self-denial involved; the crofts are far from profitable because they are managed on the same plan as the neighbouring large farms, and there are few openings for the intensively grown special products which should be the mainstay of the small holder . . . The crofters depend mainly upon raising store cattle for their larger neighbours to fatten. The admission of Canadian stores would probably finish off the Aberdeen crofters; their numbers are shrinking already through emigration, and we were informed that there are no applicants from this district for small holdings under the new land Act.[5] Most of the crofters who hold their own are engaged in some other business also — the carpenter, the mason, the postman were instanced; in many cases they do not keep a team, but get their ploughing, etc., done by contract. It is the small holder entirely dependent on his farming who tends to disappear, and the cause is really the rising standard of living and the opportunities emigration offers. For this reason the loss is not entirely to be deplored. Away in the hills, not only in the Highlands, but south of the Forth also, may be seen traces of old crofts where only the sheep and the grouse now abide. The history of these deserted holdings is to some extent being repeated now; the old men persist in the old homes, but their sons will not face the life, and it is not to the interest either of agriculture or the State to try to hold men to such ill-remunerated toil.[6]

Hall's most pregnant insight was that it was the middle peasant — 'the small holder entirely dependent on his farming' — who was in the direst straits. This fraction, previously so strong in the northeast,[7] had been the backbone of the local peasantry. The middle peasant encapsulated all the peasant virtues — it is no accident that the major northeast peasant novels focus on the small farmer rather than the crofter.[8] Through his independence, his balancing of household production and consumption without recourse to the labour market, the middle peasant asserted that the utter triumph of capitalist agriculture was not inevitable. Thus the middle peasantry gave a basis for defensive peasant institutions that rested on the need for a good reputation: bothy ballads, gossip, the clean toon, the Horseman's Society. As the middle peasantry withered in the later nineteenth and early twentieth centuries, so these defensive institutions waned. The more settled married hired labour force made the clean toon more difficult to enforce. The Horseman's Society retreated before open unionisation among farm servants. Few bothy ballads had been created in the last decades of the nineteenth century, but none appeared after 1914. Folk song moved from the farm kitchen and stable to the music hall. Consider one famous music hall song: 'Nicky Tams'. This song was written by a man who never had been on the farms. It takes up topics treated in the true bothy songs — courting the kitchie deem, eyeing the girls in the Kirk — but these topics are treated in broad caricature. One stanza concerns the secret Horseman's Society, never mentioned in true bothy ballads. 'Nicky Tams' invited a music hall audience to share with the singer in mythologising the delights of farm work that few of them had experienced. The way was open for the proudest folksong tradition in lowland Britain to slide ignominiously into the sentimental inanities of 'Bothy Nichts'. The rich local dialect went the same way: no longer anchored in the middle peasantry, the Doric declined rapidly after 1914 until today it is taught as a foreign language in evening classes with its greatest literary monument — *Johnny Gibb of Gushetneuk* — as the sacred text.

Opposition to Differentiation

By 1914 the northeast peasantry was dead as a reproducible class; but it had not died without a fight. Throughout the nineteenth century peasant fractions had tried to inhibit the polarisation of the rural northeast's class structure into capitalist farmers on the one hand and landless farm workers on the other. This opposition to differentiation took different forms among different peasant fractions. Among farm servants, we have seen, it powered opposition to farmers' increasing inclination to eat apart from their servants.[9] It also provided the most profound justification for defensive institutions like bothy ballads and the clean toon: institutions which had as more proximate aims the prevention of exploitation and victimisation of farm servants by farmers. But farm servants also joined other peasant fractions in criticising those rising consumption expectations among capitalist farmers that increasingly set muckle farmers apart from the peasantry. Thus one servant scornfully dismissed capitalist farmers' complaints of hard times in the 'great depression',

> For, looking around amongst them, you will see a good many of them living in the style of a nobleman, with two domestic servants — and in some cases a nurse and governess — to attend to their families, and running horses (used for no other purpose), and all the style and grandeur of a nobleman, each competing to be in advance of his neighbour; while in other cases a large house is taken in Aberdeen, the

mistress of the farm and family residing there while the family is attending school, a housekeeper being engaged to do the domestic work on the farm, the farmer going between, and the male servants being huddled in a bothy and made to eat brose twenty one times a week.[10]

At the end of our period the growing differentiation among farmers that was symbolised, then as now, by differences in means of travel was bitterly resented by residual northeast peasants:

> This diversity in the vehicles tends to lead to a social distinction in the grading of the families in a rural parish, not all together favourable to the old kindly ways of friendship. A crofter who comes to the market in his small cart said, 'The aul' gig fairmer aye kens ye; the braw dog cairt ane micht lat on an' speir for ye; but the man wi' the big motor he's nae time tae gie ye even a wag o' the han'. He gangs by like thunner an' lichtnin', an' he hes nae mair time than them tae speak tae a body.'[11]

In the first half of the nineteenth century this peasant opposition to differentiation was largely canalised in religious agitation. This agitation was grounded in an ambiguous attitude to agricultural improvement among urban bourgeois fractions. On the one hand the release of higher productive forces in agriculture, as in other industries, was cause for wonder. But there was also an uneasy thought that the social costs of agricultural improvement were too high. This unease was crystallised, after the 1843 Disruption, in the criticisms of rural political economy made by activists from the Free Church of Scotland. These activists rested their critique of existing rural class relations on an idealised image of class relations before the agricultural revolution — a lost 'Merrie Scotland' where lairds, muckle farmers and peasant fractions allegedly had lived together in amity, and where mutually accepted rights and obligations, rather than the coldly impersonal cash nexus, had governed social relations of production. This arcadian vision had particular power in the northeast, of course, for there the peasantry had been penetrated much less completely than in most other lowland areas, and the notion of 'kindly relations' could provide powerful ideological support for the defence of peasant interests.

The Free Church argument had two linked strands. The first attacked lairds for evicting peasant farmers in order to establish 'the large farm system' — capitalist agriculture, that is. Particular venom was reserved for those lairds who had evicted peasants in order to avoid a potentially heavy Poor Law assessment.[12] Here, as throughout the Free Church's campaign anent rural class relations, social criticism was underpinned by less than disinterested ecclesiastical concerns:

> The Free Church is specially interested in the settlement of this question. The part of the population who are sufferers [through the expansion of capitalist agriculture] are principally her members. The landlord cannot compel their return to the Establishment, but he may seriously thin our ranks in the way indicated. The vast proportion of

our country adherents is drawn from the class of small tenants. We recently visited some of the congregations in the depopulated districts, which we had visited soon after the Disruption, and were astonished by the diminution of numbers.[13]

The Free Church's second target was the typical social relations holding between capitalist farmers and farm servants. Crucial here was the Rev. Dr James Begg's crusade against the bothy. The bothy's defendants — notably Lord Kinnaird and James Robb, editor of the *North British Agriculturist*[14] — argued that capitalist agriculture (and hence productive forces) could not unfold their fullest potential in the arable districts north of the Forth without the institution of the bothy. Begg and his fellows, on the other hand, argued that the only morally acceptable form of farm service was the hinding and double-hinding system of the Lothians, where most male farm servants were married and lived in cottar houses.[15] Bothying, and by extension any mode of working farms which relied predominantly on unmarried men rather than married, was immoral. It had produced degradation already — '. . . What was formerly moral Scotland is sinking to depths of degradation as low as anything upon the continent of Europe, unless Rome herself'[16] — and would continue to corrupt hired farm workers. The bothy symbolised the increasingly impersonal relations between capitalist farmer and farm servant that developed in districts with a relatively proletarianised labour force, as social relations moved into balance with the unchallenged domination of the capitalist mode of production.

Begg was no statistician — his attempt to show a causal relationship between the mode of housing northeast farm servants and the region's scandalously high illegitimacy ratios was utterly demolished by the Registrar-General for Scotland[17] — but he was a brilliant publicist. By 1865 his view that 'bothies cause bastards' and that only the Lothian hinding system was a morally acceptable form of farm service was taken for granted in Scotland, despite its extremely shaky empirical foundations.[18] The acceptance of that view had important consequences in the northeast: it stemmed the penetration of bothying into Aberdeenshire and Banffshire,[19] and it gave a moral impetus to farmers' pressures on their lairds to build new cottar houses in the later decades of the nineteenth century.

But Begg's argument had a much more important consequence in the northeast than these. The Free Church crusaders had used an attack on the land policies of lairds, and on capitalist farmers' lack of interest in their servants' welfare, as a stick with which to beat the Auld Kirk, the Church of Scotland. By labelling the Free Church as the defender of peasant fractions — and hence, by contrast, identifying evicting lairds and grasping capitalist farmers with the Auld Kirk — Begg had turned a defence of 'kindly relations' into an assault on the established church. But Begg's argument was inverted in the northeast's great Free Church tract on rural class relations. William Alexander wrote *Johnny Gibb of Gushetneuk* in the late 1860s, only a couple of years after Begg had wound up his moral crusade over bothying. He glossed Begg's argument at many points. The heart of the novel is a systematic contrast between the socially and morally admirable relations between farmer and servants on Gushetneuk, a middle peasant farm with an incomplete farm family, and the immoral atmosphere on the neighbouring capitalist farm of Clinkstyle — an atmosphere that corrupts both the farm family and the farm servants. Alexander also attacks lairds' land policies: when Tam Meerison inseminates the kitchen maid, the newly married couple can find no farm cottage in which to set up house, for all the neighbouring lairds have pulled down croft houses and cottar houses to avoid a heavy Poor Law assessment. They are compelled to move to the Bennachie squatter colony and Tam, a skilled horseman, is forced to take to day-labouring.[20] *Johnny Gibb* is not the couthy tale of country folk — the MacArchers — that later bourgeois commentators made of it.[21] It is a diatribe against differentiation; but Alexander reverses Begg's emphasis by making conflict over church government — the novel's ostensible concern is the course of the Disruption in the Garioch — a stick with which to beat landlords and capitalist farmers. In this magnificent novel we see the defence of peasant interests moving from the religious to the political sphere. Alexander disguised the political nature of his argument, but the seeds were planted and would flower in the hothouse conditions of the 1880s.

Political Action

By the early 1860s the conflict between the Auld Kirk and the Free Church had developed a political dimension. The Church of Scotland was now seen not only as the lairds' and capitalist farmers' church, but as the ecclesiastical wing of the Tory party. The Free Church, by contrast, was identified with the Liberal party in its defence of peasant interests. These religious and class labels were far from being wholly appropriate — many northeast lairds and capitalist farmers supported the Free Church while many peasants clave to the Auld Kirk — but they set the categories within which the more openly political conflict of the second half of the nineteenth century would be carried on. At one level that conflict may be seen as the result of a steadily growing awareness of their own material interest on the part of tenant farmers.

The beginnings of the representation of specific northeast tenant interests lie in the early 1860s. The key figure in the process is the region's archetypal — and largest — tenant farmer, William McCombie, Tillyfour. In some ways McCombie was an odd figure to carry the banner of tenants' interests. The heart of his 1,100-acre farm was the small Tillyfour estate in the Vale of Alford, an estate which he leased from his brother, the minister of Lumphanan.[22] In evidence to the Select Committee on Hypothec in 1868, McCombie was unable even to state the precise rent that he paid.[23] When his brother died in 1875 he took over the estate: hence his designation 'of

Tillyfour' in his last years. These oddities apart, however, William McCombie was an ideal figurehead. His successes as a pedigree cattle breeder, and his excellence as an employer, had made 'the Grazier King' very popular. In 1862 he was given a public banquet in Aberdeen by four hundred lairds and capitalist farmers as a mark of their respect. Not to be outdone, a similar number of crofters, small farmers, craftsmen and farm servants from the Vale of Alford gave him a public dinner soon afterwards. McCombie is said to have reckoned the second dinner the greater honour.[24] When rinderpest struck northeast cattle herds in 1865, it was William McCombie who organised Aberdeenshire farmers to raise a compensation fund that made possible the rigorous slaughter policy that extirpated the disease, thus providing the model for modern disease control measures among farm stock.[25] In the same year he took a leading part in igniting agitation on the game question and on hypothec. His lieutenant in all these endeavours was J. W. Barclay, an Aberdeen merchant and Deeside capitalist farmer. In 1866 McCombie succeeded George Hope, Fenton Barns, to become the second president of the Scottish Chamber of Agriculture, a pressure group that brought together lairds and capitalist farmers to pursue their mutual interest in pushing forward the material forces of production. McCombie was no political partisan: in his agitation over game and hypothec he was at pains to emphasise that Tory farmers suffered equally with Liberal farmers, that Tory lairds were no more culpable than their Liberal counterparts. Despite this lack of strong political views, McCombie was prevailed upon to stand in the Liberal interest for West Aberdeenshire in the 1868 general election. He was returned unopposed, becoming the first Scottish, and second British, tenant farmer to sit in Parliament. When, in 1874, a Tory was unwise enough to stand against him, McCombie received 2,401 votes while his opponent, a celebrated sportsman, got a measly 326.[26] In his parliamentary career — he resigned his seat in 1876 and died in 1880 — McCombie was listened to with respect when talking about agriculture, but rarely troubled the House with his opinions on other matters.

Their recruitment of William McCombie was a master-stroke for northeast Liberals. Liberalism had been gaining strength in the region for some years,[27] and the Liberal *Aberdeen Free Press* had a near monopoly among northeast farmers and farm servants as a result of the excellent agricultural reporting of its radical editor, William McCombie, Cairnballoch, and his ultra-radical deputy, William Alexander.[28] But by contriving to persuade McCombie, Tillyfour, to nail his colours to the Liberal mast, the local party managers attached his enormous prestige among capitalist farmers and peasant fractions to the Liberal cause. Henceforth Liberalism and the representation of northeast tenant interests would be synonymous.

When William McCombie resigned his seat the parliamentary representation of northeast tenants' interests passed to his old lieutenant, J. W. Barclay, Auchlossan. Barclay was by now Liberal M.P. for Forfarshire, and in 1879 he became vice-president of the new Farmers' Alliance that was founded in

England as 'an association which should represent the tenant farmer's interests from a tenant farmer's viewpoint'.[29] Barclay was a much more political animal than McCombie had been. He eschewed the comfortable doctrine, exemplified in the Scottish Chamber of Agriculture, that the interests of lairds and tenant farmers could always be brought together. In pursuing specific tenant interests Barclay always took a strongly anti-Tory line.

Thus by the early 1880s the Liberal party provided legitimate leadership for northeast tenant farmers. Tenants' interests were represented in Parliament by J. W. Barclay and extra-parliamentary leadership was in the hands of William Alexander, who had taken the editorial chair on the *Aberdeen Free Press* when William McCombie, Cairnballoch, died in 1870.[30] Barclay was pressing in Parliament and in evidence to the Richmond Commission for the abolition of landlord's hypothec and for tenant right. Alexander supported these demands, but his lifelong defence of northeast peasant interests meant that he wanted radical reform of tenurial arrangements as well.

In the spring of 1881 tenants' leaders still felt that they had to prepare the ground for land agitation: conditions for that agitation still seemed not to be ripe. Harvests had been bad in 1873, 1875, 1876, 1877 and 1879, it is true — and the importation of prairie grain had robbed farmers of the famine prices which their light crops could otherwise have commanded. The harvest in 1880 had been much better, however, and had brought some relief. Tenants on some northeast estates had had to petition their lairds for rent relief in 1880, but in the early months of 1881 the relations between lairds and tenants still seemed fairly amicable. One leading Ellon capitalist farmer — Robert Copland, Mill of Ardlethen — was asked by a member of the Richmond Commission in April of that year whether he had 'heard of meetings to remonstrate on that point [low farming profits], and to tell the landlords that they ought to bear a part of this burden?' Copland replied that he had never heard of such a thing.[31] A little less than five months later Copland chaired a meeting at Ellon which demanded very forcefully that lairds should share the burden of low prices, and went on to demand much more.[32]

The spark that set the rural northeast alight was the realisation in the later summer of 1881 that farmers were in for yet another bad hairst. Tenants on particular estates began to hold meetings, as in 1880, to draw up petitions to their laird for temporary rent remissions. Some estates agreed — notably the benevolent (and wealthy) Haddo and Gordon Castle estates. Other estates refused to grant any remission. The tenants responded in a new and ominous way. When the Collyhill Trustees refused help to their tenants on the Barrack and West Crichie estate in New Deer, the tenants showed that they had been studying contemporary events in Ireland — they declared a rent strike.[33] Less than a week later the tenants on a neighbouring estate owned by the Boys' and Girls' Hospitals Estates threatened similar action in pursuit of a general twenty-five per cent rent remission.

But the Irish rent strike was not the only novel feature of this agitation. On the August day that the 1881 Irish Land Act received the Royal Assent, a meeting of tenant farmers was held in Skene. The demands of this meeting were very moderate — simply that lairds should take cognisance of their tenants' difficulties — but the meeting was notable in that tenants from many local estates were present. Farmers had broken out of the blinkered vision that the only form of organisation available to them was for tenants on a particular estate to press their own laird: tenants from many estates now began to perceive and pursue their common interest. This Skene meeting was followed quickly by a similar gathering of tenants in Insch and then, in September, this generalised agitation spread like a brush fire through Aberdeenshire, Banffshire and Kincardine. The usual pattern was for tenants in a given district to hold a preliminary meeting after the local market in order to arrange a later public meeting. The scale and intensity of the agitation may be judged from the fact that the preliminary meeting at Ellon, chaired by Copland, Mill of Ardlethen, attracted a crowd of four hundred farmers despite not having been advertised in any way.[34]

By early September it was clear that this spontaneous eruption of land agitation was not going to quickly fizzle out. William Alexander and other leading Liberals moved in to colonise and canalise the infant movement. Under Alexander's guidance the *Aberdeen Free Press* gave blanket coverage to tenants' meetings, and printed dozens of letters — mostly arguing for tenants to adopt a more radical stance. Alexander cajoled farmers into more radical and more openly political action. His leading article on 24 August berated the 'Insch 400' — the members of the pioneer general meeting at Insch — for their spinelessness in trying to pretend that their interests were not inevitably opposed to the interests of landlords. His leader on 8 September demanded a Land Act for England and Scotland on the lines of the new Irish measure. By 13 September he was laying out a set of demands far removed from the timid request for lower rents with which the Skene and Insch farmers had begun the agitation. Noting the ineffectiveness of existing tenants' organisations — like the Scottish Chamber of Agriculture — Alexander repeated his demand for a Land Act, which would give legal security of tenure, and argued that tenants should also press for tenant right and for the abolition of legal restrictions — entail, primogeniture and so on — which prevented land being bought and sold freely like any other commodity.[35]

This leader on 13 September set the objectives for the whole agitation. The success of Alexander's attempt to radicalise the movement was soon reflected in mass meetings in towns and villages. The cautious approach of the early meetings evaporated on 8 September when H. D. McCombie took the stage. 'H. D.' was the son of William McCombie, the first editor of the *Aberdeen Free Press,* and had taken over his father's lease on Milton of Kemnay. He was president of the West Aberdeenshire Radical Association; the meeting at Kemnay which he organised on 8 September, with the local Free Church minister as his principal lieutenant, had an openly anti-Tory colour.[36] Later meetings followed the lead of Kemnay. At Lonmay a capitalist farmer from St Fergus was cheered to the echo for a violently anti-landlord speech:

> The old must be linked into the new, but the new we must and will have. We are not to give our time, our talents, and whole life to the improvement of another man's estate and property, although our forebears have done it. We are not to live as they did — liable to be bled profusely by lawyer and factor at the end of every 19 years.[37]

A number of the local committee members at Lonmay were Directors of the Philorth Steam Cultivation and Traction Company: capitalist farmers whose community of interest with their laird had been destroyed by falling wheat prices. The same thing held in the Howe o' the Mearns, the other centre of steam ploughing in the northeast. A preliminary meeting at Laurencekirk under the chairmanship of William Alexander, Bent of Haulkerton — Kincardine's most celebrated Radical farmer and one of the northeast's most progressive — called for the abolition of entail, primogeniture and landlord's hypothec, a general revaluation of farms to match rents more closely to cash crop prices, government loans for tenants to buy their buildings if they so wished, and security and heritability of tenure with adequate compensation for tenants' improvements if they did not want to become owner-occupiers.[38] Half of the members of the Laurencekirk local committee held shares in the Kincardineshire Steam Ploughing Company: Alexander was the company's joint manager.[39] Perhaps the most striking example of how strained relations between lairds and tenants had become by 1881 is the fact that many of the tenants' representatives who had come to such a harmonious agreement with the commissioners of supply at the 1871 Aberdeen Game Conference stood on public platforms ten years later and said unpardonable things about lairds as a class and their own lairds in particular.[40]

By the end of September the main demands of the tenants' agitation were clear: revaluation of farms, reform of the land laws, security of tenure and tenant right. These demands were repeated again and again at local meetings in October and November as agitation spread to every corner of Aberdeenshire, Banffshire and Kincardine, and beyond. The climax came on 1 December, 1881, when a 'great meeting' was held in Aberdeen city, attended by 6,000 farmers — almost all from the three counties.[41] Tactics for this meeting had been prepared very carefully beforehand at a meeting of the General Council of the Aberdeen Liberal Association.[42] The resolutions at the 'great meeting' repeated the demands that had been voiced at local meetings. A committee was elected, and on 16 December this committee formed itself into a Scottish Farmers' Alliance with strong links to the Farmers' Alliance that had been founded in England in 1879. Local agitation committees formed themselves into branches of the SFA. Throughout its short life — it was reconstituted as the Scottish Land Reform Alliance in 1886 — the SFA was based firmly in the northeast. It had its offices at 123½ Union Street, Aberdeen, and always held its annual meetings in the city. It had its mass base in the northeast: a political enemy suggested that the SFA should be called the Aberdeenshire Farmers' Alliance, since it drew eighty per cent of its funds from that county.[43] But if the SFA had pinned its future on the political radicalism of northeast tenants, then those tenants had pinned their hopes for legislative redress of their grievances firmly on the Liberal party: for the SFA, like its English counterpart, was purely a Liberal front organisation. The spontaneous eruption of northeast land agitation had been tamed and channelled into political support for Gladstone and his party.[44]

To put one's faith in the Liberal party must have seemed entirely rational to members of northeast peasant fractions in the autumn of 1881, with the Irish Land Act fresh on the statute book. But it soon began to appear that this faith might be ill-founded, for the policies pursued by the SFA proved to be fatally ambiguous. One set of demands centred on tenant right, the abolition of hypothec and reform of the game and land laws. Achievement of these demands would have — and did have — the effect of removing restrictions on the most efficient investment of tenants' capital. Thus the agitation over these questions was in the interest of capitalist farmers. The SFA's second set of demands was for security and heritability of tenure under judicial rent control through a Land Court: the Irish Land Act applied to lowland Scotland. Achievement of this demand would have meant an end to rack-renting and to eviction. Peasant farmers clearly would benefit enormously from such a measure, but capitalist farmers would be unable to increase their holdings' tilled acreage through engrossment when farming profits picked up again. Thus the running battle within the SFA executive from 1882 to 1886 over which element in the organisation's programme should have primacy was a class conflict.

Land agitation in the northeast, as elsewhere in Britain, came to a head in 1886. The SFA's mass base was dwindling rapidly;[45] the change of name to the Scottish Land Reform Association was a desperate attempt to widen the potential membership and signalled a determined effort to generate support by organising farm servants' unions.[46] The mass base was dwindling partly because of the disillusion over the fratricidal conflict between right and left inside the SFA, partly because many of the right wing's demands had been met — landlord's hypothec was abolished, ground game could be shot by the farmer, the 1883 Agricultural Holdings Act had put the principle of tenant right on the statute book. Thus it is not surprising that by 1886 the SFA was firmly under radical control, and the demand for tenurial security was being pressed strongly. Things seemed to be running very well for the radicals in other ways as well. Agitation was at a high level. H. D. McCombie, the radical leader, orchestrated and ran two 'monster public meetings' at Kemnay to protest against the local laird's intention to engross a croft. At the first meeting the laird — Burnett of Kemnay — was burnt in effigy.[47] Tenants throughout the northeast petitioned their lairds for rent remissions, and if these remissions were refused — or if only large farmers received remissions[48] — then agitation started. Agitation was widespread, from Cushnie in the west through Kennethmont and the Clova estates in the Garioch to Lenabo (Longside) in Buchan.[49] A comment from Cushnie shows the mood of these months: '"Skye begun in Cushnie" is the common salutation in the cattle markets, instead of "Stormy weather and bad trade"'.[50] At Lenabo crofters threatened a rent strike.

At this high point of peasant class consciousness it seemed that the millenium was at hand when

> Nae langer this nation will thole the oppression,
> The laird and the factor will get an o'erthrow.[51]

The source of this optimism was the realistic possibility that the Crofters Holdings Bill sponsored by the Liberal government would be extended beyond the seven 'crofting counties' — Shetland, Orkney, Caithness, Sutherland, Ross and Cromarty, Inverness, and Argyll — to include the northeast. The government tried to find a reasonable basis upon which to limit the Bill to the seven counties; but each effort that they made — small average size of holding, existence of Gaelic, historical evidence of common grazings — was discredited by the parliamentary spokesmen of the SLRA, J. W. Barclay and Dr Farquharson, with evidence from Aberdeenshire provided by William Alexander.[52] It seemed not unlikely that northeast peasant farmers would get the high degree of security and heritability of tenure that their Highland brethren were soon to enjoy. But it was not to be. The Lord Advocate, despairing of finding a rational basis for limiting the area to be covered by the Bill, declared that only those counties visited by the Napier Commission would be included.[53] The SLRA spokesmen opposed this quaint decision with vigour, and put forward an amendment in committee to extend the area under the Bill. They lost the amendment by 126 votes to 87.[54]

With that vote went the hopes for legislative protection of the northeast peasantry. Gladstone had already been converted to Home Rule for Ireland, and his conversion had precipitated a general election. In that election the rural northeast clave to 'the people's Wullie'. Gladstonian Liberals were elected in all five county constituencies. Only one sitting MP declared for the Liberal Unionists, and he — MacPherson Grant of Ballindalloch, Banffshire laird, pedigree Aberdeen-Angus breeder and MP for Elgin and Nairn — was soundly beaten by a Gladstonian candidate. This loyalty was not enough, however; elsewhere the flight of the Old Whigs to the Tories meant the end of Gladstone's ministry. The concentration on Home Rule over the next three decades would take radical land reform off the agenda of British politics.[55] A Bill was brought forward in 1899 to give small Scottish tenant farmers security and heritability of tenure under a Land Court, but this smelt too Irish for the liking of Liberal Unionists and the Bill was lost.[56] A similar Bill was brought forward in 1907 by John Sinclair, Secretary of State for Scotland; it was thrown out by the Lords. Reintroduced the next year, the Bill was emasculated by the Lords and the government withdrew it.[57] When the Pentland Act finally did reach the statute book in 1912 it gave too little protection and was much too late. The northeast peasantry had been irreparably penetrated; as a class it was dead.

1886 was the turning point. The northeast peasantry was under severe pressure, but it had not yet broken. In that year a combination of factors made the achievement of security and heritability of tenure a real political possibility. The government was based on a riven party, and depended on support from agrarian radicals in Ireland, Wales, and the Scottish Highlands. A mass organisation was pushing for security of tenure and could point to ogre landlords like Burnett of Kemnay, Lumsden of Clova and Russell of Aden to prove their arguments. Half a century of peasant opposition to differentiation seemed to be about to bear fruit.

It was not to be. Northeast peasants could not mobilise sufficient political muscle to force the Liberal government to give them the same legislative protection that Highland peasants were to enjoy. The reason for this inability was not lack of numbers. It was the failure of northeast peasants clearly to realise and represent their own class interest; a failure which stemmed from the subtle and pervasive articulation of capitalist and precapitalist modes of production. Capitalist farmers were allowed to present themselves as the representatives of all farmers, to pursue their sectional interest under the guise of pursuing farmers' general interest. Thus when south Kincardine capitalist farmers organised a parliamentary petition calling for the abolition of landlord's hypothec, they prevailed on almost all the middle peasants in the district to sign it, and a great many crofters, despite the fact that the continued existence of landlord's hypothec clearly was in the peasant fractions' interest.[58] The same manipulation of peasants by their capitalist farming neighbours underlay the tragi-comic Turra Coo incident at the end of our period. Lloyd George's Insurance Act compelled farmers, like other employers, to pay national insurance contributions on their hired workers. Farmers resented this compulsion; and capitalist farmers resented it most strongly, for they had more hired workers than middle peasants. Things boiled over in 1913, when Robert Paterson, Lendrum, Turriff — a capitalist farmer and a paternalistic employer — was taken to court for failing to make insurance payments. He refused to pay the arrears, and the Sheriff issued a warrant allowing law officers to seize enough of his property to satisfy the debt. They chose to poind a white cow — the celebrated Turra Coo. In December 1913 the law officers were unwise enough to try to sell the cow by auction in Turriff Square. A riot broke out: the officers were deforced and pelted with eggs and other missiles, the cow was driven off. When the cow was recaptured it was taken by train to Aberdeen under heavy police guard. The Aberdeen marts refused to have anything to do with it, and it was sold in an underhand manner to a London dealer. He eventually sold the cow to a group of farmers who returned it, with full military honours, to Lendrum. Paterson and six other men were charged in connection with the Turriff riot, but after a hilarious week-long trial at Aberdeen the charges were found not proven.[59] It all provided a running joke at the authorities' expense: but the serious point was that, once again, capitalist farmers had organised peasant fractions in defence of specific capitalist interests:

> Last year, upon the passing of the [Insurance] Act, the district's farmers and farm servants marked their disapproval of the new measure by publicly burning, amid a gathering probably unequalled even on Porter Fair days, the effigies of the Chancellor of the Exchequer [Lloyd George] and Mr W. H. Cowan, the local member of Parliament.[60]

Farm servants had supported their employers in attacking a measure that promised the servant some measure of dignified independence in his old age — most important on the threshold of the Great War as the northeast hired labour force, becoming steadily more proletarianised, could look forward less and less to a crofting retirement. The Turriff riot was so serious because local farmers had generously given their servants a half-holiday to watch the cow being sold: once again a peasant fraction acted as capitalist farmers' shock-troops.

A few northeast peasants realised what was happening. Helen Beaton prints a standard ploughing match song from the Garioch: but this song had a sting in the tail:

> And Tilly, mind your steers and stots,
> And come nae doon here seekin' votes;
> When ye part wi' yer bunch o' notes,
> Ye'll first pairt wi' your skin, O.
>
> For ugly questions we'll be speirin',
> And at your Tory tactics sneerin',
> Ye'll find, when ower your hindmost feerin',
> An M.P. turned P.M., O.[61]

This perception of the real interests being served by the Liberal party remained rare, however. Uninterested in peasant proprietorship and unwilling to follow Irish and Highland peasants in demanding land nationalisation,[62] northeast peasant farmers put their trust in the SFA, with its ambiguous programme reflecting the northeast's complex social formation. By so doing they put their faith in men not of their own class. The leadership of the SFA at both national and branch level was in the hands of large farmers. Even the most radical of the leaders, the Irish-inspired maverick H. D. McCombie, was a capitalist farmer. The two men who led the parliamentary fight for the extension of the Crofters Holdings Bill encapsulate the problem. One, J. W. Barclay, was an Aberdeen merchant turned Deeside large farmer who would buy the Glenbuchat estate in 1901.[63] The other was Barclay's laird, Dr Farquharson of Finzean, a sporting laird who was a close friend of Burnett of Kemnay[64] and had himself been accused of evicting crofters from his estate.[65] It is not surprising, then, that the SFA was less steadfast in its opposition to 'the grasping large farmer'[66] and 'landlord oppression and infamous tyranny'[67] than was the Highland Land Law Reform Association.

West Highland peasants faced big capitalist sheep farmers with no articulation between the two groups save mutual loathing. The sharpness of the division between these two classes allowed Highland peasants clearly to recognise their own class interest. On that interest they built their own political party. The crofter MPs, like the Irish members, traded with the Liberal party. They exchanged support for the Liberal government on issues unconnected with agriculture in return for legislation on land tenure in Ireland and the Highlands.[68] Northeast peasants, by contrast, had to make do with a rather weak pressure group, ambiguously attached to their interests, within the rambling mansion of late nineteenth century Liberalism. This had some advantages — for example, the organisational skills of the party were at their disposal. But it had one crucial failing. A necessary condition for the strong assertion of peasant interests was an attack on the class interests of landowners. Such an attack could not come from the SFA, however, or from anyone working from within the Liberal party. William Alexander, for example, found himself severely constrained in his criticism of landlords. In *Johnny Gibb* he had put his own opinion in the mouth of his hero, the irascible Johnny:

> 'The tae half o' oor lairds is owre the lugs in a bag o' debt. I wud hae them roupit oot at the door, and set to some eeseful trade . . . Stechin up a kwintra side wi' them, wi' their peer stinkin' pride,' pursued Johnny, 'an them nedder able to manage their awcres themsel's, nor can get ither fowk that can dee't for them . . . I'm weel seer it was never the arreengements o' Providence that the man that tills the grun an' spen's the strength o's days upon't sud be at the merciment o' a man that never laid a han' till't, nor hardly wair't a shillin' upon't, to bid 'im bide or gyang.'[69]

In his essays on *The Aberdeenshire Crofter* Alexander was more circumspect, but he berated peasant farmers for having acquiesced in their own exploitation by lairds, '. . . for until very recently the "rights", so-called, of landed property were regarded with an almost superstitious reverence by the very class who had most reason to complain of their abuse'.[70] Even with these unimpeachable anti-landlord qualifications, however, Alexander could not openly attack landlords as a class. Many of the great northeast lairds — the Earls of Aberdeen and Fife, for example — and many smaller lairds — like Burnett of Kemnay — were Liberals (at least until the flight of the Old Whigs in 1886) and could not be attacked. Hence Alexander's glowing account of the unstinted paternalism of the huge Fife estate;[71] and the need for tenant farmers on that estate to point out that the Earl of Fife was among the most rapacious of local landlords.[72]

It is probable that the northeast peasantry could not have withstood for long the relentless pressure of a mature capitalist agriculture which no longer needed the peasant's precapitalist mode of production to ensure its own existence. The demoralisation and decay to be found today in the Irish Gaeltacht[73] and in Highland crofting areas prevents a comfortable Narodnik conclusion to this book. But the death of the northeast peasantry could have been delayed; the rapidity of its decline was ensured in 1886 by its failure to recognise clearly, and hence to represent, its own interests. Those peasants did not inherit the earth — the poor so rarely do. Their claim is prouder; their historic role was to make the land. No peasant farmer could ask for a more flattering epitaph.

7
Conclusion

> The past is intelligible to us only in the light of the present; and we can fully understand the present only in the light of the past. To enable man to understand the society of the past and to increase his mastery over the society of the present, is the dual function of history.[1]

IN this book we have seen the forces that shaped the social formation of rural northeast Scotland between 1840 and 1914. The climatic and geological endowment of different districts — notably the sandstone districts on the one hand and the central wedge of Aberdeenshire, Banffshire, and north Kincardine on the other — was modified by the incorporation of the whole region in wider British and world economic networks through the expansion of the cattle and beef trades. The interaction of these factors gave a set of farming systems differing in their emphases but all, with the exception of the rather insignificant hill sheep sector, focussing on the cattle byre.

Owner-occupation was rare in the northeast: most farmers, large and small, held their land on lease from lairds. Within the ranks of farmers a sharp division of labour appeared with the new cattle feeding industry that was made possible by steamship communication with the London market after 1828. Big farmers — capitalist farmers — quickly moved to the more profitable cattle feeding business while smaller peasant farmers continued to concentrate on cattle rearing. In the sandstone districts potential arable land was brought under the plough earlier than in other parts, and engrossment drove up the average size of holdings, making peasant farmers a small and rather insignificant class. In the northeast's central wedge things were different. Engrossment of peasant holdings was balanced by the creation of new crofts and small farms on the margin of cultivation: in this great swathe of land from Braemar to Fraserburgh most of the tilled land was held in capitalist farms, but capitalist farmers were outnumbered more than five to one by peasant farmers. Those peasant farmers and their families served invaluable functions for dominant classes. For lairds they increased estate rentals, at little or no cost to the laird, through the colonisation of waste land on improving leases. They also bore the cost of reproducing two means of production essential for the capitalist farmer — the hired labour force that lay at the heart of his mode of production, and lean cattle for fattening. Thus the capitalist farmer in the sandstone districts and in the central wedge was spared the need to bear the full cost of reproducing his means of production. This advantage was reflected in capitalist farmers' profits.

The articulation of capitalist and precapitalist modes of production was the foundation upon which was raised the cultural edifice that was such a marked feature of nineteenth century northeast farm life. Where that articulation was close and pervasive, in the central wedge, one found strong social levelling tendencies. Farm servants — themselves the children of peasant farmers — resisted attempts either to treat them less well than children in the capitalist farmer's family or to regard the relationship between a farmer and his servants as bounded simply by the cash nexus. The servants shared a vision of what relations between farmer and servant ought to be, a vision that was an idealised version of the relations between a peasant farmer and his family workers. In defence of this vision Aberdeenshire and Banffshire farm servants resisted the spread of bothying on large farms, which symbolised for them the decline of 'kindly relations' in the fermtoun. In defence of this vision servants publicised particularly scandalous abrogations of customary expectations through the northeast's unique oral wall-poster: the bothy ballads. In the sandstone districts, by contrast, articulation between capitalist and precapitalist modes of production was much weaker because the peasantry was a much less numerous and influential class. Here one found a more settled permanent farm labour force with a higher proportion of married men. Those men who were not married mostly stayed in the bothy: but in these districts the institution of the bothy was defended by its inmates. Many northeast bothymen had come to the Laigh of Moray or the Howe o' the Mearns from the central wedge: these were men who found the notion of 'kindly relations', of a close quasi-family control of servants by the farmer, stifling and constricting. Consequently, in the bothy districts one found much weaker levelling tendencies. Farm servants and local residual peasant fractions on the whole did not oppose social differentiation among farmers: the cash nexus was a perfectly acceptable basis for relations between farmer and servant.

The later decades of the nineteenth century saw a slow drift towards this polarised arrangement even in the northeast's central wedge. The difficulties of 'the great depression' bore on all classes, but they had a particularly serious effect on the peasantry. Small farmers and crofters were forced to screw yet more labour out of their family workers, thus sharpening a contradiction between independence for the farmer and obedience for his family workers that was buried within the peasant's mode of production. The contradiction dissolved as increasing numbers of peasant children refused to suffer the burden of family labour any longer, and escaped to the towns or the colonies, often through the escape-hatch offered by the new state education system. The peasantry withered internally, its indispensibility for capitalist production destroyed by developments in material forces — the importation of Irish and Canadian stores, farm mechanisation — and by lairds' lack of interest in increasing their estates' tilled acreage when they had difficulty in letting existing capitalist farms. One determined defence of the peasantry was mounted, in the 1880s. This defence failed because northeast peasant farmers did not develop their own institutions to represent their own class. They put their faith in the Liberal party, and in the capitalist farmer leaders of the Scottish Farmers' Alliance — a Liberal pressure group. Those leaders used peasant support to pursue their own class interest and then left the peasantry in the lurch. Northeast peasant farming was doomed.

What lessons does this story hold? Two sets, I think: and they centre on Carr's two functions of history that head this chapter. The first set of lessons concerns our understanding of the past.

(a) **Looking Backwards**

It is more than half a century since an Aberdeen historian wrote that

> Scottish history is at bottom a provincial history, yet it has suffered from the failure of historians to grasp this fundamental truth.[2]

Of no branch of Scottish history is this statement more true than agricultural history. Scholars have distinguished Highlands from Lowlands as a matter of course, but the fact that different lowland areas had distinctively different agrarian structures has, until the last few years, been much less widely recognised. Thus Christopher Smout, in the first modern attempt at a social history of Scotland in the seventeenth and eighteenth centuries, argues that the agricultural revolution quickly created a rural society throughout the lowlands that was polarised between capitalist farmers and landless farm workers.[3] Other scholars take a similar line.[4] It is interesting to note that most of these historians were writing from Edinburgh University, for their accounts are an accurate statement of what happened in the surrounding counties: the Lothians and Berwickshire. Smout takes his examples of the condition of farm workers after the agricultural revolution exclusively from southeastern and south-central Scotland, with the single exception of an extended reference to Hugh Miller's experience of bothy life in Easter Ross.[5]

This would not matter if the social formation of the Lothians was, in fact, identical with that of all other lowland areas. We have seen earlier, however, that this was not the case. Figure 1.5 showed that average farm size was much greater in southeast Scotland than in the northeast. Table 1.2 showed us some of the social consequences of this difference: the middle peasantry had been destroyed almost completely in East Lothian, while in the northeast it still was an important class fraction. The hired labour force differed between the two areas, too. On the arable farms of southeastern Scotland the typical hired worker was a hind or cottar: a married farm servant living in a cottage on the farm. Most of these men were the sons of men who had themselves been hired servants for all their working lives. In the northeast, by contrast, the typical male farm servant was unmarried. He was not a cottar's son;[6] until the very end of the nineteenth century he still roared round the 'ancient, strange whirlimagig'[7] of the old lowland Scots peasantry from labour on the paternal holding to hired farm service and then, for a proportion of any cohort of peasant children, to day labouring and back (with luck and remorseless thrift) to peasant farming. The rural northeast's nineteenth century social formation was radically different from that of the rural Lothians. In the Lothians something approaching a fully formed agricultural proletariat did face a small class of big capitalist farmers who monopolised the usufruct of land, the crucial means of agricultural production.[8] In the northeast, by contrast — and particularly in the central wedge of land comprising Aberdeenshire, Banffshire and north Kincardine — capitalist farmers held less than sixty per cent of the tilled acreage, and their hired servants formed a peasant fraction rather than an agricultural proletariat.

What causes the conflation of 'Lothian' and 'lowland' in the work of Edinburgh historians?[9] Part of the reason lies, no doubt, in local chauvinism; in the comforting belief that the heart of Midlothian is the centre of the world. But there is a deeper reason, a reason that is rooted in historiography. In the early nineteenth century the Lothians and Berwickshire were the most advanced region in Scottish agriculture, the region where material forces of production had been pushed forward most insistently.[10] This region also saw the rapid development of a rather sharply polarised social formation. In this respect southeastern Scotland mirrored midland and southeastern England, where one found the same pattern of developed material forces in agriculture and polarised social formation. It was easy to conclude from this conjuction that the development of capitalism in agriculture quickly and inevitably called a polarised social formation into being.[11] A Whig theory of agrarian change was born: a theory that asserted that it was both inevitable and utterly admirable that big farms should swallow small farms, that intermediate strata should be ground out of the social formation by the upper millstone of the capitalist farmer and the nether stone of the agricultural proletarian. That Whig theory still dominates policy discussions about British agriculture — hence the fixation with 'improving farm structure' (which means driving or bribing small farmers off the land). The theory has been exported to the Third World as capitalist production expanded on a world scale, where it has provided the ideological underpinning for the expansion of cash crop production for European and American markets at the expense of local subsistence fóod production. Thus, for example, increasing quantities of soyabeans have been grown in Brazil to feed cattle in the USA, while the nutritional level of the mass of the Brazilian population has fallen.[12] The same theory has imbued British agricultural history and rural sociology, where it has had two effects. The first was to make empirical investigation of regional variations appear unnecessary. Advanced areas like the Lothians held up a crystal ball to less advanced areas: what I am today, you will be tomorrow.

The second effect was to establish a particularly rigid definition of what constituted capitalist agriculture. If the development of capitalism induced the rapid establishment of a polarised social formation then, so the argument runs, if one did not find a polarised social formation in the area under study, one could not be dealing with capitalist agriculture.[13]

If we wish to avoid the intellectual sterility imposed by this excessively rigid definition, then we need to look into a rather different intellectual tradition. It is common to see in Marx's mature work not a body of new evidence but a new synthesis: a novel combination of German philosophy, French history and English (or, more properly, Scottish) political economy. Part of that political economy was what I have called the Whig philosophy of agrarian history. In the section of Engels' book on the condition of the English working class in 1844 that deals with agriculture, an early work that was written before Marx and Engels began their long collaboration, one finds a wooden account of the inevitable triumph of big farms — and the consequent proletarianisation of labour — that could have come from any agrarian commentator of the day.[14] When, two decades later, Marx published in volume one of *Capital* his analysis of primitive accumulation,[15] he chose, for good theoretical reasons, to base that analysis on a study of agrarian change. The geographical area that he chose to study was the region with the most highly developed capitalist agriculture in his time: southern England. The account of the historical development of capitalist agriculture which he gave in those splendid chapters[16] forms the prototype for all later accounts of the agricultural revolution in England, often by authors who would be horrified to discover their intellectual debt to the sage of Highgate Cemetery. Once again one has the conjunction of developed material forces and polarised social formation: but this time the analysis is underpinned by a very subtle theoretical scheme. Marx's account of the development of southern England's rural social formation is an analysis of the logical unfolding of the capitalist mode of agricultural production *within a unique set of historical circumstances.* Southern England may be the 'classic case', but there is no iron law that compels capitalist agricultural development to take precisely the same course in other settings. Social formation and mode of production are concepts that operate at different levels of generality. Marx was aware, as were socialist agrarian commentators in the generation after his death, that capitalist production could take much more diverse forms in agriculture than in manufacturing industry: agrarian capitalism was compatible with a surprisingly wide range of social formations.[17]

This point has been driven home in recent years through the growth of interest among certain French anthropologists in the articulation between capitalist and precapitalist modes of production in the Third World, and in the manner in which precapitalist production serves essential functions in maintaining the material conditions necessary for the continued existence of capitalist production.[18] In this work the failure to destroy intermediate strata — various kinds of peasant fractions, for instance — is interpreted not as a sign of weakness in the capitalist mode of production in a particular social formation, but as the most efficient way of organising production in that formation from metropolitan capitalism's point of view.[19]

This book has shown the value of this kind of analysis not in the Third World today but in understanding the historical experience of parts, at least, of advanced capitalist countries. Peasant fractions survived the agricultural revolution in northeast Scotland's central wedge not because capitalism was weakly developed there — by 1840 capitalism was the indisputably dominant mode of production throughout the region — but because the peasantry's subordinate mode of production bore the cost of reproducing many of capitalist farmers' material conditions of existence. The lessons are clear. If we are to understand the agrarian history of nineteenth century Scotland, then we must stop seeing a failure to move rapidly to a polarised social formation as evidence of social conservatism, and study the concrete articulation of different modes of production worked by different groups in the social formation. This means getting our boots dirty in local studies. One can try to force the agrarian history of the Scottish lowlands into the Procrustean bed of the Lothian social formation, but the truncated and bleeding corpse that will emerge is not likely to be able to tell us much about agrarian capitalism — a highly variable entity — in the very different conditions of Galloway, Perthshire and Caithness. Until more local studies have been undertaken we will not be able to begin to generalise about 'lowland agriculture' as a whole.

(b) Looking Forwards

Studying the social history of agricultural production in northeast Scotland is more than an antiquarian exercise. E. H. Carr's two functions of history — to help us understand the past and to increase our mastery over the present — can be separated only for analytical purposes. In reality the two functions are intimately linked.

In Britain, as throughout the western world, people tend to think — and have so thought for centuries — that life in the country is fundamentally different from life in the city. We think of the city as dynamic, dangerous, a seedbed for change. We think of the country as peaceful, idyllic, unchanging: a harmonious place where social order mirrors a natural order, where social life moves in rhythm with the turning seasons. Farming, the predominant economic activity in the countryside, seems different in kind from urban production. The farmer does not take raw materials and transform them, through labour, into a more finished product. He works with nature, not on nature. Farming is the cornerstone of a natural economy that takes its present form not as the result of human interaction in history but as a delicately judged ecological adaptation to the rural environment.

This dream of rural Britain is utter nonsense: life in the countryside never has been, and is not, like that.[20] But the dream persists, an ideology that is both pervasive and influential. Thus, for example, it provides the assumption that underpins the policies pursued by the Highlands and Islands Development Board since its establishment in 1965: the assumption that the seven crofting counties form a region 'that the various revolutions in agriculture, industry and technology have passed by'.[21] The obvious policy line is to awaken the Highlands from their Arcadian slumber, to introduce capitalist production for the first time. Capitalist development, it is confidently predicted, will bring bountiful benefits to a poor land. But what if the crofting counties were not untouched by the agricultural and industrial revolutions? What if social history can show, as it can, that the problems of remote Highland districts flow not from isolation from capitalist production but from the extent and manner in which those districts were integrated in British and international capitalist networks during the past two centuries?[22] In that case the HIDB's policy collapses under its own contradictions: the Highlands are to be developed through a massive transfusion of the substance that generated Highland underdevelopment in the first place. We can see that social history is not irrelevant to the formulation of policy today: if we wish to influence the direction of change in the social formation of the crofting counties, then an essential first step is to understand how the current social formation was shaped through time.

Highland crofters' stubborn refusal to acquiesce in their own liquidation has kept alive an account of Highland history that differs markedly from the account usually provided by sleek academic commentators.[23] The crofters' version of history is a story of class oppression, of the depredations suffered by peasant farmers at the hands of landlords and capitalist farmers. It ensures that the present social formation of the crofting counties is seen to be the outcome of struggle rather than a natural adaptation to Highland conditions, and it keeps questions about social relations of production alive in the political arena. It is in the crofting counties, alone of Scottish regions, that land ownership is a vital political issue.[24]

Things are very different in the northeast. We know that northeast peasants' failure to achieve legislative protection in 1886 opened the door to social differentiation: the average holding size has risen steadily over the years.[25] There is little more that we do know about the northeast's social formation. Our lack of knowledge on one topic is particularly illuminating. The torrent of statistical data on British agriculture that pours out of the state agricultural bureaucracies each year tells us nothing about who owns land, the crucial means of agricultural production. This is an extraordinary omission. In most Third World countries it would be taken for granted that one needed information on land ownership if one sought to move towards a more rational pattern in agriculture. The failure to collect this information in Britain is not inconsistent with the interests of groups owning land — whether lairds, owner-occupying farmers or, as has come increasingly to be the case on high-grade land in the last few years, corporations and financial institutions looking for a hedge against inflation. It is obvious that the landed interest retains considerable power in the British social formation: it is one thing to sway a political decision in one's favour when an issue gets into the political arena, but it is something else — and requires much deeper reserves of power — for a group to be able to prevent the issue ever reaching the political arena in the first place.[26]

The last occasion on which reasonably comprehensive information on land ownership was collected in Britain was the early 1870s.[27] This information provided a snapshot of the pattern of land ownership at the time, and has proved invaluable for historians.[28] But this investigation was not carried out to help future historians. It arose from contemporary political concern, mostly expressed through the radical wing of the Liberal party, over the social formation of rural Britain. Those who pressed for the enumeration of estates knew that nowhere in rural Britain would one find an Arcadian social formation with different classes combining harmoniously in a natural economy. They rested their arguments on class analysis, studying the alliances and conflicts between the separate material interests of landlords, capitalist farmers, peasant fractions and landless labourers. As the political temperature over the ownership, control and use of land rose steadily from 1865 to 1886, so more and more treatises and articles, of a scholarly or polemical nature, rolled off the press. By the 1880s the level of debate about rural matters in Scotland, and more generally in Britain, was remarkably sophisticated. By contrast, what passes for rural sociology in Britain today pales into utter insignificance.

The social history of northeast agriculture presented in this book is merely the prelude to the really important work: the analysis of the current social formation of the northeast. By showing that the agrarian structure of the region in 1914 came not from an ecological adaptation to a harsh environment, but was the result of class interaction, we cut through the ideological tap-root that nourishes the screen of leaves preventing northeast folk from recognising the true nature of the region's social formation. Stop considering the rural northeast to be a harmonious 'community', start analysing the different interests of groups in the social formation, and one begins to notice things. Many northeast farmers are still small farmers but, as in the nineteenth century, this is not true of all farmers. Many of those who are most vociferous in defence of the alleged rural virtues are big capitalist farmers dressed up to look like Walter Gabriel. The man with a battery chicken unit, the man rearing pigs intensively, the man producing barley beef by shoving as much grain as possible into young cattle that never see a field — all can argue, for their own purposes, that farming really is 'a way of life'. The most convinced agribusinessman can pull on a set of labourer's dungarees and denounce taxation policies that an urban businessman takes for granted, claiming that these policies threaten the survival of 'the rural community'. The conflation of sectional interests with general interests is an old trick: start analysing the interaction of different sectional interests and one soon penetrates the illusion.

Thus rural sociology has an important part to play in understanding the social formation of the rural northeast today. The tasks are legion. We need a full description of patterns of ownership and control in agriculture. We need to know about tenurial arrangements, and how those arrangements are changing. We need to know the nature of the labour force — the balance between hired and family labour, for instance. We need to study the membership and control of important interest groups — the Scottish National Farmers' Union, the Scottish Landowners' Federation — and analyse the articulation between such groups and national and international bureaucracies: this task grows more urgent as the state provides an increasing proportion of capital for agriculture. We need to know more about the penetration of agriculture by commercial and industrial capital not only through land purchase but also for example, through the vertical articulation of many northeast pig farmers with Lawson of Dyce's bacon factory: a factory owned not by Mr Lawson in Dyce but by Unilever in London. Then, at last, we must come to a judgement about whether tendencies manifest in all these matters are leading towards a social formation which we find desirable. If not, then we must develop new policy lines that lead towards a social future that we find more attractive. This will not be a harmonious process. Disagreements over agrarian policy in the 1880s, disagreements rooted in class interests, were fought out with bitter acrimony. Any similar argument in the 1980s would be no less acrimonious, and no less necessary.

We will finish on a professional note. Rural sociology has an important role to play in northeast Scotland, but fulfilling that role can have a vital importance for rural sociology. In the sixty years since the newly institutionalised subject of agricultural economics first began utterly to dominate discussions of British agriculture, questions about social formation have been squeezed out. To the extent that any interest in social matters has survived, it has done so through rural sociology's willing subordination to agricultural economics: rural sociology has become the study of those features which agricultural economists find interesting but not worth their own valuable time to study.[29] It is time to leave the closet, to throw away the under-labourer's apron. Rural sociologists must assert, as radical Liberals did a century ago, that the big questions about rural Britain have to do not with economics but with political economy — with the social relations of men in production. That means choosing the groups whose interests we wish to support. We must stop thinking of our subject as a purely technical enterprise, blindly pursuing ends that are defined by others for their own purposes, ends that are none of our business. It is time that British rural sociology recognised something that has become a truism in development studies, that in social life 'There are no such things as technical solutions, there are only political solutions.'[30]

Notes

A NUMBER of newspapers, journals and other sources recur frequently in the following notes and bibliography. To avoid needless repetition their titles are abbreviated as follows:

AFP	Aberdeen Free Press
AHR	Agricultural History Review
AJ	Aberdeen Journal
EcHR	Economic History Review
JA	Journal of Agriculture
JRASE	Journal of the Royal Agricultural Society of England
NSA	New Statistical Account of Scotland
OSA	[Old] Statistical Account of Scotland
PP	Parliamentary Papers
SA	Scottish Agriculture
SGM	Scottish Geographical Magazine
SHR	Scottish Historical Review
SRO	Scottish Record Office
TBFC	Transactions of the Buchan Field Club
THASS	Transactions of the Highland and Agricultural Society of Scotland
TNAPSS	Transactions of the National Association for the Promotion of Social Science

Introduction

1. See pp. 29-30.
2. A hind in Scotland, as in England, was a full-time hired farm servant who was married and — in Scotland — lived in a cottage on the farm.
3. *NSA* XII (Aberdeenshire), pp. 428-9.
4. This, like most fables, is a complete fabrication.
5. See pp. 178-9.
6. R. Duncan, 'Popular Radicalism and Working-Class Politics in Aberdeen, c. 1790-1850'; unpublished M.Litt. thesis, Aberdeen University, 1976.
7. H. Pelling, *Social Geography of British Elections, 1885-1910*, London, Macmillan, 1967, p. 390.
8. K. D. Buckley, *Trade Unionism in Aberdeen, 1878-1900*, Edinburgh, Oliver and Boyd, 1955.
9. See chapter 6.
10. In Durham and south Northumberland the dominant industry was coal mining, of course.
11. D. Buchan, *The Ballad and the Folk*, London, Routledge and Kegan Paul, 1972, p. 255.

12. For the distinction between bothy and chaumer see pp.
13. See p. 30.
14. This is a perennial problem in the social sciences, where we often find ourselves using terms which we try to define fairly tightly but which also have lay meanings. Consider terms like 'role', 'class', 'status', and many more.
15. See T. Shanin, 'The Nature and Logic of the Peasant Economy', *Journal of Peasant Studies*, 1974, I, pp.186-206.
16. See pp. 26, 109-11.
17. E. R. Wolf, 'On Peasant Rebellions', in T. Shanin (ed), *Peasants and Peasant Societies*, Harmondsworth, Penguin, 1971, pp.264-74.
18. T. Shanin, *The Awkward Class*, Oxford, Clarendon Press, 1972.
19. One northeast peasant fraction — farm servants — might appear to have been so separated, but we shall see (pp. 109-111) that farm service was just one stage in the circulation of labour from peasant agriculture into hired farm work and then back to peasant agriculture.
20. These definitions will not please everybody. The definition and logical status even of such central concepts as *mode of production* are the subject of sharp contention among scholars. Those seeking a more extended and systematic account of these concepts should consult M. Evans, *Karl Marx*, London, Allen and Unwin, 1975: a book which combines lucid exposition with a blessedly ecumenical approach.

Chapter 1

1. G. S. Keith, *General View of the Agriculture of the County of Aberdeen*, Aberdeen, Brown, 1811, p.142.
2. By political economy I mean the study of the social relations of men in production. I am aware that this definition will not be familiar in the Political Economy departments within Scottish universities.
3. J. R. Raeburn, 'Agriculture', in A. C. O'Dell and J. Mackintosh (ed), *The North-East of Scotland*, Aberdeen, Central Press, 1963, p.109.
4. R. Glentworth, 'Soils', in O'Dell and Mackintosh, *op cit*, p.38.
5. R. Gray, 'Account of the District of Buchan', *THASS*, 1832, 2nd series, III, pp.51-53. For further material on soils see R. Glentworth, *The Soils of the Country Round Banff, Huntly and Turriff*, Edinburgh, HMSO, 1954; R. Glentworth and J. W. Muir (ed), *The Soils of the Country Round Aberdeen, Inverurie and Fraserburgh*, Edinburgh, HMSO, 1963; A. C. O'Dell and K. Walton, *The Highlands and Islands of Scotland*, London, Nelson, 1962.
6. J. R. Allan, *North-East Lowlands of Scotland*, London, Hale, 1974.
7. Calculated from Board of Agriculture, Parish Totals of Crops and Stock. *SRO* AF 39/1; /4; /12; /17; /22.
8. A. Macdonald, 'The Agriculture of the Counties of Elgin and Nairn', *THASS*, 1884, 4th series, XVI, pp.14-17.
9. White crops enumerated in the 1867 parish totals were wheat, barley, oats, rye, beans and peas. All of these crops were to be found in some place in the northeast, but only oats and (to a lesser extent) barley were of any importance. Some wheat was grown in favoured lowland districts, but it was always a gambler's crop and, as we shall see in chapter 3, the wheat acreage collapsed after 1870.
10. Redrawn from L. D. Stamp (ed), *Map of Predominant Farming Types in Scotland, Explanatory Booklet*, London, Geographical Publications for the Land Utilisation Survey of Britain, 1942, p.19.

11. It must be remembered that this is a map of *predominant* farming systems. On the ground the distinctions would appear less clear.

12. Macdonald, *loc cit*, p.91. The other corn counties were Berwick, Fife, Forfar (Angus), Haddington (East Lothian), Orkney, and Ross and Cromarty.

13. For source see note 8.

14. H. M. Jenkins, 'Report on Some Features of Scottish Agriculture', *JRASE*, 1871, 2nd series, VII, p.192.

15. W. Alexander, *Northern Rural Life in the Eighteenth Century*, Edinburgh, Douglas, 1877, p.1.

16. A. Fenton, *Scottish Country Life*, Edinburgh, Donald, 1975; T. C. Smout and A. Fenton, 'Scottish Agriculture Before the Improvers — an Exploration', *AHR*, 1965, XII, pp.73-93; G. Whittington. 'Was There a Scottish Agricultural Revolution?', *Area*, 1975, VII, pp.204-6.

17. Alexander, *op cit*, pp. 69-70.

18. A. Wight, *Present State of Husbandry in Scotland*, four volumes, Edinburgh, Creech, 1778-83, IV, p.594.

19. J. Stuart (ed), *List of Pollable Persons Within the Shire of Aberdeen, 1696*, two volumes, Aberdeen, Spalding Club, 1844.

20. M. Gray, 'Scottish Emigration: the Social Impact of Agrarian Change in the Rural Lowlands, 1775-1875', *Perspectives in American History*, 1973, VII, pp.107-111.

21. Anon, 'Social Condition of our Agricultural Labourers', *JA*, 1853-5, XIX, pp.145-6. Original emphases.

22. A monopsony exists when one buyer in a market exercises such control that his purchases affect the general price level in the market.

23. See, for example, 'The Rentaill of the Lordschipe of Huntlye, 1600', in J. Stuart (ed), *Miscellany of the Spalding Club, Vol. IV*, Aberdeen, Spalding Club, 1844, pp. lxxx-lxxxi, 261-319.

24. I. F. Grant, 'An Old Scottish Handicraft Industry in the North of Scotland', *SHR*, 1921, XVIII, pp.277-289.

25. Alexander, *op cit*, p.134. In 1773 even the obtuse and astigmatic Samuel Johnson noticed that 'the women of the lower class are visibly employed in knitting': S. Johnson, *A Journey to the Western Islands of Scotland*, ed. R. W. Chapman, Oxford, Oxford University Press, 1970, p. 13.

26. Wight, *op cit*, IV, p.706.

27. J. Milne, 'The Making of a Buchan Farm', *TBFC*: 1889, I, p.16.

28. C. van Onselen 'Randlords and Rotgut, 1886-1906', *History Workshop Journal* 1976, II, pp. 34-5.

29. J. Black, 'On the Agriculture of Aberdeen and Banff Shires', *THASS*, 1870-1, 4th series, III, p.4. See also T. M. Devine, 'The Rise and Fall of Illicit Whisky-Making in Northern Scotland, c.1780-1840', *SHR*, 1975, LIV, pp.155-177; W. Paul, *Past and Present in Aberdeenshire*, Aberdeen, Smith, 1881, p.62; A. Gordon, *The Folks of Carglen, or Life in the North*, London, Fisher Unwin, 1891, pp.102, 128-30, 213; Royal Commission on the Poor Law in Scotland, Appendix, Part II, *PP* 1844 (564), XXII, pp.564, 695, 726, 738.

30. J. W. Barclay, 'The Glen and its Folk', in W. D. Simpson (ed), *The Book of Glenbuchat*, Aberdeen, Third Spalding Club, 1942, p.45.

31. H. Beaton, *At the Back of Bennachie: Life in the Garioch in the Nineteenth Century*, Aberdeen, Central Press, 1922, pp.21-2.

32. Alexander, *op cit*, pp.182-192; *PP* 1844 (564), XXII, pp.557, 563, 732, 737; Paul, *op cit*, pp.62-4.

33. Alexander, *op cit*, p.221.

34. W. Littlejohn, *Stories of the Buchan Cottars Before the Year 'One'*, Aberdeen, Milne and Hutchison, 1929, p. 40.

35. Keith, *op cit*, p. 459; I. M. Bruce, *A Century of Aberdeenshire Agriculture*, Aberdeen, *Aberdeen Journal*, 1908, p. 37.

36. J. Anderson, *General View of the Agriculture of the County of Aberdeen*, Edinburgh, no publisher stated, 1794, p.47. Until 1881 tenants on the huge Gordon Castle estate still were obliged to grind their corn at the Duke of Richmond's mills: A. J. Wilson, *Radical Cures for the Evils of Feudalism*, Aberdeen, Scottish Farmers' Alliance, 1882, pp.28-9.

37. J. A. Symon, *Scottish Farming Past and Present*, Edinburgh, Oliver and Boyd, 1959, pp.98-9.

38. Select Committee (House of Lords) on the Game Laws, Report and Evidence, *PP* 1828 (235), VIII, p.60.

39. Should the story not be clear to any reader then he will find it in many places. Among the best are Gray, *loc cit;* Symon, *op cit;* H. Hamilton, *The Industrial Revolution in Scotland*, Oxford, Clarendon Press, 1932; J. E. Handley, *The Agricultural Revolution in Scotland*, Glasgow, Burns, 1963; T. C. Smout, *A History of the Scottish People, 1560-1830*, London, Collins, 1969, pp.280-331.

40. On northeast improving lairds in general see Alexander, *op cit*, pp.101-126; H. Hamilton, *An Economic History of Scotland in the Eighteenth Century*, Oxford, Oxford University Press, 1963, pp.75-77. On Grant of Monymusk see H. Hamilton (ed), *Selections from the Monymusk Papers, 1713-1755*, Edinburgh, Edinburgh University Press for the Scottish History Society, 1945; H. Hamilton (ed), *Life and Labour on an Aberdeenshire Estate, 1735-1750*, Aberdeen, Third Spalding Club, 1946; T. P. Soper, 'Monymusk, 1770-1850', unpublished Ph.D. thesis, Aberdeen University, 1954.

41. Hamilton, *Monymusk Papers*, pp.lxxi-lxxii.

42. Wight, *op cit*, IV, pp.695-6.

43. Bruce, *op cit*, p.37.

44. Keith, *op cit*, pp.458-9.

45. Alexander, *op cit*, p.20.

46. *NSA*, XI (Kincardine), p.205.

47. J. Macdonald, 'On the agriculture of the counties of Forfar and Kincardine', *THASS*, 1884, 4th series, XIII, p. 120. See also A. Smith, *A New History of Aberdeenshire*, Aberdeen, Smith, 1875, p.1083; Royal Commission on Agricultural Interests, Reports of Assistant Commissioners, *PP* 1881 (C2778-II), XVI, p.539.

48. Keith, *op cit*, p.157.

49. Wight, *op cit*, IV, p.590.

50. *Ibid*, IV, p.608.

51. Keith, *op cit*, p.157. A generation earlier Wight had noted merchants, a bookseller and the student son of a King's College professor among the most diligent local improvers: Wight, *op cit*, IV, pp.586-601. See also T. Donnelly, 'The Development of the Aberdeen Granite Industry, 1750-1939', unpublished Ph.D. thesis, Aberdeen University, 1975, *passim*.

52. Keith, *op cit*, pp. 153-7.

53. Wight, *op cit*, IV, pp.606-7, 698-9.

54. Hamilton, *Economic History . . .*, p.75.

55. Keith, *op cit*, p.155.

56. I. F. Grant, 'Social Effects of the Agricultural Reforms and Enclosure Movement in Aberdeenshire', *EcHR*, 1926, I, p.94. See also J. Godsman, *Glass, Aberdeenshire: the Story of a Parish*, Aberdeen, Reid, 1970, *passim*.

57. *NSA*, XII (Aberdeenshire), p. 780.

58. Names of Turnpike Road and Bridge Trusts in Scotland . . ., *PP* 1850 (568), XLIX. Nairnshire made no return to this enquiry.

59. Abstract Return of the Name of each Statute Labour Trust in Scotland . . ., *PP*

1850 (303), XLIX. Commutation road got its name because it was constructed and maintained with monies that represented the commuted labour dues that farmers previously had been required to give to public authorities for road purposes.

60. J. Lindsay, 'The Aberdeenshire Canal, 1805-54', *Journal of Transport History*, 1964, VI, 150-65.

61. Select Committee on the State of Agriculture, Third Report, *PP* 1836 (465), VIII Part II, Q13 628. The consequences of the collapse of the Napoleonic war boom may be seen in evidence from Dunottar: six capitalist farms lying untenanted with the likelihood of a considerable increase in the number at the next term; some landlords sequestering for rent arrears, but others fearful so to do in case the tenant broke and the laird had yet another empty farm on his hands. See Board of Agriculture, *The Agricultural State of the Kingdom, 1816*, Bath, Adams and Dart, 1970 (1816), pp. 400-5.

62. Jenkins, *loc cit*, p. 196; Royal Commission on the Law Relating to Landlord's Right of Hypothec in Scotland, Evidence, *PP* 1865 (3546-I), XVII, pp. 156-7, 256; Royal Commission on Agricultural Interests, Evidence Part II, *PP* 1881 (C 3096), XVII, Q 42 874-5, 43 006, 43 517, 44 414. Antony Cruikshank, one of the two Quaker brothers who established the famous Sittyton shorthorn herd, was an Aberdeen hosiery merchant: Allan, *op cit*, pp. 84-5.

63. *PP* 1881 (C 3096), XVII, Q 44 404-9, 44 485, 44 498, 44 505-6.

64. *Ibid*, Q 39 151. For a similar case see *Ibid*, Q 39 515.

65. *NSA* XII (Aberdeenshire), p. 137.

66. *PP* 1881 (C 3096), XVII, Q 42 540, 42 642.

67. See for instance G. Kay, 'The Landscape of Improvement: a Case Study of Agricultural Change in North-East Scotland', *SGM*, 1962, LXXVIII, p. 104; T. C. Smout, *A History of the Scottish People, 1560-1830*, London, Collins, 1969, p. 347.

68. Calculated from Return of Owners and Heritages, Scotland, *PP* 1874 (C 1097), LXXII Part II.

69. The same is true today, of course — see J. McEwan, 'Highland Landlordism', in G. Brown (ed), *The Red Paper on Scotland*, Edinburgh, EUSPB, 1975, pp. 262-270; J. McEwan, *Who Owns Scotland? A Study in Land Ownership*, Edinburgh, EUSPB, 1977; and J. Bryden and G. Houston's inappropriately named *Agrarian Change in the Scottish Highlands*, London, Robertson, 1976, pp. 61-8. The difference today is that the landed interest, made flesh in the Scottish Landowners Federation, face such a feeble challenge that they have been able successfully to resist even such modest demands as that their holdings should be enumerated.

70. A. McN. Caird, 'Land Ownership and Tenure', in J. Wilson (ed), *Report on the Present State of the Agriculture of Scotland*, Edinburgh, Blackwood, 1878, pp. 122-3. See also Anon, *Scottish Land: the Report of the Scottish Land Enquiry Committee*, London, Hodder and Stoughton, 1914. Not all this land was tilled: the huge sheep and sporting estates of the west and north made the Scottish figures much more dramatic than they would have been if arable land alone had been counted.

71. J. Bateman, *The Great Landowners of Great Britain and Ireland*, Leicester, Leicester University Press, 1971 (1883), pp. 164, 380.

72. *SRO* AF 39/1; /4; /12; /17; /22. The thirteen parishes were Bellie, Benholm, Cluny, Crathie/Braemar, Duffus, Elgin, Fettercairn, Garvock, Kinloss, Maryculter, Marykirk, Nairn, and Peterhead.

73. Calculated from Board of Agriculture for Scotland, Agricultural Statistics 1912 Part I, *PP* 1913 (Cd 6966) LXXVI, Table 14.

74. S. H. Franklin, *The European Peasantry: the Final Phase*, London, Methuen, 1969, p. 2.

75. Provost Blaikie, 'Report of the System of Improvement followed on the Muirs of . . . Charlestown', *THASS*, 1837, 2nd series, V, p. 116.

76. W. M. Williams, *A West Country Village: Ashworthy*, London, Routledge and

Kegan Paul, 1963, pp. 47-8. See also W. M. Williams, 'The Social Study of Family Farming', in D. R. Mills (ed), *English Rural Communities: the Impact of a Specialised Economy*, London, Macmillan, 1973, pp. 116-133.

77. Returns relating to Agricultural Holdings in Great Britain in 1895, *PP* 1896 (C 8243), LXVIII, Table VI.

78. *NSA* XII (Aberdeenshire), p. 333.

79. 'Lewis Grassic Gibbon' (J. L. Mitchell), *A Scots Quair*, London, Hutchinson, 1946.

80. W. Alexander, *Johnny Gibb of Gushetneuk*, sixth edition, Edinburgh, Douglas, 1880. See also I. Carter, 'To Roose the Countra Fae the Caul' Morality o' a Deid Moderatism: William Alexander and "Johnny Gibb of Gushetneuk"', *Northern Scotland*, 1976, II, pp. 145-62; I. Carter (ed), *Aberdeenshire Peasant Life*, London, Cass, 1978, *passim*.

81. In common parlance farm sizes were given not in tilled acreages but in the number of pairs of horses needed to work them. A two-pair farm would run between 100 and 150 acres, depending on the local circumstances.

82. Calculated from Board of Agriculture, Return of the Number of Allotments detached from, and attached to, Cottages, and of Agricultural Holdings in Great Britain, *PP* 1886 (C 4848), LXX, Tables VII, X.

83. Calculated from *Ibid*, Tables VII, XI.

84. *PP* 1913 (Cd 6966), LXXVI, pp. 62-7, 70-3.

85. *PP* 1881 (C 2778-II), XVI, p. 537; A. Macdonald, *loc cit*, p. 87.

86. M. Gray, *loc cit*; M. Gray, 'Northeast Agriculture and the Labour Force, 1790-1875', in A. A. Maclaren (ed), *Social Class in Scotland: Past and Present*, Edinburgh, Donald, 1976, pp. 86-104.

87. Calculated from Board of Agriculture, Agricultural Returns for Great Britain for 1867, *PP* 1867 (3491), LXXI, pp. 6, 16-20.

88. The Highland Society collected county statistics for three years in the mid-1850s: J. H. Maxwell, 'Address on Agricultural Statistics', *THASS*, 1854, 3rd series, VI, pp. 392-9; Maxwell, 'Agricultural Statistics of Scotland, 1855, 1856, 1857', *THASS*, 1855-7, 3rd series, VII, pp. 201-22, 457-92; *THASS*, 1857-9, 3rd series, VIII, pp. 201-24. Unfortunately these figures excluded farmers paying less than ten pounds in annual rent; a criterion that would exclude something like a third of northeast farmers. The Board of Agriculture figures were first published for 1866, but livestock figures for Aberdeenshire in that year were seriously inadequate.

Chapter 2

1. J. Boswell, 'Report of the Improvement of the Farm of Swellhead, on the Estate of Kingcausie, . . . County of Kincardine', *THASS*, 1843, 2nd series, VIII, pp. 349-50.

2. Royal Commission on Agricultural Interests, Minutes of Evidence, Part II, *PP* 1881 (C 3096), XVII, Q 39 848. The comment refers specifically to cattle and beef: it comes, significantly, from lowland Moray.

3. On northeast droving see A. R. B. Haldane, *The Drove Roads of Scotland*, Newton Abbot, David and Charles, 1974, pp. 115-32; W. McCombie, *Cattle and Cattle Breeders*, Edinburgh, Blackwood, 1867; W. Alexander, *Northern Rural Life in the Eighteenth Century*, Edinburgh, Douglas, 1877, pp. 68-76.

4. H. Hamilton, *An Economic History of Scotland in the Eighteenth Century*, Oxford, Clarendon Press, 1963, p. 96.

5. G. S. Keith, *General View of the Agriculture of Aberdeenshire*, Aberdeen, Brown, 1811, p. 487.

6. R. Gray, 'Account of the District of Buchan', *THASS*, 1832, 2nd series, II, p. 9.

7. Anon, 'On the Preparation of Live-stock and Meat in Reference to their Exportation by Steam Vessels', *JA*, 1837-8, VIII, p. 247.

8. *Ibid*, p.248.
9. A. Keith, 'Aberdeenshire Agriculture, 1851-1951', *SA*, 1951, XXXI, p.2.
10. J. J. Waterman, *The Coming of the Railway to Aberdeen*, Aberdeen, Centre for Scottish Studies, 1976.
11. J. Milne, 'On the Agriculture of Aberdeenshire and Banffshire', *THASS*, 1870-1, 4th series, III, p.391.
12. *AFP*, 15 September 1871. On the competition between rail and sea see G. Channon, 'The Aberdeenshire Beef Trade with London: a Study in Steamship and Railway Competition, 1850-69', *Transport History*, 1969, II, pp.1-25. See also J. H. Smith, 'The Cattle Trade of Aberdeenshire in the Nineteenth Century', *AHR*, 1955, III, pp.114-8; R. Perren, 'The Meat and Livestock Trade in Britain, 1850-70', *EcHR*, 1975, XXVIII, pp.385-400.
13. Smith, *loc cit*, p.116.
14. W. Paul, *Past and Present of Aberdeenshire*, Aberdeen, Smith, 1881, p.93.
15. T. Lawson, *Report on the Past and Present Agriculture of the Counties of Forfar and Kincardine*, Edinburgh, n.p., 1881, pp.62-3.
16. J. Black, 'On the Agriculture of Aberdeen and Banff Shires', *THASS*, 1870-1, 4th series, III, p.12.
17. Quoted in *Ibid*, p.12.
18. J. A. Symon, *Scottish Farming Past and Present*, Edinburgh, Oliver and Boyd, 1959, pp.325-6.
19. *Ibid*, p.326. On the Cruikshank brothers see R. Bruce, 'The Late Mr Amos Cruikshank', *THASS*, 1896, 5th series, VIII, pp.214-24. For a useful summary of trends and fashions in northeast pedigree cattle breeding see I. M. Bruce, *A Century of Aberdeenshire Agriculture*, Aberdeen, Aberdeen Journal, 1908, pp.33-61.
20. McCombie, *op cit*, *passim*; H. M. Jenkins, 'Report on some Features of Scottish Agriculture', *JRASE*, 1871, 2nd series, VII, pp.199-208.
21. Black, *loc cit*, pp.15-16.
22. *NSA*, XI (Kincardine), p.96.
23. G. S. Keith, *op cit*, p.467; Paul, *op cit*, p.93.
24. J. Macdonald, 'On the Agriculture of the Counties of Forfar and Kincardine', *THASS*, 1881, 4th series, XIII, p.123.
25. Board of Agriculture, Agricultural Statistics for Great Britain for 1886, *PP* 1887 (C 5187), LXXXVIII, p.110; for 1891, *PP* 1892 (C 6743), LXXXVIII, p.134; for 1898, *PP* 1899 (C 9304), CVI, p.134. The range of prices between 1866 and 1874 are for first and second quality beef; these data do not separate British and foreign beef. The figures for the period between 1875 and 1898 are for three qualities of British beef. Prices for three qualities of foreign beef followed the general trend of British beef prices, but at rather lower levels.
26. *AFP*, 19 January 1887; Board of Agriculture, Agricultural Statistics for Great Britain for 1901, *PP* 1902 (Cd 1121), CXVI, Table XXXV; for 1906, Part III, *PP* 1907 (Cd 3653), XCVII, Table LVI; for 1911, Part III, *PP* 1912-13 (Cd 6272), CVI, Table 56; Board of Agriculture for Scotland, Agricultural Statistics, 1912, Part I, *PP* 1913 (Cd 6966), LXXVI.
27. Manuscript *Fiars Court Book for Aberdeenshire; Fiars Court Book for Kincardine*. Prices are for the grain alone, without fodder. For the method of striking fiars in each Scottish county see Departmental Committee on Fiars Prices in Scotland, Minutes of Evidence, *PP* 1911 (Cd 5764), XXIV. For a more general discussion see R. Mitchison, 'The Movement of Scottish Corn Prices in the Seventeenth and Eighteenth Centuries', *EcHR*, 1965, XVIII, pp.278-91. Aberdeenshire fiars prior to 1900 are printed in D. Littlejohn, 'Aberdeenshire Fiars', in P. J. Anderson (ed), *Miscellany of the New Spalding Club, Vol. II*, Aberdeen, New Spalding Club, 1908, pp.1-76. Fiars prices were struck each year in each Scottish county until the mid-1970s. Evidence was taken from farmers and dealers to establish the average selling price for the various kinds of grain grown in the county. This was an important matter for groups other than farmers: the stipends of ministers, for example, were paid partly in the form of a specified amount of grain which was commuted to money at the appropriate fiar's price.
28. W. Alexander, *The Rinderpest in Aberdeenshire: the Outbreak of 1865, and*

how it was Stamped Out, Aberdeen, *Free Press*, 1882.

29. *PP* 1881 (C 3096), XVII, Q 44 505-6.

30. Between 1876 and 1920 a wheat fiar was struck in Aberdeenshire only in 1878, 1884 and 1891.

31. For sources see note 27 above.

32. Select Committee (House of Lords) on the Law of Hypothec in Scotland, Report and Evidence, *PP* 1868-9 (367), IX, Q 1 705.

33. Symon, *op cit*, pp.178-89; C. S. Orwin and E. H. Whetham, *History of British Agriculture, 1846-1914*, London, Longmans, 1964, pp.95-150; J. D. Chambers and G. E. Mingay. *The Agricultural Revolution, 1750-1880*, London, Batsford, 1966, pp. 170-98.

34. Alexander, *Northern Rural Life*, p. 69.

35. McCombie, *op cit*, p.101; Symon, *op cit*, pp.177, 183; R. Gray, *loc cit*, pp.64-5; Black, *loc cit*, p.6; H. Hamilton (ed), *Third Statistical Account of Scotland: the County of Banff*, Glasgow, Collins, 1961, p.32.

36. Royal Commission on Agricultural Interests, Reports of Assistant Commissioners, *PP* 1881 (C 2778-II), XVI, p.567. Not all farmers were convinced of the advantages of bought-in cattle food: as late as the 1890s the question of whether to rely mainly on turnips and hay or to give a large supplement of cake was still debated fiercely. See J. Black, 'Methods of Rearing and Feeding Cattle in the North of Scotland', *THASS*, 1893, 5th series, V, p.39.

37. J. R. Allan, 'The Land and the People', in H. Hamilton (ed), *Third Statistical Account of Scotland: the County of Aberdeen*, Glasgow, Collins, 1960, p.48.

38. Permanent pasture was a mere 5.3 per cent of the northeast's tilled acreage in 1867.

39. Milne, *loc cit*, p.389.

40. J. Boswell, 'On the Unprofitableness of Old Pasture, Compared with New', *JA*, 1832-4, IV, pp.783-91.

41. Milne, *loc cit*, pp. 389-90.

42. Symon, *op cit*, p.358; Hamilton, *Third Statistical Account: Banff*, p.44. For the effect of 'wild white' on northeast farming see J. Cruickshank, 'Changes in the Agricultural Industry of Aberdeenshire in the Last Fifty Years', *SA*, 1936, XIX, pp.136-7.

43. G. Robertson, *General View of the Agriculture of Kincardineshire or the Mearns*, London, Phillips, 1811, pp.326-8; D. Soutar, *General View of the Agriculture of the County of Banff*, London, Nicol, 1812, pp.223-7; W. Leslie, *General View of the Agriculture of the Counties of Nairn and Moray*, London, Sherwood, Neely and Jones, 1813, pp.265-79.

44. J. Milne, 'The Making of a Buchan Farm', *TBFC*, 1889, I, p.163.

45. J. Hay, 'On Concrete Drain Tiles', *THASS*, 1843, 2nd series, VIII, pp.589-98.

46. Applications made for the Advance of Public Money, under the Provisions of the Act 9 and 10 Vict. c101, as regards England and Scotland; Distinguishing the Applications from each Country, *PP* 1847 (43, 146), XXXIX; Number of Applications that have been made for Advances of Public Money under the Act of Session 1846, c101, in England, Ireland, and Scotland, respectively . . ., *PP* 1847 (91), XXXIX.

47. Orwin and Whetham, *op cit*, p.195; J. Caird, 'General View of British Agriculture', *JRASE*, 1878, 2nd series, XIV, p.316.

48. Macdonald, *loc cit*, p. 117.

49. Black, 'Agriculture of Aberdeen and Banff Shires', p. 35; Lawson, *op cit*, pp.24-5; J. Porter, 'Report on Draining' (Monymusk), *THASS*, 1851-3, 3rd series, III, p.528; A. Thomson, 'Report on Improvement of Waste Land' (Banchory Devenick), *THASS*, 1853-5, 3rd series, V, pp. 90-8.

50. A. Smith, *A New History of Aberdeenshire*, Aberdeen, Smith, 1875, pp.500, 593, 800, 1199, 1289.

51. *Ibid*, p.1289.

52. T. J. Jamieson, 'Report on the General Principles of Reclaiming Land', *THASS*, 1855-7, 3rd series, VII, p.19.

53. Macdonald, *loc cit*, p.132.

54. Anon, 'Young on Wire Fences', *JA*, 1849-51, XVII, pp.338-42; C. Y. Michie, 'On Wire Fencing', *THASS*, 1870-1, 4th series, III, pp.446-55; Milne, 'Agriculture of

Aberdeenshire and Banffshire', p.395. By the 1880s the Laigh of Moray was fully enclosed, almost wholly by wire fences: A. Macdonald, 'On the Agriculture of the Counties of Elgin and Nairn', *THASS*, 1884, 4th series, XVI, p.90. The same was true of southern Kincardine where, it was calculated, wire fences were fifty per cent cheaper than wooden palings — the only other feasible form of enclosure in the district: Lawson, *op cit*, p.56.

55. Roberson, *op cit*, pp.180-4; G. S. Keith, *op cit*, pp.129-38; Soutar, *op cit*, pp.90-6; Leslie, *op cit*, pp.60-1.

56. Robertson, *op cit*, p.182.

57. Lawson, *op cit*, p.60; A. D. Hall, *A Pilgrimage of British Farming, 1910-12*, London, Murray, 1913, pp.374-5.

58. J. Cowie, 'Farm Steadings. Plan and Report' (St Cyrus), *THASS*, 1853-5, 3rd series, IV, pp.33-4; J. Macdonald, *loc cit*, pp.115, 131.

59. Lawson, *op cit*, pp.61-2.

60. *PP* 1881 (C 2778-II), XVI, pp.539-40; *PP* 1881 (C 3096), XVII, Q 42 578-80, 43 670, 44 435-9.

61. McCombie, *op cit*, p.19.

62. Alexander, *Northern Rural Life*, p.35.

63. J. Cowie, 'An Essay on the Comparative Advantages in the Employment of Horses and Oxen in Farm Work', *JRASE*, 1844, V, pp.52-7.

64. J. Ord, *Bothy Songs and Ballads of Aberdeen, Banff, Moray, Angus and the Mearns*, Paisley, Gardner, 1930, p.210. Reprinted John Donald Publishers, 1975.

65. *PP* 1881 (C 3096), XVII, Q 43 115.

66. Bruce, *op cit*, p.21.

67. J. Macdonald, *loc cit*, pp.160-2; A. Macdonald, *loc cit*, pp.103-4; In Aberdeenshire Clydesdales sometimes were bred into the local stock, particularly the Brangan breed: Milne, 'Agriculture of Aberdeenshire and Banffshire', pp.24-5.

68. J. Porter, 'Report on Ploughing Lea' (Monymusk), *THASS*, 1855-7, 3rd series, VII, p.30.

69. Lawson, *op cit*, pp.59-60.

70. *PP* 1881 (C 2778-II), XVI, p. 567; See also A. Fenton, *Scottish Country Life*, Edinburgh, Donald, 1976.

71. The best account of this change is A. Fenton, 'Sickle, Scythe and Reaping Machine: Innovation Patterns in Scotland', *Ethnologia Europaea*, 1974, VII, pp.35-47. See also E. J. T. Collins, 'Harvest Technology and Labour Supply in Britain, 1790-1870', *EcHR*, 1969, XXII, pp.453-73.

72. Smith, *op cit*, p.241; Black. 'Agriculture of Aberdeen and Banff Shires', p.33; Milne, 'Agriculture of Aberdeenshire and Banffshire', p.396; Lawson, *op cit*, p.58. The first reaper-binder reached Aberdeenshire in 1885: J. F. Duncan, 'Farm Servants in the Northeast, 1851-1951', *SA*, 1951, XXXI, p.14. Both back and side delivery reapers, and reaper-binders, needed scythesmen to cut a 'roadie' around the field before the machine could get started.

73. Ord, *op cit*, p.271. Willie Rae's twenty acres per day compares with the quarter acre that could be cut with a sickle in a day, and the one acre that a skilled scythesman could manage.

74. E. J. Hobsbawm and G. Rudé, *Captain Swing*, London, Lawrence and Wishart, 1969, p.359.

75. *NSA, passim;* R. Smith, 'On the Extended Application of Water and Other Power to Farm Purposes' (Huntly), *THASS*, 1841, 2nd series, VII, pp.64-8; J. Wilken, *Ellon in Bygone Days*, second edition, Ellon, Rennie, 1926, p.52.

76. Lawson, *op cit*, p.57. It was common to combine a water-powered mill with the Big Mill. The latter was called up when the farmer wanted to thresh out several stacks, and when he wanted to thresh barley — which the beater drum could not manage.

77. Smith, *op cit*, p.578.

78. A. Keith, *A Thousand Years of Aberdeen*, Aberdeen, Aberdeen University Press, 1972, pp.41-124.

79. The introduction of guano to the Garioch in the 1840s provided William Alexander with the opportunity to launch into one of the more sardonic passages in his polemical masterpiece: W. Alexander, *Johnny Gibb of Gushetneuk*, sixth edition,

Edinburgh, Douglas, 1880, pp.78-85.

80. *PP* 1868-9 (367), IX, Q 2 071. Evidence from William McCombie, Milton of Kemnay. In 1865 it was estimated that manures to the value of half the annual rent were applied by tenants each year: Royal Commission on the Law Relating to Landlord's Hypothec in Scotland, Evidence, *PP* 1865 (3546-I), XVII, p.192.

81. *PP* 1881 (C 2778-II), XVI, p.567. On the growing grip of finance capital on agriculture see W. Alexander, 'Coupar Sandy', in W. Alexander, *Life Among My Ain Folk*, Edinburgh, Douglas, 1882.

82. SRO, BT2/300; BT2/647; *PP* 1865 (3546-1), XVII, p. 186.

83. After A. C. O'Dell and K. Walton, *The Highlands and Islands of Scotland*, London, Nelson, 1962, Fig.59.

84. But not all: we can only mourn that the line projected in 1884 to connect the end of the Deeside line at Ballater with the Spey Valley through some of the most rugged country in Britain was never built. It would have lost a fortune, but it would have made a memorable trip.

85. SRO, BT2/647.

86. *PP* 1865 (3546-I), XVII, p. 181.

87. SRO, BT2/12811.

88. *PP* 1865 (3546-I), XVII, p. 182.

89. *Ibid*, p.190.

90. Black, 'Agriculture of Aberdeen and Banff Shires', p. 9

91. G. S. Keith, *op cit*, p. 463. Original emphases.

92. Alexander, *Life Among My Ain Folk*, pp.85-181.

93. McCombie, *op cit*, pp. 1-5, 55-97.

94. Alexander, *Northern Rural Life*, p. 72 fn.

95. McCombie, *op cit*, *passim*.

96. Black, 'Agriculture of Aberdeen and Banff Shires', p. 9.

97. 'A few years, indeed, after the railway was opened [Lowrin] Fair grew less and less, until it was finally abolished': H. Beaton, *At the Back o' Bennachie: Life in the Garioch in the Nineteenth Century*, Aberdeen, Central Press, 1923, p.79.

98. J. R. Barclay, 'Farming Methods in Banffshire', *THASS*, 1908, 5th series, XX, p.161.

99. A. Keith, *loc cit*, p. 3.

100. A. Macdonald, *loc cit*, pp.117-18; Cruickshank, *loc cit*, p.227.

101. Black, 'Agriculture of Aberdeen and Banff Shires', p.13. For an account of a 500-acre farm worked under this vertical integration see Jenkins, *loc cit*, pp.195-9.

102. Royal Commission on Agricultural Depression, Expenditure and Outgoings on Certain Estates in Great Britain; and Farm Accounts, *PP* 1896 (C 8125), XVI, pp. 48-9.

103. Calculated from Return of the Amount of Property assessed to Income and Property Tax . . . in each County in England, Wales, and Scotland, in each of the Years from 1842-3 to 1864-5, *PP* 1866 (511), XXXIX; 1864-5 to 1869-70, *PP* 1870 (C 454), LXI; 1880-1, *PP* 1882 (C 292), XXXVII; 1881-2, *PP* 1883 (C 206), XXXVIII; 1882-3, *PP* 1884-5 (C 25), XLV; 1883-4, *PP* 1884-5 (C 235), XLV; 1884-5 to 1889-90, *PP* 1892 (39-Sess I), XLVIII; 1889-90 to 1894-5, *PP* 1896 (C 216), XLIX.

104. Lawson, *op cit*, p. 24.

105. *Ibid*, p. 60

106. McCombie, *op cit.*, p. 52.

107. J. Milne, *Twixt Ury and Don and Round About*, Inverurie, Dufton Scott, 1947. The widespread acceptance of beater drum threshers on capitalist farms in the early nineteenth century did not render the flail redundant at a stroke: barley still had to be hand threshed until the high speed rubbing drum thresher arrived, and even then the flail was still used if the farmer wanted unbruised straw for thatching.

108. Smith, *op cit*, pp. 737, 748, 800, 915, 925, 940, 986, 1083, 1281.

109. *Ibid*, p. 474.

110. Many northeast capitalist farmers bought double-furrow ploughs when first they were introduced after 1865: fifteen years later most of these ploughs lay rusting in stackyards.

111. V. I. Lenin, 'The Capitalist System of Modern Agriculture', in V. I. Lenin, *Collected Works Vol. 16*, London, Lawrence and Wishart, 1963 (1910), pp. 442-5. Here

Lenin, wearing his cap as a rural sociologist, is investigating German agriculture: would that modern rural sociology had his combination of a firm theoretical grasp and meticulous empirical analysis.

112. H. Cockburn, *Journal*, two volumes, Edinburgh, Edmonston and Douglas, 1874, I, p.172.

113. W. Alexander, 'Aberdeenshire Agriculture — Past and Present', *TNAPSS*, 1877, p.679.

114. G. S. Keith, *op cit*, p. 404.

115. Alexander, 'Aberdeenshire Agriculture . . .', p. 679.

116. Calculated from Robertson, *op cit*, pp.61-177, *SRO*, AF 39/17.

117. Royal Commission on the Housing of the Working Classes, Second Report (Scotland), with Evidence, *PP* 1884-5 (C 4409), XXXI, Q 21 123: evidence from south Kincardine. Fettercairn's historian noted in 1899 that 'The locality was thickly peopled even down to the early decades of the present century. Besides the families of the principal tenants on the lands of Thornyhill, Cairnton and Balbegno, the writer has heard old people relate that on these lands they counted eighty or ninety "reekin' lums" (smoking chimneys), whereas at the present time they do not far exceed one-tenth of that number': A. C. Cameron, *The History of Fettercairn*, Paisley, Parlane, 1899, p. 24. See also J. Macdonald, *loc cit*, pp. 73, 130, and for the Laigh of Moray, A. Macdonald, *loc cit*, pp. 21-2.

118. *AFP*, 19 April 1886.

119. Wilken, *op cit*, p. 23.

120. Royal Commission on the Poor Laws (Scotland), Appendix, Part II, *PP* 1844 (564), XXI, pp. 566, 639, 669, 680, 691, 696, 727, 729, 734, 744, 762; *NSA* XII (Aberdeenshire), p. 235.

121. *AFP*, 29 March 1886.

122. *AFP*, 22 March, 4 May 1886.

123. Anon, 'The Large Farm System', *Free Church Magazine*, 1848, V, p.110. See also G. Kay, 'The Landscape of Improvement: A Case Study of Agricultural Change in North-East Scotland', *SGM*, 1962, LXXVIII, pp.103-7; *NSA* XII (Aberdeenshire), p.1040.

124. J. Pirie, *The Parish of Cairnie*, Banff, *Banffshire Journal*, 1906, pp. 63-4.

125. *PP*. 1844 (564), XXI, pp. 677, 746.

126. Calculated from *Valuation Rolls, Aberdeenshire*, 1859-60, 1892-3, 1912-13.

127. Calculated from Board of Agriculture, Agricultural Statistics for Great Britain for 1866, *PP* 1866 (3727), LX; for 1871, *PP* 1871 (C 460), LXIX; for 1876, *PP* 1876 (C 1635), LXXVIII; for 1881, *PP* 1881 (C 3078), XLII; for 1886, *PP* 1886 (C 4847), LXX; for 1891, *PP* 1890-1 (C 6524), XLI; for 1896, *PP* 1897 (C 8502), XLVIII; for 1901, *PP* 1902 (Cd 1121), CXVI; for 1906 Part I, *PP* 1906 (Cd 3281), CXXXIII; for 1911 Part I, *PP* 1912-13 (Cd 6021), LVI.

128. A. Wight, *Present State of Husbandry in Scotland*, four volumes, Edinburgh, Creech, 1778-83, IV, 585-602.

129. J. Ferguson, 'Report on the Improvement of the Muir of Altens' (Nigg), *THASS*, 1841, 2nd series, VII, pp.163-80; Boswell, 'Improvement of . . . Swellhead' (Maryculter); J. Yeats, 'Report on the Improvement of Waste Land' (Nigg), *THASS*, 1847-9, 3rd series, III, pp. 213-17; Sir J. Macpherson Grant. 'Report on the Improvement of the Farm of Marypark' (Inveravon), *THASS*, 1849-51, 3rd series, IV, pp. 79-94; J. Porter, 'Report on the Improvement of Waste Land' (Monymusk, Oyne, and Chapel of Garioch), *THASS*, 1855-7, 3rd series VII, pp. 291-311; Smith, *op cit*, pp. 511, 1251.

130. A. Thomson, 'Report on Improvement of Waste Land,' *THASS*, 1853-5, 3rd series, V, pp.90-8.

131. D. Davidson, 'Report on the Improvement of Waste Land' (Spynie), *THASS*, 1847-9, 3rd series, III, pp.405-8.

132. A. Cruickshank, 'On the Improvement of Forty Acres on the Farm of Sittyton . . .' (Fintray), *THASS*, 1841, 2nd series, VII, pp. 527-9; R. Gray, 'Report on the Improvement of Waste Land on the Farm of Nether Savock' (Longside), *THASS*, 1843-5, 3rd series, I, pp. 117-20; J. Cowie, 'On the Improvement of Waste Land' (Laurencekirk), *THASS*, 1843-5, 3rd series, I, pp. 424-5; J. Cruickshank, 'Report on the Improvement of Waste Lands' (Elgin), *THASS*, 1847-9, 3rd series, III, pp. 317-20; J. and J. Grant, 'Report on the Improvement of Waste Land' (Morayshire), *THASS*, 1847-9, 3rd series, III, pp. 400-1; A. Lawson, 'Report on the Improvement of Waste Land' (Morayshire), *THASS*, 1847-9, 3rd series, III, pp. 402-3; A. Reid, 'Report on the Improving of Waste Land' (Chapel of Garioch), *THASS*, 1855-7, 3rd series, VII, pp. 137-46: U. Fraser, 'Improvement of Waste Land' (Tarves), *THASS*, 1855-7, 3rd series, VII, pp. 441-5; A. Lovie, 'The Reclamation of Waste Land on the Farm of Towie' (Fraserburgh), *THASS*, 1883, 4th series, XV, pp. 65-9; *PP* 1865 (3546-1), XVII, p. 156.

133. *PP* 1881 (C 3096), XVII, Q 43 007.

134. W. Alexander, 'The Making of Aberdeenshire', *Transactions of the Aberdeen Philosophical Society*, 1892, II, pp. 102-22.

135. *PP* 1844 (564), XXI, pp. 553, 560, 703, 713, 725; *NSA* XII (Aberdeenshire), pp. 278, 602, 614, 723; Anon, 'The Large Farm System', p. 110. Intercensal population increase in the first half of the nineteenth century was attributed, in part at least, to reclamation of waste land by crofters in the parishes of Alvah, Botriphnie, Bourtie, Chapel of Garioch, Ellon, Fetteresso, Forgue, Fyvie, Gamrie, Keith, Kennethmont, King Edward, Leochel Cushnie, Marykirk, Mortlach, Nigg, Oyne, Rathen, Rathven, Rhynie, Turriff, and Tyrie: Census of Great Britain 1851, Number of Inhabitants in 1801, 1811, 1821, 1831, 1841, 1851, Scotland, *PP* 1852-3 (1632), LXXXVI, pp. 64-77.

136. K. Walton, 'The Distribution and Structure of the Population of North-East Scotland, 1696-1931', unpublished Ph.D. thesis, Aberdeen University, 1951, p. 244.

137. Black, 'Agriculture of Aberdeen and Banff Shires', pp. 33-4.

138. J. Reid, 'On the Improvement of Sixteen Acres in the Moss of Templeton . . .' (Kildrummy), *THASS*, 1841, 2nd series, VII, pp. 238-41; J. Adam, 'Report on the Improvement of Waste Land' (Banchory Ternan), *THASS*, 1847-9, 3rd series, III, pp. 403-5; J. Mackintosh, 'Report on the Improvement of Waste Land in the Parishes of Nairn and Auldearn . . .', *THASS*, 1847-9, 3rd series, III, pp. 545-55; G. Carr, 'On Improvements on the Farm of Westhill of Park . . .' (Drumoak), *THASS*, 1870-1, 4th series, III, pp. 407-8; J. Stevenson, 'On the Improvement of the Farm of Quarryhead' (Aberlour), *THASS*, 1870-1, 4th series, III, pp. 139-41.

139. *PP* 1881 (C 3096), XVII, Q 30 170,

140. Thomson, *loc cit*, p. 92.

141. Milne, 'Making of a Buchan Farm', p. 164.

142. *AFP*, 5 April, 1886. See also Carr, *loc cit.*

143. 'Lewis Grassic Gibbon' (James Leslie Mitchell) and 'Hugh MacDiarmid' (C. M. Grieve), *Scottish Scene*, London, Jarrolds, 1934, p. 235.

144. Alexander, *Johnny Gibb of Gushetneuk*, pp. 321-2.

145. C. Arensberg and S. Kimball, *Family and Community in Ireland*, London, Smith, 1968 (1940).

146. J. Hunter, *The Making of the Crofting Community*, Edinburgh, Donald, 1976, p. 74.

147. *Ibid*, pp. 122-3.

148. See table 1.2.

149. The exceptions were the great breeding herds — Sittyton, Tillyfour, and so on. But even on Tillyfour fat cattle were as important to William McCombie's profits as his famous Aberdeen-Angus breeding herd.

150. The 1696 Poll Book shows a strong correlation between farming settlement in

the Garioch and patches of deep, well-drained and fertile soil: K. Walton, 'The Distribution of Population in Aberdeeshire, 1696', *SGM*, 1950, LXVI, pp. 23-4.

151. 'There has been a quantity of land brought in; but a great number of the best farms have been arable ever since I can recollect. Some of the hill sides have been taken in and improved, and I believe that part of those hill sides should never have been improved in the world. But if you go to the Vale of Alford, the great majority of the farms have been the same ever since I recollect': *PP* 1868-9 (367), IX, Q 1734.

152. Lawson, *op cit*, p. 63; Duncan, *loc cit*, p. 14; Barclay, *loc cit*, p. 161: Pirie, *op cit*, pp, 67-8; A. Macdonald, *loc cit*, p. 101; J. Macdonald, *loc cit*, p. 125: Milne. 'Agriculture of Aberdeenshire and Banffshire', p. 392; A. D. Imper, 'The North of Scotland', in J. P. Maxton (ed), *Regional Types of British Agriculture*, London, Allen and Unwin, 1936, pp. 260-1.

153. The great capitalist farmers of the southeast tried to mitigate this unfortunate necessity, of course. Hence double-hinding, where a married servant and his son were hired jointly. Hence the perniciously exploitative bondager system, under which a hind was required to provide and lodge a female outworker for the farmer. See B. W. Robertson, 'The Border Farm Worker, 1871-1971', *Journal of Agricultural Labour Science*, 1973, II, pp.63-93; J. P. D. Dunbabin, *Rural Discontent in Nineteenth Century Britain*, London, Faber and Faber, 1974, pp. 130-172.

154. This dependence held back the development of productive forces. The scythe replaced the less efficient sickle in the Lothian corn harvest much later than was the case in the northeast. The Lothian farmer, having his harvest taken by large migrant hairst bands, could not afford experiment. His northeast counterpart, with a much more flexible organisation of harvesting, was less inhibited. See Fenton, 'Sickle, Scythe and Reaping Machine'.

155. *PP* 1844 (564), XXII, p. 695. Evidence from the Cabrach. For other parishes see *Ibid*, pp. 563 (Huntly), 564 (Glass), 557 (Inveraven), 762 (Monquitter), 685 (Glenbuchat), 732 (Birse), 737 (Crathie/Braemar), 738 (Glenmuick).

156. *NSA*, XI (Kincardine), pp. 135-6.

157. *PP* 1844 (564), XXII, p. 760 (Logie Buchan). Hence the recent judgement that by 1840 stocking knitting 'had ceased to be of any importance as a supplementary income for the payment of rents': A. A. Maclaren, *Religion and Social Class: the Disruption Years in Aberdeen*, London, Routledge and Kegan Paul, 1974, pp. 7-8.

158. Wight, *op cit*, III, pp. 613-14. Note the implication that these crofters had no lease.

159. Col. Fraser, 'Settlement of Crofters on Waste Land on the Estate of Castle Fraser, Aberdeenshire' (Cluny and Kemnay), *THASS*, 1837, 2nd series, V, p. 388.

160. Royal Commission on Agricultural Depression, Minutes of Evidence, Vol. III, *PP* 1896 (C 7400), XVII, Q 51 681. We get a thumbnail sketch of this crofter colony in Royal Commission on Labour, The Agricultural Labourer, Vol. III, Scotland, Part I, *PP* 1893-4 (C 6894-XV), XXXVI, p.117: 'As regards "orra" labour Mr Black draws it from a colony of crofters in his neighbourhood, on the reclaimed Moss of Balmuckity, who hold crofts of from two to seven acres. They built the houses and small offices for themselves, and have sat there in some cases for three generations. They pay rent to the proprietor, and they are apprehensive of questions being raised as to their right to their houses. They do not each own a horse, but own enough horses among them to work their holdings. They, and a few of their dependents, *ie* wives and daughters, work for the neighbouring farmers.'

161. J. Black, 'Report on the Cottage Accommodation in the District of Buchan', *THASS*, 1853-5, 3rd series, V, pp.92-9. I am indebted for details of Black's life to Mrs Shaw, Sheriffston.

162. *PP* 1881 (C 3096), XVII, Q 39 426-7; *PP* 1893-4 (C 6894-XV), XXXVI, p.142.

163. *PP* 1881 (C 3096), XVII, Q 39 986.

164. M. Gray, 'Scottish Emigration: the Social Impact of Agrarian Change in the Rural Lowlands, 1775-1875', *Perspectives in American History*, 1973, VII, p. 167.

165. W. Jolly, *The Life of John Duncan, Scotch Weaver and Botanist*, London, Kegan Paul, Trench, 1883.

166. Anon, 'On Reaping With the Scythe', *JA*, 1832-4, IV, p. 355.

167. Pirie, *op cit*, p. 70.

168. Ord, *op cit*, p. 264.

169. Anon, 'The Sickle, the Scythe and the Reaping Machine', *JA*, 1857-9, XXI, p. 61.

170. J. Cruickshank, *loc cit*, pp. 6-7.

171. J. Wilson, 'Farming in Aberdeenshire — Ancient and Modern', *THASS*, 1902, 5th series, XIV, p. 102.

172. *PP* 1865 (3546-I), XVII, p. 154. Evidence from A. Taylor, Cushnie, Fordoun.

173. J. Caird, 'General View of British Agriculture', *JRASE*, 1878, 2nd series, XIV, pp. 304-6; C. S. Orwin and E. H. Whetham, *History of British Agriculture, 1846-1914*, London, Longmans, 1964, pp. 164-7.

174. In 1865 Alex. Taylor held Cushnie, Fordoun, on the unexpired portion of a lease taken by his grandfather for two nineteens and a life. The security of this long lease allowed him, he said, to take a prominent part in tenant farmers' agitation over landlords' hypothec: *PP* 1865 (3546-I), XVII, p. 152. A few life rents were still to be found in Foveran a decade later (A. Smith, *op cit*, p. 577). These were unusual survivals, however. The ubiquitous nineteen-year lease was based on the mystical Metonic Cycle: it was believed that a nineteen-year period gave the farmer his fair share of every kind of weather and quality of growing season (Pirie, *op cit*, p. 66).

175. Milne, 'Agriculture of Aberdeenshire and Banffshire', p. 400.

176. J. Macdonald, *loc cit*, p. 115.

177. A. Macdonald, *loc cit*, pp. 28, 51, 86.

178. *Ibid*, p. 37; A. Smith, *op cit*, p. 689; *PP* 1881 (C 3096), XVII, Q 30 059-60.

179. It is important not to make the mistake of assuming that their legal occupation of dwarf holdings removed crofters from the dangers of extreme penury. In 1844 the Aberlour doctor reported that in the parishes of Aberlour, Knockando and Inveraven, which he knew well, 'There are a number of poor crofters, living at the bottom of the hills, in circumstances that prevent him from making any charge for attendance upon them; and he cannot distinguish them generally, by looking at their homes and mode of living, from paupers on the roll. Their mode of living and dress are altogether similar': *PP* 1844 (564), XXII, p. 551.

180. N. L. A. Campbell, 'The Story of "The Colony" on Bennachie', in A. W. M. Whitely (ed), *The Book of Bennachie*, Aberdeen, Bailies of Bennachie, 1976, pp. 104-6; A. I. McConnochie, *Bennachie*, Aberdeen, Wyllie, 1890, pp. 88-109; J. Allan, 'Agriculture in Aberdeenshire in the Sixties', *Deeside Field*, 1927, III, p. 36; Beaton, *op cit*, p. 3.

181. A.Smith, *op cit*, p. 35; J. Macdonald, *loc cit*, p. 120.

182. I can find examples of kind payments in the 1859-60 Aberdeenshire Valuation Roll only for a few farms on the Haddo estate.

183. See p. 22.

184. *NA*, XI (Kincardine), p. 18.

185. Anon, 'Rules and Regulations for the Management of the Buchan and Boyn Farmer Society, Begun at Macduff March 10th 1786', *Banffshire Journal*, 16 September 1929.

186. Bruce, *op cit*, pp. 11-12, 18.

187. Anon, *Rules and Regulations of the Aberdeenshire Agricultural Association*, Aberdeen, Chalmers, 1819. The most important and influential agricultural society in Scotland, the Highland and Agricultural Society, had the reputation in the 1840s of

being simply a landlords' body: W. G. Yourston of Garioch, 'An Inquiry into the Duties of the Landholders of Scotland to the Peasantry, and the Manner in which those Duties have been Performed', *JA*, 1841-2, XII, p. 516. The Society's Directors quickly instituted a new class of members to bring in capitalist farmers and thus cement the bond between the two fractions: Anon, 'Admission of Tenant Members. Report by the Directors to the General Meeting held on 8 January 1850,' *THASS*, 1849-51, 3rd series, II, pp. 209-11.

188. Bruce, *op cit*, pp. 40, 51.

189. Anon, *Jubilee of the Royal Northern Agricultural Society*, Banff, *Banffshire Journal*, 1893, p.19; Anon, *The Garioch Farmer Club*, Banff, *Banffshire Journal*, 1882, p.3.

190. A Farmer, 'On the Value of Agricultural Societies', *JA*, 1828-9, I, p. 344.

191. Caird, *loc cit*, p. 306.

192. Maclaren, *Religion and Social Class.*

193. See the chapter on the election of elders in Alexander, *Johnny Gibb of Gushetneuk.*

194. The Yeomanry was a favourite target for northeast levellers: 'Or if one would take a look into the Melvin Hall, Tarves, on the night of the annual volunteer ball (or "party" as they prefer to call it, as "ball" is too commonplace for them), you will see all the grandeur of lady and gentleman.' Letter to *AFP*, 9 January 1886.

195. Select Committee (House of Commons) on the Game Laws, Report and Evidence, *PP* 1872 (337), X, Q 3 408-9.

196. *AFP*, 29 June 1866.

197. *PP* 1872 (337), X, Q 3 414.

198. Anon, *Report to the Commisioners of Supply of the County of Aberdeen . . .[on] the Game Question*, Aberdeen, Chalmers, 1872, p. 23.

199. *Ibid*, pp. 25-6.

200. *PP* 1865 (3546), XVII, p. x.

201. *Ibid*, pp. xii, xiii.

202. *PP* 1868-9 (367), IX: Q 1637.

203. *PP* 1865 (3546-I), XVII, p. 152.

204. Cf. *Ibid:* 'My friends and neighbours suffer, I think, from over-competition and the admission to farms of mere adventurers.' The only northeast capitalist farmers who supported hypothec in evidence to the 1865 Royal Commission were John Garland, Cairton, Fordoun; R. Walker, Mains of Portlethen, Banchory Devenick; and W. Warrack, Newmill, Leochel Cushnie: all men who doubled muckle farming with factoring.

205. *Ibid*, p. 262.

206. *Ibid*, p. 257.

207. The secretary of the Aberdeen committee, Alex. Copland, happened also to be the manager of the Aberdeen Commercial Company — the largest manure and grain dealers in the northeast: *Ibid*, p. 181.

208. *PP* 1881 (C 3096), XVII, Q 39 903, 42 602-3; Royal Commission on Agricultural Depression, Reports of Assistant Commissioners, *PP* 1894 (C 7342), XVI, Part 1, pp. 16-18, 1895 (C 7742), XVII, P. 36; A. McN. Caird, 'Land Ownership and Tenure', in J. Wilson (ed), *Report on the Present State of the Agriculture of Scotland*, Edinburgh, Blackwood, 1878, pp. 124-6.

209. *PP* 1881 (C 3096), XVII, Q 42 469.

210. *Ibid*, Q 37 400, 44 437, 44 442-3. See also Royal Commission on Agricultural Depression, Minutes of Evidence, Vol. IV, *PP* 1896 (C 8021), XVII, Q 51 841: 'In the parish where I come from the tenants built every steading in it up till 1886.' (Evidence from lower Banffshire.)

211. Jenkins, *loc cit*, p. 153.

212. There were very few exceptions: A. Smith, *op cit*, p. 1110; Black, 'Agriculture of Aberdeen and Banff Shires', p. 35.
213. J. Cobban, 'Farm Buildings', *THASS*, 1909, 5th series, XXI, pp. 3-4.
214. See p. 43.
215. Milne, 'Making of a Buchan Farm', pp. 167-8.
216. *Ibid*, p. 165. The raising of the threshing mill had a profound symbolic significance for middle peasants: again and again it stands as a milestone on the road to the household's comfortable self-sufficiency, the end of the flail's tyranny. See, for example, Stevenson, *loc cit*, p. 140: 'The whole was finished by the end of the season 1862, when we had the satisfaction of seeing our new thrashing-mill agoing, and our cattle comfortably housed.'
217. See chapter 3. The neatest demonstration of the point is to be found in that subtle polemical masterpiece, Alexander's *Johnny Gibb of Gushetneuk*. Johnny's loans to his impecunious yet high-living laird, Sir Simon Frissal of Glensnicker, act not only as the lever with which Johnny prevents the engrossment of Gushetneuk in the contiguous capitalist farm of Clinkstyle, but also symbolise the parasitical laird's dependence on the labour of his peasant tenants.
218. *AFP*, 26 April 1886. The 'Buchan capital' referred to is Peterhead. The truth of this account is attested by an investigation into the causes of agitation among crofters at Lenabo: see the letter from A. Bath in *AFP*, 2 February 1886.
219. *PP* 1844 (564), XXI, Q 1 482-97. See above, pp.
220. *AFP*, 22 March 1886.
221. Speech by Mr Anderson, Wellhouse, Alford, to the 1882 annual meeting of the Scottish Farmers' Alliance, *AFP*, 22 December 1882.
222, The Fife estate was the glaring exception: by the 1880s it had a reputation as one of the northeast's most rapacious and eviction-prone estates.
223. *PP* 1881 (C 3096), XVII, Q 37 495. Is it too cynical to suspect that some at least of the glowing praise heaped on the Gordon Castle estate by its capitalist tenants in this source reflected the fact that they were giving evidence to a Royal Commission headed by their laird, the Duke of Richmond and Gordon?
224. G. Greig, *Folk-Song in Buchan and Folk-Song of the North-East*, Hatboro', Pennsylvania, Folklore Associates, 1963, Article 147. 'To put out your fire' was a common euphemism for the unspeakable: eviction.
225. See, for example, one of the letters with which John Bruce, Fornet, Skene, bombarded the *Aberdeen Free Press*: '. . . It bears on the face of it the hall mark of the lawyer-factor, a class of men, I say it advisedly, who have done more to damnify and ruin the tenant-farmers of this country than all the other adverse influences put together': *AFP*, 28 January 1886. Bruce was a complex character: a capitalist farmer, he was one of the leaders of the Irish-inspired pro-peasant faction in the Scottish Farmers' Alliance during the 1880s, and yet he was pilloried in a bothy ballad by his own farm servants. The ballad, 'John Bruce of the Forenit' (Fornet) will be found unexpurgated in J. Alison (ed), *Poetry of Northeast Scotland*, London, Heinemann, 1976, pp. 92-3; and, in a version bowdlerised to protect the guilty, in Gavin Greig's celebrated collection.

Chapter 3

1. G. Greig, *Folk-Song in Buchan and Folk-Song of the North-East*, Hatboro', Pennsylvania, Folklore Associates, 1963, Article 147.
2. A. Smith, *A New History of Aberdeenshire*, Aberdeen, Smith, 1875, pp. 550, 715, 1028, 1052, 1110, 1219, 1289.
3. For studies of 'the great depression' see S. B. Saul, *The Myth of the Great*

Depression, 1873-1896, London, Macmillan, 1969; P. J. Perry (ed), *British Agriculture, 1875-1914*, London, Methuen, 1973; P. J. Perry, *British Farming in the Great Depression, 1870-1914*, Newton Abbot, David and Charles, 1974.

4. H. Hamilton, *Third Statistical Account of Scotland: the County of Banff*, Edinburgh, Oliver and Boyd, 1961, pp. 43-4.

5. Royal Commission on Agricultural Interests, Reports of Assistant Commissioners, *PP* 1881 (C 2778-II), XVI, p. 568; J. R. Barclay, *The Remedy for Agricultural Distress*, Aberdeen, Scottish Farmers' Alliance, 1882, p. 5.

6. This point was not lost on contemporary socialists. See Friedrich Engels' 1886 footnote on p. 305 of F. Engels. 'The Condition of the Working Class in England' (1845), in K. Marx and F. Engels, *On Britain*, London, Lawrence and Wishart, 1962.

7. Calculated from the Board of Agriculture's parish totals for 1867 and 1911: SRO AF 39/1; /4; /12; /17; /22.

8. Calculated from Board of Agriculture, Agricultural Statistics for Great Britain for 1866, *PP* 1866 (3727), LX; for 1871, *PP* 1871 (C 460), LXIX; for 1876, *PP* 1876 (C 1635), LXXVIII; for 1881, *PP* 1881 (C 3078), XLII; for 1886, *PP* 1886 (C 4847), LXX; for 1891, *PP* 1890-1 (C 6524), XLI; for 1896, *PP* 1896 (C 8502), XLVIII; for 1901, *PP* 1902 (Cd 1121), LXVI; for 1906, Part I, *PP* 1906 (Cd 3281), LXXXIII; for 1911, Part I, *PP* 1912-13 (Cd 6021), LVI.

9. See p. 41.

10. It is difficult to place credence in the high Nairn figure in 1886. This county contained only five parishes: thus it is sensitive to small enumeration errors that would be lost in the vastness of Aberdeenshire's figures.

11. Perry, *British Farming . . .*, p. 24.

12. For sources see note 8.

13. J. Macdonald, 'On the Agriculture of the Counties of Forfar and Kincardine', *THASS*, 1881, 4th series, XIII, pp. 129-30; A. Macdonald, 'On the Agriculture of the Counties of Elgin and Nairn', *THASS*, 1884, 4th series, XVI, p. 87; Royal Commission on Agricultural Depression, Minutes of Evidence, Vol. III, *PP* 1896 (C 7400), XVII, Q 51 598.

14. J. Macdonald, *loc cit*, pp. 122-3. For the same problem in Banffshire see Royal Commission on Agricultural Interests, Minutes of Evidence, Part II, *PP* 1881 (C 3096), XVII, Q 44 480.

15. R. Gray, 'Account of the District of Buchan', *THASS*, 1832, 2nd series, V, pp. 60-1; J. Black, 'On the Agriculture of Aberdeen and Banff Shires', *THASS*, 1870-1, 4th series, III, pp. 2-3.

16. Select Committee on the State of Agriculture, Third Report, *PP* 1836 (465), VIII, Part II, Q 13 609.

17. T. Lawson, *Report on the Past and Present Agriculture of the Counties of Forfar and Kincardine*, Edinburgh, n.p. 1881. p. 40.

18. *PP* 1881 (C 3096), XVII, Q 37 443; J. R. Barclay, 'Farming Methods in Banffshire', *THASS*, 1908, 5th series, XX, p. 157: '[On Cairnton of Boyndie] the barley is threshed first . . . and the grain is sent direct to a distillery which has taken the year's crop for long time.'

19. Lawson, *op cit*, p. 51. See also *PP* 1896 (C 8021), XVII, Q 52 149; J. Macdonald, *loc cit*, pp. 141-2.

20. J. F. Tocher (ed), *The Book of Buchan*, Peterhead, Buchan Club, 1910, pp. 439-40.

21. See p. 35

22. W. Watt, *A History of Aberdeen and Banff*, Edinburgh, Blackwood, 1900, p. 334.

23. R. Perren, 'The North American Beef and Cattle Trade with Great Britain, 1870-1914', *EcHR*, 1971, XXIV, p. 436.

24. Mostly Aberdeenshire and Banffshire, no doubt.
25. For sources see note 8.
26. Lawson, *op cit*, pp. 62-3.
27. J. Black, 'Methods of Rearing and Feeding Cattle in the North of Scotland', *THASS*, 1893, 5th series, V, p. 18.
28. Lawson, *op cit*, pp.66-7.
29. J. H. Smith, 'The Cattle Trade of Aberdeenshire in the Nineteenth Century', *AHR*, 1955, III, p. 118.
30. *PP* 1881 (C 3096), XVII, Q 39 331, 39 594, 39 776, 44 003.
31. J. H. Maxwell, 'Agricultural Statistics of Scotland, 1855', *THASS*, 1855-7, 3rd series, VII, p. 201; Board of Agriculture, Agricultural Statistics for Great Britain for 1910, Part II, *PP* 1911 (Cd 5604), XLV, Part I, Tables 30, 31, 32. Oat yields on an Aberdeenshire capitalist farm rose throughout 'the great depression': J. A. Symon, 'Cairnhill, Turriff, 1861-1926, Part II', *SA*, 1951, XXX, p. 26. See also P. S. Craigie, 'On Recent Changes in Scottish Agriculture', *Transactions of the British Association for the Advancement of Science*, 1886, pp.1162-4.
32. *PP* 1881 (C 3096), XVII, Q 30 057, 30 077.
33. A. Macdonald, *loc cit*, p. 83; Royal Commission on Agricultural Depression, Minutes of Evidence, Vol. IV, *PP* 1896 (C 8021), XVII, Q 52 149; *PP* 1896 (C 7400), XVII, Q 51 530-5.
34. *PP* 1881 (C 3096), XVII, Q 29 983; *PP* 1896 (C 7400), XVII, Q 51 530-5.
35. We do not know the bankruptcy rate before 1870, of course.
36. *PP* 1896 (C 8021), XVII, Q 51 809-10.
37. *Ibid*, Q 51 920-1.
38. Royal Commission on Agricultural Depression, Reports of Assistant Commissioners, *PP* 1894 (C 7342), XVI, PartI, p. 7.
39. See pp. 115-9.
40. R. Molland and G. Evans, 'Scottish Farm Wages from 1870 to 1900', *Journal of the Royal Statistical Society*, 1950, CXIII, pp.200-7.
41. See pp. 109-11.
42. *PP* 1881 (C 3096), XVII, Q 39 617-8, 40 042.
43. Royal Commission on Agricultural Depression, Expenditure and Outgoings on Certain Estates in Great Britain; and Farm Accounts, *PP* 1896 (C 8125), XVI, pp. 48-9.
44. *PP* 1896 (C 7400), XVII, Q 51 655-70.
45. A. Macdonald, *loc cit*, p.83.
46. See pp. 76-7.
47. Royal Commission on Agricultural Depression, Reports of Assistant Commissioners, *PP* 1895 (C 7742), XVII, pp. 22-3.
48. *AFP*, 26 February 1886.
49. *AFP*, 9 July, 1891.
50. A. Keith, 'Aberdeenshire Agriculture, 1851-1951', *SA*, 1951, XXXI, p. 2.
51. SRO BT2/240.
52. *Montrose, Arbroath and Brechin Review*, 29 December 1865. Some people were unwise enough to put these precepts into practice: see the description of a southern English farm worked entirely by steam in R. Jeffries, *Hodge and His Masters*, two volumes, London, MacGibbon and Kee, 1966 (1880), I, pp.19-27.
53. Philorth Steam Cultivation and Traction Company (Limited) — hereafter PSCTCL — manuscript *Sederunt Book*, p.1.
54. *AJ*, 24 April 1872.
55. Black, 'Agriculture of Aberdeen and Banff Shires', p. 30.
56. PSCTCL *Sederunt Book*, pp. 3-5.
57. *Ibid.*
58. Smith, *op cit*, pp. 1219-21.

59. SRO BT2/348.
60. *Ibid.*, J. Cruickshank, 'Changes in the Agricultural Industry of Aberdeenshire in the last Fifty Years', *SA*,1936, XIX, p. 132.
61. SRO BT2/240.
62. PSCTCL *Sederant Book*, Directors' meeting, 6 June 1873; 2nd Annual General Meeting, 13 August, 1873.
63. *Ibid*, Directors' meetings, 8 June, 25 June 1880.
64. SRO BT2/240. The Edinburgh-based Scottish Steam Cultivation company had fared even worse; it was wound up in January, 1881. See SRO BT2/348.
65. Cruickshank, *loc cit*, p.133.
66. Anon, 'Report of a Special Committee . . . on the Various Methods of Cultivating Land by Steam Power in East Lothian', *THASS*, 1870-1, 4th series, III, p. 289.
67. Royal Commission on Agricultural Interests, Minutes of Evidence, Part I, *PP* 1881 (C 2778-I), XV, Q 6 440-6.
68. Cruickshank, *loc cit*, p. 133. Only the engine drivers, ploughman and foreman came with the tackle: the farmer had to provide the rest of the labour team.
69. Socialist agrarian commentators invariably took steam ploughing as an index of capitalist agricultural development. See, for example, V. I. Lenin, 'Capitalism in Agriculture' (1889), in Lenin, *Collected Works*, Vol. IV, London, Lawrence and Wishart, 1960, p. 142.
70. See pp. 23, 51.
71. *PP* 1896 (C 8021), XVII, Q 51 860.
72. *PP* 1896 (C 7400), XVII, Q 51 537-41, 51 558, 51 723.
73. *PP* 1881 (C 3096), XVII, Q 43 287.
74. A cottar house is the farm cottage given to a married farm servant as part of his wages. The name shows the strong perception of continuity between the poor peasant subtenant in the sixteenth and seventeenth centuries and the married farm servant of the nineteenth and twentieth centuries.
75. *PP* 1881 (C 3096), XVII, Q 29 959, 37 394, 39 216-7, 39 525, 40 057-63, 42 912; *PP* 1881 (C 2778-II), XVI, pp. 536-9, 569.
76. *PP* 1881 (C 3096), XVII, Q 39 465, 39 517-9, 42 614, 42 946, 42 957, 42 983-7, 43 644-7.
77. *Ibid*, Q 39 220-3, 39 908-11, 42 656-8, 43 881.
78. *Ibid*, Q 39 570, 44 021; J. Milne, *Compensation for Improvements*, Aberdeen, Scottish Farmers' Alliance, 1882; G. Bruce, *The Value of Tenants' Improvements*, Aberdeen, Scottish Farmers' Alliance, 1883.
79. Quoted in Anon, *Notes on the Land Question*, Aberdeen, Scottish Farmers' Alliance, 1883, pp. 7-8.
80. *PP* 1881 (C 3096), XVII, Q 44 021.
81. Landlords had been able to contract out of the 1875 Act. In Wales almost all had done so: C. S. Orwin and E. H. Whetham, *History of British Agriculture, 1846-1914*, London, Longmans, 1964, p.172.
82. *AFP*, 12 April 1886. The episode shows that, as before 1870, peasants and capitalist farmers had some community of interest in the achievement of tenant right.
83. *PP* 1894 (C 7342), XVI, Part I, p. 13. See also J. W. Barclay, *op cit*, p.7.
84. *PP* 1881 (C 3096), XVII, Q 29 962, 37 587, 39 558, 40 074, 42 590-5; A. Macdonald, *loc cit*, p. 87; *PP* 1895 (C 7742), XVII, pp. 20, 52.
85. On northeast dissatisfaction with the 1883 Agricultural Holdings Act see *PP* 1894 (C 7342), XVI, Part I, pp. 18-21; *PP* 1895 (C 7742), XVII, pp. 21, 38; *PP* 1896 (C 8021) XVII Q 51 876-99. Many of these difficulties were forseen in J. Esslemont, *The Agricultural Holdings (Scotland) Bill*, Aberdeen, Scottish Farmers' Alliance, 1883.
86. *PP* 1895 (C 7742), XVII, p. 19.

87. The situation in the west Highlands in the late eighteenth and early nineteenth centuries, where landlords established and maintained the crofting system as a means of allowing peasants to produce their own subsistence while lairds took as rent the peasants' entire money income from gathering and burning kelp: M. Gray, 'The Kelp Industry in the Highlands and Islands', *EcHR*, 1951, IV, pp. 197-209; J. Hunter, *The Making of the Crofting Community*, Edinburgh, Donald, 1976, pp. 15-49.

88. See pp. 61-2.

89. *AFP*, 2 February 1886.

90. *PP* 1896 (C 7400), XVII, Q 51 753.

91. *PP* 1895 (C 7742), XVII, p. 22.

92. J. Milne, 'The Making of a Buchan Farm', *TBFC*, 1889, I, p. 164.

93. A. Mitchell, *Recollections of a Lifetime*, privately printed, 1911.

94. I. Carter (ed), *Aberdeenshire Peasant Life*, London, Cass, forthcoming.

95. The use of a professional son to reflect glory on the extended family of a farmer is a running thread in nineteenth century Scottish literature, from the exquisite sourness of William Alexander's treatment of the priggish Benjie Birse in *Johnny Gibb of Gushetneuk*, Edinburgh, Douglas, 1880, to the sugary sentimentality of Ian Maclaren's kailyard novels: *Beside the Bonny Brier Bush*, eighth edition, London, Hodder and Stoughton, 1895; *The Days of Old Lang Syne*, London, Hodder and Stoughton, 1895: *Afterwards and Other Stories*, second edition, London, Hodder and Stoughton, 1898. Like so much else in kailyard literature, this use of a professional son to hike up family status is guyed in the unrelieved gloom of George Douglas, *The House with the Green Shutters*, London, Cassell, 1967 (1901). See I. Carter, 'To Roose the Countra Fae the Caul Morality o' a Deid Moderatism: William Alexander and *Johnny Gibb of Gushetneuk*', *Northern Scotland*, 1976, II, pp. 145-62; I. Carter, 'Kailyard: the Literature of Decline in Nineteenth Century Scotland', *Scottish Journal of Sociology*, 1976, I, pp. 1-14.

96. Work on farm tenancies in Newmachar between 1901 and 1930 shows some evidence of a farming ladder, particularly at the bottom end of the farm size hierarchy; but the ladder is both shorter and less broad than the ideology of the lad o' pairts would lead us to expect. See J. Brown, 'An enquiry into social mobility within the farming industry, 1900-30', unpublished M.A. dissertation, Department of Sociology, University of Aberdeen, 1971. I replicated Brown's work in a W.E.A. class at Cove Bay, Nigg, and came up with similar results. Both Newmachar and Nigg lie within the Aberdeen dairying belt, of course: it may be that the abnormally high rents in these parishes inhibited movement up the farming ladder more than in other parts of the northeast. The major study of social mobility within British farming is J. A. Nalson, *The Mobility of Farm Families*, Manchester, Manchester University Press, 1968.

97. In 1886 one hundred acres of the Hill of Dudwick, Ellon, still lay unreclaimed and would — it was argued — yield fair crops, 'only the laird put a stop to the takin' in, cause they were encroachin' on his sheetin''. *AFP*, 26 April 1886.

98. *PP* 1894 (C 7342), XVI, Part I, p. 14.

99. *PP* 1896 (C 8021), XVII, Q 52 034.

100. H. Brody, *Inishkillane: Change and Decline in the West of Ireland*, London, Allen Lane, 1973, pp. 71-2.

101. *Ibid*, pp. 99-100; E. Morin, *Plodémet*, London, Allen Lane, 1971, pp. 93-4; S. H. Franklin, *Rural Societies*, London, Macmillan, 1971, pp. 35-6.

102. *PP* 1896 (C 8021), XVII, Q 51 829; *PP* 1896 (C 7400), XVII, Q 51 717.

103. A. R. Mortimer, *Notes on Farm Kitchen Work*, Elgin, *Courier and Courant*, 1910, p. 52.

104. Royal Commission on Labour, The Agricultural Labourer, Vol. III, Scotland, Part I, *PP* 1893-4 (C 6894-XV), XXXVI, pp. 109, 121.

105. Royal Commission on the Housing of the Industrial Population of Scotland,

Rural and Urban, Minutes of Evidence, 1921, Q 29 091, 29 123.

106. I. MacPherson, *Shepherd's Calendar*, London, Cape, 1931; 'Lewis Grassic Gibbon' (James Leslie Mitchell), *Sunset Song*, (1932) in *A Scots Quair*, London, Hutchinson, 1946. See also I. Carter, 'Dorset, Kincardine, and Peasant Crisis', *Journal of Peasant Studies*, 1975, II, pp. 483-8.

107. Alexander, *Johnny Gibb of Gushetneuk*, pp. 110-16.

108. R. C. on Housing, Evidence, 1921, p. 1371.

109. See pp. 135-6.

110. See chapter 6.

Chapter 4

1. 'Lewis Grassic Gibbon' (J. L. Mitchell) and 'Hugh MacDiarmid' (C. M. Grieve), *Scottish Scene*, London, Jarrolds, 1934, p. 297.

2. This phrase encapsulates much better than any English equivalent the element of command over household or hired labour by peasant or capitalist farmer. I will use it as a shorthand term to avoid the endless repetition of the cumbersome phrase 'capitalist farmers, middle peasants and poor peasants'.

3. Calculated from Census of Great Britain 1841, Occupations Abstract 1841: Part II, Scotland, *PP* 1844 (588) XXVII: Census of Great Britain 1851, Ages, Civil Condition, Occupations and Birthplaces, Vol II, *PP* 1852-3 (1691-II), LXXXVIII Part II; Census of Scotland 1861, Population Tables and Report, Vol. II, *PP* 1864 (3275) LI; Census of Scotland 1871, Report and Tables, Vol. II, *PP* 1873 (C 841) LXXII; Census of Scotland 1881, Report and Tables, Vol. II, *PP* 1883 (C 3637) LXXXI; Census of Scotland 1891, Report and Tables, Vol. II, Part II, *PP* 1893-4 (C 7134) CVII; Census of Scotland 1901, Report and Tables, Vol. III, *PP* 1904 (Cd 1798) CVIII; Census of Scotland 1911, Report and Tables: the Counties in Alphabetical Order, *PP* 1912-13 (Cd 6097), CXIX-CXX.

4. For sources see note 3.

5. The point is made in W. Cramond, *Illegitimacy in Banffshire; Facts, Figures and Opinions*, Banff, *Banffshire Journal*, 1888, p. 22. See also *PP* 1864 (3275) LI, p. liii.

6. J. Kitteridge, 'Country Work Girls in Nineteenth-Century England', in R. Samuel (ed), *Village Life and Labour*, London, Routledge and Kegan Paul, 1975, pp. 75-138.

7. G. Greig, *Folk-Song in Buchan and Folk-Song of the North-East*, Hatboro, Pennsylvania, Folklore Associates, 1963, Article 92. This song dates from 1880.

8. Anon. 'The Physical Condition of the People — the Rural Labourer', *JA:* 1857-9, XXI, p. 626.

9. Royal Commission on the Employment of Women and Children in Agriculture, Fourth Report, Appendix Part I, *PP* 1870 (C 221) XIII, p. 34. Note that his family was not included in a northeast married farm servant's bargain with the farmer, as in southeast Scotland: B. W. Robertson, 'The Border Farm Worker, 1871-1971', *Journal of Agricultural Labour Science*, 1973, II, pp. 65-93.

10. *PP* 1870 (C 221) XIII. Appendix Part II, pp. 48-9. A. Macdonald, 'On the Agriculture of the Counties of Elgin and Nairn', *THASS:* 1884, 4th series, XVI, p. 119 asserts that, in those counties at least, work previously done by female outworkers was being taken over by unmarried male farm servants.

11. *PP* 1870 (C221) XIII, Appendix Part II, pp. 48-9: evidence from Mortlach, Speymouth and Banchory Ternan.

12. *PP* 1870 (C 221) XIII, Appendix Part I, p. 34.

13. *PP* 1870 (C 221), XIII, Appendix Part II, pp. 48-9: evidence from Birse, Cawdor and Tarland.

14. J. W. Paterson, 'Rural Depopulation in Scotland', *THASS:* 1883, 5th series, IX,

p. 266; Royal Commission on Agricultural Interests, Minutes of Evidence, Part II, *PP* 1881 (C 3096), XVII, Q 37 466.

15. See p. 95.

16. Royal Commission on Agricultural Interests, Reports of Assistant Commissioners, *PP* 1881, (C 2778-II), XVI, p. 540.

17. *PP* 1881 (C 3096), XVII, Q 39 549-50; *PP* 1881 (C 2778-II) XVI, p. 657; Macdonald , *loc cit*, p. 118; Royal Commission on Agricultural Depression, Minutes of Evidence, Vol. III, *PP* 1896 (C 7400), XVII, Q 51 696, Vol. IV, *PP* 1896 (C 8021), XVII, Q 51 829; Report by Mr. Wilson Fox on the Wages, Earnings and Conditions of Employment of Agricultural Labourers in the United Kingdom, *PP* 1900 (Cd 346), LXXXII, pp. 54, 68.

18. *AFP*, 18 November 1882; *PP* 1900 (Cd. 346), LXXXII, pp. 54, 68; A. R. Mortimer, *Notes on Farm Kitchen Work*, Elgin, *Courant and Courier*, 1910, p. 52; J. F. Duncan, 'The Scottish Agricultural Labourer', in D. T. Jones, J. F. Duncan, H. M. Conacher and W. R. Scott, *Rural Scotland During the War*, Oxford, Clarendon Press, 1926, p. 199.

19. The question whether to include *chefs d'entreprise* in the family labour force can be answered only in the context of knowledge about an area's agrarian structure. In East Lothian, for example, with an average farm size above 200 acres in 1912, we are safe to exclude farmers from the labour force. In the northeast, by contrast, the proportion of *chefs* who did not work alongside their hired and family workers was rather small.

20. For sources see note 3.

21. H. Hamilton, *Third Statistical Account of Scotland: the County of Banff*, Edinburgh, Oliver and Boyd, 1961, pp. 64-5.

22. See p. 101

23. See pp. 99-100

24. See pp. 30-31

25. For sources see note 3.

26. It is thus in W. Alexander, *Johnny Gibb of Gushetneuk*, sixth edition, Edinburgh, Douglas, 1880: Mrs Birse of Clinkstyle machinates to have Gushetneuk, engrossed in Clinkstyle, and she will then retire with her husband to the Gushetneuk crofthouse.

27. One finds a literary example of this arrangement in I. MacPherson, *Shepherd's Calendar*, London, Cape, 1931.

28. Calculated from *PP* 1912-13 (Cd 6097), CXIX-CXX, Tables XXVI, XXVII, XXVIII.

29. For source see note 28.

30. For source see note 28.

31. Macdonald, *loc cit*, p.28.

32. *PP* 1896 (C 8021), XVII, Q 51 826.

33. Calculated from *PP* 1883 (C 3657), LXXXI, pp. 871-3.

34. For source see note 33.

35. Robertson, *loc cit*. For differences between Scottish regions in average labour squad size in recent times see A. Geddes, 'The Agricultural Unit: the Farm Labour-Team', *Planning Outlook*, 1949, I, pp. 1-17.

36. Calculated from *PP* 1864 (3275), LI.

37. Calculated from *PP* 1852-53 (1691-II), LXXXVIII Part II, p. 987.

38. Calculated from *PP* 1904 (Cd 1718), CVIII, p. 90.

39. J. F. Duncan, 'Organising Farm Workers', *Journal of Agricultural Economics*, 1935-7, IV, p. 253.

40. M. Gray, 'North-East Agriculture and the Labour Force, 1790-1875', in A. A. Maclaren (ed), *Social Class in Scotland: Past and Present*, Edinburgh, Donald, 1976,

pp. 86-104; J. F. Duncan, 'Farm Workers in the North-East, 1851-1951', *SA*, 1951, XXX, p. 14.

41. A. Mitchell, *Recollections of a Lifetime*, privately printed, 1911.

42. *PP* 1870 (C 221), XIII, Appendix Part I, p. 34, Part II, pp. 47-8.

43. 'David Toulmin' (J. Reid), *Straw into Gold*, Aberdeen, Impulse, 1973, pp. 26-60.

44. A. G. Wilken, *Peter Laing, the Elgin Centenarian*, second edition, Elgin, Yeadon, 1887, p.15.

45. *Ibid*, p. 24.

46. For Gray's career see W. Muir, 'Biographical Sketch', in A. Gray, *Talks With Our Farm Servants*, Edinburgh, Clark, 1906, pp. xi-xxxv; Marquess of Aberdeen, *Why Are Aberdeenshire Folk Proud of their County?* Dundalk, Dundalgan Press, 1929, pp. 11-13.

47. A. Gray, *op cit*, p. 24.

48. *PP* 1881 (C 3096), XVII, Q 42 501; J. Pirie, *The Parish of Cairnie*, Banff, *Banffshire Journal*, 1906, pp. 69-70.

49. J. Black, 'On the Agriculture of Aberdeen and Banff Shires', *THASS*, 1870-1, 4th Series, III, p. 32; Duncan, 'Scottish Agricultural Labourer', p. 195.

50. M. Gray, 'Scottish Emigration: the Social Impact of Agrarian Change in the Rural Lowlands', *Perspectives in American History*, 1973, VII, pp. 139-41.

51. J. Donaldson, *General View of the Agriculture of the County of Elgin or Moray*, London, Clarke, 1794, p. 24. E. Cameron, *Reform and Economy*, Inverurie, Kemp, 1865, p. 9 asserts that the usual yokings in the Garioch in 1839 were three hours in the morning and five in the afternoon.

52. H. M. Jenkins, 'Report on some Features of Scottish Agriculture', *JRASE*, 1871, 2nd series, VII, pp. 197-8.

53. Greig, *op cit*, Article 4.

54. Horses could be worked in the northeast on between 220 and 240 days in the year, depending on local circumstances: G. Brown, 'Agricultural Costs in Scotland', *THASS*, 1891, 5th series, III, p. 272.

55. On seasonal changes in labour routine on northeast farms see *PP* 1893-94 (C 6894-XV), XXXVI, pp. 111, 132.

56. See, for example, 'the Banffshire Ploughman's' objection to 'the custom, in practice here, of making the ploughmen undergo all the drudgery of the farm; such as thrashing (for "the weary flinging tree" is still more common here than thrashing mills), shearing, turning dunghills, etc, etc. Must it not be galling for a young fellow like me, Mr Editor, after following his plough and darling horses for a whole morning, to be obliged to wield the flail in a dusty barn till yoking-time again, while my horses are resigned to some careless cowherd, ignorant and uninterested in their welfare? Anon. Hints by the Banffshire Ploughman', *Farmer's Magazine*, 1806, VII, p. 54.

57. Duncan, 'Scottish Agricultural Labourer', pp. 194-5. This was used as an argument by farmers resisting demands from farm servants for a half-holiday: horsemen and orramen, it was argued, would not look after cattle properly. *AFP*, 1 February 1886.

58. *AFP*, 27 February 1886 (Tarland); 18 March 1886 (Newhills, Tarves); 20 March 1886 (Fyvie); 22 March 1886 (Forgue); 23 March 1886 (Banchory Ternan, Fyvie); 25 March 1886 (Echt); 2 April 1886 (Drumblade).

59. *PP* 1893-4 (C 6894-XV), XXXVI, pp. 111, 123-6, 132, 136-9.

60. Feeing markets were the usual route through which northeast farm servants were hired, but other arrangements were to be found at times. See pp. 146-7.

61. For a discussion of wage variations within one market see R. Molland and G. Evans, 'Scottish Farm Wages from 1870 to 1900'; *Journal of the Royal Statistical Society*, 1950, CXIII, p. 221.

62. *AFP*, 19 January 1887.

63. It may well be that these two farms were run by a single farmer: the source does not help us on this point. For a discussion by counties of Scottish farm labour costs in 1890, distinguishing the cost of cash wages and perquisites, see Brown, *loc cit*, pp. 282-3.

64. Not all of these variations have to do with money wages: it is likely that these paradoxical cases result from the different value of perquisites given to married and to unmarried servants.

65. Expressed from Molland and Evans, *loc cit*, Table 3.

66. Data on money wages between 1840 and 1869 are taken from *AJ*; between 1870 and 1920 from G. Evans, 'Trade Unionism and the Wage Level in Aberdeen', unpublished PhD thesis, Aberdeen University, c. 1950, Appendix I, Table 3. These data are controlled with indices of (a) average retail prices 1850-1902 (1850 = 100) and (b) cost of living 1880-1920 (1914 = 100) in order to arrive at a measure of real wages. These indices are taken from B. R. Mitchell and P. Deane, *Abstract of British Historical Statistics*, Cambridge, Cambridge University Press, 1962, pp. 343-5; A. L. Bowley, 'Index-Numbers of Wage-Rates and Cost of Living', *Journal of the Royal Statistical Society*, 1952, CXV, pp. 500-6.

67. After 1880 one usually finds overseas emigration quoted in press reports as one of the prime causes of increases in ruling prices at a particular feeing market.

68. *PP* 1900 (Cd 346) LXXXII, p. 74.

69. See pp.

70. Royal Commission on the Housing of the Industrial Population of Scotland, Rural and Urban, Report, *PP* 1917-18 (Cd 8731), XIV, p. 172.

71. W. Alexander, *Life Among My Ain Folk*, second edition, Edinburgh, Douglas, 1882, pp. 204-30; Alexander, *Johnny Gibb of Gushetneuk*, pp. 15-22; J. Ord, *Bothy Songs and Ballads of Aberdeen, Banff, and Moray, Angus and the Mearns*, Paisley, Gardner, 1930, pp. 247-8.

72. J. R. Allan, *Farmer's Boy*, London, Methuen, 1935, pp. 46-7. This description comes from the very end of our period. Though cheerless, the conditions described were more comfortable than had been the case earlier.

73. I. Carter, 'Illegitimacy Rates and Farm Service in North-East Scotland', paper given to Section N, British Association for the Advancement of Science Annual Meeting, Stirling, 1974; I. Carter, 'Illegitimate Births and Illegitimate Inferences', *Scottish Journal of Sociology*, 1977, I, 125-35.

74. See pp.

75. *PP* 1893-4 (C 6894-XV), XXXVI, p. 141. Evidence from H. D. McCombie, Milton of Kemnay: in this parish most servants were chaumered.

76. An English visitor saw the Aberdeenshire farm kitchen as 'very much a humble kind of club': Jenkins, *loc cit*, p. 198.

77. The men slept two to a bed.

78. Quoted in J. P. Watt, *First Annual Report of the Medical Officer of Health for Aberdeenshire*, Aberdeen, *Free Press*, 1891, p. 53.

79. J. Allan, 'Agriculture in Aberdeenshire in the Sixties', *Deeside Field*, 1927, III, p. 33.

80. 'An Agricultural Labourer', *Duty to Farm Servants*, Aberdeen, Bennet, 1859, p. 7. For other first-hand accounts of life in northeast chaumers see, *inter alia*, J. Alexander, *Prize Essay . . . on Farm Servants in Scotland*, Aberdeen, Bennet, 1852, p. 14; G. B. Watt, *On the Improvement of Farm Servants*, Inverurie, Kemp, 1865, p. 10; Anon, *Eleven Years at Farm Work*, Aberdeen, *Free Press*, 1879; Mitchell, *op cit*, 'David Toulmin' (J. Reid), *op cit*, pp. 44-5.

81. J. R. Allan, *op cit*, pp. 111-12.

82. Bothying is touched on in Anon, *Eleven Years . . .*, and Mitchell, *op cit*. See also A. Fraser, 'Essay', pp. 17-18, and J. Cassie, 'Essay', p. 40 in *Essays by Agricultural*

Labourers on the Condition and Improvement of their Class, Aberdeen, Brown, 1859; Cameron, *op cit*, p. 8.

83. R. H. Campbell, *Scotland Since 1707: the Rise of an Industrial Society*, Oxford, Blackwell, 1965, pp. 167-8; T. C. Smout, *A History of the Scottish People, 1560-1830*, London, Collins, 1969, p. 322; E. Gauldie, *Cruel Habitations: A History of Working Class Housing, 1780-1918*, London, Allen and Unwin, 1974, p. 66.

84. H. Miller, 'The Bothy System', *Witness*, 22 September 1841, reprinted in H. Miller, *Essays*, Edinburgh, Nimmo, 1890, pp. 203-4. See also Miller's reworking of the same material in his *My Schools and Schoolmasters*, Edinburgh, Nimmo, 1880, pp. 115-18.

85. Anon, 'Bothies', *Reformed Presbyterian Magazine*, March 1859, p. 81. See also, among other accounts at the mid-century, J. Cowie et al, 'Digest of Essays on the Bothy System of Maintaining Single Farm Servants', *THASS*, 1842, 2nd series, XIV, p. 133; W. Watson, *Remarks on the Bothie System and Feeing Markets*, Aberdeen, Davidson and King, 1849, p. 3; D. Esdaile, 'Report by a Committee of the Synod of Angus and Mearns as to Agricultural Labourers', *JA*, 1856, XX, p. 400.

86. Rev. H. Stuart, *Agricultural Labourers, as they were, are, and should be*, Edinburgh, Blackwood, 1853, pp. 46-53; Anon, *First Annual Report of the Association for Promoting Improvement in the Dwellings and Domestic Conditions of Agricultural Labourers in Scotland* (hereinafter *Cottage Association*), Edinburgh, Blackwood, 1856, pp. 25-8; *Second Annual Report, Cottage Association*, 1856, p. 36; T. Lawson, *Report on the Past and Present Agriculture of the Counties of Forfar and Kincardine*, Edinburgh, n.p., 1881, p. 76; J. Macdonald, 'On the Agriculture of the Counties of Forfar and Kincardine', *THASS*, 1881, 4th series, XII, p. 170.

87. *PP* 1893-4 (C 6894-XV), XXXVI, pp. 114, 118, 120, 121, 122; Royal Commission on the Housing of the Industrial Population of Scotland, Rural and Urban, Evidence, 1921, Q 30 638, 31 729.

88. *PP* 1893-4 (C 6894-XV), XXXVI, pp. 111, 123, 132; Mr Watt, 'The Condition of the Labouring Poor', *Poor Law Magazine*, 1860, II, p. 235; W. A. Macnaughton, *Fourth Annual Report upon the Health and Sanitary Condition of the County of Kincardine*, Stonehaven, Waldie, 1894, p.18.

89. Royal Commission on the Poor Law in Scotland, Appendix, Part II, *PP* 1844 (564), XXII, Q 817; *Fourth Annual Report, Cottage Association*, 1858, pp. 33, 38.

90. *PP* 1893-4 (C 6894-XV), XXXVI, pp. 112, 117, 118, 120, 121, 122, 123, 125, 131, 136, 137, 139, 140, 142.

91. R. C. on Housing, Evidence, 1921, Q 29 177.

92. *Ibid*, Q 31 875.

93. See for example Jenkins, *loc cit*, p. 198: 'One result (of the stigmatising of bothying) is, that Scotch farmers — who thoroughly appreciate the result of giving a dog a bad name — now designate as 'Barracks' those bothies which are used as bedrooms, and as 'kitchens' those in which the labourers (sic) get their food and spend their evenings.'

94. J. Donaldson, *General View of the Agriculture of the County of Kincardine*, London, Philanthropic Reform, 1794, p. 25.

95. G. Robertson, *General View of the Agriculture of Kincardineshire or the Mearns*, London, Phillips, 1810, p. 423; Robertson, *Rural Recollections*, Irvine, 1829, p. 420; Select Committee on the State of Agriculture, Third Report, *PP* 1836 (465) VIII Part II, Q 13 640.

96. *NSA* XI (Kincardine), pp. 42, 94, 139, 203-4; *PP* 1844 (564) XXII, Q 815-7.

97. *NSA* XI (Kincardine), p. 42. Original emphases.

98. *PP* 1870 (C 221), XIII, p. 40.

99. *Ibid*, pp 55, 57.

100. *PP* 1893-4 (C 6894-XV), XXXVI, pp. 135, 136, 138, 140, 142.

101. G. S. Keith, *General View of the Agriculture of Aberdeenshire,* Aberdeen, Brown, 1811, p. 514.
102. *PP* 1835 (465), VII Part II, Q 10 633-4.
103. *NSA* XII (Aberdeen), p. 1000.
104. *Ibid,* pp. 204-5 (St. Fergus), 419 (Towie), 428 (Rayne), 505 (Alford), 574-5 (Chapel of Garioch).
105. Watson, *op cit,* p. 3.
106. J. Robb, *The Cottage, the Bothy, and the Kitchen,* Edinburgh, Blackwood, 1861, pp. 51-79.
107. *PP* 1870 (C 221), XIII, pp. 54-6. Bothies were unknown in the parishes of Alford, Birse, Forgue, Huntly, Kincardine O'Neil, King Edward, Old Deer, Tarland and Strichen.
108. *PP* 1893-4 (C 6894-XV), XXXVI, p. 140.
109. *Ibid,* p. 139.
110. Information from Mr W. Cook, Little Meldrum, Tarves.
111. *PP* 1893-4 (C 6894-XV), XXXVI, pp. 135-43.
112. *Ibid,* p. 141.
113. *Ibid,* pp. 136, 141.
114. R. C. on Housing, Evidence, 1921, Q 31 875.
115. *Ibid,* Q 29 035-7; 29 088; 31 766, p. 1261.
116. *PP* 1870 (C 221), XIII, pp. 54, 56. Bothying was unknown in Inveravon, Mortlach, and Grange.
117. *PP* 1893-4 (C 6894-XV), XXXVI, pp. 121-2.
118. *Ibid,* pp. 117, 118, 121, 124, 126.
119. J. Donaldson, *General View of the Agriculture of the County of Nairn,* London, Clarke, 1794, p. 16; Donaldson, *General View . . . Moray,* p. 25.
120. *PP* 1893-4 (C 6894-XV), XXXVI, p. 123.
121. *PP* 1870 (C 221), XIII, pp. 55, 57-58.
122. A. Macdonald, *loc cit,* pp. 118-9.
123. *PP* 1893-4 (C 6894-XV), XXXVI, pp. 114, 116, 118, 120, 121, 123, 125; R. C. on Housing, Evidence, 1921, Q 30 654-5.
124. *PP* 1917-18 (Cd 8731), XIV, p. 162.
125. L. J. Saunders, *Scottish Democracy, 1815-40,* Edinburgh, Oliver and Boyd, 1950, p. 73; J. A. Symon, *Scottish Farming Past and Present,* Edinburgh, Oliver and Boyd, 1959, pp. 160-1; A. Fenton, 'Farm Servant Life in the 17th-19th centuries', *SA,* 1964-5, XLIV, p. 283; A. Fenton, *Scottish Country Life,* Edinburgh, Donald, 1976, pp. 188-9; Smout, *op cit,* p. 321.
126. R. C. on Housing, Evidence, 1921, Q 31 885.
127. *Ibid,* Q 31 358: 'I felt that (the bothy) was not a thing that should have been, but I could not see my way to do otherwise. I arranged with the grieve's wife to make the best of it by having a good fire on and the kettle boiling.' Many Howe farmers have confirmed to me that immigrant northern farmers tried, and failed, to destroy bothying on their farms after 1900.
128. This experiment was tried on the Haddo estate in the 1860s. The fifth Earl of Aberdeen was willing to undertake this — from the estate's point of view — laborious policy as part of his doomed attempt to extirpate illegitimacy in the area: Rev. E. B. Elliott, *Memoir of Lord Haddo, in his Later Years Fifth Earl of Aberdeen,* fifth edition, London, Seeley, Jackson and Halliday, 1869, p. 387.
129. *PP* 1893-94 (C 6894-XV), XXXVI, pp. 112, 124, 126.
130. Calculated from Board of Agriculture, Return of the Number of Allotments Detached from and Attached to Cottages, and of Agricultural Holdings in Great Britain, *PP* 1886 (C 4848), LXX, Tables I, II.
131. *PP* 1870 (C 221), XIII, p. 35; 'These allowances and privileges vary so much in

different districts, and depend so often on the peculiarities and tastes of the farmers, that it seems to me impossible to estimate their value accurately.'

132. 'Your men have got good gardens, or you give them potato ground? — I do both. I give them 1000 yards of a drill of potatoes, and as much garden ground as they wish. I have told them I will extend their gardens as much as they like, and they say they do not want any more.' *PP* 1896 (C7400), XVII, Q 51 695. Evidence from James Black, Sherriffston.

133. W. Alexander, *Northern Rural Life in the Eighteenth Century*, Edinburgh, Douglas, 1877, pp. 7-12; J. W. Barclay, 'The Glen and its Folk', in W. D. Simpson (ed), *The Book of Glenbuchat*, Aberdeen, Third Spalding Club, 1942, pp. 43-4. See also the letter of 23 February 1859 from the Earl of Kintore's factor to G. Bruce, Heatherwick, Keithhall concerning a croft to be engrossed in Heatherwick: 'It seems to me that James Watt's houses will not be required for the accommodation of the conjoined farm, and I think I must stipulate for the removal by you of the material of the offices [steading], leaving you to retain the dwelling house which will be useful for a married servant.'

134. J. Black, *Report on the Cottage Accommodation in the District of Buchan, Aberdeenshire*, Edinburgh, Blackwood, 1851, pp. 3-4. This essay won the Highland Society's Gold Medal: it is also to be found in *THASS*, 1851, 3rd Series, V, pp. 92-9.

135. Robertson, *Agriculture . . . Kincardine or the Mearns*, facing p. 184.

136. See the description of an improved cottage on Slack for which the Garioch Farmer Club gave a prize in 1831: 'Length of house forty and a half feet; breadth sixteen and a half feet; height seven feet; stone and lime built and neatly harled; plastered and whitewashed inside; glass windows three feet by two and a half feet; roof very neatly thatched with straw; two apartments, beside a centre closet, neatly and compactly floored with clay; garden well arranged and laid out; dunghill properly concealed and at a proper distance from the house': I. M. Bruce, *A Century of Aberdeenshire Agriculture*, Aberdeen, *Aberdeen Journal*, 1908, p. 31. This house, while still not palatial with its thatched roof and earthen floor, was a great improvement on what had gone before.

137. Elliott, *op cit*, p. 303.

138. *PP* 1881 (C 3096), XVII, Q 39 942; *PP* 1893-4 (C 6894-XV), XXXVI, p. 115; A. Macdonald, *loc cit*, p. 89.

139. *PP* 1896 (C 8021), XVII, Q 51 873.

140. *Ibid.*

141. H. Stephens, *The Book of the Farm*, Edinburgh, Blackwood, 1844, Vol. I, pp. 211-20; Vol. III, pp. 1368-80.

142. H. Stephens, *The Book of the Farm*, sixth edition, ed J. Macdonald, Edinburgh, Blackwood, 1908, Vol III, pp. 340-75.

143. *Second Annual Report, Cottage Association*, p. 36; Elliott, *op cit*, p. 387,

144. *PP* 1870 (C 221), XIII, p. 37.

145. *PP* 1893-4 (C 6894-XV), XXXVI, p. 132.

146. *PP* 1870 (C 221), XIII, p. 38.

147. *PP* 1893-4 (C 6894-XV), XXXVI, pp. 112, 132. A. Macdonald, *loc cit* shows that by the 1880s most lowland Moray estates had sufficient farm cottages.

148. R. C. on Housing, Evidence, 1921, Q 31 922, 31 725, 31 318-39.

149. In Tarves in 1892-3, for instance, there were 129 cottar houses on farms. 21 were vacant and a further 18 were occupied by people who were not farm servants. In Logie Buchan seven out of 48 cottar houses were vacant in the same year, and a further six were not held by farm servants. In Strathdon two out of fifteen houses were vacant and a further ten were not occupied by farm servants.

150. See, among many others, W. Ruxton, *Essay*, Inverurie, Kemp, 1865, pp. 7-9; A. Gray, *op cit*, p. 81; Alexander, *Life Among My Ain Folk*, pp. 9-10.

151. M. Gray, 'North-East Agriculture . . .', p. 99.

152. Lawson, *op cit*, pp. 77-8.

153. *PP* 1844 (564), XXII, pp. 692-3. Accounts from parish after parish report marked similarities in the diet of poor peasants, farm servants and paupers.

154. *Ibid*, pp. 510-11 (Duffus), 534 (Peterhead), 539 (Nairn). In Tough, we are told, a little dried fish was eaten (*Ibid*, p. 676), and many Echt peasants made a weekly journey to Aberdeen market to buy fish (*Ibid*, p. 735).

155. *Ibid*, p. 737 (Crathie/Braemar). Much of this meat was braxy mutton.

156. *NSA* XII (Aberdeen), p. 137.

157. A. Fenton, 'The Place of Oatmeal in the Diet of Scottish Farm Servants in the Eighteenth and Nineteenth Centuries', in J. Szabadfalvi and Z. Ujváry (ed), *Studia Ethnographica et Folkoristica in Honorem Béla Gunda*, 1971, pp. 87-101.

158. J. Allan, *loc cit*, p. 32. On potatoes see that masterpiece of comparative sociology, R. N. Salaman, *The History and Social Influence of the Potato*, Cambridge, Cambridge University Press, 1949.

159. See the fascinating evidence in Fig. 57 of A. C. O'Dell and K. Walton, *The Highlands and Islands of Scotland*, London, Nelson, 1962, p. 176.

160. J. F. Duncan, 'Farm Workers in the North East, 1851-1951', *SA*, 1951, XXX, p. 16.

161. Ord. *op cit*, p. 277. Evidently a song about the bothy, not the farm kitchen. Brose was made by mixing dry oatmeal with hot water (or the water in which vegetables had been boiled), salt and perhaps milk. The criterion of good brose was that the spoon would stand up in it. Full culinary instructions are to be found in Fenton, 'The Place of Oatmeal . . .'

162. J. Tait, 'The Physiological Distinctions in the Condition of the Scottish Peasantry', *THASS*, 1883, 4th series, XV, pp. 4-7. See also J. Allan, *loc cit*, p. 32: 'On this diet I weighed 14 stones 4 lbs at eighteen years of age.' For more examples of the food of northeast farm servants see R. Hutchison, 'Report on the Dietaries of Scottish Agricultural Labourers', *THASS*, 1869, 4th series, II, 1-29; Hutchison, 'On the Dietary of the English Agricultural Labourer in contrast to the Scottish', *THASS*, 1870-1, 4th series, III, 349-78.

163. Fenton, 'Farm Servant Life . . .'. p. 282; H. Henderson, 'The Bothy Ballads', *Journal of Peasant Studies*, 1975, II, p. 499.

164. J. Cruickshank, 'Changes in the Agricultural Industry of Aberdeenshire in the last Fifty Years', *SA*, 1935, XIX, p. 231.

165. W. Diack, 'The Scottish Farm Labourer', *Independant Review*, 1905, VII, pp. 323-4.

166. Anon, 'Bothies', p. 81.

167. Northeast cottars seem to have had a prejudice against pigs — the southern English cottager's main buttress against want. Thus while the Haddo estate put no obstacles in the path of cottars seeking to keep pigs, few actually did so: R. C. on Housing, Evidence, 1921, p. 1270.

168. J. A. Symon, 'Cairnhill, Turriff, 1861-1926: Part II', *SA*, 1951, XXX, p. 25.

169. A. Macdonald, *loc cit*, p. 119; J. Macdonald, *loc cit*, p. 171.

170. R. C. on Housing, Evidence, 1921, Q 31 358.

171. Diack, *loc cit*, p. 322.

Chapter 5

1. J. Ord, *Bothy Songs and Ballads of Aberdeen, Banff and Moray, Angus and the Mearns*, Paisley, Gardner, 1930, pp. 211-12. A song from the Howe of Cromar, the bowl of arable land around Tarland. Reprinted by John Donald Publishers Ltd., Edinburgh.

2. See pp. 102-4.
3. Expressed from G. Greig, *Folk-Song in Buchan and Folk-Song of the North-East*, Hatboro', Penn, Folklore Associates, 1963, Article 92.
4. Unless the farm was too small to employ a grieve, and his supervisory functions were performed by the foreman. This was the usual arrangement in the northeast, with its small number of huge farms. Even when the foreman ruled the roost, however, it was only he who could give orders to a cattleman: a second horseman never could do so.
5. A. R. Mortimer, *Farm Kitchen Work*, Elgin, *Courant and Courier*, 1910.
6. Greig, *op cit*, Article 92.
7. See p. 110.
8. See Figures 4.4 and 4.5, pp. 116, 117.
9. J. R. Allan, *Farmer's Boy*, London, Methuen, 1935, p. 113. Here, as elsewhere in his delightful book, Allan calls the chaumer a bothy. Some accounts assert that even the seating arrangements round the kitchen fire in the evening were determined by the internal status hierarchy of the labour squad: A. Gordon, *The Folks of Carglen, or Life in the North*, London, Fisher Unwin, 1900, p. 134.
10. By John Mearns, Aberdeen.
11. W. Alexander, 'The Peasantry of North-East Scotland', *United Presbyterian Magazine*, 1884, I, p. 427.
12. 'David Toulmin', (J. Reid), *Straw into Gold*, Aberdeen, Impulse, 1973, pp. 26-60.
13. Greig, *op cit*, Article 92.
14. See p. 112.
15. Jimmy MacBeath, quoted in H. Henderson, 'The Bothy Ballads', *Journal of Peasant Studies*, 1975, II, p. 497.
16. Interview with John Reid, Aberdeen: a dairy cattleman who claims that he never could get on with horses. See the account — slightly fictionalised — of his struggles with a cantakerous 'orra beast' in 'David Toulmin' (J. Reid), *Hard Shining Corn*, Aberdeen, Impulse, 1972, pp. 118-25. This fine short story bears the expressive title 'I Wadna Be a Loon Again'.
17. A. Mitchell, *Recollections of a Lifetime*, privately printed, 1911; Mr Cook, manuscript *Diary*.
18. The newspapers of the time took an interest in breach of promise cases that was quite as salacious as the interest of the *News of the World* today, and cloaked in a similarly hypocritical mantle of pure morality. The rural breach of promise cases always involved illegitimate births, and the man was always found working on a farm many miles from the place where he had sown his seed. The best treatment of the topic is W. Alexander, 'Bawbie Huie's bastard geet', in W. Alexander, *Life Among My Ain Folk*, Edinburgh, Douglas, 1882, pp. 204-30, a short story showing an astoundingly unpunitive attitude to the girl for one of the author's time and sect; Alexander was an elder of the Free Church of Scotland, See I. Carter, 'Introduction', to I. Carter (ed), *Aberdeenshire Peasant Life*, London, Cass, forthcoming.
19. G. B. Currie, manuscript *Annals of Insch*, 1889-1929, p. 1 (V).
20. *NSA* XI (Kincardine), p. 49; A. C. Cameron, *The History of Fettercairn*, Paisley, Parlane, 1899, p. 268.
21. Hairst labour was often still recruited in the atrophying fairs: St. Sair's Fair continued to be a hairst market until at least the early 1890s.
22. Royal Commission on the Poor Law in Scotland, Appendix Part II, *PP* 1844 (564), XXI, p. 531.
23. Interview with John Reid, Aberdeen.
24. Interview with W. Cook, Little Meldrum, Tarves. The best literary account of negotiations in the feeing market is W. Alexander, *Johnny Gibb of Gushetneuk*, sixth edition, Edinburgh, Douglas, 1880, pp. 52-5. Earlier in the same novel (pp. 3-4),

Johnny Gibb fees 'a stoot young folla, from the Upper Garioch' at Pitmachie feeing market, but only after agreeing to the loon's stipulation that 'ye maun gie's an ouk at the Walls (Macduff) aifter the neep seed'.

25. Royal Commission on the Housing of the Industrial Population of Scotland, Rural and Urban, Report, *PP* 1917-18 (Cd 8731), XIV, p. 162.

26. G. Houston, 'Labour Relations in Scottish Agriculture before 1870', *AHR*, 1958, VI, pp. 28-41; W. Diack, 'The Scottish Farm Labourer', *Independent Review*, 1905, VII, p. 327. It was possible for a servant to sue a farmer for having broken his agreement, but cases of this kind were rare. Partly this came from servants' timidity before the law, but a more important reason was the great difficulty in proving that the farmer had broken his bargain.

27. *AFP*, 18 August 1891.

28. W. Cairnie, *Reporting Reminiscences*, Aberdeen, Aberdeen University Press, 1902, pp. 3-4.

29. *AFP*, 20 November 1882.

30. Anon, 'The Scottish Farm Labourer', *Cornhill Magazine*, 1864, X, pp. 619-20.

31. *Witness*, 12 February 1859.

32. *AFP*, 15 May 1891.

33. See — among many others — A. Harvey, *The Agricultural Labourer: His Present Condition and Means for his Amelioration*, Aberdeen, Brown, 1858, p. 22; Anon, 'The Homes of the Working Poor', *Poor Law Magazine*, 1859, I, p. 260; W. Watson, *Remarks on the Bothie System and Feeing Markets*, Aberdeen, Davidson, 1849, p. 4; J. Cumming, 'Essay', in *Essays by Agricultural Labourers on the Condition and Improvement of their Class*, Aberdeen, Brown, 1859.

34. Anon, 'A Register for Farm Servants', *JA*, 1841-2, XII, pp. 296-9.

35. Anon, 'Report by a Committee of Directors on Hiring Markets', *THASS*, 1849-51, 3rd series, II, p. 11.

36. *AJ*, 2 January 1867. This association had managed to arrange only 359 engagements during the year.

37. *AFP*, 7 April, 1871.

38. A. Forbes Irvine, 'Report on Hiring Markets by a Committee of the Society', *THASS*, 1873, 4th series, V, pp. 312-13.

39. *AFP*, 15 May, 21 May 1891.

40. J. Black, 'On the Agriculture of Aberdeen and Banff Shires', *THASS*, 1870-1, 4th series, III, p. 31.

41. T. Lawson, *Report on the Past and Present Agriculture of the Counties of Forfar and Kincardine*, Edinburgh, n.p., 1881, p. 80. Press advertisements were a more important method of recruiting men in Kincardine than in other northeast counties: see Royal Commission on Labour, The Agricultural Labourer, Vol. III, Scotland, Part I, *PP* 1893-4 (C 6894-XV), XXXVI, pp. 130, 137.

42. Departmental Committee on Farm Workers in Scotland, Report, *PP* 1935-6, (Cmd 5217), VII, p. 10.

43. Gordon, *op cit*, pp. 69-70.

44. Interview with W. Cook, Little Meldrum, Tarves.

45. Lawson, *op cit*, p. 80.

46. A. Mitchell, *Recollections of a Lifetime*, privately printed, 1911.

47. Interview with John Reid, Aberdeen.

48. 'Mr Esslemont, Culsalmond, thought feeing markets an expeditious method of doing business. He had sometimes got a bad man in the market; but, generally, he found no difficulty in getting plenty of good hands, and he could get all he wanted within an hour's time, while he would perhaps have to ride sixty miles on horseback before he could get one man by the registration system': *AFP*, 7 April 1871. See also *AFP*, 10 February 1886, letter from 'A Reader'. For the servant the attraction of the

market was its untrammelled nature: '. . . servants seem to like the freedom of an open market, where they can bring their commodity of labour to the best account' (Lawson, *op cit*, p. 80).

49. *OSA* XV, p. 469. This reverend gentleman was no friend of farm servants; the passage quoted continues: 'The same silly idea leads [farmers] to give way to the grossest abuses in their domestic concerns. A farmer must often rise from bed at 3 or 4 o'clock in a winter's morning, to admit his servants, who have been junketing all night in the neighbourhood; and he must perform all the morning work of a farm, in tending cattle, etc. long before they get up, to assist him . . . In short, the common meaning of language here is totally reversed, and the servants do not so much serve, as rule and tyrannise over their master' *(Ibid*, pp. 469-70). One must have serious doubts about this account, which controverts every other piece of evidence that we have about the relations of farmers and servants. Many northeast ministers, in both Statistical Accounts, show a much more sympathetic — if often patronising — attitude to farm servants.

50. Terry Byres' version of 'Turra Market'. For other songs about amiable deems, and the farm loons' successful attempts to get at them, see Ord, *op cit*, pp. 246, 247-8. See also Alexander, *Life Among My Ain Folk*, pp. 207-9. Songs about courting the deem are heavily under-represented in the published collections: most of them are — or were — far too bawdy to pass on to Gavin Greig, a great collector but something of a moralist. See T. J. Byres, 'Scottish Peasants and their Song', *Journal of Peasant Studies*, 1976, III, pp. 236-51.

51. Ord, *op cit*, p. 249. Ord claims that Mill of Boyndie had twenty pairs of horse in 1860. To have been foreman of such a 'toon' was cause for justified pride. A later stanza suggests that the song's composer achieved this eminence at the age of 21 — again we see how young was the hired labour force on northeast farms. Being 'the best man in the Boyne' meant being champion ploughman in the district.

52. C. A. Mollyson, *The Parish of Fordoun*, Aberdeen, Smith, 1893, p. 109: 'Rarely a country feeing market passes but the recruiting sergeant succeeds in persuading some promising son of the soil to accept the "shilling" and take the oath of fidelity to his sovereign.'

53. Greig, *op cit*, Article 176.

54. J. Allan, 'Agriculture in Aberdeenshire in the Sixties', *Deeside Field*, 1927, III, pp. 32-3. 'Regarding our food in farm service, I had no complaint to make; it was clean and wholesome . . . For sauce we had the very best — namely, a keen appetite engendered by hard work.'

55. The classic literary example is the passage in *Johnny Gibb*, once so popular as a recitation, when the Clinkstyle servants discover that their supper is to be neep brose yet again and go into the kitchen lowing like cattle. Alexander, *Johnny Gibb*, pp. 55-6.

56. Ord, *op cit*, pp. 257-8. Many other songs concentrate their critical attention on food. See, for example, *ibid*, p. 212 ('The Weary Farmers'), 213 ('The Scranky Black Farmers'), 215 ('Barnyards o' Delgaty'), 231 ('The Barns o' Beneuchies'), 261 ('Cameloun').

57. Henderson, *loc cit*, p. 500.

58. Many songs were sung which simply replaced Drumdelgie and Cairnie with the name of another farm and parish; but I hear strong echoes of 'Drumdelgie' in many other songs as well. See, for example, Ord, *op cit*, p. 256 ('Harrowing Time' — which was sung to the same tune as 'Drumdelgie' according to Ord), and pp. 260-1 ('Cameloun'). Gavin Greig *(op cit*, Article 179) credits 'Nethermill' to the pen of William Forsyth, Mintlaw; but this song clearly shows its ancestry in 'Drumdelgie'.

59. Ord, *op cit*, pp. 226-7. 'Sleepytown' is an interesting song for a number of reasons. Firstly, we know that it was composed by a man serving on the farm at the time — the 'Poet Clark', remembered by a fellow servant as 'awfu' learnt' (Greig, *op*

cit, Article 133). This gives a keen edge to the song's criticism both of 'hashing' and of bad food — the farmer orders his servants to scrape sacks to get the oatmeal for their food. Secondly, this song shows how far songs could travel. Sleepytown is in Kennethmont, just above the village of Insch; yet Greig collected versions from Maud, New Deer, Bruckley and Fyvie: Greig, *op cit,* Articles 127, 133.

60. Greig, *op cit,* Article 138. Swaggers has the dubious honour of being the villain in two songs; 'Nethermill' *ibid,* Article 179) is also about him and serves to identify his farm.

61. Mitchell, *op cit,* p. 35: 'If there was a disagreement at any farm, [the farm servants] sent Johnnie [Milne] particulars, and he would compose verses and sell them at the feeing market.

62. Ord, *op cit,* p. 220. The villainous Swaggers once more.

63. Alexander, 'Peasantry of North-East Scotland', p. 428; *PP* 1893-4 (C 6894-XV), XXXVI, p. 110.

64. Mr Watt (Stonehaven), 'The Condition of the Labouring Poor', *Poor Law Magazine,* 1859, II, p. 231. See also Alexander, *Life Among My Ain Folk,* pp. 240-8.

65. J. Allan, *loc cit,* p. 31.

66. W. Mair, 'Biographical sketch', in A. Gray, *Talks with Our Farm Servants,* Edinburgh, Clark, 1906, p. xv: 'His character as a man and a servant, and his victories in the rivalries of farm work, gained [Gray] such influence among farm men that all over Aberdeenshire his name was a household word with them.

67. J. Macdonald, 'On the Agriculture of the County of Caithness', *THASS,* 1875, pp. 32-3.

68. Ord, *op cit,* p. 241. An existing song about a ploughing match often was altered to fit a new match by changing the names of competing horsemen.

69. *PP* 1893-4 (C 6894-XV), XXXVI, p. 122; *PP* 1935-6 (Cmd 5217), VII, pp. 11-12.

70. J. F. Duncan, 'The Scottish Agricultural Labourer', in D. T. Jones, J. F. Duncan, H. M. Conacher and W. R. Scott, *Rural Scotland During the War,* Oxford, Clarendon Press, 1926, p. 191.

71. Ord, *op cit,* pp. 231-2. Kempie is the grieve.

72. Greig, *op cit,* Article 92.

73. Interview.

74. Interview with John Reid, Aberdeen.

75. J. R. Allan, *The Seasons Return,* London, Hale, 1955, p. 61. See also 'David Toulmin' (J. Reid), *Hard Shining Corn,* pp. 26-36. The structural position of the grieve or foreman echoes that of the foreman in industrial settings. See, for example, C. Fletcher, 'Men in the Middle', *Sociological Review,* 1969, XVII, pp. 341-54.

76. Hence the heroic myths about grieves: 'The legendary ones had a wonderful physique and did a power of work. Mack o' the Walls used a fork so long and broad an ordinary man could hardly lift it. Geordie Gill once filled 100 cartloads of muck out of the midden in a day, with the help of the carters, of course. They set a pace which other men had to follow, and I guess they often set that pace too fast.' J. R. Allan, *The Seasons Return,* pp. 58-9.

77. Ord, *op cit,* p. 220.

78. Alexander, *Johnny Gibb,* p. 103.

79. Anon, 'The Horseman's Society: what it could Achieve', *People's Journal,* 5 April 1902: 'This society is one of the most secret in existence. Even in the country, where it might be supposed a tolerably clear knowledge would be found prevailing in regard to it, only among those who are initiated into its mysteries are its true aims and aspirations understood.'

80. J. M. MacPherson, *Primitive Beliefs in the North-East of Scotland,* London, Longmans Green, 1929, pp. 290-1.

81. T. Davidson, 'The Horseman's Word: a rural initiation ceremony', *Gwerin,*

1956, I, pp. 71-4; G. E. Evans, 'The horse and magic', *New Society*, 14 March 1963; *The Pattern Under the Plough*, London, Faber and Faber, 1966, p. 235; *The Days That We Have Seen*, London, Faber and Faber, 1975, pp. 35-43.

82. W. Singer, *An Exposition of the Miller and Horseman's Word, or the True System of Raising the Devil*, sixth edition, Aberdeen, Anderson, 1865; Anon, *Eleven Years at Farm Work*, Aberdeen, Free Press, 1869; J. F. S. Gordon, *The Book of the Chronicles of Keith*, Glasgow, Forrester, 1880, p. 149; 'Neil Roy' (A. D. Russell), *The Horseman's Word*, London, Macmillan, 1895, pp. 92-9. The Horseman's Oath was taken directly from freemasonry: 'I now hereby in the presence of God and these witnesses promise to keep the great secrets of Horsemanry. Furthermore I vow and swear that I shall all hereby heal conceal and never reveal to any he she or them to any alive save to a brother horseman. Furthermore I vow and swear that I shall neither write it nor indite it cut it nor carve it on marble wood snow or sand or so much as to wave a single letter of it in the air that can be taken notice of neither print it nor engrave it on anything movable or immovable under the whole canopy of heaven . . . And in failing to do this may my body be quartered in four quarters with a horseman's knife and buried in the sand of the sea thirty fathoms from the shore where the tide ebbs and flows twice every twenty-four hours or may I be torn to pieces between two wild horses and now O God enable me to perform these my duties and obligations as a true horseman' (Excerpts from undated ms Horseman's Oath, Alexander Robertson, Glack of Clunymore, Mortlach, Banffshire). For published northeast versions of the Oath see Evans, *Pattern Under the Plough*, pp. 230-1; Anon, *The Horseman's Oath, as Written Down by a Buchan Horseman in 1908*, Edinburgh, Scottish Country Life Museums Trust, 1972; A. Fenton, *Scottish Country Life*, Edinburgh, Donald, 1976, pp. 223-4.

83. J. Davidson, *Inverurie and the Earldom of the Garioch*, Edinburgh, Douglas, 1878; Mollyson, *op cit*, pp. 145-6.

84. Singer, *op cit.*

85. It may be more accurate to say that the Horseman's Word evolved out of the Miller's Word. J. F. S. Gordon, *op cit*, states that the Miller's Word gave power to reist horses (stop them immovably in their tracks) — the prerogative of the Horseman's Word in later days. This is supported by interview evidence: Frank Hendry told me the story of Paul Gordon, who lived in the Cabrach about 1850. He lived in a thackit hoose and had a considerable reputation as a 'skeely man'. He had the Horseman's Word, but it is evident that he also had the Miller's Word; for he fee'd one winter to a local farmer and was sacked for making the water wheel on the threshing mill turn when the mill dam was empty in order to avoid having to thresh with the flail.

86. A Herd Loon, *The Kingdom of Forgue*, Aberdeen, Fraser, 1903, p. 67.

87. I.e. third horseman.

88. 'Nicky Tams' is a music hall song, not a true bothy song. The Horseman's Word is never mentioned in the bothy songs, despite the fact that is was so widespread.

89. Singer, *op cit*, pp. 20-1. Can this be the explanation of the northeast's astronomical illegitimacy ratios?

90. Anon, 'The Horseman's Word: a Red Letter Day for a Young Horseman', *People's Journal*, 29 March 1902. The anonymous author was made a horseman in the Auld Castle of Gight, Fyvie. The initiation ceremony was always held at midnight in some secluded place, but it was usually a farm steading rather than a ruined castle.

91. G. E. Evans, *The Horse in the Furrow*, London, Faber and Faber, 1960, pp. 231-75.

92. Gray, *op cit*, p. xiv.

93. Interview with John Reid, Aberdeen.

94. G. Robertson, *Rural Recollections*, Irvine, 1829, p. 420. See also G. Robertson, *General View of the Agriculture of Kincardineshire or the Mearns*, London, Phillips,

1810, pp. 424-5.

95. H. Henderson, 'The Oral Tradition', *Scottish International*, 1973, p. 31. We saw above (p. 108) that roughly three northeast male farm servants in five worked with horses.

96. Henderson, *loc cit*, p. 31. See also Henderson, 'A Slight Case of Devil Worship', *New Statesman*, 14 June 1952.

97. A. Fenton, 'Farm Servant Life in the 17th-19th centuries', *SA*, 1964-5, LXIV, p. 283.

98. C. Bell and H. Newby, 'The Sources of Variation in Agricultural Workers' Images of Society', *Sociological Review*, 1973, XXI, pp. 231-253.

99. See the song 'Newmill' quoted above, pp. 149-50.

100. T. Shanin, *The Awkward Class*, Oxford, Clarendon Press, 1972. For examples of fee'd northeast peasant children's outrage at being fed differently from the farm family see Mitchell, *op cit*, p. 33 — practically the only criticism made by this amiable man — and, inevitably, Alexander, *Johnny Gibb of Gushetneuk*.

101. William Alexander captures this status anxiety exquisitely in his vitriolic portrait of Mrs Birse, the would-be genteel wife of a capitalist farmer. At one point she perches uncomfortably on the horns of a dilemma after a local schoolmaster is evicted from his school by the laird. It would be socially elevating to employ the master to tutor her son, but how could he be lodged on the farm? He could not be admitted to the parlour company, but it would be socially defiling for Benjie Birse's tutor to be chaumered along with the farm servants. See Alexander, *Johnny Gibb of Gushetneuk*, p. 203.

102. See pp. 148-51.

103. See p. 109.

104. It is remarkable how often farm servants were unable to explain why they moved so frequently. Alex. Mitchell *(op cit)* was quite unable to give any account of his reasons for leaving farms where he had been very happy: but leave he did. A manuscript letter in the Country Life Archive, National Museum of Antiquities, Edinburgh, makes a similar point. In talking about a Banffshire farm servant, part of the letter reads: 'He wasn't married until he was thirty-five and except for three years when he worked at home, never stayed more than six months at one place. It wasn't done.' The expectation that a man would shift at the term, like the stronger expectation that a farm's whole labour squad would leave if the most senior hired man left, points to a degree of collective organisation among farm servants — but organisation built around culture rather than politics or economics.

105. *PP* 1893-4 (C 6894-XV), XXXVI, pp. 111-26.

Chapter 6

1. 'Lewis Grassic Gibbon' (James Leslie Mitchell), 'Sunset Song', in *A Scots Quair*, London, Hutchinson, 1946, p. 193.

2. J. R. Allan, *North-East Lowlands of Scotland*, London, Hale, 1974, pp. 78-9.

3. J. Hunter, *The Making of the Crofting Community*, Edinburgh, Donald, 1976.

4. See pp. 94, 96.

5. Hall means the 1912 Pentland Act. The 1892 Small Holdings Act had required the new County Councils to advertise the possibility of creating allotments or small holdings where the demand warranted. Anybody interested had to petition the council. Banffshire, Kincardine and Nairn received no petitions. Aberdeenshire County Council received four petitions, signed by 58 people. Moray County Council received two petitions. Neither the Aberdeenshire nor the Moray council thought that the demand warranted the establishment of new holdings. See Return showing, for each

county, (a) the number and date of the Petitions presented under Section 5 of the Small Holdings Act, 1892, with the Resolutions of the County Council thereon; (b) the amount of Land acquired under Section 3 of the Act, with the Parish in which it is situate; (c) the number of Small Holdings provided, with the Acreage of each, and the terms of Sale or Letting, *PP* 1895 (C 407), LXXXIV, pp. 23, 26, 29.

6. A. D. Hall, *A Pilgrimage of British Farming, 1910-1912*, London, Murray, 1913, pp. 383-4.

7. See pp. 28-30.

8. Gibbon, *op cit;* W. Alexander, *Johnny Gibb of Gushetneuk*, sixth edition, Edinburgh, Douglas, 1880; I. MacPherson, *Shepherd's Calendar*, London, Cape, 1931.

9. See pp. 157-8.

10. *AFP*, 9 January 1886.

11. W. S. Bruce, *The Nor' East*, London, Hodder and Stoughton, 1915, p. 44.

12. See p. 54.

13. Anon, 'The Large Farm System', *Free Church Magazine*, 1848, V. p. 112.

14. Anon, *Fourth Annual Report of the Association for the Improvement of the Dwellings and Domestic Conditions of Agricultural Labourers in Scotland*, Edinburgh, Blackwood, 1858, p. 25; *North British Agriculturist*, 27 March 1863 (letter from Lord Kinnaird); J. Robb, *The Cottage, the Bothy, and the Kitchen*, Edinburgh, Blackwood, 1861, p. 76; Robb, 'On hinds' houses and bothies', *TNAPSS*, 1863, pp. 761-2.

15. There is a very extensive periodical and pamphlet literature supporting this view. The major references are H. Miller, 'The Cottages of our Hinds', *Witness*, 22 January 1842, and 'The Bothy System', *Witness*, 22 September 1841, reprinted in H. Miller, *Essays*, Edinburgh, Nimmo, 1890, pp. 187-207; R. S. Skirving, *Landlords and Labourers*, Edinburgh, Blackwood, 1862; Skirving, 'Farm Labour and Labourers', in J. Wilson (ed), *Report on the Present State of the Agriculture of Scotland*, Edinburgh, Blackwood, 1878, pp. 134-46; the reports of Begg's significantly titled 'Committee on the Houses of the Working Classes with Special Reference to Social Morality' in the *Proceedings of the General Assembly of the Free Church of Scotland* between 1859 and 1867; J. Begg, *Lecture on 'Our Social Evils'*, Aberdeen, King, 1859; Begg, 'Obstacles to Cottage-Building in Scotland', *TNAPSS*, 1859, pp. 691-3; Begg, 'The Bothy System', *TNAPSS*, 1860, pp. 881-2; Anon, 'The Homes of the Working Poor', *Poor Law Magazine*, 1859, I, pp. 258-61. In their eulogy of the 'family system' of hinding Begg and his supporters failed to notice that it was intimately associated with the bondager system of female field labour, perhaps the most perniciously exploitative form of wage labour in nineteenth century rural Scotland. See B. Robertson, 'The Border Farm Worker, 1871-1971', *Journal of Agricultural Labour Science*, 1973, II, pp. 65-93.

16. Begg, *Lecture . . .*, p. 15. For an evangelical Disruption dogfighter like Begg, a comparison with Rome was, of course, the ultimate sign of moral collapse.

17. T. C. Smout, 'Aspects of Sexual Behaviour in Nineteenth Century Scotland', in A. A. Maclaren (ed), *Social Class in Scotland: Past and Present*, Edinburgh, Donald, 1976, pp. 55-85; I. Carter, 'Illegitimate Births and Illegitimate Inferences', *Scottish Journal of Sociology*, 1977, I, pp. 125-135.

18. See, for example, W. Cramond, *Illegitimacy in Banffshire: Facts, Figures and Opinions*, Banff, *Banffshire Journal*, 1888. Begg's argument underlies the discussion of modes of housing farm servants in Royal Commission on the Housing of the Industrial Population of Scotland, Rural and Urban, Report, *PP* 1917-18 (Cd 8731), XIV, pp. 161-75 — the result of Joe Duncan's belief in Begg's argument, which is evident in the questions which he put to witnesses. See also Carter, *loc cit*, p. 128.

19. See p. 126.

20. For a more extended appreciation of Alexander's multi-faceted masterpiece see I. Carter, 'To Roose the Countra fae the Caul' Morality o' a Deid Moderatism: William Alexander and "Johnny Gibb of Gushetneuk"', *Northern Scotland*, 1976, II, pp. 145-

62.

21. See in particular the *Festschrift* produced to celebrate the centenary of Alexander's birth: *TBFC*, 1926, XIII.

22. W. McC. Smith, *Memoir of the Families of MacCombie and Thoms*, second edition, Edinburgh, Blackwood, 1890, pp. 119-133.

23. Select Committee (House of Lords) on the Law of Hypothec in Scotland, Report and Evidence, *PP* 1868-9 (367), IX, Q 1 636.

24. Anon, *In Memoriam William McCombie of Tillyfour*, Aberdeen, privately printed, 1880, pp. 24-5.

25. W. Alexander, *The Rinderpest in Aberdeenshire, the Outbreak of 1865, and how it was stamped out*, Aberdeen, *Free Press*, 1882.

26. F. H. McCalmont, *McCalmont's Parliamentary Poll Book: British Electoral Results, 1832-1918*, eighth edition, ed J. Vincent and M. Stenton, Brighton, Harvester Press, 1971.

27. The point is made through election results. A Tory represented Aberdeenshire from 1832-1852, but from 1852 until the constituency was divided in 1867 a Liberal was returned. After the division West Aberdeenshire returned a Liberal at every election until 1914. In East Aberdeenshire a Tory was returned in 1875 and 1880, and a Liberal Unionist in 1900: those elections apart, however, the Liberals held this seat as well. In Banffshire and in Kincardine a Tory held the seat in 1832, but after 1837 in Banffshire and 1865 in Kincardine both seats were impregnable Liberal strongholds. Elgin and Nairn was held by the Tories from 1832 to 1874, but thereafter the Liberals lost control only in the 1895 and 1900 elections. See McCalmont, *op cit.*

28. W. Alexander, *Twenty-Five Years: a Personal Retrospect*, Aberdeen, n.p., 1878.

29. Quoted in J. P. D. Dunbabin, *Rural Discontent in Nineteenth Century Britain*, London, Faber and Faber, 1974, p. 174.

30. By 1870 this William McCombie — the cousin of the 'Grazier King' — had given up the lease of Cairnballoch, Alford, and had taken Milton of Kemnay.

31. Royal Commission on Agricultural Interests, Minutes of Evidence, Part II, *PP* 1881 (C 3096), XVII, Q 39 748.

32. *AFP*, 6 September 1881.

33. *AFP*, 13 September 1881.

34. *AFP*, 6 September, 1881.

35. These demands for abolition of entail, changes in the law of settlement, abolition of primogeniture and so on had been a familiar chorus from the Radical wing of the Liberal party for a number of years: H. J. Perkin, 'Land reform and class conflict in Victorian Britain', in J. Butt and I. F. Clarke (ed), *The Victorians and Social Protest: a Symposium*, Newton Abbot, David and Charles, 1973, pp. 191-4. See also Dunbabin, *op cit;* R. Douglas, 'God gave the land to the people', in A. J. A. Morris (ed), *Edwardian Radicalism, 1900-1914*, London, Routledge and Kegan Paul, 1974, pp. 148-61; J. Brown, 'Scottish and English land legislation, 1905-11', *SHR*, 1968, XLVII, pp. 72-85.

36. *AFP*, 9 September 1881.

37. *AFP*, 19 September 1881.

38. *AFP*, 20 September 1881.

39. SRO BT2/240; *AFP*, 20 September 1881.

40. At least seven of the 1871 tenants' representatives sat on local agitation committees in 1881: Anderson, Wellhouse; Barclay, Auchlossan; Bruce, Fornet; Copland, Mill of Ardlethen; Marr, Uppermill; Skinner, Cottown; and Walker, Bithnie.

41. *AFP*, 2 December 1881. The number would have been even greater but for the Caledonian Railway's refusal to run special trains from the south. National newspapers took a keen interest in the northeast agitation, and divided strictly on party lines — Liberal papers in support, Conservative against. The *Times* reported that between 2000

and 3000 people were at the 'great meeting' (Dunbabin, *op cit*, p.174). In 1881, as in 1978, any event outside London was, at best, only half as significant as an event in London.

42. *AFP*, 30 November 1881.

43. Speech by Lord Kintore to the Aberdeen Working Men's Conservative Association, reported in *AFP*, 22 March 1883.

44. It is important to note that this pattern was repeated in a whole cluster of northeast institutions. Thus the Mutual Improvement Association movement could be seen in many ways as a primitive Liberal branch organisation (I. Carter, 'The Mutual Improvement Movement in North-East Scotland in the Nineteenth Century', *Aberdeen University Review*, 1976, XLVI, pp. 383-92). Attempts to organise northeast farm servants were largely sponsored by the Liberal party too, as a means of generating political support.

45. *AFP*, 29 January 1886.

46. *AFP*, 29 January 1886; 27 February 1886; G. Evans, 'Farm Servants' Unions in Aberdeenshire Between 1870 and 1900', *SHR*, 1952, XXXI, pp. 29-40.

47. *AFP*, 9 March, 26 March 1886.

48. For an account of discriminatory remissions on the Durris estate see *AFP*, 29 January, 2 and 4 February 1886: for the huge Fife estate see *AFP*, 8 April 1886.

49. *AFP*, 2, 27 February; 12, 16, 19, 25 March; 2, 5, 7, 20, 27, 29 April 1886.

50. *AFP*, 12 March 1886. The comment refers to the Highland land war raging in Skye and other areas at the time. See Hunter, *op cit.*

51. G. Greig, *Folk-Song in Buchan and Folk-Song of the Northeast*, Hatboro', Penn, Folklore Associates, 1963, Article 147.

52. See, in particular, *AFP*, 15 March, 4 April 1886.

53. *AFP*, 20 April 1886.

54. *AFP*, 20 April 1886.

55. Perkin, *loc cit.*

56. Small Tenants (Scotland) Bill *PP* 1899 (129), VII, p. 139.

57. P. Rowland, *The Last Liberal Governments: The Promised Land, 1905-1910*, London, Barrie and Rockcliffe, 1968, pp. 114, 122; R. Douglas, *The History of the Liberal Party, 1895-1970*, London, Sidgwick and Jackson, 1971, p. 39: 'No doubt this would infuriate the people of Scotland but Scotland only returned 12 Unionists out of 72 constituencies, and the issue was not one on which the Government could appeal with confidence to an electorate which was predominantly English.' The argument has a familiar ring.

58. Royal Commission on the Law relating to Landlord's Hypothec in Scotland, Evidence, *PP* 1865 (3546-I), XVII, p. 153.

59. *AJ*, 11, 13, 17 December 1913; 7, 12, January 1914.

60. *AJ*, 11 December 1913.

61. H. Beaton, *At the Back of Bennachie, or Life in the Garioch in the Nineteenth Century*, Aberdeen, Central Press, 1922, pp. 137-9. 'Tilly', is, of course, William McCombie, Tillyfour: Liberal MP for West Aberdeenshire.

62. At the height of the 1881 agitation Michael Davitt, the apostle of land nationalisation in Ireland, spoke at a public meeting in Aberdeen. He aroused nobody but the university's medical students, who tried to prevent him from speaking. In the Highlands, by contrast, Davitt was lionised.

63. *PP* 1881 (C 3096), XVII, Q 43 007; W. D. Simpson (ed), *The Book of Glenbuchat*, Aberdeen, Third Spalding Club, 1942, p. iii.

64. R. Farquharson, *In and Out of Parliament: Reminiscences of a Varied Life*, London, Williams and Norgate, 1911, pp. 185-6.

65. *AFP*, 9, 20, 25 March 1886.

66. *AFP*, 15 March 1886.

67. *AFP*, 13 March 1886.

68. The HLLRA became the Highland Land League in 1886. When, in the 1890s, the HLL changed its strategy and became a Liberal pressure group of the kind that the SFA had been between 1881 and 1886 it became a much less effective organisation: J. Hunter, 'The politics of Highland land reform, 1873-1895', *SHR*, 1974, LIII, pp. 45-68. See also Hunter, 'The Gaelic connection: the Highlands, Ireland and nationalism', *SHR*, 1975, LIV, pp. 178-204.

69. Alexander, *Johnny Gibb of Gushetneuk*, pp. 9, 10, 322.

70. *AFP*, 22 March 1886.

71. *AFP*, 10 March 1886.

72. *AFP*, 17 May 1886; Royal Commission on Agricultural Depression, Minutes of Evidence, Vol. IV, *PP* 1896 (C 8021), XVII, Q 51 851, 51 872-3.

73. H. Brody, *Inishkillane: Change and Decline in the West of Ireland*, London, Allen Lane, 1973.

Chapter 7

1. E. H. Carr, *What is History?* Harmondsworth, Penguin, 1961, p. 55.

2. W. D. Simpson, *The Castle of Kildrummy*, Aberdeen, Wyllie, 1923, p. viii.

3. T. C. Smout, *A History of the Scottish People, 1560-1830*, London, Collins, 1969, p. 347. In this passage Smout makes it clear that he believes that the northeast, even upland districts in the northeast, shared this polarised social formation.

4. R. Mitchison, *A History of Scotland*, London, Methuen, 1970, pp. 293, 328-9, 349-50; A. Birnie, *An Economic History of the British Isles*, London, Methuen, 1935, p. 263; B. Lenman, *An Economic History of Modern Scotland, 1660-1975*, London, Batsford, 1977, pp. 195-6.

5. Smout, *op cit*, pp. 321-2.

6. We saw in chapter 4 that cottars were rather less uncommon in the sandstone districts than in the northeast's central wedge.

7. 'Lewis Grassic Gibbon' (J. L. Mitchell) and 'Hugh Macdiarmid' (C. M. Grieve), *Scottish Scene*, London, Jarrolds, 1934, p. 302.

8. We saw in Table 1.3 that East Lothian capitalist farmers held more than ninety-five per cent of the county's tilled acreage.

9. It is important to note that some historians do take account of regional variations within lowland agriculture. See, for example, R. H. Campbell, *Scotland since 1707: the Rise of an Industrial Society*, Oxford, Blackwell, 1965, pp. 163-5; M. Gray, 'Scottish Emigration: the Social Impact of Agrarian Change in the Scottish Lowlands, 1775-1875', *Perspectives in American History*, 1973, VII, 95-174; A. Fenton, *Scottish Country Life*, Edinburgh, Donald, 1976. None of these men works from Edinburgh University.

10. Sir J. Sinclair, *Account of the Systems of Husbandry Adopted in the More Improved Districts of Scotland*, third edition, two volumes, Edinburgh, Constable, 1814.

11. Hence the typical view of the English farm servant as a precapitalist relic, since day labouring apparently was a more completely proletarian form of labour. See, for example, J. Thirsk, *English Peasant Farming: the Agrarian History of Lincolnshire from Tudor to Recent Times*, London, Routledge and Kegan Paul, 1957, p. 271; F. E. Green, *A History of the English Agricultural Labourer, 1870-1920*, London, King, 1920, p. 17; W. Hasbach, *A History of the English Agricultural Labourer*, London, King, 1908, pp. 68-9.

12. S. George, *How the Other Half Dies*, Harmondsworth, Penguin, 1976, pp. 91-4.

13. R. Frankenberg, *Communities in Britain*, Harmondsworth, Penguin, 1966; H. Newby, 'Agricultural Workers in the Class Structure', *Sociological Review*, 1972, XX, p. 413.

14. F. Engels, 'The Condition of the working-class in England', (1845), in K. Marx and F. Engels, *On Britain*, London, Lawrence and Wishart, 1962, pp. 297-306.

15. Primitive accumulation is the process through which precapitalist production is penetrated and resources are accumulated and organised in a novel fashion to form mature capitalism.

16. K. Marx, *Capital*, Vol. I, ed. E. Mandel, Harmondsworth, Penguin, 1976, pp. 873-940.

17. *Ibid*, p. 876; V. I. Lenin, 'The Development of Capitalism in Russia' (1899), in V. I. Lenin (ed), *Collected Works*, Vol. III, London, Lawrence and Wishart, 1960, p. 111; J. Banaji, 'Summary of Selected Parts of Kautsky's *The Agrarian Question*', *Economy and Society*, 1976, V, pp. 2-49. The important theoretical point is this: to recognise that the capitalist mode of production is compatible with a range of social relations in different social formations is to make social relations a dependent variable of mode of production. Class analysis requires that this be the case. But to argue, as many British agricultural historians and rural sociologists do argue, that unless one has a polarised social formation, then one is not dealing with capitalist production, is to make mode of production a dependent variable of relations of production — an absurd position.

18. The most accessible source for this work is N. Long, *An Introduction to the Sociology of Rural Development*, London, Tavistock, 1977, pp. 71-104.

19. This work builds on the connection between capitalist development and imperialism that has seen such spectacular growth in development studies during the last decade. See, for example, S. Amin, *Accumulation on a World Scale: A critique of the Theory of Underdevelopment*, New York, Monthly Review Press, 1974; H. Bernstein (ed), *Underdevelopment and Development*, Harmondsworth, Penguin, 1973; E. de Kadt and G. Williams (ed), *Sociology and Development*, London, Tavistock, 1974; I. Oxaal, A. Barnett and D. Booth (ed), *Beyond the Sociology of Development*, London, Routledge and Kegan Paul, 1975; Long, *op cit*.

20. R. Williams, *The Country and the City*, London, Chatto and Windus, 1973, elaborates and then demolishes this antithesis between town and country, using a consummately elegant combination of literary and historical scholarship.

21. Highlands and Islands Development Board, *First Annual Report*, Inverness, HIDB, 1967, Foreword.

22. I. Carter, 'The Highlands of Scotland as an Underdeveloped Region', in E. de Kadt and G. Williams (ed), *Sociology and Development*, London, Tavistock, 1974, pp. 279-314; I. Carter, 'A Socialist Strategy for the Highlands', in G. Brown (ed), *The Red Paper on Scotland*, Edinburgh, EUSPB, 1975, pp. 247-53; J. Hunter, *The Making of the Crofting Community*, Edinburgh, Donald, 1976.

23. Hunter, *op cit*, codifies the crofters' view. For the epitome of sleekness, with an unusually open conflation of Highland landlords' sectional interests with the national interest, see P. Gaskell, *Morvern Transformed*, Cambridge, Cambridge University Press, 1968.

24. J. McEwan, 'Highland Landlordism', in G. Brown (ed), *op cit*, pp. 262-70; J. McEwan, *Who Owns Scotland? A Study in Land Ownership*, Edinburgh, EUSPB, 1977; J. Bryden and G. Houston, *Agrarian Change in the Scottish Highlands*, London, Robertson, 1976, pp. 61-8; Highlands and Islands Development Board, *Highland Agriculture and Land Use*, Inverness, HIDB, 1977, pp. 22-6. The vitality of the land question in the Highlands is shown not only in attempts like these to number estates and to judge the part played by estate policies in the rural Highlands, but also by more openly polemical events: the 7.84 Company's barnstorming success with their anti-landlord revue, 'The Cheviot, the Stag and the Black, Black Oil', for instance; or the

remarkable early success of the West Highland Free Press — a success that was built on a principled opposition to landlords' interests.

25. D. Turnock, 'Small Farms in North Scotland', *SGM*, 1975, XLI, pp. 170-7.

26. S. Lukes, *Power: a Radical View*, London, Macmillan, 1974, pp. 16-25.

27. Return of Owners of Land, England and Wales, *PP* 1874 (C 1097), LXXII, Part I and II; Return of Owners of Land and Heritages, Scotland, *PP* 1874 (C 899), LXXII, Part III; Return of Owners of Land, Ireland, *PP* 1876 (C 422), LXXX.

28. This information was organised by counties. Its value was enhanced when parcels of land owned by an individual in different counties were brought together to show his estate's true acreage: see J. Bateman, *The Great Landowners of Great Britain and Ireland*, Leicester, Leicester University Press, 1971, (1883).

29. The point is elaborated — in a deplorably polemical manner — in I. Carter, 'Sociology and Upland Britain', in J. C. Bowman (ed), *The Future of Upland Britain*, Reading, Centre for Agricultural Strategy, forthcoming.

30. P-M. Henry, 'Politics and Development', in G. Hunter, A. H. Bunting and A. Bottrall (ed), *Policy and Practice in Rural Development*, London, Croom Helm, 1976, p. 58.

Bibliography

THIS Bibliography contains items cited in chapter references, plus a few important items consulted but not cited. It is organised under the following heads.

1. Manuscript Sources.
2. Theses and Dissertations.
3. Newspapers.
4. Parliamentary Papers.
5. Other Official Reports.
6. Pamphlets.
7. Books and Articles.

1. Manuscript Sources.

At the Scottish Record Office, Edinburgh
Aberdeen Commercial Company, Annual Reports, BT 2/300.
Aberdeen Lime Company, Annual Reports BT 2/647.
Banff and Moray Agricultural Company Limited, Annual Reports, BT2/12811.
Board of Agriculture, parish totals of crops and stock, 1866-1911,
Aberdeenshire AF 39/1
Banffshire AF 39/4
Kincardine AF 39/17
Moray AF 39/12
Nairn AF 39/22
Kincardine Steam Ploughing Company (Limited), Annual Reports, 1866-85, BT 2/240.
Scottish Steam Cultivation and Traction Company, Annual Reports, BT 2/348.

At King's College Library, Aberdeen University
G. B. Currie, *Annals of Insch.*

At the Sheriff Clerk's Office, Aberdeen
Fiars' Court Book, Aberdeenshire.

At the Sheriff Clerk's Office, Stonehaven
Fiars' Court Book, Kincardine.

Private Collections
Mr Cook, *Diary, 1865-96,* (Mr W. Cook, Little Meldrum, Tarves).
Fintray Mutual Instruction Class, *Minute Book, Vol. 2,* (Mrs Walker, Fintray).
W. Gall, Oldtown, Atherb, *Diary,* (Country Life Archive, National Museum of Antiquities of Scotland).
G. McWillie, *Diary, 1829-65,* (Col. Gordon-Duff, Drummuir Castle).
Philorth Steam Cultivation and Traction Company (Limited), *Sederunt Book, 1871-88,* (Mrs Ramsay, Cairnbulg Castle, Fraserburgh).
A. Robertson, *Horseman's Oath,* (Mrs P. Gordon-Duff, Cabrach).

Rhynie Literary and Debating Club, *Minute Book, 1833-5,* (Mr Troup, Rhynie).
Rhynie Mutual Instruction Class, *Minute Book, 1846-97,* (Mr Troup, Rhynie).

2. Theses and Dissertations.

Brown, J., 'An enquiry into social mobility within the farming industry, 1900-30', (M.A. dissertation, Department of Sociology, Aberdeen University, 1971).
Buchan, D. D. 'The ballad and the folk: studies in . . . the northeast of Scotland', (Ph.D. thesis, Aberdeen University, 1965).
Collie, J. P., 'A study of the treatment of the life of northeast Scotland by Scottish novelists', (Ph.D. thesis, Aberdeen University, 1954).
Donnelly, T., 'The Development of the Aberdeen Granite Industry, 1750-1939', (Ph.D. thesis, Aberdeen University, 1975).
Duncan, R., 'Popular radicalism and working class movements in Aberdeen, c 1790-1850', (M. Litt, thesis, Aberdeen University, 1976).
Dyer, M. C., 'The politics of Kincardineshire', (Ph.D. thesis, Aberdeen University, 1974).
Evans, G., 'Trade unionism and the wage level in Aberdeen between 1870 and 1920', (Ph.D. thesis, Aberdeen University, c 1950).
Lindsay, J., 'The operation of the poor law in the north-east of Scotland, 1745-1846', (Ph.D. thesis, Aberdeen University, 1962).
Munro, R., 'The farmworkers of the north-east of Scotland, 1860-1914', (M.A. dissertation, Department of History, Edinburgh University, 1975).
Maclaren, A. A., 'Religion and social class in mid-nineteenth century Aberdeen', (Ph.D. thesis, Aberdeen University, 1971).
Soper, T. P., 'Monymusk, 1770-1850: a study of the economic development of a Scottish estate', (Ph.D. thesis, Aberdeen University, 1954).
Walton, K., The distribution and structure of the population of north-east Scotland, 1696-1931', (Ph.D. thesis, Aberdeen University, 1951).

3. Newspapers.

Aberdeen Free Press
Aberdeen Herald
Aberdeen Journal
Aberdeen Press and Journal
Banffshire Journal
Montrose, Arbroath and Brechin Review
North British Agriculturist
North of Scotland Gazette
Onward and Upward
People's Journal
Scotsman
Witness

4. Parliamentary Papers.

Reports

Board of Agriculture.
Report on the Decline in the Agricultural Population of Great Britain, 1881-1906. *PP* 1906 (Cd 3273), XCVI.

Board of Trade.
Report by Mr Wilson Fox on the Wages, Earnings and Conditions of Employment of Agricultural Labourers in the United Kingdom. *PP* 1900 (Cd 346), LXXXII.
Report of an Enquiry by the Board of Trade into the Earnings and Hours of Labour of Workpeople in the United Kingdom, Part V, Agriculture in 1907. *PP* 1910 (Cd 5460), LXXXIV.
Departmental Committee on Farm Workers in Scotland.
Report. *PP* 1935-6 (Cmd 5217), VII.
Departmental Committee on Fiars Prices in Scotland.
Evidence. *PP* 1911 (Cd 5764), XXIV.
Royal Commission on Agricultural Interests.
Minutes of Evidence. Part I, *PP* 1881 (C 2778-I), XV.
Part II, *PP* 1881 (C 3096), XVII.
Reports of Assistant Commissioners, *PP* 1881 (C 2778-II), XVI.
Royal Commission on Agricultural Depression.
Expenditure and Outgoings on Certain Estates in Great Britain; and Farm Accounts. *PP* 1896 (C 8125), XVI.
Minutes of Evidence. Vol. III, *PP* 1896 (C 7400), XVII.
Vol. IV. *PP* 1896 (C 8021), XVII.
Reports of Assistant Commissioners. *PP* 1894 (C 7342), XVI Part I.
PP 1895 (C 7742), XVII.
Royal Commission on the Employment of Children, Young Persons and Women in Agriculture.
Fourth Report. Appendix. Parts I and II. *PP* 1870 (C 221), XIII.
Royal Commission on the Housing of the Industrial Population of Scotland, Rural and Urban.
Report, *PP* 1917-18, (C 8731), XIV.
Evidence, six volumes, 1921, (Not a parliamentary paper).
Royal Commission on the Housing of the Working Classes.
Second Report. Scotland. *PP* 1884-5 (C 4409), XXXI.
Royal Commission on Labour.
The Agricultural Labourer, Vol. III. Scotland. Part I. *PP* 1893-4 (C 6894-XV), XXXVI.
Royal Commission on the Law relating to Landlord's Hypothec in Scotland.
Report. *PP* 1865 (3546), XVII.
Minutes of Evidence. *PP* 1865 (3546-I), XVII.
Royal Commission on the Poor Laws in Scotland.
Appendix. Part II. *PP* 1844 (564) XXI.
Part III. *PP* 1844 (565), XXII.
Part IV. *PP* 1844 (597) XXIII.
Part V. *PP* 1844 (598) XXIV.
Part VI. *PP* 1844 (543), XXV.
Select Committee on the Game Laws.
Report, with Evidence. *PP* 1828 (235), VIII.
Select Committee on the Game Laws.
First Report, with Evidence, *PP* 1872 (C 337), X.
Second Report, with Evidence, *PP* 1873 (C 285), XIII.
Select Committee on the Law of Hypothec in Scotland.
Report, with Evidence. *PP* 1868-9 (367), IX.
Select Committee on Small Holdings.
Report, with Proceedings and Minutes of Evidence. *PP* 1889 (C 313), XII.
Select Committee on the State of Agriculture.
Third Report, with Evidence. *PP* 1836 (465), VIII Part II.

Population Census
Census of Great Britain, 1841.
Occupation Abstract, 1841. Part II. Scotland. *PP* 1844 (588), XXVII.
Census of Great Britain, 1851.
Number of Inhabitants 1801-51. Vol. II. *PP* 1852-3 (1632), LXXXVI.
Ages, Civil Condition, Occupations and Birthplaces. Vol. II. *PP* 1852-3 (1691-II), LXXXVIII. Part II.
Religious Worship and Education. Reports and Tables. *PP* 1854 (1764), LIX.
Census of Scotland, 1861.
Population Tables and Report. Vol. II. *PP* 1864 (3275), LI.
Census of Scotland, 1871.
Report and Tables Vol. II. *PP* 1873 (C 841), LXXII.
Census of Scotland, 1881.
Report and Tables. Vol. II. *PP* 1883 (C 3657) LXXXI.
Census of Scotland, 1891.
Report and Tables Vol. II. Part II. *PP* 1893-4 (C 7134), CVII.
Census of Scotland, 1901.
Report and Tables Vol. III. *PP* 1904 (Cd 1798) CVIII.
Census of Scotland, 1911.
Report and Tables: the Counties in Alphabetical Order. *PP* 1912-13 (Cd 6097), CXIX-CXX.

Agricultural statistics
Board of Agriculture.
Agricultural Statistics for Great Britain for
1866. *PP* 1866 (3727), LX.
1867. *PP* 1867 (3491), LXXI.
1871. *PP* 1871 (C 460), LXIX.
1876. *PP* 1876 (C 1635), LXXVIII.
1881. *PP* 1881 (C 3078), XCII.
1886. *PP* 1886 (C 4847), LXX.
1887. *PP* 1887 (C 5187), LXXXVIII.
1891. *PP* 1890-1 (C 6524), LCI.
1896. *PP* 1897 (C 8502), XCVIII.
1898. *PP* 1899 (C 9304), CVI.
1901. *PP* 1902 (Cd 1121), CXVI.
1906. Part I. *PP* 1906 (Cd 3281), CXXXIII.
Part III. *PP* 1907 (Cd 3653), XCVII.
1910. Part II. *PP* 1911 (Cd 5604), XLV, Part I.
1911. Part I. *PP* 1912-13 (Cd 6021), CVI.
Part III. *PP* 1912-13 (Cd 6272), CVI.
Board of Agriculture for Scotland.
Agricultural Statistics for 1912. Part I. *PP* 1913 (Cd 6966), LXXVI.

Miscellaneous
Abstract Return of the Name of each Statute Labour Trust in Scotland. *PP* 1850 (303), XLIX.
Applications made for the advance of Public Money, under the Provisions of the Act 9 and 10 Vict c 101, as regards England and Scotland; distinguishing the Applications from each country. *PP* 1847 (43), XXXIX; 1847 (146), XXXIX.
Board of Agriculture.
Return of the number of Allotments detached from and attached to cottages and of Agricultural Holdings in Great Britain. *PP* 1886 (C 4848), LXX.
Board of Agriculture.

Returns relating to Agricultural Holdings in Great Britain in 1895. *PP* 1896 (C 8243), LXVII.
Names of Turnpike Road and Bridge Trusts in Scotland . . . *PP* 1850 (568), XLIX.
Number of Applications that have been made for Advances of Public Money, under the Act of Session 1846, c 101, in England, Ireland and Scotland respectively . . . *PP* 1847 (91), XXXIX.
Return of Owners of Land and Heritages, Scotland, *PP* 1874 (C 1097), LXXII Part III.
Return of Owners of Land, England and Wales, *PP* 1874 (C 1097), LXXII Parts I and II.
Return of Owners of Land, Ireland. *PP* 1876 (C 422), LXXX.
Return of the amount of Property assessed to Income and Property Tax . . . in each County of England and Wales, and Scotland, in the year
1842-3 to 1864-5. *PP* 1866 (511), XXXIX.
1864-5 to 1869-70. *PP* 1870 (C 454), XLI.
1880-1, *PP* 1882 (C 292), XXXVII.
1881-2. *PP* 1883 (C 206), XXXVIII.
1882-3. *PP* 1884-5 (C 25), XLV.
1883-4. *PP* 1884-5 (C 235) XLV.
1884-5 to 1889-90. *PP* 1892 (39-Sess I), XLVIII.
1889-90 to 1894-5. *PP* 1896 (C 216), XLIX.
Return showing, for each County, . . . the Number and Date of the Petitions presented under Section 5 of the Small Holdings Act, 1892 . . . *PP* 1895 (C 407), LXXXIV.

5. Other Official Reports.

Highlands and Islands Development Board,
First Annual Report, Inverness, HIDB, 1967.
Highland Agriculture and Land Use, Inverness, HIDB, 1977.
MacNaughton, W. A., *Annual Reports upon the Health and Sanitary Condition of the County (of Kincardine)*. Stonehaven, Waldie, 1891-1909.
Watt, J. P. *Annual Reports of the Medical Officer of Health, Aberdeenshire*, Aberdeen, *Free Press* (1892), Cornwall (1893-9), n.p. (other years), 1892-1911.
Valuation Roll, Aberdeenshire, 1859-60, 1892-3, 1912-13.

6. Pamphlets.

Aberdeen Association for the Promotion of Social Morality,
An Earnest Address by the Committee to Heads of Families and Well-Wishers of Society, Aberdeen, King, no date.
Aberdeen Association for the Improvement of the Dwellings of the Labouring Classes, *Reports 1-4*, Aberdeen, Cornwall, 1863-6.
Aberdeen, Ishbel, Countess of, *Our Farm Servant Girls*, Aberdeen, Wyllie, 1882.
Aberdeen, Marquess of, *Why Are Aberdeenshire Folk Proud of Their County?* Dundalk, Dundalgan Press, 1929.
Alexander, J., *Prize Essay on the Present Condition of Farm Servants in Scotland with Means to be Adopted for its Amelioration*, Aberdeen, Bennett, 1852.
Alexander, W., *Twenty-Five Years: a Personal Retrospect*, Aberdeen, n.p., 1878.
Aliquis, *Landlords, Land Laws, and Land Leagues: Being a Humble Contribution to Contemporary Politics*, Edinburgh, Douglas, 1881.
An Agricultural Labourer, *Duty to Farm Servants, Being an Essay on the Present Condition of the Agricultural Population in Their Relation to the Soil*, Aberdeen, Bennett, 1859.
An Aul' Coo Baillie, *Farm Servants as they Are*, Aberdeen, *Aberdeen Free Press*, n.d.

Anon, *Administration of Landed Property: the Hatton Estates,* Banff, *Banffshire Journal,* 1887.

A Well-Meant Word to the Women of Aberdeenshire, and the Other North-Eastern Counties, Aberdeen, Smith, n.d.

Constitution, Rules and Regulations of the Kincardineshire Ploughman Friendly Society in Auchenblae, Instituted June 22 1812, Montrose, *Chronicle* Office, 1825.

Farm Servants' Excursions, n.p., c 1860.

Jubilee of the Monquitter Agricultural Society, Banff, *Banffshire Journal,* 1902.

Jubilee of the Royal Northern Agricultural Society, Banff, *Banffshire Journal,* 1893.

Notes on the Land Question, Aberdeen, Scottish Farmers' Alliance, 1883.

Pastoral Address by the Synod of Aberdeen on the Moral Condition of the Rural Population, Aberdeen, Chalmers, 1865.

Report to the Commissioners of Supply of the County of Aberdeen . . . (on) . . . the Game Question, Aberdeen, Chalmers, 1872.

Rules and Regulations for the Management of the Buchan and Boyn Farmer Society, Begun at Macduff, 10 March 1786, Banff, *Banffshire Journal,* 1929.

Rules and Regulations of the Aberdeenshire Agricultural Association, Aberdeen, Chalmers, 1819.

The Aberdeenshire Land Agitation: Thoughts on the Questions Agitated at Farmers' Meetings in Aberdeenshire, Edinburgh, Blackwood, 1881.

The Garioch Farmer Club, Banff, *Banffshire Journal,* 1882.

The Horseman's Oath, as Written Down by a Buchan Horseman in 1908, Edinburgh, Scottish Country Life Museums Trust, 1972.

Association for the Improvement of the Dwellings and Domestic Conditions of Agricultural Labourers in Scotland (the Cottage Association), *1st to 7th Annual Reports,* Edinburgh, Blackwood, 1855-61.

Association for the Promotion of Social Morality, *Fourth Report,* Edinburgh, Lindsay, 1865.

Barclay, J. W., *Farmers' Grievances and their Remedies,* Aberdeen, Scottish Farmers' Alliance, 1883.

The Remedy for Agricultural Distress, Aberdeen, Scottish Farmers' Alliance, 1882.

Begg, J., *Lecture on 'Our Social Evils',* Aberdeen, King, 1859.

Black, J., *Report on Cottage Accommodation in Buchan,* Edinburgh, Blackwood, 1851.

Braik, A., *On the Condition of Agricultural Labourers and the Means of their Elevation,* Insch, Insch Mutual Improvement Association, 1861.

Bruce, G., *The Value of Tenants' Improvements,* Aberdeen, Scottish Farmers' Alliance, 1883.

Cameron, E., *Reform and Economy: an Essay,* Inverurie, Kemp, 1865.

Cassie, J., 'Essay', in *Essays by Agricultural Labourers on the Condition and Improvement of their Class,* Aberdeen, Brown, 1859, pp. 38-52.

Cramond, W., *Illegitimacy in Banffshire: Facts, Figures and Opinions,* Banff, *Banffshire Journal,* 1888.

Cumming, J., 'Essay', in *Essays by Agricultural Labourers on the Condition and Improvement of their Class,* Aberdeen, Brown, 1859, pp. 55-66.

Duncan, J. B., *Folk Songs of Aberdeenshire,* London, 1967.

Escott, H., *Beacons of Independency: Religion and Life in Strathbogie and Upper Garioch in the Nineteenth Century,* Huntly, *Huntly Express,* 1940.

Esslemont, J., *The Agricultural Holdings (Scotland) Bill,* Aberdeen, Scottish Farmers' Alliance, 1883.

Forbes, J. S., *Short Appeal for the Cottar's Ingle,* Edinburgh, Blackwood, 1854.

Fraser, A., 'Essay', in *Essays by Agricultural Labourers on the Condition and*

Improvement of their Class, Aberdeen, Brown, 1859, pp. 7-35.
Free Church of Scotland Committee on the Houses of the Working Classes, with Special Reference to Social Morality, 'Annual Reports', in the Appendix of the *Proceedings of the General Assembly of the Free Church of Scotland.* 1860-5.
Gerrard, J., *Rural Labourers in the North of Scotland; their Medical Relief and House Accommodation as they Affect Pauperism and Illegitimacy*, Banff, Smith, n.d.
Harvey, A., *The Agricultural Labourer: his Present Condition and Means for his Amelioration*, Aberdeen, Brown, 1858.
Jamieson, T., *Restrictions in Cultivation and Sale*, Aberdeen, Scottish Farmers' Alliance, 1883.
Marr, G., *Essay on the Condition of the Agricultural Population, and the Best Means of Ameliorating their State, Morally and Socially*, Aberdeen, Smith, 1858.
Milne, John (Mains of Laithers), *Compensation for Improvements*, Aberdeen, Scottish Farmers' Alliance, 1882.
Morrice, J., *Female Degradation: the Bane of Society*, Peterhead, Taylor, 1861.
Mortimer, A. R., *Farm Kitchen Work*, Elgin, *Courant and Courier*, 1910.
R. M., *A Book for Farm-Servants, or Hints for their Self Improvement*, Edinburgh, Blackwood, 1881.
Robb, J., *The Cottage, the Bothy, and the Kitchen: Being an Inquiry into the Condition of Agricultural Labourers in Scotland*, Edinburgh, Blackwood, 1861.
Ruxton, W., *Essay by a Farm Servant in Aberdeenshire*, Inverurie, Kemp, 1865.
Singer, W., *An Exposition of the Miller and Horseman's Word, or the True System of Raising the Devil*, sixth edition, Aberdeen, Anderson, 1865.
Skirving, R. S., *Landlords and Labourers*, Edinburgh, Blackwood, 1862.
Stuart, H. A. M., *Agricultural Labourers as they Were, Are, and Should Be, in their Social Condition*, Edinburgh, Blackwood, 1853.
Synod of Moray, *Statement and Address Relative to Farm Servants*, Edinburgh, Blackwood, 1859.
Thomson, A., *On the Licentiousness of Scotland*, London, Nisbet, 1861.
Waterman, J. J. *The Coming of the Railway to Aberdeen*, Aberdeen, Centre for Scottish Studies, 1976.
Watson, W., *Remarks on the Bothie System and Feeing Markets*, Aberdeen, Davidson, 1849.
Watt, G. R., *On the Improvement of Farm Servants*, Inverurie, Kemp, 1865.
Wilson, A. J., *Radical Cures for the Evils of Feudalism*, Aberdeen, Scottish Farmers' Alliance, 1882.

7. Books and Articles.

Note: for abbreviations used in this section see p. 185.

Aberdeen, Ishbel, Countess of, 'Household clubs: an experiment', *Nineteenth Century*, Jan-June 1892, XXXI, pp. 391-8.
A Buchan Farmer, 'On the husbandry of Buchan', *Farmer's Magazine*, 1807, VIII, pp. 344-8.
Acland, T. D., 'On lodging and boarding labourers, as practised on the farm of Mr Sotherton, M.P.', *JRASE:* 1849, X, pp.379-81.
Adam, J., 'Report on the improvement of waste land', *THASS*, 1847-9, 3rd series, III, pp. 403-5.
A Farmer, 'On the value of agricultural societies', *JA*, 1828-9, I, pp. 343-5.
A Herd Loon, *The Kingdom of Forgue*, Aberdeen, Fraser, 1903.
Alexander, W., 'Aberdeenshire agriculture — past and present', *TNAPSS*, 1877, pp. 677-86.

Johnny Gibb of Gushetneuk, Edinburgh, Douglas, 1880.

Life Among My Ain Folk, Edinburgh, Douglas, 1882.

Northern Rural Life in the Eighteenth Century, Edinburgh, Douglas, 1877.

'The Making of Aberdeenshire', *Transactions of the Aberdeen Philosophical Society*, 1892, II, 102-22.

'The peasantry of north-east Scotland', *United Presbyterian Magazine*, 1884, I, pp. 377-9, 426-9.

The Rinderpest in Aberdeenshire: the Outbreak of 1865, and how it was stamped out, Aberdeen, *Free Press*, 1882.

Alison, J. (ed), *Poetry of Northeast Scotland*, London, Heinemann, 1976.

Allan, J., 'Agriculture in Aberdeenshire in the Sixties', *Deeside Field*, 1927, III, pp. 29-36.

Allan J. R., *Farmer's Boy*, London, Methuen, 1935.

North-East Lowlands of Scotland, London, Hale, 1974.

'The land and the people', in H. Hamilton (ed), *Third Statistical Account of Scotland: the County of Aberdeen*, Glasgow, Collins, 1960, pp. 47-118.

The Seasons Return: Impressions of Farm Life, London, Hale, 1959.

Allardyce, A. D., *The Goodwife at Home, Illustrating the Dialect of the North-West District of Aberdeenshire*, Aberdeen, Smith, 1918.

Allardyce, J., *Byegone Days in Aberdeenshire*, Aberdeen, Central Press, 1913.

Amin, S., *Accumulation on a World Scale: a Critique of the Theory of Underdevelopment*, New York, Monthly Review Press, 1974.

Anderson, J., *General View of the Agriculture of the County of Aberdeen*, Edinburgh, n.p., 1794.

Anderson, R., 'An Aberdeenshire author', *Caledonia*, 1895, I, pp. 47-53, 137-43.

Anon., 'Admission of tenant members. Report by the Directors to the general meeting held on 8 January 1850', *THASS*, 1849-51, 3rd series, II, pp. 209-11.

'A farm servants' meeting', *Gateway*, 1918, VI, pp. 8-11.

'Agriculture at the meeting of the Association for the Promotion of Social Science', *JA*, 1864, XXIV, pp. 269-86.

'A register for farm servants', *JA*, 1841-2, XII, pp. 296-9.

'Bothies', *Reformed Presbyterian Magazine*, 1859, pp. 79-83.

Eleven Years at Farm Work, Being a True Tale of Farm Servant Life from 1863 Onwards, Aberdeen, *Free Press*, 1879.

'Hints by the Banffshire ploughman', *Farmer's Magazine*, 1806, VII, pp. 53-5.

In Memoriam William McCombie of Tillyfour, Aberdeen, privately printed, 1880.

'Labourers' houses', *Quarterly Review*, 1860, CVII, pp. 267-97.

'Life among my ain folk', *Gateway*, 1917, VI, pp. 7-10.

'On reaping with the scythe', *JA*, 1832-4, IV, pp. 350-69.

'On the preparation of live-stock and meat in reference to their exportation by steam vessels', *JA*, 1837-8, VIII, pp. 241-8.

'On the social and political importance of small holdings', *JA*, 1847-9, XVI, pp. 485-509.

'Our farm-labourers and their dwellings', *JA*, 1857-9, XXI, pp. 493-8.

'Report by a committee of Directors on hiring markets', *THASS*, 1849-51, 3rd series, II, pp. 9-15.

'Report by the committee . . . appointed to consider the means of improving the lodging of the peasantry', *THASS*, 1841, 2nd series, VII, pp. 534-41.

'Report by the committee . . . on . . . the engagement of farm-labourers', *THASS*, 1859-61, 3rd series, IX, pp. 387-92.

'Report of a special committee . . . on the various methods of cultivating land by steam power in East Lothian', *THASS*, 1870-1, 4th series, III, pp. 274-89.

Scottish Land: the Report of the Scottish Land Enquiry Committee, London,

Hodder and Stoughton, 1914.
'Social condition of our agricultural labourers', *JA*, 1853-5, XIX, pp. 143-59.
The agricultural labourer of Scotland', *Fraser's Magazine*, 1871, new series, III, pp. 641-53.
'The condition of the agricultural labourer', *JA*, 1859-61, XXII, pp. 721-36.
'The cottage, the bothy and the kitchen', *JA*, 1861-3, XXIII, pp. 274-7.
'The homes of the working poor', *Poor Law Magazine*, 1859, I, pp. 258-61.
'The Horseman's Society: what it could achieve', *People's Journal*, 5 April 1902.
'The Horseman's Word: a red letter day for a young horseman', *People's Journal*, 29 March 1902.
'The large farm system', *Free Church Magazine*, 1848, V, pp. 109-12.
The Life and Death of Jamie Fleeman, the Laird of Udny's Fool, Aberdeen, Smith, 1838.
'The physical condition of the people — the rural labourer', *JA*, 1857-9, XXI, pp. 623-41.
'The Scottish farm labourer', *Cornhill Magazine*, 1864, X, pp. 609-22.
'The sickle, the scythe and the reaping-machine', *JA*, 1857-9, XXI, pp. 61-3.
'Young on wire fencing', *JA*, 1849-51, XVII, pp. 338-42.
Arch, J., *Autobiography*, (1898), London, Macgibbon and Kee, 1966.
Arensberg, C. and Kimball, S., *Family and Community in Ireland*, London, Smith, 1968.
AZ, 'On the comparative advantages of keeping married and unmarried servants upon farms', *Farmer's Magazine*, 1802, III, pp. 1-8.
Bain, G., *History of Nairnshire*, second edition, Nairn, *Telegraph*, 1928.
Banaji, J., 'Backward capitalism, primitive accumulation, and modes of production', *Journal of Contemporary Asia*, 1973, pp. 393-413.
'For a theory of colonial modes of production', *Economic and Political Weekly*, 1972, VII, pp. 2498-2502.
'Summary of selected parts of Kautsky's *The Agrarian Question*', *Economy and Society*, 1976, V, pp. 2-49.
Barclay, J. R., 'Farming methods in Banffshire', *THASS*, 1908, 5th series, XX, pp. 155-80.
Barclay, J. W., 'The Glen and its folk', in W. D. Simpson (ed), *The Book of Glenbuchat*, Aberdeen, Third Spalding Club, 1942, pp. 39-48.
Bateman, J., *The Great Landowners of Great Britain and Ireland* (1883), Leicester, Leicester University Press, 1971.
Beaton, H., *At the Back of Bennachie, or Life in the Garioch in the Nineteenth Century*, Aberdeen, Central Press, 1923.
Begg, J., 'Houses of the working-classes of Scotland: the bothy system', *TNAPSS*. 1858, pp. 621-4.
'Obstacles to cottage-building in Scotland', *TNAPSS*, 1859, pp. 690-6.
'The bothy system', *TNAPSS*, 1860, pp. 881-2.
'The houses of the working classes in Scotland, rural and urban', *TNAPSS*, 1874, pp. 908-15.
'The necessity for appointing public inspectors for rural cottages', *TNAPSS*, 1863, pp. 763-5.
Bell, C. and Newby, H., *Community Studies*, London, Allen and Unwin, 1971.
'Husbands and wives: the dynamics of the deferential dialectic', paper given to the 1974 Annual Conference of the British Sociological Association, Aberdeen.
'The sources of variation in agricultural workers' images of society', *Sociological Review*, 1973, XXI, pp. 229-53.
Bendix, R., 'Tradition and modernity reconsidered', *Comparative Studies in Society and History*, 1966, IX, pp. 292-346.

Bernstein, H. (ed), *Underdevelopment and Development*, Harmondsworth, Penguin, 1973.
Birnie, A., *An Economic History of the British Isles*, London, Methuen, 1935.
Black, J., 'Methods of rearing and feeding cattle in the north of Scotland', *THASS*, 1893, 5th series, IV, pp. 18-80.
'On clovers and grasses best suited for two or three years pasture', *THASS*, 1851-3, 3rd series, III, pp. 161-72.
'On the agriculture of Aberdeen and Banff shires', *THASS*, 1870-1, 4th series, III, pp. 1-36.
'Report on the cottage accommodation in the district of Buchan, Aberdeenshire', *THASS*, 1853-5, 3rd series, V, pp. 92-9.
Blaikie, Provost, 'Report on the system of improvement followed on the muirs of . . . Charlestown, Kincardine . . . by the settlement of crofters on improving leases', *THASS*, 1837, 2nd series, V, pp. 97-121.
Board of Agriculture, *The Agricultural State of the Kingdom, 1816*, London, Adams and Dart, 1970, (1816).
Booth, A., 'On the improvement of 70 acres 2 roods 30 poles of the Farm of Auchmaleddy, in the parish of New Deer, Aberdeenshire', *THASS*, 1841, 2nd series, VII, pp. 524-7.
Boswell, J., 'On the unprofitableness of old pastures, compared with new', *JA*, 1832-4, IV, pp. 783-91.
'Report of the improvement of the farm of Swellhead, on the estate of Kingcausie, parish of Maryculter, and County of Kincardine', *THASS*, 1843, 2nd series, VIII, pp. 349-57.
Bowley, A. L., 'Index-numbers of wage-rates and cost of living', *Journal of the Royal Statistical Society*, 1952, CXV, pp. 500-6.
Brody, H., *Inishkillane: Change and Decline in the West of Ireland*, London, Allen Lane, 1973.
Brown, G., 'Agricultural costs in Scotland', *THASS*, 1891, 5th series, III, pp. 266-85.
Brown, J.; 'Scottish and English land legislation, 1905-11', *SHR*, 1968, XLVII, pp. 72-85.
Bruce, I. M., *A Century of Aberdeenshire Agriculture*, Aberdeen, *Aberdeen Journal*, 1908.
Bruce, R., 'The late Mr Amos Cruickshank', *THASS*, 1896, 5th series, VIII, pp. 214-24.
Bruce, W. S., *The Nor' East*, second edition, London, Hodder and Stoughton, 1915.
Bryce, J., *The Story of a Ploughboy*, London, Bodley Head, 1912.
Bryden, J., and Houston, G., *Agrarian Change in the Scottish Highlands*, London, Robertson, 1976.
Buchan, D. D., *The Ballad and the Folk*, London, Routledge and Kegan Paul, 1972.
Buckley, K. D., *Trade Unionism in Aberdeen, 1878-1900*, Aberdeen, Aberdeen University Press, 1955.
Bullock, J. M., 'Johnny Gibb of Gushetneuk', *TBFC*, 1926, XIII, pp. 87-90.
Burnett, J., *A Century of Agricultural Statistics: Great Britain 1866-1966*, London, HMSO, 1968.
Byres, T. J., 'Scottish peasants and their song', *Journal of Peasant Studies*, 1976, III, pp. 236-51.
Caird, A. McN., 'Land ownership and tenure', in J. Wilson (ed), *Report on the Present State of the Agriculture of Scotland*, Edinburgh, Blackwood, 1878, pp. 134-46.
Caird, J., 'General view of British agriculture', *JRASE*, 1878, 2nd series, XIV, pp. 271-332.
Cameron, A. C., *The History of Fettercairn,*, Paisley, Parlane, 1899.
Campbell, I., 'Chris Caledonia: the search for an identity', *Scottish Literary Journal*, 1974, I, 2, pp. 46-57.

Campbell, N. L. A., 'The story of "The Colony" on Bennachie', in A. W. M. Whiteley (ed), *The Book of Bennachie*, Aberdeen, Baillies of Bennachie, 1976, pp. 104-6.

Campbell, R. H., *Scotland Since 1707: the Rise of an Industrial Society*, Oxford, Blackwell, 1965.

Carnie, W., *Reporting Reminiscences*, Aberdeen, Aberdeen University Press, 1902.

Carr, E. H., *What is History?*, Harmondsworth, Penguin, 1961.

Carr, G., 'On improvements on the farm of Westhill of Park, Kincardineshire', *THASS*, 4th series, III, pp. 407-8.

Carter, I. R., 'Agricultural workers in the class structure: a critical note', *Sociological Review*, 1974, XXII, pp. 271-9.

'A socialist strategy for the Highlands', in G. Brown (ed), *The Red Paper on Scotland*, Edinburgh, EUSPB, 1975, pp. 247-53.

'Dorset, Kincardine, and peasant crisis', *Journal of Peasant Studies*, 1975, II, pp. 483-8.

'Economic models and the recent history of the Highlands', *Scottish Studies*, 1971, XV, pp. 99-120.

'Illegitimacy rates and farm service in north-east Scotland, *Section N, British Association for the Advancement of Science*, 1974, mimeo.

'Illegitimate births and illegitimate inferences', *Scottish Journal of Sociology*, 1977, I, pp. 125-35.

'Kailyard: the literature of decline in nineteenth century Scotland', *Scottish Journal of Sociology*, 1976, I, pp. 1-14.

'Social differentiation in the Aberdeenshire peasantry, 1696-1870', *Journal of Peasant Studies*, 1977, V, pp. 48-65.

'Sociology and upland Britain', in J. C. Bowman (ed), *The Future of Upland Britain*, Reading, Centre for Agricultural Strategy, forthcoming.

'The Highlands of Scotland as an underdeveloped region', in E. de Kadt and G. Williams (ed), *Sociology and Development*, London, Tavistock, 1974, pp. 279-314.

'The mutual improvement movement in north-east Scotland in the nineteenth century', *Aberdeen University Review*, 1976, XLVI, pp. 383-92.

'To roose the countra fae the caul' morality o' a died Moderatism: William Alexander and "Johnny Gibb of Gushetneuk"', *Northern Scotland*, 1976, II, pp. 148-62.

(ed), *Aberdeenshire Peasant Life*, London, Cass, forthcoming.

Chambers, J. D. and Mingay, G. E., *The Agricultural Revolution, 1750-1880*, London, Batsford, 1966.

Channon, G., 'The Aberdeenshire beef trade with London: a study in steamship and railway competition, 1850-69', *Transport History*, 1969, II, pp. 1-24.

Checkland, S. G., *The Rise of Industrial Society in England, 1815-1885*, London, Longmans, 1964.

Clapham, J. H., *An Economic History of Modern Britain: Free Trade and Steel, 1850-1886*, Cambridge, Cambridge University Press, 1932.

Cobban, J., 'Farm buildings', *THASS*, 1909, 5th series, XXI, pp. 1-23.

Cockburn, H., *Journal, 1831-1854*, two volumes, Edinburgh, Edmonston and Douglas, 1884.

Collins, E. J. T., 'Harvest technology and labour supply in Britain, 1790-1870', *EcHR*, 1969, XXII, pp. 453-73.

'Migrant labour in British agriculture in the nineteenth century', *EcHR*, 1976, XXIX, pp. 38-59.

Cook, A. S., *Pen Sketches and Reminiscences of Sixty Years*, Aberdeen, Taylor and Henderson, 1901.

Cowie, J., 'An essay on the comparative advantages in the employment of horses and

oxen in farm work', *JRASE*, 1844, V, pp. 52-7.
'Farm steadings', *THASS*, 1853-5, 3rd series, VI, pp. 33-9.
'On the improvement of waste land', *THASS*, 1843-5, 3rd series, I, pp. 452-5.
Et al, 'Digest of essays on the bothy system of maintaining single farm servants', *THASS*, 1843, 2nd series, XIV, pp. 133-44.

Craig, D., 'Novels of peasant crisis', *Journal of Peasant Studies*, 1974, I, pp. 47-68.

Craigie, P. G., 'On recent changes in Scottish agriculture', *Transactions of the British Association for the Advancement of Science*, 1886, pp. 1162-4.

Cramond, W., 'Illegitimacy in Banffshire', *Poor Law Magazine*, 1892, 2nd series, II, pp. 571-90.

Cruickshank, J. (Cruden Bay), 'Changes in the agricultural industry of Aberdeenshire in the last fifty years', *SA*, 1936, XIX, pp. 130-9, 225-39.

Cruickshank, J., (Elgin), 'Report on the improvement of waste lands', *THASS*, 1847-9, 3rd series, III, pp. 317-20.

Cruikshank, A., 'On the improvement of 40 acres on the farm of Sittyton', *THASS*, 1841, 2nd series, VII, pp. 527-9.

Davidson, D., 'Report on the improvement of waste land', *THASS*,1847-9, 3rd series, III, pp. 405-8.

Davidson, J., *A Topographical and Historical Account of Inverurie and the Earldom of the Garioch*, Edinburgh, Douglas, 1878.

Davidson, T., 'The Horseman's Word: a rural initiation ceremony', *Gwerin*, 1956, I, pp. 67-74.

de Kadt, E., and Williams, G. (ed), *Sociology and Development*, London, Tavistock, 1974.

Devine, T. M., 'The rise and fall of illicit whisky-making in northern Scotland, c 1780-1840', *SHR*, 1975, LIV, pp. 155-77.

Diack, H., *Boy in a Village*, Nottingham, Palmer, 1962.
That Village on the Don, Nottingham, Palmer, 1965.

Diack, W., 'The Scottish farm labourer', *Independent Review*, 1905, VII, pp. 315-27.

Dod, C. R., *Electoral Facts from 1832 to 1853 Impartially Stated* (1872), ed H. J. Hanham, Brighton, Harvester Press, 1971.

Donaldson, J., *General View of the Agriculture of the County of Banff*, Edinburgh, Ruddiman, 1794.
General View of the Agriculture of the County of Elgin or Moray, London, Clarke, 1794.
General View of the Agriculture of the County of Kincardine, London, Philanthropic Reform, 1795.
General View of the Agriculture of the County of Nairn, London, Clarke, 1794.

Douglas, G., *The House With the Green Shutters* (1901),London, Cassell, 1967.

Douglas, R., 'God gave the land to the people', in A. J. A. Morris (ed), *Edwardian Radicalism, 1900-1914*, London, Routledge and Kegan Paul, 1974, pp. 148-61.
The History of the Liberal Party, 1895-1970, London, Sidgwick and Jackson, 1971.

Dunbabin, J. P. D., *Rural Discontent in Nineteenth Century Britain*, London, Faber and Faber, 1974.
'The incidence and organisation of agricultural trade unionism in the 1870s', *AHR*, 1968, XVI, pp. 114-41.
'The revolt of the field', *Past and Present*, 1963, XXVI, pp. 68-97.

Dunbar, E., *Social Life in Former Days, Chiefly in the Province of Moray*, 2 volumes, Edinburgh, Douglas, 1865.

Duncan, J. F., 'Farm workers in the north-east, 1851-1951', *SA*, 1951, XXX, pp. 13-29.
'Organising farm workers', *Journal of Agricultural Economics*, 1935-7, IV, pp. 250-8.
'The farm cottage in Scotland', *SA*, 1930, XIII, pp. 140-53.

'The Scottish agricultural labourer', in D. J. Jones, J. F. Duncan, H. M. Conacher, and W. R. Scott, *Rural Scotland During the War*, Oxford, Clarendon Press, 1926, pp. 188-220.

Dyer, M. C., 'Why Tory stronghold crumbled', *Scotsman*, 24 October 1974.

Elliott, E. B., *Memoir of Lord Haddo, in his Latter Years Fifth Earl of Aberdeen*, fifth edition, London, Seeley, Jackson and Halliday, 1869.

Emmett, I., *A North Wales Village*, London, Routledge and Kegan Paul, 1964.

Engels, F., 'The condition of the working-class in England' (1845), in K. Marx and F. Engels, *On Britain*, London, Lawrence and Wishart, 1962.

Ernle, Lord, *The Land and its People: Chapters in Rural Life and History*, London, Hutchinson, 1925.

Esdaile, D., 'Report by a committee of the synod of Angus and Mearns as to agricultural labourers', *JA*, 1855-7, XX, pp. 397-406.

Evans, G., 'Farm servants' unions in Aberdeenshire between 1870 and 1900', *SHR*, 1952, XXXI, pp. 29-40.

Evans, G. E., *The Days That We Have Seen*, London, Faber and Faber, 1975.

'The horse and magic', *New Society*, 14 March 1963.

The Horse in the Furrow, London, Faber and Faber, 1960.

The Pattern Under the Plough, London, Faber and Faber, 1966.

Evans, M., *Karl Marx*, London, Allen and Unwin, 1975.

Farquharson, R., *In and Out of Parliament: Reminiscences of a Varied Life*, London, Williams and Norgate, 1911.

The House of Commons from Within, and Other Memories, London, Williams and Norgate, 1912.

Fay, C. R., *Great Britain from Adam Smith to the Present Day: an Economic and Social Survey*, London, Longmans, 1928.

Fenton, A., 'Farm servant life in the 17th-19th centuries', *SA*, 1964-5, LXIV, pp. 281-5.

'Sickle, scythe and reaping machine: innovation patterns in Scotland', *Ethnologia Europaea*, 1974, VII, pp. 35-47.

Scottish Country Life, Edinburgh, Donald, 1976.

'The history of rural Scotland', *SA*, 1971, L, pp. 90-5.

'The place of oatmeal in the diet of Scottish farm servants in the eighteenth and nineteenth centuries', *Studia Ethnographia et Folkloristica in Honorem Bela Gunda*, 1971, pp. 87-101.

'The scope of regional ethnology', *Folk Life*, 1973, XI, pp. 5-14.

Ferguson, J., 'Report on the improvement of the muir of Altens', *THASS*, 1841, 2nd series, VII, pp. 163-80.

Ferguson, R. C. M. 'Cheap cottages', *THASS*, 1907, 5th series, XIX, pp. 93-7.

Ferguson, T., *Scottish Social Welfare*, Edinburgh, Livingstone, 1958.

Findlay, W. M., *Oats, their Cultivation and Use from Ancient Times to the Present Day*, Aberdeen, Aberdeen University Press, 1955.

Fletcher, C., 'Men in the middle', *Sociological Review*, 1969, XVII, pp. 341-54.

Fletcher, T. W., 'The great depression of English agriculture, 1873-96', *EcHR*, 1961, XIII, pp. 417-32.

Flinn, M. W., and Smout, T. C. (ed), *Essays in Social History*, Oxford, Clarendon Press, 1974.

Forbes Irvine, A., 'Report on hiring markets by a committee of the Society', *THASS*, 1873, 4th series, V, pp. 311-5.

Forbes, J. S., 'On the constitution and statistics of the friendly societies in the counties of Aberdeen, Banff and Kincardine', *THASS*, 1853, 3rd series, V, pp. 65-91.

Frank, A. G., *Capitalism and Underdevelopment in Latin America*, New York, Monthly Review Press, 1967.

Latin America: Underdevelopment or Revolution?, New York, Monthly Review

Press, 1970.

Frankenberg, R., *Communities in Britain: Social Life in Town and Country*, Harmondsworth, Penguin, 1966.

Franklin, S. H., *Rural Societies*, London, Macmillan, 1971.

The European Peasantry: the Final Phase, London, Methuen, 1969.

Franklin, T. B., *A History of Scottish Farming*, London, Nelson, 1952.

Fraser, Col., 'Settlement of crofters on waste land on the estate of Castle Fraser, Aberdeenshire', *THASS*, 1837, 2nd series, V, pp. 387-90.

Fraser, U., 'Improvement of waste land', *THASS*, 1855-7, 3rd series, VII, pp. 441-5.

Galeski, B., *Basic Concepts of Rural Sociology*, Manchester, Manchester University Press, 1972.

Gallagher, J., and Robinson, R., 'The imperialism of free trade', in A. G. L. Shaw (ed), *Britain and the Colonies, 1815-1865*, London, Methuen, 1970.

Galtung, J., *Theory and Methods of Social Research*, London, Allen and Unwin, 1967.

Garry, F., *Bennygoak and Other Poems*, third edition, Aberdeen, Rainbow Books, 1975.

Gaskell, P., *Morvern Transformed*, Cambridge, Cambridge University Press, 1968.

Gauldie, E., *Cruel Habitations: a History of Working-Class Housing, 1780-1918*, London, Allen and Unwin, 1974.

Geddes, A., 'The agricultural unit: the farm labour team', *Planning Outlook*, 1949, I, pp. 1-17.

and Forbes, J., 'Rural communities of fermtoun and baile in the lowlands and highlands of Aberdeenshire, 1696', *Aberdeen University Review*, 1947, XXXII, pp. 98-104.

George, S., *How the Other Half Dies*, Harmondsworth, Penguin, 1976.

'Gibbon, Lewis Grassic', (Mitchell, James Leslie), *A Scots Quair*, London, Hutchinson, 1946.

and 'MacDiarmid, Hugh', (Grieve, C. M.), *Scottish Scene*, London, Jarrolds, 1934.

Giles, P., 'William Alexander and "Johnny Gibb of Gushetneuk"', *TBFC*, 1926, XIII, pp. 74-86.

Glentworth, R., 'Soils', in A. C. O'Dell and J. Mackintosh (ed), *The North-East of Scotland*, Aberdeen, Central Press, 1963.

The Soils of the Country Round Banff, Huntly and Turriff, Edinburgh, HMSO, 1954.

and Muir, J. W. (ed), *The Soils of the Country Round Aberdeen, Inverurie, and Fraserburgh*, Edinburgh, HMSO, 1963.

Godsman, J., *Glass, Aberdeenshire: the Story of a Parish*, Aberdeen, Reid, 1970.

Goldthorpe, J., Lockwood, D., Bechofer, F., and Platt, J., 'The affluent worker and the thesis of embourgeoisement: some preliminary research findings', *Sociology*, 1967, I, pp. 11-32.

Goode, W.,'Illegitimacy, anomie and cultural penetration', *American Sociological Review*, 1961, XXVI, pp. 910-25.

Gordon, A., *The Folks of Carglen, or Life in the North*, London, Fisher Unwin, 1891.

Gordon, Sir A., *The Earl of Aberdeen*, London, Sampson, Low, Marston, 1893.

Gordon, J. F. S., *The Book of the Chronicles of Keith, Grange, Ruthven, Cairney, and Botriphnie: Events, Places, and Persons*, Glasgow, Forrester, 1880.

Graham, H. G., *The Social Life of Scotland in the Eighteenth Century*, two volumes, London, Black, 1899.

Grant, G., 'On the reclamation of waste land on the farm of Ballimore, in the county of Banff', *THASS*, 1879, 4th series, XI, pp. 87-90.

Grant, I. F., 'An old Scottish handicraft industry in the north of Scotland', *SHR*, 1921, XVIII, pp. 277-89.

'Social effects of the agricultural reforms and enclosure movement in

Aberdeenshire', *EcHR*, 1926-9, I, pp. 89-116.
Grant, J., and Grant, J., 'Report on the improvement of waste land', *THASS*, 1847-9, 3rd series, III, pp. 400-1.
Gray, A., (Auchterless), *Talks with our Farm Servants*, Edinburgh, Clark, 1906.
Gray, A. (Peterhead), 'On the improvement of the estates of Auchtigal and Collielaw, parish of Peterhead, Aberdeenshire', *THASS*, 1841, 2nd series, VII, pp. 258-60.
Gray, J., 'Mao Tse-Tung's strategy for the collectivisation of Chinese agriculture', in E. de Kadt and G. Williams (ed), *Sociology and Development*, London, Tavistock, 1974, pp. 39-66.
'The two roads: alternative strategies of social change and economic growth in China', in S. Schram (ed), *Authority, Participation and Cultural Change in China*, Cambridge, Cambridge University Press, 1973, pp. 109-58.
Gray, M., 'North-east agriculture and the labour force, 1790-1875', in A. A. Maclaren (ed), *Social Class in Scotland: Past and Present*, Edinburgh, Donald, 1976, pp. 86-104.
'Scottish emigration: the social impact of agrarian change in the rural lowlands, 1775-1875', *Perspectives in American History*, 1973, VII, pp. 95-174.
'The kelp industry in the Highlands and Islands', *EcHR*, 1951, IV, pp. 197-209.
Gray, R., 'Account of the district of Buchan', *THASS*, 1832, 2nd series, III, pp. 49-70.
'Report on the improvement of waste land on the farm of Nether Savock', *THASS*, 1843-5, 3rd series, I, pp. 117-20.
Green, F. E., *A History of the English Agricultural Labourer, 1870-1920*, London, King, 1920.
Gregor, W., *An Echo of the Olden Time from the North of Scotland*, Edinburgh, Menzies, 1874.
'Kilns, mills, millers, meal and bread', *TBFC*, 1894, III, pp. 125-59.
Notes on the Folk-lore of the North-East of Scotland, London, Stock, 1881.
Greig, G., *Folksong in Buchan, and Folksong of the North-East* (1914), Hatboro', Pennsylvania, Folklore Associates, 1963.
Last Leaves of Traditional Ballads and Ballad Airs, edited by A. Keith, Aberdeen, Aberdeen University Press, 1925.
Grose, F., 'A chiel's amang ye', *Gateway*, 1913, I, pp. 16-19.
Groves, R., *Sharpen the Sickle! The History of the Farm Workers' Union*, London, Porcupine Press, 1949.
H., 'An essay on the proper size of farms', *Farmer's Magazine*, 1801, I, pp. 376-86.
Haldane, A. R. B., *The Drove Roads of Scotland*, Newton Abbot, David and Charles, 1973.
Hall, A. D., *A Pilgrimage of British Farming, 1910-1912*, London, Murray, 1913.
Hamilton, H., *An Economic History of Scotland in the Eighteenth Century*, Oxford, Clarendon Press, 1963.
Selections from the Monymusk Papers, 1713-1755, Edinburgh, Edinburgh University Press, 1945.
The Industrial Revolution in Scotland, Oxford, Clarendon Press, 1932.
Ed, *Life and Labour on an Aberdeenshire Estate, 1735-50*, Aberdeen, Third Spalding Club, 1946.
The Third Statistical Account of Scotland: the County of Aberdeen, Glasgow, Collins, 1960.
The Third Statistical Account of Scotland: the County of Banff, Glasgow, Collins, 1961.
The Third Statistical Account of Scotland: the Counties of Moray and Nairn, Glasgow, Collins, 1965.
Handley, J. E., *Scottish Farming in the Eighteenth Century*, London, Faber and Faber, 1953.

The Agricultural Revolution in Scotland, Glasgow, Burns, 1963.

Hardy, Thomas, 'The Dorsetshire Labourer' (1883), in Thomas Hardy, *Stories and Poems,* London, Dent, 1970, pp. 3-19.

Harrison, M., 'Chayanov and the economics of the Russian peasantry', *Journal of Peasant Studies,* 1975, II, pp. 389-417.

Hasbach, W., *A History of the English Agricultural Labourer,* London, King, 1908.

Hay, J., 'On concrete drain tiles', *THASS,* 1843, 2nd series, VIII, pp. 589-98.

Henderson, H., 'A slight case of devil worship', *New Statesman,* 14 June 1952.

'The bothy ballads', *Journal of Peasant Studies,* 1975, II, pp. 497-501.

'The oral tradition', *Scottish International,* 1973, VI, I, pp. 27-32.

Hendry, J., 'The language of Johnny Gibb', *TBFC,* 1925, XIII, pp. 57-67.

Henriques, U. R. Q., 'Bastardy and the new poor law', *Past and Present,* 1967, XXXVII, pp. 103-29.

Henry, P-M., 'Politics and development', in G. Hunter, A. H. Bunting and A. Bottrall (ed), *Policy and Practice in Rural Development,* London, Croom Helm, 1976, pp. 57-8.

Hill, C., *Reformation to Industrial Revolution,* Harmondsworth, Penguin, 1969.

Hinton, W., *Fanshen: a Documentary of Revolution in a Chinese Village,* Harmondsworth, Penguin, 1972.

Hobsbawm, E. J., *Industry and Empire,* Harmondsworth, Penguin, 1969.

and Rudé, G., *Captain Swing,* London, Lawrence and Wishart, 1969.

Hofstee, E. W., 'Development and rural social structure', *Sociologia Ruralis,* 1968, VIII, pp. 240-55.

Holderness, B. A., '"Open" and "close" parishes in England in the eighteenth and nineteenth centuries', *AHR,* 1972, XX, pp. 126-39.

Horn, P. R. L., *Joseph Arch,* Kineton, Roundwood Press, 1971.

Houston, G. F. B., 'A farmworker's journal of the 1890s', *SA,* 1960, XXXIX, pp. 124-6.

'Agricultural statistics in Scotland before 1866', *AHR,* 1961, IX, pp. 93-7.

'Labour relations in Scottish agriculture before 1870', *AHR,* 1958, VI, pp. 27-41.

Howie, A., 'Agriculture', in R. Glentworth and J. W. Muir (ed), *The Soils of the Country Round Aberdeen, Inverurie and Fraserburgh,* Edinburgh, HMSO, 1963, pp. 222-31.

Howie, G. W., 'Work among the Ploughmen and Quarriers in a Forfarshire parish', *Missionary Record of the United Free Church of Scotland,* 1908, pp. 104-5.

Hudson, K., *Patriotism with Profit: British Agricultural Societies in the Eighteenth and Nineteenth Centuries,* London, Evelyn, 1972.

Hunter, J., 'The Gaelic connection: the Highlands, Ireland, and nationalism', *SHR,* 1975, LIV, pp. 178-204.

The Making of the Crofting Community, Edinburgh, Donald, 1976.

'The politics of Highland land reform, 1873-1895', *SHR,* 1974, LIII, pp. 45-68.

Hutchinson, R., 'On the dietary of the English agricultural labourer in contrast to the Scottish', *THASS,* 1870-1, 4th series, II, pp. 349-78.

'Report on the dietaries of Scotch agricultural labourers', *THASS,* 1869, 4th series, II, pp. 1-29.

Imper, A. D., 'The north of Scotland', in J. P. Maxton (ed), *Regional Types of British Agriculture,* London, Allen and Unwin, 1935, pp. 253-70.

Jamieson, T. F., 'Report on the general principles of reclaiming land', *THASS,* 1855-7, 3rd series, VII, pp. 9-29.

Jefferies, R., *Hodge and His Masters,* (1880), two volumes, London, Macgibbon and Kee, 1966.

Jenkins, D., 'Farming and community in south Cardiganshire during the late nineteenth century', *Local Historian,* 1970, IX, pp. 178-83.

The Agricultural Community in South-West Wales at the Turn of the Twentieth

Century, Cardiff, University of Wales Press, 1971.

Jenkins, G. (ed), *Studies in Folk Life*, London, Routledge and Kegan Paul, 1969.

Jenkins, H. M., 'Report on some features of Scottish agriculture', *JRASE*, 1871, 2nd series, VII, pp. 145-219.

Johnson, Samuel, *A Journey to the Western Islands of Scotland*, (1775), ed R. W. Chapman, Oxford, Oxford University Press, 1970.

Johnston, T., *The History of the Working Classes in Scotland*, Glasgow, Forward Publishing Company, 1920.

Jolly, W., *The Life of John Duncan, Scotch Weaver and Botanist*, London, Kegan Paul, Trench, 1883.

Jones, E. L., *The Development of English Agriculture, 1815-73*, London, Macmillan, 1968.

Kay, G., 'The landscape of improvement: a case study of agricultural change in north-east Scotland', *SGM*, 1962, LXXVIII, pp. 100-11.

Keith, A., 'Aberdeenshire agriculture, 1851-1951', *SA*, 1951, XXX, 1-5.

A Thousand Years of Aberdeen, Aberdeen, Aberdeen University Press, 1972.

'William Alexander—the artist', *TBFC*, 1926, XIII, pp. 91-5.

Keith, G. S., *General View of the Agriculture of Aberdeenshire*, Aberdeen, Brown, 1811.

Kerr, B., *Bound to the Soil*, London, Baker, 1968.

'The Dorset agricultural labourer, 1750-1850', *Proceedings of the Dorset Natural History and Archaeological Society*, 1962, LXXXIV.

Kerr, J. *Memories Grave and Gay: Forty Years of School Inspection*, Edinburgh, Blackwood, 1902.

Khera, S., 'Social stratification and land inheritance among Austrian peasants', *American Anthropologist*, 1973, LXXV, pp. 814-23.

Kinnear, G. H., *Kincardineshire*, Cambridge, Cambridge University Press, 1921.

Kitteridge, J., Country work girls in nineteenth century England', in R. Samuel (ed), *Village Life and Labour*, London, Routledge and Kegan Paul, 1975, pp. 73-135.

Kuhn, T. S., *The Structure of Scientific Revolutions*, Chicago, Chicago University Press, 1962.

Landsberger, H. A., (ed), *Rural Protest: Peasant Movements and Social Change*, London, Macmillan, 1974.

Lawson, A., 'Report on the improvement of waste lands', *THASS*, 1847-9, 3rd series, III, pp. 402-3.

Lawson, J., 'Comparative experiments on the sowing of wheat by drilling and by broadcast', *THASS*, 1821, VI, pp. 221-8.

Lawson, T., *A Report on the Past and Present Agriculture of the Counties of Forfar and Kincardine*, Edinburgh, n.p., 1881.

Leatham, J., 'An Aberdeenshire classic — centenary of Dr William Alexander', *TBFC*, 1926, XIII, pp. 123-34.

Lee, S. (ed), *Dictionary of National Biography*, London, Smith and Elder, 1893.

Lenin, V. I., 'The development of capitalism in Russia' (1899), in V. I. Lenin, *Collected Works*, Vol. III, London, Lawrence and Wishart, 1960, pp. 23-607.

'Capitalism in agriculture' (1899), in V. I. Lenin, *Collected Works*, Vol. IV, London, Lawrence and Wishart, 1960, pp. 105-59.

'The capitalist system of modern agriculture' (1910), in V. I. Lenin, *Collected Works*, Vol. XVI, London, Lawrence and Wishart, 1963, pp. 423-46.

Lenman, B., *An Economic History of Modern Scotland, 1660-1975*, London, Batsford, 1977.

Leslie, W., *General View of the Agriculture of the Counties of Nairn and Moray*, London, Sherwood, Neely and Jones, 1813.

Lindsay, J., 'The Aberdeenshire canal, 1805-54', *Journal of Transport History*, 1964,

VI, pp. 150-65.
Little, H. J., 'The agricultural labourer', *JRASE*, 1878, 2nd series, XIV, pp. 761-802.
Littlejohn, D., 'Aberdeenshire fiars', in P. J. Anderson (ed), *Miscellany of the New Spalding Club, Vol. II*, Aberdeen, New Spalding Club, 1908, pp. 1-76.
Littlejohn, J., *Westrigg: the Sociology of a Cheviot Parish*, London, Routledge and Kegan Paul, 1963.
Littlejohn, W., *Stories of the Buchan Cottars Before the Year 'One': Life and Character in a Buchan Parish in Aberdeenshire in the Olden Times*, Aberdeen, Milne and Hutchison, 1929.
Lockwood, B., 'Sources of variation in working-class images of society', *Sociological Review*, 1966, XIV, pp. 249-67.
and Goldthorpe, J. 'Affluence and the British class structure', *Sociological Review*, 1963, XI, pp. 133-63.
Long, N., *An Introduction to the Sociology of Rural Development*, London, Tavistock, 1977.
Lovie, A., 'The reclamation of waste land on the farm of Towie', *THASS*, 1883, 4th series, XV, pp. 65-9.
Lukes, S., *Power: a Radical View*, London, Macmillan, 1974.
Lumsden, J., 'Report on draining and subsoil ploughing on the farm of Braco', *THASS*, 1849-51, 3rd series, II, pp. 188-91.
McCalmont, F. M., *McCalmont's Parliamentary Poll Book: British Electoral Results, 1832-1918*, eighth edition, ed J. Vincent and M. Stenton, Brighton, Harvester Press, 1971.
McCombie, W., *Cattle and Cattle Breeders*, Edinburgh, Blackwood, 1867.
McConnochie, A. I., *Bennachie*, Aberdeen, Wyllie, 1890.
McCulloch, J., 'On providing a sufficient supply of labour during press of agricultural work', *THASS*, 1880, 4th series, XII, pp. 229-37.
Macdonald, A., 'On the agriculture of the counties of Elgin and Nairn', *THASS*, 1884, 4th series, XVI, pp. 1-123.
Macdonald, J., 'On the agriculture of the counties of Forfar and Kincardine', *THASS*, 1881, 4th series, XIII, pp. 53-173.
'On the agriculture of the county of Caithness', *THASS*, 1875.
McEwan, J., 'Highland landlordism', in G. Brown (ed), *The Red Paper on Scotland*, Edinburgh, EUSPB, 1975, pp. 262-70.
McEwan, J., *Who Owns Scotland? A Study in Land Ownership*, Edinburgh, EUSPB, 1977.
McKilligan, A., 'Johnny Gibb of Gushetneuk and its author', *TBFC*, 1926, XIII, pp. 96-122.
Mackintosh, J., 'Report on the improvement of waste land in the parishes of Nairn and Auldearn, in the County of Nairn', *THASS*, 1847-9, 3rd series, III, pp. 545-55.
Maclaren, A. A., *Religion and Social Class: the Disruption Years in Aberdeen*, London, Routledge and Kegan Paul, 1974.
Ed, *Social Class in Scotland: Past and Present*, Edinburgh, Donald, 1976.
'McLaren, Ian' (Watson, John MacLaren), *Beside the Bonnie Brier Bush*, eighth edition, London, Hodder and Stoughton, 1895.
The Days of Auld Lang Syne, London, Hodder and Stoughton, 1895.
Afterwards and Other Stories, second edition, London, Hodder and Stoughton, 1898.
Macleod, W., 'Report on ploughing lea', *THASS*, 1855-7, 3rd series, VII, pp. 154-61.
McPherson, I., *Shepherd's Calendar*, London, Cape, 1931.
McPherson, Grant, Sir J., 'Report on the improvement of the farm of Marypark', *THASS*, 1849-51, 3rd series, IV, pp. 79-94.
McPherson, J. M., *Primitive Beliefs in the North-East of Scotland*, London, Longmans

Green, 1929.

McQuiston, J. R., 'Tenant right: farmer against landlord in Victorian England, 1847-1883', *Agricultural History*, 1973, XLVII, pp. 95-113.

Mann, P. H. 'Life in an agricultural village in England', *Sociological Papers*, 1904, pp. 163-93.

Marshall, J. D., 'The Lancashire rural labourer in the early nineteenth century', *Transactions of the Lancashire and Cheshire Antiquarian Society*, 1961, LXXI.

Martin, E. W., *The Shearers and the Shorn: a Study of Life in a Devon Community*, London, Routledge and Kegan Paul, 1965.

Marx, K., *Capital*, Vol. I, ed E. Mandel, Harmondsworth, Penguin, 1976.

The Eighteenth Brumaire of Louis Napoleon, (1852), Moscow, Progress Publishers, 1967.

Matthews, A. H. H., *Fifty Years of Agricultural Politics, Being the History of the Central Chamber of Agriculture, 1865-1915*, London, King, 1915.

Maxwell, J. H., 'Address on agricultural statistics', *THASS*, 1854, 3rd series, VI, pp. 392-9.

'Agricultural Statistics of Scotland, 1855', *THASS*, 1855-7, 3rd series, VII, pp. 201-22.

'Agricultural Statistics of Scotland, 1856', *THASS*, 1855-7, 3rd series, VII, pp. 547-92.

'Agricultural Statistics of Scotland, 1857', *THASS*, 1857-9, 3rd series, VIII, pp. 201-24.

May, T., *Agriculture and Rural Society in Britain, 1846-1914*, London, Arnold, 1973.

Michie, C. Y., 'On wire fencing', *THASS*, 1870-1, 4th series, III, pp. 446-54.

Miller, H., *Essays*, Edinburgh, Nimmo, 1890.

My Schools and Schoolmasters, Edinburgh, Nimmo, 1880.

Mills, D. R., 'English villages in the eighteenth and nineteenth centuries: a sociological approach', *Amateur Historian*, 1965, VI, pp. 271-8.

Milne, James, *Twixt Ury and Don and Round About*, Inverurie, Dufton Scott, 1947.

Milne, John (Atherb), 'The making of a Buchan Farm), *TBFC*, 1889, I, pp. 159-72.

Milne, John (Mains of Laithers), 'On the agriculture of Aberdeenshire and Banffshire', *THASS*, 1870-1, 4th series, III, pp. 378-401.

Mintz, S., 'A note on the definition of peasantries', *Journal of Peasant Studies*, 1973, I, pp. 91-106.

Mitchell, A., *Recollections of a Lifetime*, privately printed, 1911.

Mitchell, B. R., and Deane, P., *Abstract of British Historical Statistics*, Cambridge, Cambridge University Press, 1962.

Mitchison, R., *A History of Scotland*, London, Methuen, 1970.

'The movement of Scottish corn prices in the seventeenth and eighteenth centuries', *EcHR*, 1965, XVIII, pp. 278-91.

Moisley, H. A., 'The Highlands and Islands: a crofting region?', *Transactions of the Institute of British Geographers*, 1962, XXXI, pp. 83-95.

Molland, R., and Evans, G., 'Scottish farm wages from 1870 to 1900', *Journal of the Royal Statistical Society*, 1950, CXIII, pp. 220-7.

Mollyson, C. A., *The Parish of Fordoun*, Aberdeen, Smith, 1893.

Morin, E., *Plodemet*, London, Allen Lane, 1971.

Munro, I. S., *Leslie Mitchell: Lewis Grassic Gibbon*, Edinburgh, Oliver and Boyd, 1966.

Murray, W., 'On the cost of stocking a small farm', *JA*, 1840-1, XI, pp. 76-81.

Nalson, J. A., *Mobility of Farm Families*, Manchester, Manchester University Press, 1968.

Nelson, L., 'The rise of rural sociology: the pre-Purnell period', *Rural Sociology*, 1965, XXX, pp. 407-27.

New Statistical Account of Scotland, fifteen volumes, Edinburgh, Blackwood, 1845.

Newby, H., 'Agricultural workers in the class structure', *Sociological Review,* 1975, XXIII, pp. 51-60.

'Deference and the agricultural worker', *Sociological Review,* 1975, XXIII, pp. 51-60.

'The dangers of reminiscence', *Local Historian,* 1973, X, pp. 334-9.

'The deferential dialectic', *Comparative Studies in Society and History,* 1975, XVII, pp. 139-64.

Nurkse, R., *Problems of Capital Formation in Underdeveloped Countries,* Oxford, Oxford University Press, 1958.

O'Dell, A. C., and Walton, K., *The Highlands and Islands of Scotland,* London, Nelson, 1962.

Ogg, W. S. and Muir, A., *Aberdeenshire,* London, Land Utilisation Survey of Britain, 1946.

Ord, J., *Bothy Songs and Ballads of Aberdeen, Banff and Moray, Angus and the Mearns,* Paisley, Gardner, 1930. Reprinted Edinburgh, Donald, 1973.

Ortiz, S., 'Reflections on the concept of "peasant culture" and "peasant cognitive systems"', in T. Shanin (ed), *Peasants and Peasant Societies,* Harmondsworth, Penguin, 1971, pp. 322-36.

Uncertainties in Peasant Farming: a Colombian Case, London, Athlone Press, 1973.

Orwin, C. S., and Whetham, E. H., *History of British Agriculture, 1846-1914,* London, Longmans, 1964.

Oxaal, I., Barnett, A., and Booth, D., (ed), *Beyond the Sociology of Development,* London, Routledge and Kegan Paul, 1975.

Paterson, J. W., 'Rural depopulation in Scotland', *THASS,* 1897, 5th series, IX, pp. 236-78.

'Rural depopulation in Scotland', *THASS,* 1904, 5th series, XVI, pp. 21-34.

Paul, W., *Past and Present in Aberdeenshire, or Reminiscences of Seventy Years,* Aberdeen, Smith, 1881.

Pelling, H., *Social Geography of British Elections, 1885-1910,* London, Macmillan, 1967.

Perkin, H. J., 'Land reform and class conflict in Victorian Britain', in J. Butt and I. F. Clarke (ed), *The Victorians and Social Protest: a Symposium,* Newton Abbot, David and Charles, 1973, pp. 177-217.

Perren, R., 'Changes in Aberdeenshire farm livestock, 1750-1850', *The Ark,* 1975, II, pp. 287-91.

'The meat and livestock trade in Britain, 1850-70', *EcHR,* 1975, XXVIII, pp. 385-400.

'The north American beef and cattle trade with Great Britain, 1870-1914', *EcHR,* 1971, XXIV, pp. 430-44.

Perry, P. J., *British Farming in the Great Depression, 1870-1914,* Newton Abbot, David and Charles, 1974.

Ed, *British Agriculture, 1875-1914,* London, Methuen, 1973.

Pirie, J., *The Parish of Cairnie,* Banff, *Banffshire Journal,* 1906.

Porter, J., 'Report on draining', *THASS,* 1851-3, 3rd series, III, pp. 528-38.

'Report on ploughing lea', *THASS,* 1855-7, 3rd series, VII, pp. 30-6.

'Report on the improving of waste land', *THASS,* 1855-7, 3rd series, VII, pp. 291-311.

'Report on the management of a home farm', *THASS,* 1857-9, 3rd series, VIII, pp. 225-35.

Pratt, J. B., *Buchan,* Aberdeen, Smith, 1901.

Pringle, R. H., 'The agricultural labourer of Scotland', *THASS,* 1894, 5th series, VI, pp. 238-71.

Pye, L., *Aspects of Political Development*, Boston, Little Brown, 1966.
Raeburn, J. R., 'Agriculture', in A. C. O'Dell and J. Mackintosh (Ed), *The North-East of Scotland*, Aberdeen, Central Press, 1963, pp. 107-117.
Razzell, P. E., and Wainwright, R. W., (ed), *The Victorian Working Class*, London, Cass, 1973.
Reed, H., 'The cattle plague', *JRASE*, 1866, 2nd series, II, pp. 230-88.
Rees, A. D., *Life in a Welsh Countryside*, Cardiff, University of Wales Press, 1940.
Reid, A., 'Report on improvement of waste land', *THASS*, 1855-7, 3rd series, VII, pp. 137-46.
Reid, H. G., *Past and Present*, Edinburgh, Edmonston and Douglas, 1871.
Reid, J., 'On the improvement of sixteen acres in the Moss of Templeton, in the parish of Kildrummy, district of Alford, Aberdeenshire', *THASS*, 2nd series, VII, pp. 238-41.
Richards, E., *The Leviathan of Wealth: the Sutherland Fortune in the Industrial Revolution*, London, Routledge and Kegan Paul, 1973.
Robb, J., 'On hinds houses and bothies', *TNAPSS*, 1863, pp. 760-2.
Robbie, W., *Mains of Yonderton: A Study of Domestic Life in the Buchan District*, Aberdeen, Milne and Hutchison, 1928.
Robertson, B. W., 'The Border farm worker, 1871-1971', *Journal of Agricultural Labour Science*, 1973, II, pp. 65-93.
Robertson, G., *General View of the Agriculture of Kincardineshire or the Mearns*, London, Phillips, 1810.
Rural Recollections, Irvine, 1829.
Robertson Scott, J. W., *The Dying Peasant, and the Future of his Sons*, London, Williams and Norgate, 1926.
Rowland, P., *The Last Liberal Government: the Promised Land, 1905-1910*, London, Barrie and Rockcliffe, 1968.
'Roy, N.' (Russell, A. D.), *The Horseman's Word*, London, Macmillan, 1895.
Salaman, R. N., *The History and Social Influence of the Potato*, Cambridge, Cambridge University Press, 1949.
Saul, S. B., *The Myth of the Great Depression*, London, Macmillan, 1969.
Saunders, L. J., *Scottish Democracy, 1815-1840*, Edinburgh, Oliver and Boyd, 1950.
Sayce, R. U., 'Food in the highland zone of Britain in the eighteenth century', *Folk-Life*, 1948-9, XII-XIII, pp. 199-207.
Scott, J., and Hughes, M., 'The Scottish ruling class: problems of analysis and data', in A. A. Maclaren (ed), *Social Class in Scotland: Past and Present*, Edinburgh, Donald, 1976, pp. 166-88.
Shanin, T., *The Awkward Class*, Oxford, Clarendon Press, 1972.
'The nature and change of peasant economies', *Sociologia Ruralis*, 1973, XIII, pp. 141-71.
'The nature and logic of the peasant economy — diversity and change', *Journal of Peasant Studies*, 1974, I, 186-206.
'The peasantry as a political factor', in T. Shanin (ed), *Peasants and Peasant Societies*, Harmondsworth, Penguin, 1971, pp. 238-63.
Shillinglaw, D., 'Land reform and peasant mobilisation in southern China, 1947-50', in D. Lehmann (ed), *Agrarian Reform and Agrarian Reformism: Studies of Peru, Chile, China and India*, London, Faber and Faber, 1974, pp. 121-66.
Simpson, I. J., *Education in Aberdeenshire Before 1872*, London, University of London Press, 1947.
Simpson, W. D., *The Castle of Kildrummy*, Aberdeen, Wyllie, 1923.
Ed, *The Book of Glenbuchat*, Aberdeen, Third Spalding Club, 1942.
Sinclair, Sir J. (ed), *Statistical Account of Scotland (Old Statistical Account)*, 21 volumes, Edinburgh, Creech, 1791-9.

Sinclair, Sir J., *Account of the Systems of Husbandry Adopted in the More Improved Districts of Scotland*, third edition, two volumes, Edinburgh, Constable, 1814.

Skirving, R. S., 'Farm labour and labourers', in J. Wilson (ed), *Report on the Present State of the Agriculture of Scotland*, Edinburgh, Blackwood, 1878, pp. 134-46.

'Rural labourers', *TNAPSS*, 1863, pp. 762-3.

Small, A., 'The small villages of the Howe of the Mearns', *Folk Life*, 1966, IV, pp. 22-9.

Smeaton, G., *Memoir of Alexander Thomson of Banchory*, Edinburgh, Edmonston and Douglas, 1869.

Smith, A. (ed), *A New History of Aberdeenshire*, two volumes, Aberdeen, Smith, 1875.

Smith, A. (Mains of Crombie), 'On the improvement of 152 acres 2 roods Scotch, on the Mains of Crombie, parish of Marnoch, Banffshire', *THASS*, 1841, 2nd series, VII, pp. 249-51.

Smith, J. H., *Joe Duncan: the Scottish Farm Servants and British Agriculture*, Edinburgh, RCSS and the Scottish Labour History Society, 1973.

'The cattle trade of Aberdeenshire in the nineteenth century', *AHR*, 1955, III, pp. 114-8.

Smith, R., 'On the extended application of water and other power to farm purposes', *THASS*, 1841, 2nd series, VII, pp. 64-8.

Smith, R. H., *An Aberdeenshire Village Propaganda, Forty Years Ago*, Edinburgh, Douglas, 1889.

Smith, T., *Memoir of James Begg, D.D.*, two volumes, Edinburgh, Gemmel, 1885-8.

Smith, W. McC., *Memoir of the Families of McCombie and Thoms*, second edition, Edinburgh, Blackwood, 1890.

Smout, T. C., *A History of the Scottish People, 1560-1830*, London, Collins, 1969.

'Aspects of sexual behaviour in nineteenth century Scotland', in A. A. Maclaren (ed), *Social Class in Scotland: Past and Present*, Edinburgh, Donald, 1976, pp. 55-85.

'Scottish landowners and economic growth, 1650-1850', *Scottish Journal of Political Economy*, 1964, XI, pp. 218-34.

'The landowner and the planned village in Scotland, 1730-1830', in N. T. Phillipson and R. Mitchison (ed), *Scotland in the Age of Improvement*, Edinburgh, Edinburgh University Press, 1970, pp. 73-106.

and Fenton, A., 'Scottish agriculture before the improvers — an exploration', *AHR*, 1965, XIII, pp. 73-93.

Soutar, D., *General View of the Agriculture of the County of Banff*, Edinburgh, Nicol, 1812.

Stamp, L. D., (ed), *Map of Predominant Farming Types in Scotland, with Explanatory Booklet*, London, Geographical Publications for the Land Utilisation Survey of Britain, 1942.

Stavenhagen, R., *Social Classes in Agrarian Societies*, New York, Anchor Books, 1975.

Stephens, H., *The Book of the Farm*, first edition, three volumes, Edinburgh, Blackwood, 1844.

The Book of the Farm, sixth edition (ed. Macdonald), three volumes, Edinburgh, Blackwood, 1908.

Stern, W. M., *Britain Yesterday and Today*, London, Longmans, 1962.

Stevenson, J., 'On improvements on the farm of Quarryhead', *THASS*, 1870-1, 4th series, III, pp. 139-41.

Stuart, John (ed), *List of Pollable Persons within the Shire of Aberdeen, 1696*, two volumes, Aberdeen, Bennett, 1844.

'The rentaill of the Lordschipe of Huntlye *alias* Strauthbogye', in J. Stuart (ed), *Miscellany of the Spalding Club, Vol. IV*, Aberdeen, Spalding Club, 1844,

pp. lxxx-lxxxi, 261-319.
Symon, J. A., 'Cairnhill, Turriff, 1861-1926: Part II', *SA*, 1951, XXXI, pp. 24-9.
Scottish Farming Past and Present, Edinburgh, Oliver and Boyd, 1959.
Tait, J., 'The physiological distinctions in the condition of the Scottish peasantry', *THASS*, 1883, 4th series, XV, pp. 1-19.
Taylor, J., 'On the comparative merits of different modes of reaping grain', *THASS*, 1843-5, 3rd series, I, pp. 259-71.
Thirsk, J., *English Peasant Farming: the Agrarian History of Lincolnshire from Tudor to Recent Times*, London, Routledge and Kegan Paul, 1957.
Thompson, E. P., 'Anthropology and the discipline of historical context', *Midland History*, 1972, I, pp. 41-55.
The Making of the English Working Class, Harmondsworth, Penguin, 1968.
Thomson, A., 'On the settlement of crofters', *THASS*, 1837, 2nd series, V, pp. 379-83.
'Report on the improvement of waste land', *THASS*, 1853-5, 3rd series, IV, pp. 90-8.
Social Evils: Their Causes and Their Cures, London, Nisbet, 1852.
Tocher, J. F., (ed), *The Book of Buchan*, Peterhead, Buchan Club, 1910.
'Toulmin, David', (Reid, J.), *Hard Shining Corn*, Aberdeen, Impulse, 1972.
Straw Into Gold, Aberdeen, Impulse, 1973.
Turnock, D., 'Depopulation in north-east Scotland with reference to the countryside', *SGM*, 1968, LXXXIV, pp. 256-68.
'Small farms in north Scotland', *SGM*, 1975, XCI, pp. 164-81.
van Onselen, C., 'Randlords and Rotgut, 1886-1903', *History Workshop Journal*, 1976, II, pp. 33-89.
Wallace, A. R., *Land Nationalisation: its Necessity and Aims*, London, Swan Sonnenschein, 1892.
Walton, K., 'Population changes in north-east Scotland, 1696-1951', *Scottish Studies*, 1961, V, pp. 149-80.
'The distribution of population in Aberdeenshire, 1696', *SGM*, 1950, LXVI, pp. 17-26.
Watson, J. A. S., *Rural Britain Today and Tomorrow*, Edinburgh, Oliver and Boyd, 1934.
'The agricultural revolution in Scotland, 1750-1810', *THASS*, 1929, 5th series, XLI, pp. 1-20.
Watson, W., *Glimpses of Auld Lang Syne*, Aberdeen, Aberdeen University Press, 1929.
Watt, Mr., 'The condition of the labouring poor', *Poor Law Magazine*, 1860, II, pp. 229-36.
Watt, W., *A History of Aberdeen and Banff*, Edinburgh, Blackwood, 1900.
Whetham, E. H., 'Livestock prices in Britain, 1851-93', *AHR*, 1962, XI, pp. 27-35.
'The changing cattle enterprises of England and Wales, 1870-1910', *Geographical Journal*, 1963, CXXIX, pp. 378-80.
Whittington, G., 'Was there a Scottish agricultural revolution?', *Area*, 1975, VII, pp. 204-6.
Wight, A., *Present State of Husbandry in Scotland*, four volumes, Edinburgh, Creech, 1778-83.
Wilken, A. G., *Peter Laing, the Elgin Centenarian*, second edition, Elgin, Yeadon, 1887.
Wilken, J., *Ellon in Bygone Days*, second edition, Ellon, Rennie, 1926.
Wilkes, T. C., 'Bastardy in our rural districts — the causes and remedies', *TNAPSS*, 1859, pp. 733-734.
Wilkinson, Canon, 'Some frien's and neebors o' Johnny Gibb', *TBFC*, 1926, XIII, pp. 135-41.
Will, W., *Song and Story of Aberdeen, Banff, and Kincardine*, Aberdeen, Aberdeen

University Press, 1939.
Williams, R., *The Country and the City*, London, Chatto and Windus, 1973.
Williams, W. M., *A West Country Village: Ashworthy*, London, Routledge and Kegan Paul, 1963.
'The social study of family farming', in D. R. Mills (ed), *English Rural Communities: the Impact of a Specialised Economy*, London, Macmillan, 1973, pp. 116-34.
The Sociology of an English Village: Gosforth, London, Routledge and Kegan Paul, 1956.
Wilson, Jacob, 'Reaping machines', *THASS*, 1865, 3rd series, XXV, pp. 123-49.
Wilson, James, 'Farming in Aberdeenshire — ancient and modern', *THASS*, 1902, 5th series, XIV, pp. 76-102.
Wilson, John, 'Farming of the east and north-eastern districts', in J. Wilson (ed), *Report on the Present State of the Agriculture of Scotland*, Edinburgh, Blackwood, 1878, pp. 23-59.
Withrington, D. J., 'The 1851 census of religious worship and education: with a note on church accommodation in mid-19th century Scotland', *Records of the Scottish Church History Society*, 1973, XVIII, pp. 133-48.
Wolf, E. R., 'On peasant rebellions', in T. Shanin (ed), *Peasants and Peasant Societies*, Harmondsworth, Penguin, 1971, pp. 264-74.
Peasants, Englewood Cliffs N.J., Prentice-Hall, 1966.
Yeats, J., 'Report on the improvement of waste land', *THASS*, 1847-8, 3rd series, III, pp. 213-7.
Young, D., *Beyond the Sunset: a Study of James Leslie Mitchell*, Aberdeen, Impulse, 1973.
Young, R., *The Parish of Spynie*, Elgin, *Elgin Courant*, 1871.
Yourston, W. G., 'An inquiry into the duties of the landholders of Scotland to the peasantry and the manner in which these duties have been performed', *JA*, 1841-2, XII, pp. 509-56.

Index